Philippines
a country study

Foreign Area Studies
The American University
Edited by
Frederica M. Bunge
Research completed
August 1983

RIZAL

On the cover: The foremost national hero of the Philippines,

José Rizal. The leading articulator of growing Filipino national consciousness in the late nineteenth century, Rizal was executed by the
Spanish in 1896.

Third Edition, 1983; First Printing, 1984

Library of Congress Cataloging in Publication Data

Bunge, Frederica M.
　Philippines, a country study.

　(Area handbook series) (DA pam; 550-72)
　Bibliography: p.
　Includes index.
　1. Philippines. I. Title. II. Series. III. Series:
DA pam; 550-72.
DS655.B86 1984　　959.9　　84-6382

Headquarters, Department of the Army
DA Pam 550-72

For sale by the Superintendent of Documents, U.S. Government Printing Office
Washington, D.C. 20402

Foreword

This volume is one of a continuing series of books prepared by Foreign Area Studies, The American University, under the Country Studies/Area Handbook Program. The last page of this book provides a listing of other published studies. Each book in the series deals with a particular foreign country, describing and analyzing its economic, national security, political, and social systems and institutions and examining the interrelationships of those systems and institutions and the ways that they are shaped by cultural factors. Each study is written by a multidisciplinary team of social scientists. The authors seek to provide a basic insight and understanding of the society under observation, striving for a dynamic rather than a static portrayal of it. The study focuses on historical antecedents and on the cultural, political, and socioeconomic characteristics that contribute to cohesion and cleavage within the society. Particular attention is given to the origins and traditions of the people who make up the society, their dominant beliefs and values, their community of interests and the issues on which they are divided, the nature and extent of their involvement with the national institutions, and their attitudes toward each other and toward the social system and political order within which they live.

The contents of the book represent the views, opinions, and findings of Foreign Area Studies and should not be construed as an official Department of the Army position, policy, or decision, unless so designated by other official documentation. The authors have sought to adhere to accepted standards of scholarly objectivity. Such corrections, additions, and suggestions for factual or other changes that readers may have will be welcomed for use in future new editions.

William Evans-Smith
Director, Foreign Area Studies
The American University
Washington, D.C. 20016

Acknowledgments

The authors are grateful to individuals in various Philippine and United States government offices, multilateral agencies, and private institutions who gave of their time, research materials, and special knowledge to provide data and perspective. Without associating them in any way with responsibility for the contents of this study, the team wishes to thank a number of consultants, including Filipinos living in the United States, whose observations provided a rich breadth of perspective to the team in its research. Edward W. Doherty of the United States Catholic Conference graciously made available material bearing on the role of the church as cited in the bibliography of Chapter 4.

The team also thanks members of the Foreign Area Studies staff who contributed directly to the preparation of the manuscript. These include Dorothy M. Lohmann, Kathryn R. Stafford, and Andrea T. Merrill, who edited the manuscript and the accompanying figures and tables; Harriett R. Blood and Farah Ahannavard, who prepared the graphics; and Gilda V. Nimer, librarian. The team appreciates as well the assistance provided by Ernest A. Will, publications manager, and Eloise W. Brandt and Wayne W. Olsen, administrative assistants. Margaret Quinn typed the manuscript and gave valuable help in various phases of production. Special thanks are owed to Regina Faul-Jansen, who designed the illustrations for the cover of this volume and for the title pages of the chapters. The inclusion of photographs in this book was made possible by the generosity of various individuals and public and private agencies. The authors acknowledge their indebtedness especially to those persons who contributed original work not previously published.

Acknowledgments

Contents

List of Figures

Preface

Since 1976, when the *Area Handbook for the Philippines* was published, the country has continued under the leadership of President Ferdinand E. Marcos. On the surface, until August 1983, the political, economic, and social milieu remained much as it had been when the handbook was published, despite the lifting of martial law in 1981. After the assassination of Benigno "Ninoy" Aquino, Jr., on August 21, 1983, however, discontent with continued authoritarian measures, economic setbacks, corruption, and alleged abuses by the military in exercising its duties shattered the surface calm in an outpouring of protest. A crisis atmosphere prevailed thereafter, not only in Manila but also in outlying urban centers. Although no one could foresee the full consequences of this development, the point was nonetheless an appropriate one at which to take stock of Philippine society as it headed into a highly uncertain future.

The purpose of this volume, *Philippines: A Country Study*, like that of its predecessor, is to treat in a compact and objective manner the dominant social, economic, political, and national security forces at work and to give readers insight into the attitudes and values of the people. Sources of information used in its preparation included scholarly works, official reports of governmental and international organizations, journals, and newspapers. Brief comments on some of the more valuable sources for further reading appear at the end of each chapter. Full references to these and other sources used by the authors are included in the Bibliography. Interpretations are offered on a tentative basis as befits research undertaken without field study in a nation undergoing change and without the advantage of a completely free press.

The spelling of place-names follows that used by the United States Board on Geographic Names, as set forth in the official gazetteer published in 1953. Readers may refer to the Glossary for conversion rates between the United States dollar and the Philippine peso and for frequently used terms. Diacritics have been omitted from Spanish personal names except in sections of the book pertaining to the colonial period.

Measurements are given in the metric system; a conversion table is provided to assist those readers who are unfamiliar with metric measurements (see table 1, Appendix). The Appendix provides other tabular material that will be of interest particularly to students of economic and security matters.

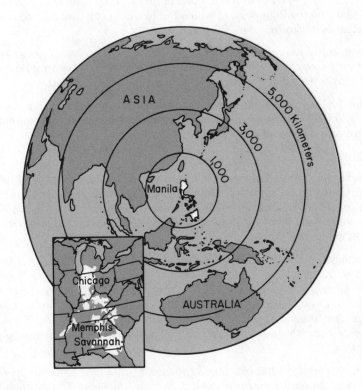

Country

Formal Name: Republic of the Philippines.

Term for Citizens: Filipinos.

Capital: Quezon City (National Capital City), one of four cities within Metro Manila (National Capital Region), designated capital by law. Another of the four cities, Manila, functions as de facto capital.

Flag: Two horizontal bands upon which an equilateral triangle is superimposed on the left. Blue band (uppermost in peacetime) stands for high political purpose; red band for courage. Positions reverse in wartime. White triangle contains centered gold sun and gold stars in each angle.

Geography

Size: Archipelago of some 7,100 islands extending about 1,850 kilometers from north to south separating South China Sea from Philippine Sea and Pacific Ocean beyond. Occupies claimed Exclusive Economic Zone (EEZ) of 496,400 square nautical miles. Total land area of about 300,000 square kilometers, of which the two largest islands, Luzon and Mindanao, make up about 65 percent.

Topography: Largely mountainous, creating narrow coastal plains and interior valleys and plains. Major plains include those of central Luzon, northeastern Cagayan valley, and Agusan Basin in far south.

Climate: Tropical climate; mean annual sea-level temperatures rarely fall below 27°C. Two seasons, wet and dry, determined by monsoon conditions. Frequent typhoons.

Society

Population: Population unofficially estimated in mid-1983 at 50.4 million. Growth rate during 1975-80 period 2.6 percent. In early 1980s density of 160 persons per square kilometer compared with 139 in 1973 for country as a whole; but more than half (54.4 percent) of population found on Luzon.

Language: English and Pilipino (a variant of Tagalog) the official languages. English widely used in commerce, government, and international relations and as medium of instruction. Expanding usage of Pilipino, lingua franca of central Luzon. Diversity of other indigenous languages, including (besides Pilipino) Ilocano and Cebuano. Knowledge of Spanish and Arabic significant among some population elements.

Ethnic Groups: Filipinos a blend principally of Malay, Chinese, Spanish, Negrito, and American stock. Cleavages in society based mainly on religious (Muslims versus Lowland Christians), sociocultural (upland tribes versus lowland peoples), and urban-rural differences rather than ethnic or racial ones.

Religion: About 85 percent of population Roman Catholic. Philippine-based Iglesia ni Kristo has substantial number of followers. Small numbers of believers adhere to other indigenous Christian churches, to Protestant groups originally established by foreign missionaries, or to various small sects and cults. Filipino Muslim minority (Moros) makes Islam important in southern portion of archipelago.

Education: Literacy estimated at over 89 percent in 1981 in official government publications. Total enrollment in academic year 1980-81 of 12.6 million students, including 8.3 million primary-level pupils. Free education at elementary level; partly subsidized secondary level. Higher education provided mainly by private sector. More than 1 million students in higher education in early 1980s.

Health: Public and private medical and health services concentrated in urban areas, but in 1981 over 4,500 *barangay* (see Glossary) health stations and nearly 2,000 rural health units assist in reaching remainder of population. In 1980 70 percent said to be reached by health care delivery system. Infant mortality 53 per 1,000 in 1981; life expectancy 63 years. 43 percent of population has access to safe water.

Economy

Gross National Product (GNP): About US$40.2 billion in 1982 (US$792 per capita). Growth rate declined from average of more than 6 percent per year in 1972-79 period to less than 3 percent in 1982. Most of growth from increased public and private investment, which rose from 16 percent of GNP in 1972 to 26 percent of GNP in 1981.

Resources: Abundant minerals—copper, coal, gold, chromite, cement materials, nickel, and low-grade iron ores. Petroleum and natural gas limited to a few small wells, but excellent potential for hydroelectric and geothermal energy. Good timber and fishery resources, as well as extensive plantations of coconuts. Except on Mindanao and Palawan, arable land at or near ecological limits.

Agriculture, Forestry, and Fishing: In 1981 produced 23 percent of gross domestic product (GDP) and in 1980 employed about 46 percent of labor force. Staple crops: rice and corn. Sugarcane, coconuts, bananas, pineapples, livestock, tropical hardwoods, tuna, and brackish-water shrimp also important.

Industry: Manufacturing produced 25 percent of GDP in 1981; mining, construction, and utilities another 13 percent. Industry engaged only 17 percent of labor force in 1980. Mostly concentrated in Metro Manila. Processing of food, beverages, tobacco, and other agricultural products and of mineral products predominates. Machinery manufacturing mostly assembly from imported components.

Services: Wholesale and retail trade produced 24 percent of GDP in 1981; transportation, storage, communications, finance, government, and other services additional 17 percent. Most modern business and financial services located in Metro Manila. Most service employment in small-scale wholesale and retail trade.

Exports: Merchandise exports about US$5 billion in 1982. Major products: semiconductors and other electronic equipment, coconut products, copper, sugar products, textiles, and other agricultural and mineral products. Other important receipts from export of construction labor to Middle East and from tourism.

Imports: Merchandise imports about US$7.8 billion in 1982. Major items: petroleum and other mineral fuels, intermediate goods and raw materials, and capital equipment for energy and transportation.

Balance of Payments: Current account deficit reached US$3.3 billion in 1982, raising total external foreign debt to nearly 35 percent of GNP. Interest payments on this debt some 25 percent of all export earnings in 1982.

Exchange Rate: Major devaluation of currency in July 1983 brought rate to ₱11 per US$1 (for value of the peso—see Glossary). Floating rate pegged to United States currency generally depreciating.

Transportation and Communications: Roads covered about 155,000 kilometers in 1981, but only 18 percent all-weather surfaces. Railroads, diminishing in importance, consisted of about 1,060 kilometers of meter-gauge track in 1981; double tracking and construction of overhead rails in Metro Manila. Some 34 significant ports nationwide, of which Manila, Cebu, Iloilo, Davao, and Iligan are the most important. About one telephone per 74 people in 1980; most telecommunications facilities in Metro Manila. International airport in Manila and 39 secondary airports, of which five handle some international traffic.

Government and Politics

Government: Based on the Constitution of 1973, amended in 1976 and 1981, providing for a centralized, presidential form of government and separation of powers. President may rule by decree in national emergencies, as was true under Ferdinand E. Marcos, from proclamation of martial law in September 1972 to its lifting in January 1981. President—head of state and chief executive of the government—directly elected for unlimited number of terms of six years each. Prime minister nominated by president for formal confirmation by national legislature, dominated since 1978 by ruling political party, New Society Movement.

Administrative Divisions: Seventy-three provinces and provincial-level Metro Manila at top of territorial administrative structure. Provinces grouped into 12 regions for purpose of developmental planning and coordination; Metro Manila identified as thirteenth region, officially called National Capital Region. Provincial-level divisions subdivide into cities, municipalities (also called towns), and *barangays*, known as barrios until officially renamed in 1974.

Politics: Partisan politics, suspended 1972-77, resumed in 1978 when Marcos formed New Society Movement as government party. Opposition groups numerous but fragmented organizationally; suffer from endemic factionalism and paucity of resources.

The Judiciary: Whole judicial system in state of transition since enactment of Judicial Reorganization Law in 1981. Reorganization aimed at streamlining judicial structure and process and eliminating incompetence and corruption among judges. Court hierarchy topped by Supreme Court, which supervises courts at lower levels. Justice at grass-roots level administered informally through *barangay* conciliation courts.

Foreign Affairs: Member of United Nations and Association of Southeast Asian Nations (ASEAN), regional grouping with Indonesia, Malaysia, Singapore, and Thailand. Observer to Nonaligned Movement (see Glossary). Maintains mutual defense treaty and other defense agreements with United States, which has two major military bases—Clark Air Base and Subic Bay Naval Base—in Philippines. Supports continued military presence of United States in Asia as essential to maintenance of balance of power in region, as well as to continued peace and stability therein.

National Security

Insurgency: Two basic sources—communist and Moro. Major communist group Maoist Communist Party of the Philippines-Marxist Leninist (CPP-ML), active in most of nation; strength of its military arm, New People's Army regulars estimated at between 6,000 and 10,000 or more in 1983. Separate pro-Soviet communist party, Philippine Communist Party (commonly known as the PKP) less than 200 strong. Moro insurgents, most in Moro National Liberation Front, estimated at 10,000 to 15,000 in 1983 and concentrated in southern portions of nation.

Armed Forces: Comprised army, navy, air force, and Philippine Constabulary (PC). Total estimated strength in 1983 of 146,300; army, 70,000; navy 26,000; air force, 16,800; and PC, 33,500. Reserves estimated at 1 million.

Major Tactical Units: Army: four light infantry divisions, one unconventional warfare brigade, two engineer brigades, one light armored regiment, four artillery regiments, and one Hawk surface-to-air missile unit. Forming one ranger regiment in 1983. Navy: fleet (Naval Operating Force), coast guard, and two marine brigades. Air: 21 squadrons, including three fighter squadrons and four counterinsurgency squadrons. PC: personnel deployed throughout nation in regional, provincial, and local detachments.

Major Equipment Suppliers: In 1983 bulk of all equipment of United States origin. Additional sources included Australia, Britain, Federal Republic of Germany (West Germany), Italy, Netherlands, Republic of Korea (South Korea), and Singapore. Philippines developing indigenous defense industry, much through license agreements.

National Defense Spending: Rose from near 10 percent of total budget in 1969 to over 19 percent in 1976-77 period; thereafter declined steadily to around 12 percent of total in 1980 (totals not including United States military assistance grants and credits).

Police and Paramilitary Forces: Integrated National Police personnel strength 51,000 in 1980, including about 5,000 fire and prison officials. Paramilitary forces included Civilian Home Defense Forces, estimated at 71,000 in 1981.

Foreign Military Alliances: Maintained close military relations with United States through agreements covering United States use of military bases in Philippines, United States assistance to Philippine armed forces, and 1951 Mutual Defense Treaty Between the Republic of the Philippines and the United States of America. Philippines also a signatory to Southeast Asia Collective Defense Treaty of 1954 along with United States, Thailand, and others, which remained valid even though structure formed by it, Southeast Asia Treaty Organization (SEATO), was phased out in 1975-77 period.

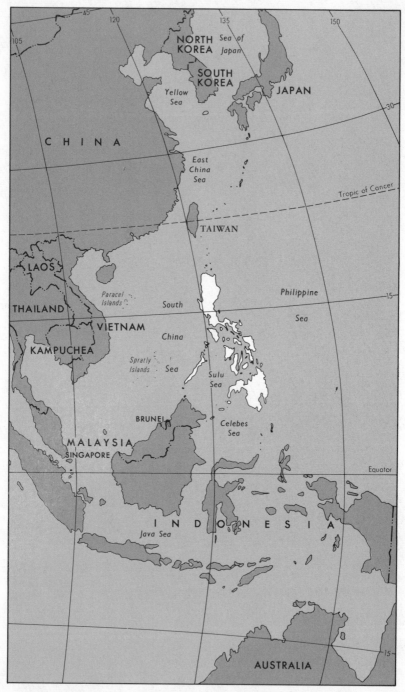

Figure 1. Philippines in Its Asian Setting, 1983

Introduction

IN LATE SUMMER 1983 the Philippines was gripped by uncertainty amid mounting signs of a troubled political future. President Ferdinand E. Marcos had been in power for nearly 18 years, ruling for more than a decade with tight-fisted authority, which he defended as essential to achieve the broad goals of his administration. Yet the lofty aims of what through 1980 he had called the "New Society" program remained largely unfulfilled. The middle class was frustrated by the impact of the latest economic setbacks: and labor (both urban and agricultural) was discouraged by widespread unemployment and its own abject poverty contrasted with the wealth and lavish consumption of a privileged elite. Adding fuel to the discontent were corruption and the widely reported excesses in some areas of government security personnel.

In this milieu, the assassination of opposition leader Benigno "Ninoy" Aquino, Jr., who had just returned from several years as an expatriate in the United States, precipitated a crisis potentially more threatening to the regime than any it had previously faced. The killing of Aquino at close range while in the hands of government security authorities at Manila International Airport in circumstances not fully explained brought masses of angry protesters into the streets, unleashing an outpouring of antigovernment sentiment among moderate opposition elements, including office workers from the Makati business district of Manila and others who hitherto had been neither articulate nor highly visible on the political scene. Fear of the consequences of increasing polarization between them and the stability-minded senior military officers in the ruling circle gave rise to renewed calls by Roman Catholic clergy for "national reconciliation." For the government, the graver threat, however, lay in the perceived possibility of a joining of forces between leftist insurgents and alienated elements of the moderate opposition, including students, professionals, and the business community.

In many respects the acrimony and disorder prevailing in late summer 1983 were products of the later years of Marcos' rule, during which time the nation underwent a thoroughgoing political reconfiguration. The apparent successes of the political order of the 1950s and 1960s had made the Philippines at one time "the showcase of democracy in Asia" (see fig. 1). Marcos himself had risen through the system of free and open partisan political competition, stepping from the legislature to the presidency in 1965 and winning an unprecedented second—and constitutionally last—four-year term in 1969, by a wide margin.

In late 1972, near the close of his second term, however, Marcos declared martial law. To support his action, he invoked the troubling realities of the period: unrest over socioeconomic inequities and the failure of successive administrations to deal with the need for land reform; confrontations in Muslim-inhabited areas of the predominantly Roman Catholic Philippines; and communism, disorder, corruption, and violence in the political arena.

At the time, the action was not without public support, but tolerance wore thin as years passed and alleged abuses of authority increased. Although a degree of political normalization had been achieved by 1978 and martial law was finally lifted in 1981, Marcos' wide-ranging authority remained all but absolute. The political opposition was in disarray, left without meaningful channels of expression. Some activists were confined to prison on dubious grounds; the press offered only guarded comment; and civil rights abuses, including disappearances and killings by the military, were reported. Of all the changed features of the political scene, however, the most conspicuous were the rise of the influence of the military and the concentration of power around Marcos, particularly in the personages of the First Lady, Imelda Romualdez Marcos, and some of their closest associates.

The impact of the Marcos years notwithstanding, the instability and tension characterizing the society in late 1983 could also be traced to features of the national life spawned in the pre-Marcos era and the colonial past. Among these, dependence on a few critical agricultural exports was noteworthy. First under Spain, then under the United States, which in 1898 had disestablished the Spanish colonial administration, the economy of the archipelago had been developed chiefly to meet the requirements of commercial and industrial interests of the colonial power. During the American occupation, policies culminating in free trade between the United States and the Philippines were intended to produce a favorable climate for American trade and investment and to yield inexpensive raw materials and a market for American goods. After independence in 1946, the difficulties of the new state in steering its own course were compounded by this economic legacy, especially insofar as preferences in tariff regulations allowed the United States to retain enormous economic leverage in the archipelago. Even after those trade arrangements—bitterly resented by many Filipinos—lapsed and new economic strategies were developed, continued dependence on agricultural exports still left the nation's economic planners at the mercy of extreme fluctuations in the international market, although the country has been engaged in a program of diversification that offers prospects of alleviating the problem over the long term.

Still another source of tension and instability in the contemporary Philippines was deeply rooted in circumstances of the past—the painful disparity between an affluent upper social stratum and the mass of low-income, often impoverished, Filipinos. The disparity, generating pressure for reform among twentieth-century political and social activists, had arisen gradually over the past 300 years in traditionally rural Philippine society.

Under Spanish rule, lasting from the first settlement under Miguel López de Legazpi in 1565 to 1898, friars of various Roman Catholic orders, acting as surrogates of the Spanish crown, had integrated the scattered peoples of the *barangays* (see Glossary) into a single administrative entity and firmly implanted Roman Catholicism among them as the dominant faith—except in the southern Muslim-dominated portion of the archipelago. Over the centuries the orders had acquired huge landed estates and become wealthy, sometimes corrupt, and highly powerful. Eventually, their estates were acquired by *principales* (literally, principal ones; term for indigenous colonial elite) and Chinese mestizos (see Glossary) eager to take advantage of expanding opportunities in agriculture and commerce. The way of life of the increasingly prosperous regional oligarchy was far removed from that of the people of the barrios, although the harshest effects of poverty were somewhat mitigated by the impact of the prevailing patterns of reciprocal obligation between patron and client in all walks of life. Accumulating wealth, the new entrepreneurs and landlords were able to educate their children, and these sons and daughters formed the nucleus of an emerging, largely provincially based, sociocultural elite—the *ilustrados* ("enlightened ones")—who dominated almost all aspects of the national life in later generations.

Meanwhile, opposition to Spanish rule was taking the form of periodic millenarian revolt by people of the barrios struggling against their growing impoverishment on the great landed estates and persistent demands by reform-minded *ilustrados* for better treatment of the colony and its eventual assimilation with Spain. In the late nineteenth century, inflamed by the martyrdom of three Filipino priests and by other developments, a number of young *ilustrados* took up the nationalist cause in their writings, published chiefly in Europe. During the struggle for independence against Spain (1896-98), *ilustrados* and peasants made common cause against the colonial power, but not before a period of *ilustrado* vacillation, reflecting doubts about the outcome of a confrontation that had begun as a mass movement among workers and peasants in the environs of Manila. Once in the struggle, however, the *ilustrados* took over, becoming the articulators and leaders of the fight for independence—first against Spain, then against the United States. Rapidly overcome by superior American forces in 1899, peasant guerrillas continued their revolutionary activity, holding out in the hills for several years, but the leadership opted for accommodation in the seemingly futile situation.

Once again, *ilustrados* found themselves in an intermediary position as arbiters between the colonial power and the rest of the population. *Ilustrados* responded eagerly to the tutelage in Western democratic processes and values provided by the United States as it prepared the Philippines for eventual self-rule, and soon, in return for their allegiance, American authorities began to yield control to them. Although a massive American-sponsored popular education program exposed millions of Filipinos to the basic workings of democratic government, political leadership at the regional and national level continued thereafter to remain almost entirely the province of families of the sociocultural elite. A number of family-centered political dynasties grew up, including the Laurels of Batangas Province and the Aquinos of Tarlac Province, which generation after generation produced men who rose to national prominence. Marcos himself came out of this same elite tradition.

For its part, the peasantry continued to stage periodic uprisings in protest against its difficult situation, which, as the twentieth century progressed, was to worsen owing to population growth, usury, the spread of absentee landlordism, and the weakening of the traditional patron-client bonds of reciprocal obligation. Agrarian distress was particularly acute in the rice-growing areas of Luzon.

Whereas the economic legacy of colonialism, including the relative impoverishment of so large a segment of the population, left seeds of dissension in its wake, not all the enduring features of colonial rule were forces of destabilization. Improvements in education and health had enhanced the quality of life. More important in the context of stabilizing influences was the profound impact of Roman Catholicism. The great majority of the Filipino people became adherents of the faith, and the influence of prelates of the church on the society was profound.

After independence in 1946 the church had been a source of stability to the infant nation as it was to continue to be in later periods. Throughout the era of constitutional government lasting until 1972, however, the church remained outside the realm of secular affairs; its largely conservative clergy was occupied almost exclusively with matters of the church.

As a new nation, the Philippines continued to be closely linked to the United States in economic and security matters. Landlords in the archipelago pressed for free trade between the two countries, given the great dependence of agricultural products on American markets. Trade relations as agreed upon did provide for the free entry of most Philippine goods until 1954, with the imposition of rising tariffs thereafter, but the agreement also provided "parity" rights giving American investors equal rights along with Filipinos to develop the islands' resources, a circumstance bitterly resented by many Filipinos. Mutual security arrangements were also guaranteed by treaty, and the United States was allowed to operate military installations in the Philippines, including extensive facilities at Subic Bay and Clark Air Base. United States help was given in putting down the Huk (see Glossary) rebellion in central Luzon.

Pro-American sentiment had run high in the initial years of nationhood, based on Philippine appreciation of its tutelage in democratic processes and on Philippine pride in its enormous and costly contribution to winning the war in the Pacific alongside the American military. As the country gained self-confidence, however, a growing number of Filipinos expressed the view that trade arrangements and security ties between the Philippines and the United States contained what they called inequities and ambiguities. Impetus arose for a reassessment of the relationship between the two countries in keeping with the dignity of the Philippines as a sovereign republic. Thus, in the period of parliamentary government, the country's initial dependence on the United States and its Western orientation in foreign affairs were gradually tempered by growing nationalist sentiment and pressures for a new emphasis on Asian regionalism. Trade agreements with the United States lapsed in 1974, and bases agreements were eventually renegotiated to provide a greater measure of Philippine sovereignty over them.

Before 1972 the Philippines functioned, if not altogether smoothly, as a working democracy. National elections were regularly held under the framework of a constitution written in 1935 providing for checks and balances between the principal branches of government. Vigorous competition between two loosely structured political parties put one or the other at the apex of power in a remarkably consistent cycle of alternation. The electorate grew from 1.6 million in 1946 to 8 million in 1969, the year that Marcos received his emphatic mandate for a second term. The political process was characterized by free-wheeling, occasionally violent, exchange and a quid pro quo basis of interaction. Marcos demonstrated his mastery of its intricacies in a triumph attributable to his public impact programs—"Marcos means more rice," "Marcos means more roads"—and his judicious use of an enormous campaign fund distributed through traditional patronage networks. Beyond this, his political success owed much to skill in preventing defections from the hierarchy of his party, no mean feat insofar as a tendency to challenge or desert the party leader had been a repeated pattern in national political life.

Economic performance in the decade before the imposition of martial law in 1972 was generally lackluster. Overall economic growth averaged about 5.2 percent in real terms during the 1960s. Heavily protected infant manufacturing industries grew despite their inefficiencies, and the country's economic management generally enjoyed the respect of international observers. Bureaucratic inefficiency impeded progress, however, and government economic planners were frustrated by the vulnerability of agricultural and extractive industry exports to world price fluctuations.

Discontent rooted in economic conditions was a concern at the start of the martial law era. The scarcity of arable land and the seeming inability of the government to come to grips with land reform and economic redistribution, together with the perception among students and others that powerful and corrupt oligarchs were profiting at public expense, brought protest in the streets and fanned leftist agitation in Manila. Demands for autonomy by Muslims, triggered in part by disputes over land with Christian colonizers to Mindanao, and problems of unemployment among the urban poor in the burgeoning slums of the metropolitan centers contributed to worsening conditions.

A turning point came in the aftermath of a bomb attack on a major opposition party rally in Manila in August 1971 that left many opposition senatorial candidates seriously injured. Marcos reacted by suspending the writ of habeas corpus, foreshadowing the declaration of martial law a year later after an assassination attempt against a cabinet minister. Using emergency powers available to him under the 1935 constitution, which was scheduled for early replacement by a new charter under preparation by a constitutional convention, the president cited economic decline, disorder, and the threat of a communist overthrow in justifying the action. In return for lost freedoms, he promised to break what he described as the stranglehold of the "Old Society" on the nation and to bring greater economic equality to the people under the banner of the New Society.

Having established martial law, Marcos set about securing his hold on the levers of power. Wasting no time, he began an offensive to forestall challengers to martial law rule so that the envisioned reforms could be set in motion. To counter violence and disorder, which he described as challenges to "the very stability of the country," immediate "extreme measures for survival" were taken. Under presidential orders, the military closed down certain elements of the media and arrested a number of opposition leaders, including Aquino, his strongest political rival at the time, as well as journalists, labor leaders, and several thousand protesters, many later tried by martial law military tribunals. Firearms were confiscated, private armed guards of regional political rivals and wealthy landowners were abolished, and extensive military intelligence surveillance was initiated.

Gradually, but systematically, Marcos then directed a thorough overhaul of the political system. Political parties were banned, and the legislature was closed. The draft constitution that had been in preparation was hastily ratified in January 1973 in a show of hands by members of local government bodies established only days earlier, and then only in certain parts of the country. The new charter called for a parliamentary form of government to be headed by a prime minister and a largely ceremonial president. Also strengthening Marcos' hand were "transitory" provisions giving him the power of both the prime minister and the president: he was empowered to convene an interim legislature and could remove any member of the executive or judiciary at his discretion. Most importantly, the decrees he issued during the transitory period were to have the force of law indefinitely.

Even before 1972 the technocrats serving in the Marcos administration had concluded that the distributional and employment problems were not well served by the import substitution strategy followed by previous administrations. Population growth, ineffectually controlled in a Roman Catholic country, and stagnant rural incomes had created a flood tide of migration to expanding squatter settlements in burgeoning metropolitan centers, especially Manila. Even though it was protected by extreme trade barriers, domestic industry was not expanding rapidly enough to absorb this migration, which was increasingly turning to relatively unproductive service sector employment. To arrest this course of development and on the recommendation of the World Bank (see Glossary) and other major foreign aid donors, the Marcos administration decided, in a radical shift of policy, to support labor-intensive export industries. After 1972 this new trade and market-oriented strategy became one of the fundamental underpinnings of the New Society program.

By 1978, using the military as his prime instrument to enforce the law, combat insurgency, and control the legal opposition, Marcos had further strengthened his formidable powers under a continuing martial law regime. Extensive purges rid the government of politically unreliable or corrupt bureaucrats. The press was under tight rein; some newspapers had been closed down and ceased publication. Around the president and First Lady Imelda Marcos, a select circle of supporters had collected—technocrats, businessmen, politicians, and ranking military officers, many of them kin to the president or Imelda Marcos or linked to the two families by common regional origin.

As First Lady, governor of Metro Manila (see Glossary), and minister of human settlements, Imelda Marcos occupied a preeminent position in the circle. She lent incalculable support as a highly visible spokesperson for New Society aspirations and accomplishments, although the Marcos' wealth, hers in particular, was a source of some resentment.

Having been pressured the summer of 1977 by domestic and foreign critics to relax the harsher aspects of martial law, Marcos had indicated plans for formation of an interim National Assembly, and in early 1978 he lifted the ban on political parties. In a scramble for patronage, his supporters hastily organized as the New Society Movement (Kilusang Bagong Lipunan—KBL). In the April elections the enfeebled opposition made a generally poor showing; most refused to participate in elections they regarded as fraudulent. Only Aquino, campaigning from prison, where he had been preparing an appeal against charges including murder and provision of arms to communist guerrillas predating his 1972 arrest, made a credible, though unsuccessful, showing against a KBL slate in Metro Manila headed by the First Lady. Opening the new interim legislature, Marcos told his audience—all but 14 of whom were KBL members—that his administration was defying a historic trend that asserted the irreversibility of a drift toward authoritarianism and centralism.

Efforts to bring about economic reform were less quickly and less easily engineered than political changes. Able Philippine technocrats and outside advisers, who had agreed on the need for long-term planning, foresaw a period of at least a generation before substantial relief of agrarian distress and urban poverty and modification of the lopsided distribution of wealth could be accomplished. In the meantime, the proportion of households unable to meet their own basic needs had risen from 38 percent in 1971 to 45 percent in 1975. A five-year plan covering the 1978-82 period addressed eight major areas of concern: inadequacy in basic needs; income inequality; unemployment and underemployment; rapid population growth; balance of payments and price instability; energy constraints; environmental problems; and regional growth disparities. Optimistic plans for meeting these challenges outlined goals for promotion of social development: attainment of self-sufficiency in food and improved domestic supply of energy; pursuit of sustained high growth; improvements in price levels; improvement in domestic resource mobilization and the balance of payments; and attention to housing and lagging regional development. All this was premised on sustained political stability.

The administration launched the optimistic plans despite disappointment over severe blows to the economy from unanticipated external developments since 1973. For a brief interval after the declaration of martial law, commodity prices of Philippine exports had boomed. The sharp increase in world oil prices in 1973, however, badly hurt the Philippines, which until the early 1980s imported as much as 90 percent of its energy requirements, depleting foreign exchange resources and creating inflation. Additionally, the economy was hit by export failure, primarily because of the collapse of sugar, coconut, and copper prices. The island of Negros and other sugar-producing areas were hard hit. The unrelenting population growth exerted further pressures on strained metropolitan job markets. In the distressed agricultural sector, fragmentation of ownership through inheritance, the weakening of traditional landlord-tenant obligations, and erratic price shifts in basic commodities caused severe hardship.

Two bright notes in the agricultural picture were moderate government achievements in land reform and more bountiful crops attributable to administration efforts to raise productivity. Land reform was confined to rice- and corn-growing areas and to the holdings of relatively large landowners, but it went further than did the efforts of any previous regime.

The cost of the Muslim insurgency in the southern Philippines, moreover, was a diminishing burden. The Moro National Liberation Front, founded in 1968, had grown to an organization of 50,000 to 60,000 guerrillas by 1974 and was launching sporadic terrorist attacks on government forces from its hideaways in the hinterlands. Negotiations between high-level Philippine spokesmen and representatives of the international Islamic community in Jidda in 1974 and in Tripoli in 1976 provided greater cultural autonomy to the Muslim Filipinos (Moros), which together with high-image infrastructure projects in Mindanao and the decline of foreign assistance to the Moros significantly reduced the level of tension in that area by the early 1980s.

Curtailment of Muslim insurgency, modest economic growth, and land reform and other agricultural successes failed, however, to abate an undercurrent of criticism against the government in 1979 and 1980, in the light of continuing allegations of government inaction in failing to respond to urgent needs of the population, political repression, human rights violations, and military abuses. Voices expressing dissatisfaction, even cynicism, underlining the conviction of the persistence of corruption and dishonesty in the affairs of the nation, came from a wide spectrum of society. From the redoubt of the enormously powerful, and hitherto generally conservative, Roman Catholic Church, members of the Catholic Bishops Conference of the Philippines (CBCP), priests, and lay church-workers, joined by members of religious orders, had begun from the mid-1970s to press for sociopolitical changes leading to greater social justice and human dignity.

Mutually beneficial and close economic and security ties with the United States at the start of the 1980s also drew criticism from Marcos opponents. A small but vocal group of Philippine nationalists charged that these links relegated their country to a continuing neocolonial status and undermined, rather than enhanced, its overall strategic position. Indeed, United States and multilateral aid and investment were crucial inputs in Philippine economic growth. Marcos, meanwhile, was broadening the base in foreign affairs, seeking wider ties with other Asian countries and nations of the Middle East. Japan had become a trading partner of almost equal importance to the United States.

Another problem for the Marcos government was spreading communist insurgency, even though the movement appeared to have little or no outside sources of support, and observers gave it almost no chance—acting independently—of staging a successful government takeover. Militarily, the threat was mounted by forces of the New People's Army (NPA), an adjunct of the outlawed Communist Party of the Philippines-Marxist Leninist (CPP-ML). Press accounts in the early 1980s reported that NPA forces had infiltrated more than one-half of the country's 73 provinces, especially remote parts of eastern Mindanao, Samar, and northern and southeastern Luzon, where they engaged in sporadic terrorist attacks, sometimes supported by peasant elements.

Although church leaders were less strident in expressing their grievances than during the previous year, 1980 presented the martial law government with expressions of tension on other fronts—urban terrorism, student demonstrations, and the threat of a general strike. Beginning in August, a spate of bombings rocked Manila over a three-month period, responsibility being claimed by a small dissident group. Meanwhile, more than 70 opposition leaders succeeded in joining forces to issue the Covenant for National Freedom, urging basic reforms in the political process.

Political relaxation notwithstanding, Marcos remained a formidable figure on the national scene. His position was buttressed not only by emergency powers backed by military force but also by bureaucratic and grass-roots support from those who had benefited from his programs. He gained enormous leverage from the traditional mutual give-and-take between himself and some of his more powerful supporters, who had substantial vested interests in manufacturing industries. Access to funds for patronage and other political uses also counted heavily among his political assets, particularly considering the relative dearth of funds available to the opposition. In the presidential election of June

16, 1981—the first since 1969—Marcos, as the standard-bearer of the KBL—received 88 percent of the vote.

Because of its institutional strength and the adherence of an overwhelming majority of the Philippines' more than 50 million people, Marcos correctly respected the power of the church. For a time after martial law was lifted—especially in the aftermath of the visit of Pope John Paul II to the Philippines in February 1981—members of the clergy focused on the aspects of their carefully balanced "critical collaboration" policy that emphasized both qualified cooperation and criticism. In early 1983 as Jaime Cardinal Sin, archbishop of Manila, asserted that a climate of fear in the country had stifled dissent, the CBCP issued a joint pastoral letter read in 3,000 churches across the nation. In it, the 112 bishops identified as the sources of their "difficulties with the government" the arrest and detention of clergy and others working in social action programs and the deeper issues of poverty and the suppression of dissent. Putting forward their "dialogue for peace," the bishops urged the government to "seek out, in all possible objectivity, root causes of disturbances" and to "apply genuine remedies while seeking to accept a certain pluralism of positions in the way [the] people strive for justice according to their faith." At the same time, they cautioned the clergy and members of religious orders against taking "an exaggerated interest" in temporal affairs.

In the summer of 1983, mounting economic difficulties and the prospect of the May 1984 parliamentary elections occupied Filipino businesspeople, professionals, and political leaders. Rumors that Marcos was in ill health rebounded in Manila in early August. In the United States, Marcos' longtime opponent, Aquino, was preparing to return to the islands to bolster the moderate opposition efforts in the forthcoming elections, despite intensive efforts by Marcos to delay or impede his return. Even Imelda Marcos herself had flown to the United States where, in a personal encounter, she had attempted to dissuade him by warning of plots against his life. Aquino, however, was determined, and citing the need for national reconciliation and restoration of rights and freedoms through nonviolence, he boarded a plane for Manila, intent on rejoining the opposition in an all-out push against the 18-year-old Marcos regime. Moments after he was escorted from the plane by military authorities, however, Aquino lay on the tarmac of Manila International Airport, shot dead reportedly from less than a yard away by an unidentified assailant. In the aftermath of an act that by its utter brutality had produced a storm of outrage at home and abroad, the danger of polarization in Philippine society had exponentially increased, and to many observers it appeared likely that the assassination would serve as a catalyst for dramatic political and social change. The Marcos regime had proved itself not to be trifled with on more than one occasion in the past, however, demonstrating its power and tenacity and the exceptional political astuteness of its core leadership.

Thus, in the days immediately after Aquino's death, the situation remained extremely fluid, and the ultimate outcome of this, the latest crisis for Marcos' leadership, remained conjectural at best.

August 1983

Turbulence and uncertainty continued to characterize the scene as this book went to press in April 1984, some seven months after research had been completed. In the aftermath of the assassination, the political arena was characterized by a high degree of volatility. Anger and resentment against the Marcos administration, long held in check, were now expressed without hesitation in street demonstrations. Protesters demanded that Marcos resign and condemned his administration for lax security at the airport, seen as having cost Aquino his life. Some 2 million Filipinos filed past the body of the slain opposition leader or joined the funeral procession.

After the prolonged period of public mourning, opposition groups formed. Protests were organized against Marcos' long years of harsh rule, the erosion of rights and freedoms, and the militarization of the countryside. Participation of middle-class elements in the opposition demonstrations, now joined by a growing number of previously acquiescent Makati business district leaders, sounded a new and ominous note for the government. In late September public dissent culminated in a violent street clash between critics and army and police, claiming 11 lives. Amid the turmoil, the Philippines leg of a planned visit to Southeast Asia by the United States president, Ronald Reagan, was postponed indefinitely; official releases cited the press of business at home as the reason. Showing his usual political astuteness, Marcos managed to sidestep demands for his resignation, but persistent rumors that he was gravely ill brought renewed calls for a constitutional amendment clarifying the succession question.

Meanwhile, political instability had compounded previously existing monetary problems, leading to a full-blown economic crisis. Contributing to the crisis was a massive capital flight, symptomatic of a growing concern within the financial community about the uncertain future of the Marcos leadership. An estimated US$200 million had been diverted out of the country by early October, and the flight was continuing. Difficulties in management of the foreign debt escalated. A drop in export prices and rising international interest rates had already pushed the country's balance of payments deficit to 8.5 percent of the gross national product in 1982, while during the first three quarters of 1983 a total deficit of US$1.3 billion had already been accumulated. Marcos was compelled to announce a second currency devaluation for the year in late 1983, as well as a new economic policy calling for austerity measures considerably beyond those that international creditors had already demanded earlier in the year. A 90-day moratorium was imposed on the foreign debt, while national leaders scrambled to arrange rescheduling with international lending agencies. Efforts were initially unsuccessful, but the moratorium was extended in mid-January 1984 for 90 days. Adding to the consternation was the discovery of a major miscalculation in assessing the foreign debt, indicative of an actual total of US$25 billion rather than the US$19 billion for 1983 previously reported by the Central Bank. Worse still, it was revealed that the bank had overstated its reserves by about US$600 million.

On the eve of the 1984 parliamentary elections, Marcos remained the dominant political figure, but there was little doubt of erosion in his power base. The threshold of popular tolerance of frustration and resentment over political constraints had been progressively lowered. Relations with the United States remained cordial, but the Reagan administration gave courteous attention to visiting opposition spokesmen. Moreover, in response to continuing demands that the question of presidential succession be resolved, a constitutional amendment bill was passed, designating the Speaker of the National Assembly as interim successor, pending restoration of the office of vice president in 1987. The enactment satisfied opposition and other elements who feared that, in the event of the death or incapacity of the president, Imelda Marcos herself might step into the breach with the support of a clique within the military. Another widely expressed fear was that General Ver and his supporters might try to seize power themselves.

Inquiry into the Aquino assassination compounded Marcos' problems. A Marcos-appointed investigatory commission disbanded within weeks after its organization, having failed to win public confidence. Respected appeals court judge Corazon Julian Agrava accepted responsibility for heading a new commission. The new fact-finding body's meticulous investigation only served, however, to undermine further public confidence. Testimony that it elicited from a number of heretofore reluctant witnesses cast further doubt on the reliability of the government claim that Rolando Galman, a small-time criminal having communist links, was responsible for the murder. By mid-April the government contention that Galman had fired the fatal shots had been largely discredited. Moreover, new evidence was reinforcing public suspicion of government complicity in the murder, pointing to the possibility that elements of the military were to blame.

With the parliamentary elections less than a month away, Marcos, although not himself a candidate, headed a tightly organized, well-financed campaign on behalf of KBL candidates. An impressive margin of victory could perhaps regenerate confidence in his administration among foreign lenders, from whom he was seeking an additional US$4 billion in financing. Procurement of such a loan, however, might depend on Marcos' willingness to undertake economic and administrative reforms that would almost certainly diminish the power and influence of members of his ruling circle, among them his wife. Imelda Marcos had already declared her intention not to run again for the National

Assembly, but she was reportedly highly displeased at the possibility of the dismantling of the government ministry she headed.

Opposition leaders, meanwhile, including Salvador Laurel and Aquino's brother, Agapito, traveled to the United States in search of support. Laurel and others were publicly received by senior government officials in a seeming effort to keep communication lines open with the opposition while pressuring Marcos toward democratic reforms and helping to shore up the country's finances. The opposition remained sharply divided on the issue of participation in the elections. Some, including Agapito Aquino, former senator Lorenzo Tañada, and former president Diosdado Macapagal, called for a boycott, citing controversy and claims of fraud surrounding earlier elections. Others, including Aquino's widow, Corazon, came out—after some hesitation—in favor of participation, saying it was the best strategy for restoring democracy. Marcos, appearing to be in better health than in past months, continued to address large crowds assembled by party organizers. Only time would tell whether his administration could successfully respond to opposing sentiment for increased freedom and democratic rights.

April 1984   Frederica Bunge

Chapter 1. Historical Setting

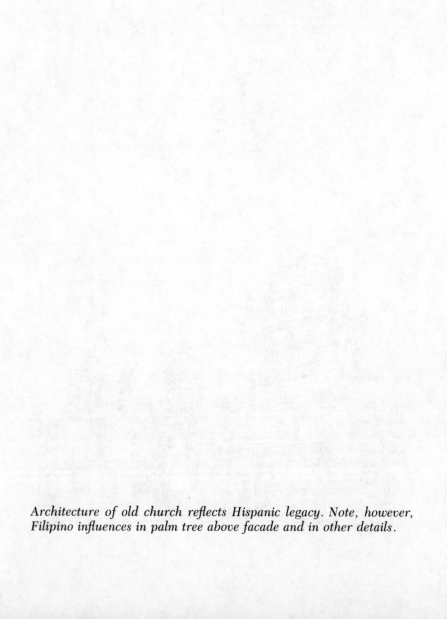

Architecture of old church reflects Hispanic legacy. Note, however, Filipino influences in palm tree above facade and in other details.

THE PHILIPPINES EVOLVED as a result of the blending of Spanish cultural elements, principally those associated with Roman Catholic Christianity, and older indigenous cultural patterns. The period of Spanish rule, most firmly established in the lowland areas of Luzon and the Visayan Islands, lasted for over three centuries, from 1565 to 1898. Although colonial rule was at times harsh, "Hispanicization" of the people was accomplished peacefully through the medium of the friar members of the Catholic religious orders engaged in missionary work in the barrios, or villages. The Islamic sultanates in the Sulu Archipelago and on Mindanao, however, successfully resisted Spanish penetration and Christianization.

By the late nineteenth century the development of a cash crop and an export economy, as well as greater contact with the outside world, had stimulated the growth of a Westernized Filipino elite, the *ilustrados* ("enlightened ones"), who began to demand a more equal relationship between Filipinos and Spanish. A central issue was the inclusion of a greater number of Filipino priests in the islands' Roman Catholic parishes. These were controlled by Spanish priests of the religious orders, the friars, who also had a privileged position in the economic and political system of the colony and stubbornly resisted change. *Ilustrado* members of the Propaganda Movement, based largely in Europe and influenced by liberal and democratic ideas, advocated moderate reform. Harsh suppression of dissent by the Spanish, however, led to the formation of a revolutionary movement, the Katipunan, in 1892; four years later, it initiated a revolt against Spain, calling for total independence.

The December 10, 1898, Treaty of Paris, which concluded the Spanish-American War, transferred control of the Philippines from Spain to the United States. Although opposed at first by revolutionaries who had declared the independence of the islands in June 1898, the new colonial rulers gained the support of the landowning and *ilustrado* elite. Representative institutions were established in the first decade of United States rule to prepare the people for eventual independence. Progress in this direction was rapid. On November 15, 1935, the self-governing Commonwealth of the Philippines was established, and full independence was to be granted by 1946. The cash-crop economy of the islands, however, was increasingly dependent on American markets, and *ilustrado* and landowner domination of the political system meant that needed social reforms were never implemented. The Japanese occupation of the Philippines in the 1942-45 period and United States recapture of the islands inflicted great suffering on the population, and there were bitter divisions over the issue of political leaders' collaboration with the Japanese.

During the 1946-72 period Philippine society was pluralistic, and competing political parties, a free press, and constitutionally defined representative institutions were modeled on those of the United States. Political power remained a monopoly of the old elite, and problems of poverty and extreme inequality persisted. In response to what he perceived as a rising tide of lawlessness and an active conspiracy on the part of leftist elements to overthrow the government, President Ferdinand E. Marcos proclaimed martial law on September 21, 1972. His New Society program, a largely successful effort to gain central control over competing political forces, was to last until January 1981.

Early History

Negrito, Proto-Malay, and Malay peoples were the principal contributors to the population of the Philippine archipelago. The Negritos are believed to have migrated by land bridges during the last glacial period. Later migrations were by water and took place over several thousand years in repeated movements before and after the start of the Christian era.

The social and political organization of the population in the widely scattered islands evolved into a generally common pattern. There was only a vaguely developed concept of territoriality other than that among the permanent-field rice farmers of northern Luzon. The basic unit of settlement was the *barangay* (see Glossary), originally a kinship group headed by a *datu* (chief; pl., *datu*). Within the *barangay* the broad social divisions consisted of nobles, which included the *datu;* freemen; and a group described before the Spanish period as dependents. Dependents included a number of categories with differing degrees of dependency: landless agricultural workers; those who had lost freeman status because of indebtedness or punishment for crime; and slaves, most of whom appear to have been captives of war.

Trade relations between the Philippines and both mainland Asia and the islands to the south started early in the Christian era; trade first centered mainly in the Sulu region, reaching the northern islands later. The earliest foreign traders were Hindus, Indonesians, and possibly Arabs. By the tenth century the Chinese were engaged in trade with the Philippines, and they were joined in the fifteenth century by the Japanese, who, like the Chinese, established resident trading communities.

Islam was brought to the Philippines by traders and proselytizers coming from the Indonesian islands. By 1500 Islam was established in the Sulu Archipelago and spread from there to Mindanao; it reached the Manila area by 1565. Muslim immigrants introduced a political concept of territorial states ruled by rajas or sultans who exercised suzerainty over the *datu*. Neither the political state concept of the Muslim rulers nor the limited territorial concept of the sedentary rice farmers of Luzon, however, spread beyond their original boundaries. When the Spanish arrived in the sixteenth century, the majority of the estimated 500,000 persons in the islands still lived in *barangay* settlements.

The Early Spanish Period, 1521-1762

The European discovery of the Philippines took place on March 16, 1521, during Ferdinand Magellan's circumnavigation of the globe, when he landed on Cebu and claimed the land for Charles I of Spain. A month later he was killed by a local chief. The Spanish crown sent several expeditions to the archipelago during the next decades. Permanent settlement was finally established in 1565 when Miguel López de Legazpi, the first royal governor, arrived in Cebu from Mexico. Six years later, after defeating a local Muslim ruler, he established his capital at Manila, a location that offered the excellent harbor site of Manila Bay, a large population, and proximity to the ample food supplies of the central Luzon rice lands. Manila remained the center of Spanish civil, military, religious, and commercial activity in the islands. The islands were given their present-day name in honor of Philip II of Spain, who reigned from 1556 to 1598.

Spanish policy toward the Philippines, Spain's only colony in Asia, had three objectives: acquisition of a share in the spice trade, development of contacts with China and Japan in order to further Christian missionary efforts there, and conversion of the Filipinos to Christianity. Only the third objective was eventually realized, and this not completely because of the active resistance of both the Muslims in the south and the Igorot, the upland tribal peoples in the north.

Philip II explicitly ordered that Spanish pacification of the Philippines be bloodless, avoiding a repetition of Spain's sanguinary conquests on the American mainland. The ideal was not completely attained, but the Spanish occupation of the islands was accomplished with relatively little bloodshed. The achievement was facilitated by the absence of initial armed resistance by most of the population except the Muslims. Church and state were inseparably linked in carrying out Spanish policy. The state assumed administrative responsibility—expenditures and selection of personnel—for the new ecclesiastical establishments and in turn assigned responsibility for conversion of the natives to the several religious orders—the Dominicans, Franciscans, Jesuits, and Augustinians—the members of which were known as friars.

At the lower levels of their colonial administration, the Spanish built on traditional village organization, thereby co-opting and confirming the status of traditional leaders over their followers and dependents. The *barangay* (renamed *visita* and, later, barrio) was kept as the lowest administrative unit; the position of *datu* was retained and renamed the *cabeza de barangay* (headman) and initially made hereditary. The next highest level was that of the *pueblo*, the forerunner of the municipality, made up of several *barangays* and incorporating a principal town, where the parish church was located. Through a semielective procedure, a *pueblo* magistrate was selected, known as the *gobernadorcillo* (petty governor); the local church and Spanish authorities also had considerable say in his appointment. The office of *gobernadorcillo* was the highest that could be held by a Filipino. At a higher level was the province, governed by an *alcalde mayor*, a Spanish official reporting directly to Manila and responsible for all administrative, military, and judicial affairs in his region.

The system of indirect rule helped create in rural areas a Filipino upper class, referred to as the *principalía* or the *principales* (principal ones). This group came to combine local wealth, high status and prestige, certain privileges such as exemption from taxes, lesser roles in the parish church, and appointment to local offices. Somewhat enlarged from the preconquest nobility, the *principalía* succeeded in creating and perpetuating an oligarchic system of local control. Among the most significant and enduring changes under Spanish rule was the replacement of the Filipino idea of communal use and ownership of land with the concept of private, individual ownership. The Filipinos gradually adopted the principle of individual ownership of land, which in practice meant that members of the *principalía* acquired titles.

Religion played an intimate part in Spanish relations with, and attitudes toward, the indigenous population. The Spaniards considered conversion through baptism a symbol of allegiance to their authority. Although they were interested in gaining a profit from the colony, the Spanish recognized at the same time a responsibility to protect the property and personal rights of these new Christians.

The church's work of conversion of Filipinos was facilitated by the absence of other organized religions, except for Islam in the south. The missionaries had their greatest success among women and children, although the pageantry of the church had a wide appeal. Its appeal was reinforced by the incorporation of Filipino social customs into religious observances, for example, in the fiestas celebrating the patron saint of a barrio (see Religious Life, ch. 2). The eventual outcome was a new cultural community of the main Malay lowland population, from which the Muslims (known by the Spanish as Moros, or Moors) and the upland tribal peoples of Luzon remained detached and alienated.

The Spanish found neither spices nor exploitable precious metals in the Philippines. The ecology of the islands was little changed by Spanish importations and technical innovations, with the exception of corn cultivation and some extension of irrigation in order to increase rice supplies for the growing urban population. The colony was not profitable. A long war with the Dutch in the seventeenth century and intermittent conflict with the Moros nearly bankrupted the colonial treasury. Annual deficits were made up by a subsidy from New Spain (Mexico). Colonial income derived mainly from entrepôt trade: the "Manila Galleons" sailing from Acapulco on the west coast of New Spain brought shipments of silver bullion and minted coin that were exchanged for return cargoes of Chinese goods, mainly silk textiles. There was no direct trade with Spain. Failure to exploit indigenous natural resources and investment of virtually all official, private, and

Multilevel rice terraces on Luzon were established
centuries ago by Ifugao tribal peoples.
Courtesy Embassy of the Republic of the Philippines, Washington

Ferdinand Magellan's commemorative cross on Cebu reflects
the historic circumnavigation of the globe by one of
his ships, which carried the news of his discovery
of the Philippines in 1521 to Europe.
Courtesy Tourist Research and Planning

7

church capital in the galleon trade were mutually reinforcing tendencies. Loss or capture of the galleons or Chinese junks en route to Manila represented a financial disaster for the colony.

The thriving entrepôt trade quickly attracted growing numbers of Chinese to Manila. The Chinese, in addition to managing trade transactions, assumed necessary functions in provisioning and providing services for the capital. The Spanish regarded them with mixed distrust and acknowledgment of their indispensable role. During the first decades of Spanish rule, the Chinese in Manila became more numerous than the Spanish, who tried to control them by residence restrictions, periodic deportations, and actual or threatened violence sometimes degenerating into riots and massacres of Chinese during the period between 1603 and 1762.

The Later Period of Spanish Rule, 1762-1898

In 1762 Spain became involved in the Seven Years' War (1756-63) on the side of France against Britain; in October 1762 forces of the British East India Company captured Manila after fierce fighting. Spanish resistance continued under Lieutenant Governor Simón de Anda, based at Bacolor in Pampanga Province, and Manila was returned to the Spanish in May 1764 in conformity with the Treaty of Paris, which formally ended the war. The British occupation nonetheless marked, in a very significant sense, the beginning of the end of the old order. Spanish prestige suffered irreparable damage because of the defeat at British hands. A number of rebellions broke out, of which the most notable was that of Diego Silang in the Ilocos area of northern Luzon. In December 1762 Silang expelled the Spanish from Vigan and set up an independent government. He established friendly relations with the British and was able to repulse Spanish attacks on Vigan, but he was assassinated in May 1763. The Spanish, tied down with fighting the British and the rebels, were unable to control the raids of the Moros of the south on the Christian barrios of the Visayan Islands and Luzon. Thousands of Christian Filipinos were captured as slaves, and Moro raids continued to be a serious problem through the remainder of the century. The Chinese community, resentful of Spanish policies of discrimination, for the most part enthusiastically supported the British, providing them with laborers and armed men who fought de Anda in Pampanga.

After Spanish rule was restored, José Basco y Vargas (1778-87), one of the ablest of Spanish administrators, implemented a series of reforms designed to promote the economic development of the islands and make them independent of the subsidy from New Spain. In 1781 he established the Economic Society of Friends of the Country, which, through its checkered history extending over the next century, encouraged the growth of new crops for export—such as indigo, tea, silk, opium poppies, and abaca (hemp)—and the development of local industry. A government tobacco monopoly was established in 1782. Areas of the country, principally the Cagayan valley, Nueva Vizcaya, and the

Ilocos region in northern Luzon and the island of Marinduque, were set aside for tobacco cultivation, and farmers were obliged to deliver fixed quotas of tobacco to officials. The monopoly brought in large profits for the government and made the Philippines a leader in world tobacco production; it also resulted in great hardship for the cultivators in the tobacco regions because they were fined if they could not deliver the quota and were subjected to the constant abuse of officials ostensibly seeking to curtail black market trade.

The venerable galleon trade between the Philippines and New Spain continued as a government monopoly until 1815, when the last official galleon from Acapulco docked at Manila. The Royal Company of the Philippines, chartered by the Spanish king in 1785, promoted direct trade between the islands and Spain. All Philippine goods were given tariff-free status, and the company, hand in hand with Basco y Vargas' Economic Society, encouraged the growth of a cash-crop economy by investing a portion of its early profits in the cultivation of sugar, indigo, peppers, and mulberry trees for silk, as well as in textile factories.

Economic and Social Transformation, 1820-72

As long as the Spanish Empire on the eastern rim of the Pacific remained intact and the galleons sailed to and from Acapulco, there was little incentive on the part of the colonial authorities to promote the development of the Philippines, despite the initiatives of Basco y Vargas, a man much maligned by conservatives during his career as governor in Manila. After his departure, the Economic Society was allowed to fall on hard times, and the Royal Company showed decreasing profits. The independence of Spain's Latin American colonies, particularly Mexico in 1821, forced a fundamental reorientation of policy. Cut off from the Mexican subsidies and protected Latin American markets, the islands had to pay for themselves. The result, in terms of commerce, was an end to the isolation that had been breaking down anyway in the late eighteenth century.

Growing numbers of foreign merchants in Manila spurred the integration of the Philippines into an international commercial system linking industrialized Europe and North America with sources of raw materials and markets in the Americas and Asia. In principle, non-Spanish Europeans were not allowed to reside in Manila or elsewhere in the islands, but in fact British, American, French and other foreign merchants got around this prohibition by flying the flags of Asian states or conniving with local officials. There were enough foreigners in the capital by 1820 that, during a cholera epidemic, Spanish reactionaries, fearing the foreigners' growing influence, spread rumors among the populace that foreigners had spread the epidemic; this resulted in riots in which a number of Europeans and Chinese were killed. The old isolationism, however, could not be restored, and in 1834 the crown abolished the Royal Company of the Philippines and formally recognized free trade, opening the port of Manila to unrestricted foreign commerce.

By 1856 there were 13 foreign trading firms in Manila, of which seven were British and two American; between 1855 and 1873 the Spanish opened new ports, including Iloilo on Panay, Zamboanga in the western portion of Mindanao, Cebu on Cebu, and Legazpi in the Bicol area of southern Luzon, to foreign trade. The growing prominence of steam over sail navigation and the opening of the Suez Canal in 1869 contributed to spectacular increases in the volume of trade. In 1851 exports and imports totaled some ₱8.2 million; 10 years later they had risen to ₱18.9 million and by 1870 were ₱53.3 million, exports growing by 20 million in the 1861-70 period. British and American merchants dominated Philippine commerce, the former in an especially favored position owing to their bases in Singapore and Hong Kong. The growth of British commercial colonies in northern Borneo brought them into intimate—and in Spanish eyes distressing—contact with the sultan of Sulu. It was only through diplomatic pressure on London that a treaty between the sultan and James Brooke, "White Raja" of Sarawak, making the sultanate a British protectorate, was not ratified in 1849. In 1877 an agreement was concluded between Spain, Britain, and Germany in which Spain granted Britain free trade privileges in the Sulu Archipelago in return for its recognition of Spanish control over the sultanate. After centuries of defiance the sultan recognized Spanish suzerainty in 1878.

By the late nineteenth century three crops—tobacco, abaca, and sugar—dominated Philippine exports. The government monopoly on tobacco had been abolished in 1880, but Philippine cigars maintained their high reputation, fumigating Victorian parlors in Britain, the European continent, and North America. Because of the growth of worldwide shipping, Philippine abaca, which was considered the best material for ropes and cordage, grew in importance and after 1850 alternated with sugar as the islands' most important export. Americans dominated the abaca trade; raw material was made into ropes first at plants in New England and then in the Philippines. Principal regions for the growing of abaca were the Bicol areas of southeastern Luzon and the eastern portions of the Visayan Islands.

Sugarcane had been produced and refined using crude methods at least as early as the beginning of the eighteenth century. The opening of the port of Iloilo on Panay in 1855 and the encouragement of the British vice consul in that town, Nicholas Loney (described by a modern writer as "a one-man whirlwind of entrepreneurial and technical innovation"), led to the development of the previously unsettled island of Negros as the center of the Philippines sugar industry that exported its product to Britain and Australia. Loney arranged liberal credit terms for local landlords to invest in the new crop, encouraged the migration of labor from the neighboring and overpopulated island of Panay, and introduced stream-driven sugar refineries that replaced the traditional method of producing low-grade sugar in loaves. The population of Negros tripled. Local "sugar kings"—the owners of the sugar plantations—were to grow into a potent political and economic force by the end of the century.

Other important crops for export included indigo dye, coffee, tropical woods, and coconut products. It was a mark of the Philippines' evolution into a cash-crop export economy that the islands, traditionally an exporter of rice, principally to China, by 1870 became a net importer of the grain that formed the basis of the people's diet.

Chinese and Chinese Mestizos

A more tolerant official attitude toward Chinese immigration and activities within the archipelago evolved in the late eighteenth and early nineteenth centuries as a deep-seated Spanish suspicion of the Chinese gave way to recognition of their potentially constructive role in economic development. Chinese expulsion orders had been issued in 1755 and 1766, and many Chinese moved south to Sulu or Mindanao to resume their craft or trading activities, but the edicts were repealed in 1788. Chinese remained concentrated in towns around Manila, particularly Binondo and Santa Cruz, the provinces having been emptied of Chinese by the expulsion orders. In 1839, however, the government issued a decree granting them freedom of occupation and residence. In the latter half of the century immigration into the archipelago, largely from the maritime province of Fujian on the southeastern coast of China, increased, and a growing proportion went into outlying areas. In 1849 more than 90 percent of the approximately 6,000 Chinese lived in or around the capital, while in 1886 this decreased to 77 percent of the 66,000 Chinese at that time, declining still further in the last decade of Spanish rule. The Chinese presence in the hinterland went hand in hand with the transformation of the insular economy. Spanish policy was to encourage immigrants to become agricultural laborers, but most, with the exception of gardeners who supplied vegetables to the towns, shunned the fields and set themselves up as small retailers and moneylenders.

While British, American and, to a lesser extent, European trading companies dominated Philippine trade on the national level, the Chinese gained a central position in the cash-crop economy on the provincial and local levels. Chinese often acted as agents for *cabecillas* (wholesalers) based in Manila, exchanging imported goods—particularly textiles—for produce at small *tiendas de sari-sari* (general stores); the produce was then transported to the *cabecilla*, who sold it to foreign merchants. In exchange for loans Chinese moneylenders acquired land from Filipino cultivators, which they then rented out, a situation that was particularly prevalent in the tobacco region of the Cagayan valley after the monopoly was abolished. Chinese obtained contracts from the government to serve as "tax farmers" in the villages, making huge profits, and owned rice mills and abaca plantations. Their position in the late nineteenth century economy was so secure that the conservative Spanish echoed earlier warnings that the islands were turning into "a Chinese colony with a Spanish flag."

Of equal, if not greater, significance for subsequent political, cultural, and economic developments were the Chinese mestizos (see Glossary). At the beginning of the nineteenth century they composed about 5 percent of the total population of around 2.5 million and were concentrated in the most developed provinces of central Luzon and in Manila and its environs. A much smaller number lived in the more important towns of the Visayan Islands, such as Cebu and Iloilo, and on Mindanao. Converts to Catholicism and speakers of Filipino languages or Spanish rather than Chinese dialects, the mestizos enjoyed a legal status as subjects of Spain that was denied the Chinese. In the words of historian Edgar Wickberg, they were considered, unlike the mixed-Chinese of other Southeast Asian countries, not "a special kind of local Chinese" but "a special kind of Filipino."

The eighteenth-century expulsion edicts gave the Chinese mestizos the opportunity to enter retailing and the skilled craft occupations formerly dominated by the Chinese. The growing competition of new Chinese immigrants, however, drove mestizos out of the commercial sector, with the apparent result that many invested in land, particularly in central Luzon. The estates of the religious orders were concentrated in this region, and mestizos became *inquilinos* (lessees) of these lands, subletting them to cultivators; a portion of their rent was given by the *inquilino* to the friar estate. Like the Chinese, the mestizos were moneylenders and acquired land when debtors defaulted.

By the late nineteenth century prominent mestizo families, despite the inroads of the Chinese, were noted for their wealth and formed the major component of a truly Filipino elite. As the export economy grew and foreign contact increased, the mestizos and other members of this Filipino elite, known collectively as *ilustrados*, obtained higher education (in some cases abroad), entered professions such as law or medicine, and were particularly receptive to the liberal and democratic ideas that were beginning to reach the Philippines despite the efforts of a generally reactionary—and friar-dominated—Spanish establishment.

The "Friarocracy"

The power of religious orders remained one of the great constants, over the centuries, of Spanish colonial rule. Even in the late nineteenth century the friars of the Augustinian, Dominican, Franciscan, and Recollect orders conducted many of the executive and control functions of government on the local level. They were responsible for education and health measures, kept the census and tax records, reported on the character and behavior of individual villagers, supervised the selection of local police and town officers, and were responsible for maintaining "public morals" and reporting incidences of sedition to the authorities. Contrary to the principles of the church, they commonly used information gained in confession to pinpoint troublemakers. Given the very small number of Spanish living outside the capital even in the nineteenth century, the friars were regarded as indispensable instruments of Spanish rule that contemporary critics labeled a "friarocracy" (*fri-alocracia*).

Persistent themes in Philippine church history were the controversies over visitation and secularization. Visitation involved the authority of the bishops of the church hierarchy to inspect and discipline the religious orders, a principle laid down in church law and practiced in most of the Catholic world. The friars were successful in resisting the efforts of the archbishops of Manila to impose visitation; consequently they operated under no formal supervision except that of their own "provincials," or regional heads. Secularization meant the replacement of the friars, who came exclusively from Spain, with Filipino, or diocesan, secular priests. This, again, was successfully resisted, as friars through the centuries kept up the argument, often couched in crude racial terms, that Filipino secular priests were of too poor quality to take on parish duties. Although the church practice was for the parishes of countries converted to Christianity to be relinquished by the religious orders to native seculars, in 1870 only 181 out of 792 parishes in the islands had Filipino priests. With its national and racial dimensions, the secularization issue became linked at that time with broader demands for political reform.

The economic position of the orders was secured by their extensive landholdings, which generally had been donated to them for the support of their churches, schools, and other establishments. Given the general lack of interest on the part of Spanish colonials—clustered in Manila and dependent on the galleon trade—in developing agriculture, the religious orders had become by the eighteenth century the largest landholders in the islands, their estates being concentrated in the central Luzon region. Land rents—paid often by Chinese mestizo *inquilinos*, who planted cash crops for export—provided them with the sort of income that enabled many friars to live like princes in palatial establishments. Filipino resentment of the growth of friar estates is evident from at least the mid-eighteenth century; titles to land were vague, and when the friars began occupying native lands in the Tagalog area of central Luzon around Manila, there was such a violent popular reaction in 1745-46 that the Spanish king ordered a special investigation into the friars' abuses. This was sabotaged, however, by their refusal to submit their land deeds to official examination.

Central to the friars' dominant position was their monopoly of education on all levels and thus their control over cultural and intellectual life. In 1863 the Spanish government decreed that a system of free public primary education be established in the islands, which could have been interpreted as a threat to this monopoly. By 1867 there were 593 primary schools enrolling 138,990 students; by 1877 this had grown to 1,608 schools and 177,113 students, and in 1898 there were 2,150 schools and over 200,000 students out of a total population of approximately 6 million. The friars, however, were given the responsibility of supervising the system on both the local and the national levels, while the Jesuits were given control of the teacher-training colleges. The religious orders were strongly opposed to the teaching of modern foreign languages (including Spanish) and scientific and technical subjects to the *indios* (literally, Indians; the Spanish term for Filipinos); in 1898 the University of Santo Tomás taught essentially the same courses that it did in 1611, when it was founded by the Dominican order, 21 years before Galileo was hauled before the Inquisition for publishing the idea that the earth revolved around the sun.

The "friarocracy" seems to have had more than its share of personal irregularities, and the priestly vow of chastity was often honored in the breach. In the eyes of educated Filipino priests and laymen, however, most inexcusable was the friars' open attitude of contempt toward the people. By the late nineteenth century their attitude was one of blatant racism. In the words of one friar, responding to the challenge of the *ilustrados*, "the only liberty the Indians want is the liberty of savages. Leave them to their cock-fighting and their indolence, and they will thank you more than if you load them down with old and new rights."

Resistance to Spanish Rule: The Early Phase

Insurrections had periodically broken out in the villages from the very first days of Spanish rule, as Filipinos rebelled against its harsher aspects, such as the *polo* (corvée labor) and *vandala* (forced sale of local products to the government) systems, or against individual abuses of power by friars, Spanish officials, or *gobernadorcillos*. Most rebellions were extremely limited in scope. The Ilocos' "wine revolt" of 1807 was sparked by popular opposition to the government wine monopoly and the prohibition of the much-beloved *casi* (palm wine). Even Diego Silang, who saw great opportunities in the British occupation of Manila, never formally renounced his allegiance to the Spanish king.

On the fringes of Spanish rule, local leaders were sometimes able to seize and maintain control. The most striking example of this was the revolt of Francisco Dagohoy on Bohol in the southern Visayan Islands. Its immediate cause was the refusal in 1744 of a Spanish friar to bury Dagohoy's brother, a police constable, on consecrated ground. Dagohoy raised an army, expelled the Spanish, killed friars, and established a virtually independent regime on Bohol that lasted until 1829, when the Spanish were finally able to reassert control.

The Muslim sultanates of Sulu, Buayan, and Maguindanao were the most successful in resisting Spanish rule. Attempting to extend their dominance into southern Mindanao and the Sulu Archipelago, the Spanish encountered well-organized resistance, for the formerly feuding sultans of the region had banded together in opposition to the invaders. The Spanish were gradually able to establish Christian enclaves on Palawan and parts of the Zamboanga Peninsula. The sultan of Sulu capitulated to the Spanish in 1878, but Spanish control over the Moros was never complete. A fierce pride in their culture and independence motivated Moro resistance to Christian authority, and the triumph of western gunboats and cannons in the southern islands led to last-ditch struggles waged by individual Muslim fighters known as *juramentados* ("those who have sworn an oath," i.e., to conduct holy war against the infidel) in the late nineteenth and early twentieth centuries (see Islam, ch. 2).

The Cofradía de San José

Apolinario de la Cruz, a Tagalog who led the 1841 Cofradía de San José revolt, embodied the religious aspirations and disappointments of the Filipinos. A pious individual who sought to enter a religious order, his repeated applications were turned down by the racially conscious friars, and he was left with no alternative but to become a humble lay brother at a charitable institution in Manila, performing menial tasks. While serving in that capacity he started the *cofradía* (confraternity or brotherhood), a society to promote Catholic devotion among Filipinos. In 1839-40 Brother Apolinario sent representatives to his native Tayabas, south of Laguna de Bay, to recruit members, and the movement rapidly spread as "cells" were established throughout the southern Tagalog area. Originally, it was apparently neither anti-Spanish nor nativist in religious orientation, though native elements were prevalent among its provincial followers. Yet its emphasis on secrecy, the strong bond of loyalty its members felt for Brother Apolinario, and above all the fact that it barred Spanish and mestizos from membership aroused the suspicions of the authorities. The *confradía* was banned by the authorities in 1840.

In the autumn of 1841 Brother Apolinario left Manila and gathered his followers, numbering several thousands and armed with rifles and bolos (heavy, single-bladed knives), at bases in the barrios around the town of Tayabas; as a spiritual leader, he preached that God would deliver the Tagalog people from slavery. Spanish accounts describe him as having proclaimed himself pope or "king of the Tagalogs," living in luxury and surrounded by beautiful female attendants. Although the rebel force, aided by Negrito hill tribesmen, was able to defeat a detachment led by the provincial governor in late October, a much larger Spanish force composed of soldiers from Pampanga Province—the elite of the Filipino military establishment and traditional enemies of the Tagalogs—took the *confradía* camp at Alitao after a great slaughter on November 1, 1841.

The insurrection was effectively over upon the betrayal and capture of Brother Apolinario and his execution on November 5. Survivors of the movement became *remontados* ("those who go back into the mountains"), leaving their villages to live on the slopes of the volcanic Mount San Cristobal and Mount Banahao, within sight of Alitao. These mountains, where no friar ventured, became folk religious centers, places of pilgrimage for lowland peasants, and the birthplace of religious communities known as Colorums (see Glossary).

15

The Development of a National Consciousness

Rural folk religious movements expressed an inchoate desire to be rid of the Spanish and discover a Promised Land that would reflect memories of a world that existed before the coming of the Spanish. Nationalism in the modern sense developed in an urban context, in Manila and the major towns and perhaps more significantly in Spain and other parts of Europe where Filipino students and exiles were exposed to modern intellectual currents. Folk religion, for all its power, could not form the basis of a national ideology. Yet the millenarian tradition of rural revolt would merge with the Europeanized nationalism of the *ilustrados* to spur a truly national resistance, first against Spain in 1896 and then against the Americans in 1899.

In many colonialized countries the struggle for independence drew much of its impetus from appeals to the precolonial tradition. This was true in the Philippines, but its case was different from that of other Southeast Asian countries in that there was no precolonial history of centralized kingship (save in the Moro regions) or priestly hierarchy upon which to build a strong sense of unique national identity. Nationalism evolved in the last decades of the nineteenth century on the foundation of the unity created by three centuries of Spanish rule and the Christianization of the lowland peoples by the friars. The *ilustrado* class, which came to embody Philippine aspirations—first within the Spanish colonial order and then in revolt against it—looked culturally and intellectually to Europe. It drew on nineteenth-century liberal ideas and a much older tradition of natural law derived from Catholic scholastic philosophy.

Reform and Reaction

Following the Spanish revolution of September 1868, in which the unpopular Queen Isabella II was deposed, the new government appointed General Carlos María de la Torre governor of the Philippines. An outspoken liberal, de la Torre extended to Filipinos the promise of reform. In a break with established practice, he fraternized with Filipinos, inviting them to the governor's palace and riding with them in official processions. Filipinos in turn welcomed de la Torre warmly, holding a "liberty parade" to celebrate the adoption of the liberal 1869 Spanish constitution and establishing a Reform Committee to lay the foundations of a new order. Prominent among de la Torre's supporters in Manila were professional and business leaders of the *ilustrado* community and, perhaps more significantly, Filipino secular priests. These included the learned Father José Burgos, a Spanish mestizo, who had published a pamphlet, *Manifesto to the Noble Spanish Nation*, criticizing those racially prejudiced Spanish who barred Filipinos from the priesthood and government service. For a brief time the tide seemed to be turning against the friars. In December 1870 the archbishop of Manila, Gregorio Meliton Martínez, wrote to the Spanish regent advocating secularization and warning that discrimination against Filipino priests would encourage anti-Spanish sentiments.

According to historian Austin Coates, "1869 and 1870 stand distinct and apart from the whole of the rest of the period as a time when for a brief moment a real breath of the nineteenth century penetrated the Islands, which till then had been living largely in the seventeenth century." De la Torre abolished censorship of newspapers and legalized the holding of public demonstrations, free speech and assembly being rights guaranteed in the 1869 constitution. Students at the University of Santo Tomás formed an association, the Liberal Young Students (Juventud Escolar Liberal), and in October 1869 held demonstrations protesting the abuses of the university's Dominican friar administrators and teachers.

The liberal period came to an abrupt end in 1871. Friar and conservative Spanish interests in Manila managed to engineer the replacement of de la Torre by a more conservative figure, Rafael de Izquierdo, who, following his installation as governor in April 1871, reimposed the severities of the old regime. He is alleged to have boasted that he came to the islands "with a crucifix in one hand and a sword in the other." Liberal laws were rescinded, and the enthusiastic Filipino supporters of de la Torre came under political suspicion.

The final blow came after the Cavite mutiny of January 20, 1872, when about 200 Filipino dockworkers and soldiers revolted and killed their Spanish officers apparently in the mistaken belief that a general uprising was in progress among Filipino regiments in Manila. Grievances connected with the government revocation of old privileges—exemption from tribute service—inspired the revolt, which was put down by January 22. The authorities, however, began weaving a tale of conspiracy between the mutineers and prominent members of the Filipino community, particularly secular priests. The governor asserted that a secret junta, with connections to liberal parties in Spain, existed in Manila and was ready to overthrow Spanish rule. A military court sentenced three Filipino priests most closely associated with liberal reformism—José Burgos, Mariano Gómez, and Jacinto Zamora—to death and exiled a number of prominent *ilustrados* to Guam or the Marianas (then Spanish possessions), whence they would escape to carry on the struggle in Hong Kong, Singapore, or Europe.

Manila archbishop Martínez requested that the governor commute the priests' death sentence and refused the governor's order that they be defrocked. Martínez' efforts were in vain, however, and on February 17, 1872, they were publicly executed with the brutal garrote on the Luneta (the broad park facing Manila Bay). The archbishop ordered that Manila church bells toll a requiem for the victims which, it turned out, was also a requiem for Spanish rule in the islands. Dr. José Rizal, the most prominent of Filipino nationalist thinkers, described Spanish policy after de la Torre with the Latin phrase *quos vult perdere Jupiter, prius dementat* ("those whom Jupiter wishes to destroy, he first makes mad"). Although a policy of accommodation would have won the loyalty of peasant and *ilustrado* alike, intransigence—particularly on the question of the secularization of the clergy—led increasing numbers to question the need for a continuing association with Spain.

José Rizal and the Propaganda Movement

Between 1872 and 1892 the focus of a growing national consciousness was largely outside the Philippines in the freer atmosphere of Europe where small communities of Filipino émigrés—those liberals exiled in 1872 and Filipino students taking courses in European universities—formed the vaguely defined Propaganda Movement. Literary and cultural rather than political in an organizational sense, the movement, which included upper class Filipinos from all the Lowland Christian areas, strove to "awaken the sleeping intellect of the Spaniard to the needs of our country" and create a closer, more equal association of the islands and the motherland. Among their specific goals were representation of the Philippines in the Cortes, or parliament; secularization of the clergy; legalization of Spanish and Filipino equality; creation of a public school system independent of the friars; abolition of the *polo* and *vandala*; guarantee of basic freedoms of speech and association; and equal opportunity for Filipinos and Spanish to enter government service.

The most outstanding of the Propagandists was Rizal—physician, scholar, scientist, and writer. Born in 1861 into a prosperous Chinese mestizo family in Laguna Province, he displayed remarkable talents at an early age. After several years of medical study at the University of Santo Tomás, he went to Spain in 1882 to finish his studies at the University of Madrid. During the decade that followed, Rizal's career spanned two worlds: the small communities of Filipino students in Madrid and other European cities, among whom he gained a position of leadership as their most eloquent spokesman, and the wider world of European science and scholarship—particularly in Germany—where he formed close relationships with prominent natural and social scientists. The new discipline of anthropology was of special interest to him; he was committed to refuting friars' stereotypes of Filipino racial inferiority with scientific arguments. His greatest impact on the development of a Filipino national consciousness, however, was his publication of two novels—*Noli Me Tangere* in 1886 and *El Filibusterismo* in 1891. Drawing upon Rizal's personal experiences, these books depicted the conditions of Spanish rule in the islands and particularly the abuses of the friars. Although the friars had them banned, they were smuggled into the Philippines and rapidly gained a wide readership.

Other important Propagandists included Graciano López Jaena, a noted orator and pamphleteer who had left the islands for Spain in 1880 after the publication of his satirical short novel, *Fray Botod* (which can be translated as "Brother Fatso"), an unflattering portrait of a provincial friar. In 1889 he established a biweekly newspaper in Barcelona, *La Solidaridad*, which became the principal mouthpiece of the Propaganda Movement, having audiences both in Spain and in the

Ruins of Fort Santiago with Rizal Museum in background
Courtesy Tourist Research and Planning

islands. Its contributors included Rizal, Dr. Ferdinand Blumentritt, an Austrian geographer and ethnologist whom Rizal had met in Germany, and Marcelo del Pilar. Del Pilar, a reform-minded lawyer who was active in the antifriar movement in the islands until obliged to flee to Spain in 1888, became editor of *La Solidaridad* and assumed leadership of the Filipino community in Spain.

In 1887 Rizal returned briefly to the islands, but because of the furor surrounding the appearance of *Noli Me Tangere* the previous year, he was advised by the governor to leave, returning to Europe by way of Japan and North America to complete his second novel and an edition of Antonio de Morga's seventeenth-century work, *Sucesos de las Islas Filipinas* (History of the Philippine Islands). The latter project stemmed from an ethnological interest in the cultural connections between the peoples of the pre-Spanish Philippines and those of the larger Malay region (including modern Malaysia and Indonesia) and the closely related political objective of encouraging national pride. The broad-minded Morga, unlike later Spanish writers, had much to say in a positive vein about the islands' early inhabitants, and his account of pre-Christian religion and social customs was one of the few reliable ones.

19

After a stay in Europe and Hong Kong, Rizal returned to the Philippines in June 1892. This was partly owing to family considerations; the Dominican friars had evicted his father and sisters from the land they leased from the friar estate at Calamba, in Laguna Province. He was also convinced that the struggle for reform could no longer be conducted effectively from overseas. In July he established the Liga Filipina (Philippine League), designed to be a truly national, but nonviolent, organization. It was dissolved, however, following his arrest and exile to the remote town of Dapitan in northwestern Mindanao.

After Rizal's arrest and the collapse of the Liga Filipina, the Propaganda Movement languished. *La Solidaridad* went out of business in November 1895, and in 1896 both del Pilar and López Jaena died in Barcelona, worn down by poverty and disappointment. An attempt was made to reestablish the Liga Filipina, but the national movement had become split between *ilustrado* advocates of reform and peaceful evolution (the *compromisarios*, or "compromisers") and a plebeian constituency that wanted revolution and national independence. Because the Spanish refused to allow genuine reform, the initiative quickly passed from the former group to the latter.

The Katipunan

After Rizal's arrest and exile, Andres Bonifacio, a self-educated man of humble origins, founded a secret society, the Katipunan, in Manila. This organization was committed from the beginning to winning independence from Spain. It was modeled in part on Masonic lodges. Rizal, López Jaena, del Pilar, and other leaders of the Propaganda Movement had been Masons, and Masonry was regarded by the church as heretical. The Katipunan, like the Masonic lodges, had secret passwords and ceremonies, and its members were organized into ranks or "degrees," each having different colored hoods and different passwords and secret formulas. New members went through a rigorous initiation, which concluded with the *pacto de sangre*, or "blood compact."

The Katipunan spread gradually from the Tondo district of Manila, where Bonifacio had founded it, to the provinces, and by August 1896—on the eve of the revolt against Spain—it had some 30,000 members, including both men and women. Most of them were members of the lower and lower middle-income strata, including peasants. The nationalist movement had effectively moved from the closed circle of prosperous *ilustrados* to a truly popular base of support.

The 1896 Uprising and Rizal's Execution

During this time Rizal remained in lonely exile at Dapitan. He had promised the Spanish governor that he would not attempt an escape, which, in that remote part of the country, would have been relatively easy. Such a course of action, however, would have both compromised the moderate reform policy that he still advocated and confirmed the suspicions of reactionary Spanish. Whether he came to support Philippine independence during his period of exile is difficult to determine.

He retained, to the very end, a faith in the decency of Spanish "men of honor," which made it difficult for him to accept the revolutionary course of the Katipunan.

Revolution had broken out in Cuba in February 1895, and Rizal applied to the governor to be sent to that yellow fever-ridden island as an army doctor, believing that it was the only way he could keep his word to the governor and yet get out of his exile. His request was granted, and he was preparing to leave for Cuba when the Katipunan revolt broke out in August 1896. An informer had tipped off a Spanish friar about the society's existence, and Bonifacio, his hand forced, proclaimed the revolution, attacking Spanish military installations on August 29, 1896. Rizal was allowed to leave Manila on a Spanish steamship. The governor, however, apparently forced by reactionary elements, ordered Rizal's arrest en route, and he was sent back to Manila to be tried by a military court as an accomplice of the insurrection.

The rebels were poorly led and had few successes against colonial troops. Only in Cavite Province did they make any headway. Commanded by Emilio Aguinaldo, the 27-year-old mayor of the town of Cavite who had been a member of the Katipunan since 1895, the rebels defeated Civil Guard and regular colonial troops between August and November 1896 and made the province the center of the revolution.

Under a new governor who apparently had been sponsored as a hard-line candidate by the religious orders, Rizal was brought before a military court on fabricated charges of involvement with the Katipunan. The events of 1872 were repeating themselves. The brief trial was held on December 26 and—with little chance to defend himself— he was found guilty and sentenced to death. On December 30, 1896, he was brought out to the Luneta and executed by a firing squad.

Rizal's death filled the rebels with new determination, but the Katipunan was becoming divided between supporters of Bonifacio, who was revealing himself to be an increasingly ineffective leader, and its rising star, Aguinaldo. At a convention held at Tejeros—the Katipunan's headquarters—in March 1897, delegates elected Aguinaldo president and demoted Bonifacio to the post of director of the interior. Bonifacio withdrew his supporters and formed his own government. After fighting broke out between Bonifacio's and Aguinaldo's troops, Bonifacio was arrested, tried, and on May 10, 1897, executed by order of Aguinaldo.

As 1897 wore on, Aguinaldo himself suffered reverses at the hands of Spanish troops, being forced from Cavite in June and retreating to Biak-na-Bato in Bulacan Province. The futility of the struggle was becoming apparent, however, on both sides. Although Spanish troops were able to defeat insurgents on the battlefield, it was impossible to suppress guerrilla activity. In August armistice negotiations were opened between Aguinaldo and a new Spanish governor. By mid-December an agreement was reached in which the governor would pay Aguinaldo ₱800,000 and the rebel leader and his government would go into exile. Aguinaldo established himself in Hong Kong, and the Spanish bought themselves time. Within the year, however, their more than three centuries of rule in the islands would come to an abrupt and unexpected end.

Spanish-American War and Philippine Resistance

Spain's rule in the Philippines came to an end as a result of United States involvement with Spain's other major colony, Cuba. American business interests were anxious for a resolution—with or without Spain— of the insurrection that had broken out there in February 1895. Moreover, public opinion in the United States had been aroused by newspaper accounts of the brutalities of Spanish rule.

When the United States declared war on Spain on April 25, 1898, Acting Secretary of the Navy Theodore Roosevelt ordered Commodore George Dewey, commander of the Asiatic Squadron, to sail to the Philippines and destroy the Spanish fleet anchored in Manila Bay. Spanish naval history, which had seen its apogee in the building of a global empire "upon which the sun never sets" in the sixteenth century, came to an inglorious end on May 1, 1898, as Spain's antiquated armada, including ships with wooden hulls, was sunk by the guns of Dewey's flagship, the *Olympia* and other American warships. More than 380 Spanish sailors died, but there was only one American fatality.

As Spain and the United States had moved toward war over Cuba in the last months of 1897, negotiations of a highly tentative nature began between United States officials and Aguinaldo in both Hong Kong and Singapore. When war was declared, the revolutionary—a partner, if not an ally, of the United States—was urged by Dewey to return to the islands as quickly as possible. Arriving in Manila on May 19, Aguinaldo reassumed command of rebel forces. Insurrectionists overwhelmed demoralized Spanish garrisons around the capital, and links were established with other movements throughout the islands.

In the eyes of the Filipinos, their relationship with the United States was that of two nations joined in a common struggle against Spain. As allies, the Filipinos provided American forces with valuable intelligence (that, for instance, the Spanish had no mines or torpedoes with which to sink warships entering Manila Bay), and Aguinaldo's 12,000 troops kept a slightly larger Spanish force bottled up inside Manila until American troop reinforcements could arrive from San Francisco in late June. Aguinaldo was unhappy, however, that the Americans would not commit to paper a statement of support for Philippine independence.

The Navy Department by late May had ordered Dewey, who had been promoted to rear admiral, to distance himself from Aguinaldo lest he make untoward commitments. The war with Spain was still going on, and the future of the Philippines remained uncertain. The immediate objective was to capture Manila, and it was thought best to do that without the assistance of the insurgents. By late July there were some 12,000 United States troops in the area, and relations between them and rebel forces deteriorated rapidly.

By the summer of 1898 Manila had become the focus not only of the Spanish-American conflict and the growing suspicions of the Americans and Filipino rebels but also of a rivalry that encompassed the European powers. Following Dewey's victory, Manila Bay was filled with the warships of Britain, Germany, France, and Japan. The German fleet of eight ships, ostensibly in Philippine waters to protect German interests (a single import firm), acted provocatively—cutting in front of American ships, refusing to salute the American flag (according to naval courtesy), taking soundings of the harbor, and landing supplies for the besieged Spanish. Germany, hungry for that ultimate of status symbols, a colonial empire, was eager to take advantage of whatever opportunities the conflict in the islands might afford. Dewey called the bluff of the German admiral, threatening a fight if his aggressive activities continued. Fortunately, the Germans backed down, for Dewey's squadron was supported by a friendly British squadron.

The Spanish cause was doomed, but Fermin Jaudenes, Spain's last governor in the islands, had to devise a way to salvage the honor of his country. Negotiations were carried out through British and Belgian diplomatic intermediaries. A secret agreement was made between the governor and American military commanders in early August 1898 concerning the capture of Manila: American forces in their assault would neither bombard the city nor allow the insurgents to take part (the Spanish continued to fear that the Filipinos plotted to massacre them all); the Spanish, in turn, would put up only a show of resistance and, on a prearranged signal, would then surrender. This way the governor would be spared the ignominy of giving up without a fight, and both sides would be spared casualties. The mock battle was staged on August 13. The attackers rushed in, and by afternoon the American flag was flying over Intramuros, the ancient walled city that had been the seat of Spanish power for over 300 years.

The agreement between Jaudenes and Dewey marked a curious reversal of roles. At the beginning of the war, Americans and Filipinos had been allies against Spain in all but name; now Spanish and Americans were in a partnership that excluded the insurgents. Fighting between American and Filipino troops almost broke out as the former moved in to dislodge the latter from strategic positions around Manila on the eve of the attack. Aguinaldo was told bluntly by the Americans that his army could not participate and would be fired upon if it crossed into the city. The insurgents were infuriated at being denied triumphant entry into their own capital, but Aguinaldo bided his time. Relations continued to deteriorate, however, as it became clear to Filipinos that the Americans were in the islands to stay.

The Malolos Constitution and the Treaty of Paris

After returning to the islands, Aguinaldo wasted little time in setting up an independent government. On June 12, 1898, a declaration of independence, modeled on the American one, was proclaimed at his headquarters in Cavite. It was at this time that Apolinario Mabini, lawyer and political thinker, came into prominence as Aguinaldo's principal adviser. Born into a poor *indio* family but educated at the University of Santo Tomás, his advocacy of "simultaneous external and internal revolution" unsettled the more conservative landowners and *ilustrados* who initially supported Aguinaldo. In fact, Mabini meant that true independence for the Philippines would consist not simply in liberation from Spain (or any other colonial power) but in the education of the people for self-government and the abandonment of the paternalistic, colonial mentality that the Spanish had cultivated over the centuries. Mabini's *The True Decalogue,* published in July 1898 in the form of the Ten Commandments, used this medium, somewhat paradoxically, to promote critical thinking and a reform of customs and attitudes. His *Constitutional Program for the Philippine Republic,* published at the same time, elaborated his ideas on political institutions.

On September 15, 1898, a revolutionary congress was convened at Malolos, a market town located 32 kilometers north of Manila, in order to draw up a constitution for the new republic. A document was approved by the congress on November 29, 1898. Modeled on the constitutions of France, Belgium, and Latin American countries, it was promulgated at Malolos on January 21, 1899, and two days later Aguinaldo was inaugurated as president.

American observers traveling on Luzon commented that the areas controlled by the republic seemed peaceful and well governed. The Malolos congress had set up schools, a military academy, and the Literary University of the Philippines. Government finances were organized, and new currency was issued. The army and navy were established on a regular basis, having regional commands. The relative accomplishments of the Filipino government, however, counted for little in the eyes of the great powers as the transfer of the islands from Spanish to American rule was arranged in the closing months of 1898. In late September, treaty negotiations were initiated between Spanish and American representatives in Paris. The Treaty of Paris was signed on December 10, 1898. Among its conditions was the cession of the Philippines, Guam, and Puerto Rico to the United States (Cuba was granted its independence); in return, the United States would pay Spain a sum of US$20 million. The nature of this payment is rather difficult to define; it was paid neither to purchase Spanish territories nor as a war indemnity. In the words of historian Leon Wolff, "it was . . . a gift. Spain accepted it. Quite irrelevantly she handed us the Philippines. No question of honor or conquest was involved. The Filipino people had nothing to say about it, although their rebellion was thrown in (so to speak) free of charge."

The Treaty of Paris aroused anger among Filipinos. Reacting to the US$20 million sum paid to Spain, *La Independencia,* a newspaper published in Manila by a revolutionary, General Antonio Luna, stated that "people are not to be bought and sold like horses and houses. If the aim has been to abolish the traffic in Negroes because it meant the sale of persons, why is there still maintained the sale of countries with inhabitants?" Tension and ill feeling were growing between the American troops in Manila and the insurgents surrounding the capital. A second pressure point was Iloilo, the main port on the island of Panay, where an American force stood poised to capture the city from the rebels and where the Revolutionary Government of the Visayas was proclaimed on November 17, 1898. Upon the announcement of the treaty, the radicals, Mabini and General Luna prepared for war, and provisional articles were added to the constitution giving the president, Aguinaldo, dictatorial powers in times of emergency. President William McKinley issued a proclamation on December 21, 1898, declaring American policy to be one of "benevolent assimilation" in which "the mild sway of justice and right" would be substituted for "arbitrary rule." When this was published in the islands on January 4, 1899, references to "American sovereignty" having been prudently deleted, Aguinaldo issued his own proclamation condemning American "violent and aggressive seizure" and threatening war.

War of Resistance

Hostilities broke out on the night of February 4, 1899, after two American privates on patrol killed three Filipino soldiers in a suburb of Manila. Thus began a war that would last for more than two years. Some 126,000 American troops would be committed to the conflict, 4,234 of whom lost their lives, while 16,000 Filipino soldiers died.

The troops of the Philippine Republic, armed with old rifles and bolos and carrying *anting-anting* (magical charms), were no match for American troops in open combat, but they were formidable opponents in guerrilla warfare. For General Ewell S. Otis, commander of American forces, who had been appointed military governor of the Philippines, the conflict began auspiciously with the expulsion of the rebels from Manila and its suburbs by late February and the capture of Malolos, the revolutionary capital, on March 31, 1899. Aguinaldo and his government escaped, however, establishing a new capital at San Isidro in Nueva Ecija Province. The Filipino cause suffered a number of reverses. The attempts of Mabini and his successor as president of Aguinaldo's cabinet, Pedro Paterno, to negotiate an armistice in May 1899 ended in failure because Otis insisted on unconditional surrender. Still more serious was the murder of General Luna, Aguinaldo's most capable military commander, in June. Hot-tempered and cruel, Luna collected a large number of enemies among his associates and, according to rumor, Aguinaldo himself ordered his death.

With his best commander dead and his troops suffering continued defeats as American forces pushed into northern Luzon, Aguinaldo in November 1899 dissolved the regular army and ordered the establishment of decentralized guerrilla commands in each of several military zones. More than ever, United States soldiers knew the miseries of fighting an enemy that, like Mao Zedong's proverbial "fish in water," was able to move at will within the civilian population in the barrios. Civilians, caught between Americans and rebels, suffered horribly.

According to historian Gregorio Zaide, as many as 200,000 of them died, largely the result of famine and disease, by the end of the war. Atrocities were committed on both sides.

Although Aguinaldo's government did not have effective authority over the whole archipelago and resistance was strongest and best organized in the Tagalog area of the central portion of Luzon, the notion entertained by many Americans that independence was supported only by the "Tagalog tribe" was refuted by the fact that there was sustained fighting in the Visayan Islands and on Mindanao. Although the ports of Iloilo on Panay and Cebu on Cebu were captured in February 1899 and Tagbilaran, capital of Bohol, in March, guerrilla resistance continued in the mountainous interiors of these islands. Only on the sugar-growing island of Negros did local authorities peacefully accept American rule. On Mindanao the United States Army faced the determined opposition of Christian Filipinos loyal to the republic.

Aguinaldo was captured at Palanan on March 23, 1901, by a force of Philippine Scouts loyal to the United States and was brought back to Manila. Convinced of the futility of further resistance, he swore allegiance to the United States and issued a proclamation calling on his compatriots to lay down their arms. Yet insurgent resistance continued in various parts of the Philippines until 1903.

The Moros on Mindanao and in the Sulu Archipelago, suspicious of both Christian Filipino insurrectionists and Americans, remained for the most part neutral. In August 1899 an agreement was signed between General John C. Bates and the sultan of Sulu, Jamal-ul Kiram II, pledging a policy of noninterference on the part of the United States. In 1903, however, a Moro province was established by the American authorities and a more forward policy implemented: slavery was outlawed, schools that taught a non-Muslim curriculum were established, and local governments challenging the authority of traditional community leaders were organized. A new legal system replaced the sharia, or Islamic law. United States rule, even more than that of the Spanish, was seen as a challenge to Islam, a religion that prescribes not only personal beliefs but also social and political institutions. Armed resistance grew, and the Moro province remained under United States military rule until 1914, by which time the major Muslim groups had been subjugated (see Muslim Filipinos (Moros), ch. 2).

The First Phase of American Rule, 1899-1935

On January 20, 1899, President McKinley appointed the First Philippine Commission, a five-man group headed by Dr. Jacob Schurman, president of Cornell University, and including Admiral Dewey and General Otis, to investigate conditions in the islands and make recommendations. In the report that they issued to the president the following year, the commissioners acknowledged Filipino aspirations for independence (in Manila, they had conferred with emissaries of the Aguinaldo government) but declared that they were not ready for it. Specific recommendations included the establishment of civilian government as rapidly as possible (the American chief executive in the islands at that time was the military governor), including a bicameral legislature; the creation of autonomous governments on the provincial and municipal levels; and the organization of a system of free public elementary schools. The Second Philippine Commission (Taft Commission), appointed by McKinley on March 16, 1900, and headed by William Howard Taft, was granted legislative as well as limited executive powers. Between September 1900 and August 1902 it issued 499 laws. A judicial system was established, including an insular supreme court, a legal code was drawn up to replace antiquated Spanish ordinances, and a civil service was organized. The 1901 Municipal Code provided for popularly elected presidents, vice presidents, and councillors to serve on municipal boards; these officials had the responsibilities of collecting taxes, maintaining municipal properties, and undertaking necessary construction projects. The municipal board members elected provincial governors. In July 1901 the Philippine Constabulary (PC) was organized as an islands-wide police force to control brigandage and deal with the remnants of the insurgent movement. After military rule was terminated on July 4, 1901, the PC gradually took over from United States Army units the responsibility for suppressing guerrilla and bandit activities.

From the very beginning, United States presidents and their representatives in the islands defined their colonial mission in terms of tutelage: a process of preparing the Philippines for eventual independence. Except for a small group of "retentionists," the issue was not whether they would be granted self-rule, but when and under what conditions. Thus, political development in the islands was rapid and particularly impressive in light of the complete lack of representative institutions under the Spanish. The Philippine Organic Act of July 1902 stipulated that, upon the achievement of peace, a legislature would be established composed of a lower house, the Philippine Assembly, which would be popularly elected, and an upper house consisting of the Philippine Commission, which was appointed by the president of the United States. The two houses would share legislative powers, although the upper house alone was responsible for passing laws relating to the Moros and other non-Christian peoples. The act also provided for extension of the United States Bill of Rights to cover Filipinos and the sending of two Filipino resident commissioners to Washington to attend sessions of the United States Congress. In July 1907 the first elections for the assembly were held, and it opened its first session on October 16, 1907. Political parties were organized, and although open advocacy of independence had been banned during the insurgency years, criticism of government policies in the local newspapers was tolerated.

Taft, the Philippines' first civilian governor, outlined a comprehensive development plan that he described in sum as "the Philippines for the Filipinos"—that "every measure, whether in the form of a law or an executive order, before its adoption, should be weighed in the light of this question: does it make for the welfare of the Filipino people, or does it not?" Its main features included not only the broadening of representative institutions but also the expansion of a system of free public elementary education and economic policies designed to promote the islands' development. Filipinos widely interpreted Taft's pronouncements as a promise of independence. But in fact the governor, personally disillusioned with the "shallowness" of the westernized elite, felt that the people were totally unprepared for the responsibilities of self-rule. With the condescension of a person overly sure of himself and his benevolent intentions, he wrote that "the character of the people contains many discouraging defects which can only be cured by careful tutelage and widespread education."

Religious Issues

Opposition to the Spanish friars was a point of view shared by practically all Filipinos, and in the first years of United States rule the prospects of the Catholic church were in some doubt. Aguinaldo had appointed Gregorio Aglipay, a Filipino secular priest, "Spiritual Head of the Nation under Arms." Catholic bishops, because of their Spanish nationality, were declared deposed by the revolutionists, and parish priests who remained loyal to them were also relieved of their responsibilities.

The 1902 Philippine Organic Act disestablished the Catholic church. The United States government, in an effort to resolve the friar issue, negotiated with the Vatican; the church agreed to the sale of the friar estates and promised gradual substitution of non-Spanish and Filipino priests for the friars. It refused, however, to withdraw the religious orders from the islands immediately, in part for fear of offending Spain. In 1904 the administration bought for US$7.2 million the major part of the friars' holdings, amounting to some 166,000 hectares, of which one-half was in the vicinity of Manila. The land was eventually resold to Filipinos, some of them tenants but the majority of them estate owners.

Anger over the Vatican's continued resistance to appointing Filipino priests contributed to the rapid growth of the Iglesia Filipina Independiente (Philippine Independent Church), which Aglipay, breaking with the Catholic church, and journalist Isabelo de los Reyes had established in 1902. The desertion to Aglipay's church of one out of every 16 priests and, by 1904, one-quarter to one-third of the total Christian population testified to the magnitude of popular disaffection with Catholicism. His movement's fortunes waned, however, owing to internal dissension and government suspicions; Aglipay had taken an active part in guerrilla resistance and was considered subversive. In 1906 the Philippine Supreme Court ruled that property seized by the Aglipayans be returned to the Catholic church.

In 1907 Pope Pius X appointed a Benedictine monk as papal delegate to preside over the Philippine Provincial Council, a council of bishops and other religious officials. The council, held in Manila during 1907 and 1908, set in motion a counterreformation in response to the challenges of Aglipayanism, Protestantism brought by American missionaries, and the declining influence of the church in Philippine society. Largely as a result of its reforms, Philippine Catholicism acquired greater vigor and more unity than it had had for a long time. Members of the clergy were forbidden to accept government positions. For the first time, Catholic education was made available to the majority of Filipino children of both sexes in more than 1,200 schools. By 1927 there were more than 1,000 boys and men preparing for the priesthood. By the early 1930s a major portion of those priests who had joined the Iglesia Filipina Independiente had returned to Catholicism. The friars ceased to be an issue after the government purchased their estates, for most of them returned to Spain.

A Collaborative Philippine Leadership

The most important step in the establishment of a new political system was successful co-optation of the Filipino elite—the "policy of attraction." Wealthy and conservative *ilustrados*, the self-described "oligarchy of intelligence," had been from the outset reluctant revolutionaries, suspicious of the Katipunan and willing to negotiate with either Spain or the United States. Trinidad H. Pardo de Tavera and Benito Legarda, the former a descendant of Spanish nobility and the latter a rich landowner and capitalist, had quit Aguinaldo's government in 1898 as a result of disagreements with Mabini. Subsequently, they worked closely with the Schurman and Taft commissions, advocating acceptance of American rule. In December 1900 they established the Federalista Party, advocating statehood for the islands. The following year they were appointed the first Filipino members of the Philippine Commission. In such an advantageous position, they were able to influence the appointment of Federalistas to provincial governorships, the Supreme Court, and top positions in the civil service. Although the party could boast a membership of 200,000 by May 1901, its proposal to make the islands a state of the United States had limited appeal, both in the islands and in the United States, and it was widely regarded as opportunistic. In 1905 the party revised its program over the objections of its leaders, calling for "ultimate independence" and changing its name to the National Progressive Party.

The Nacionalista Party, which was established in 1907, dominated the Philippine political process until the beginning of World War II. It was led by a new generation of politicians, not *ilustrado* but by no means radical. Manuel Quezon came from a family of moderate wealth. An officer in Aguinaldo's army, he studied law, passed his bar examination in 1903, and entered provincial politics, becoming governor of Tayabas in 1906 before being elected to the Philippine Assembly the following year. His success at an early age was attributable to consummate political skills and the support of influential Americans. His Nacionalista Party associate and sometime rival was Sergio Osmeña, the college-educated son of a shopkeeper. This former journalist's thoroughness and command of details made him a perfect complement to

29

Quezon. Like Quezon, Osmeña had served as provincial governor (in his home province of Cebu) before being elected in 1907 to the assembly and, at age 29, selected as its first Speaker.

Although the Nacionalista Party's platform at its founding called for "immediate independence," dubious American observers described Osmeña and Quezon as using this appeal just to get votes; in fact, their policy toward the Americans was highly accommodating. Thus in 1907 an understanding was reached with an American official that the two leaders would block any attempt by the Philippine Assembly to demand independence. Osmeña and Quezon, who were the dominant political figures in the islands up to World War II, were genuinely committed to independence. The failure of Aguinaldo's revolutionary movement, however, had taught them the pragmatism of a conciliatory policy.

The appearance of the Nacionalista Party in 1907 marked the emergence of a party system that worked with remarkable effectiveness, though the dissolution of the opposition Democratic Party (a left-wing breakaway group of Nacionalistas) in 1932 left the party without an effective rival until the emergence of the Liberal Party in 1945. Much of the system's success (or, rather, the Nacionalistas' success) depended on the linkage of modern political institutions with traditional social structures and practices. Most significantly, it involved the integration of local-level elite groups into the new political system. Philippine parties have been described by political scientist Carl Landé as organized "upward" rather than "downward": national followings were put together by party leaders working in conjunction with local elite groups—in many cases the descendants of the *principalía* of Spanish times—who controlled constituencies tied to them in patron-client relationships. The issues of independence, its date, and the conditions under which it would be granted generated considerable passion in the national political arena; however, the decisive factors in terms of popular support, according to Landé, were more often local and particularistic issues rather than national or ideological concerns. Filipino political associations depended upon intricate networks of personalistic ties, directed upward to Manila and the national legislature.

The linchpins of the system created under American tutelage were the village- and province-level notables (often labeled "bosses" or "caciques" by colonial administrators) who garnered support by exchanging specific favors for votes. Most often they were large landholders who formed personal ties with their tenants or sharecroppers. Reciprocal relations between inferior and superior (involving the concept of *utang na loob*, or repayment of debts) or kinship ties formed the basis of support for village-level factions led by the notables (see The Social System, ch. 2). It was they who decided political party allegiance. The abolition of both property requirements and the poll tax, the growth of literacy, and the granting of women's suffrage (they first voted in 1938) increased the electorate considerably. The elite, however, was largely successful in monopolizing the support of the newly enfranchised, and a genuinely populist alternative was never really established within the system.

Integration of the notables, the "policy of attraction," ensured the success of what colonial administrators called the political education of the Filipinos. It was, however, also the cause of its greatest failure. Osmeña and Quezon, as the acknowledged representatives, were not genuinely interested in social reform. Thus, serious problems involving land reform, tenancy, and the highly unequal distribution of wealth were largely ignored. The growing power of the Nacionalista Party, particularly in the period after 1916, when it gained almost complete control of a bicameral Filipino legislature, barred the inclusion of effective nonelite interests in the political system. Not only revolution but also moderate reform of the social and economic systems were precluded. Discussions of policy alternatives became less salient to the political process than the dynamics of personalism and the "ethic" of give and take.

The Jones Act

The term of Governor General Francis Burton Harrison (1913-21) was one of particularly harmonious collaboration between Americans and Filipinos. Harrison's attitudes (he is described as having regarded himself as a "constitutional monarch" presiding over a "government of Filipinos") reflected the relatively liberal stance of Woodrow Wilson's Democratic administration. In 1913 Wilson had appointed five Filipinos to the Philippine Commission, giving them a majority for the first time. Harrison undertook rapid "Filipinization" of the civil service, much to the anger and distress of Americans in the islands, including superannuated officials. In 1913 there had been 2,623 American and 6,363 Filipino officials; in 1921 there were 13,240 Filipino and only 614 American administrators. Critics accused Harrison of transforming a "colonial government of Americans aided by Filipinos" into a "government of Filipinos aided by Americans" and of being the "plaything and catspaw of the leaders of the Nacionalista Party."

A major step was taken in the direction of independence when the United States Congress passed a second organic law, in 1916, commonly referred to as the Jones Act, which replaced the 1902 law. Its preamble stated explicitly the intent to grant Philippine independence as soon as a stable government was established. By this act, the Philippine Senate replaced the Philippine Commission as the upper house of the legislature. Unlike the commission, the Senate was popularly elected, although two of its 24 members (and nine of the 90 representatives in the lower house, now called the House of Representatives) were appointed by the governor general to represent the non-Christian peoples. The legislature's actions were subject to the veto of the governor general, and it could not pass laws affecting the rights of United States citizens. The Jones Act brought the legislative branch under Filipino control. The executive was still firmly under the control of an appointed governor general, and most Supreme Court justices, who were appointed by the United States president, were in 1916 still Americans.

In elections held for the two houses in 1916, the Nacionalista Party made almost a clean sweep. All but one seat in the Senate and 83 out of 90 in the House were won by their candidates, leaving the National Progressive Party (the former Federal Party) a powerless opposition. Quezon was chosen president of the Senate, while Osmeña continued as Speaker of the House.

The Jones Act remained the basic legislation for the administration of the Philippines until the United States Congress passed new legislation in 1934 establishing the Commonwealth of the Philippines. Its provisions were differently interpreted, however, by the governors general. Under Harrison, the legislature was rarely challenged by his use of the veto power. His successor, General Leonard Wood (1921-27), was convinced that American withdrawal from the islands would be as disastrous for the Filipinos as it would be for the interests of the United States in the western Pacific. He aroused the intense opposition of the Nacionalistas by his use of the veto power 126 times in his six years in office. The opposition created a political deadlock when ranking Filipino officials resigned in 1923 and remained out of office until Wood's term ended with his death in 1927. His successors, however, reversed his policies and reestablished effective working relations with Filipino politicians.

Although the Jones Act of 1916 did not transfer responsibility for the Moro regions (reorganized in 1914 under the Department of Mindanao and Sulu) from the American governor to the Filipino-controlled legislature, Muslims perceived the rapid Filipinization of the civil service and United States commitment to eventual independence as serious threats. In the view of the Moros, an independent Philippines would be dominated by Christians, their traditional enemies. United States policy from 1902 had been to break down the historic autonomy of the Muslim territories. Immigration of Christian settlers from Luzon and the Visayan Islands to the relatively unsettled regions of Mindanao was encouraged, and the new arrivals began supplanting the Moros in their own homeland. Large areas of the island were opened to economic exploitation. There was no legal recognition of Muslim customs and institutions. In March 1935 Muslim *datu* petitioned United States president Franklin D. Roosevelt, asking that "the American people should not release us until we are educated and become powerful because we are like a calf who, once abandoned by its mother, would be devoured by a merciless lion." Any suggestion of special status for or continued United States rule over the Moro regions, however, met the vehement opposition of Christian Filipino leaders who, when the Commonwealth of the Philippines was established, gained virtually complete control over government institutions (see Muslim Filipinos (Moros), ch. 2).

Economic and Social Developments

The Taft Commission of 1900 had seen economic development, along with education and the establishment of representative institutions, as one of the three pillars of the American program of tutelage. Its members had ambitious plans to build railroads and highways, improve harbor facilities, open greater markets for Philippine goods through the lowering or elimination of tariffs, and stimulate foreign investment in mining, forestry, and cash-crop cultivation. In 1901 some 93 percent of the islands' total land area was public land, and it was hoped that a portion of this area could be sold to American investors.

Their plans were frustrated, however, by powerful agricultural interests in the United States Congress who feared the competition of Philippine sugar, coconut oil, tobacco, and other exports. Although Taft argued for more liberal terms, the United States Congress, in the 1902 Land Act, set a limit of 16 hectares of public land to be sold or leased to individuals and 1,024 hectares to corporations by the government. This act and tight financial markets in the United States discouraged the development of large-scale, foreign-owned plantations such as were being established in British Malaya, the Dutch East Indies, and French Indochina.

The commission argued that tariff relief was essential if the islands were to be developed. In August 1909 Congress passed the Payne-Aldrich Tariff Act, which provided for free entry of all Philippine products except rice, sugar, and tobacco. Rice imports were subjected to regular tariffs, while quotas were established for sugar and tobacco. In 1913 the Underwood Tariff Act removed all restrictions. The principal result of these acts was to make the islands increasingly dependent on American markets; between 1914 and 1920 the portion of Philippine exports going to the United States rose from 50 to 70 percent. By 1939 it had reached 85 percent, and 65 percent of imports came from the United States.

In 1931 there were between 80,000 and 100,000 Chinese in the islands active in the local economy; many of them had arrived after American rule had been established. Some 16,000 Japanese were concentrated largely in the Mindanao province of Davao (the incorporated city of Davao was labeled by local boosters the "Little Tokyo of the South") and were predominant in the abaca industry. Yet the immigration of foreign laborers never reached a volume sufficient to threaten indigenous control of the economy or the traditional social structure as it did in British Malaya and Burma. There, Chinese and Indians displaced the native populations in the colonial economy, and indigenous leaders expressed fears for the continued existence of their national and cultural communities.

The Problem of Tenancy

The limited nature of American intervention in the economy and elite dominance of the Filipino political system through the medium of the Nacionalista Party ensured that the status quo in terms of the

33

relationship between landlord and tenant would be maintained, even if certain of its traditional aspects changed. A government attempt to establish "homesteads" on the model of the American West in 1903 did next to nothing to alter landholding arrangements. Although different regions of the archipelago had their own specific arrangements and different proportions of tenants and small proprietors, the *kasama* (share tenancy system), was the most prevalent, particularly in the rice-growing areas of central Luzon but also in the Visayan Islands. Under this arrangement the landowners supplied seed and cash necessary to tide cultivators over during the planting season while the cultivator provided tools and work animals and was responsible for one-half the expense of crop production. Usually, owner and sharecropper each took one-half of the harvest, although only after the former deducted a portion for expenses; terms might be more liberal in frontier areas where owners needed to attract cultivators to clear the land. Sometimes land tenancy arrangements were three tiered. An original owner would lease land to an *inquilino*, who would then sublet it to *kasamas* (sharecroppers). In the words of historian David R. Sturtevant: "Thrice removed from their *proprietario*, affected *taos* [peasants] received ever-diminishing shares from the picked-over remains of harvests."

Cultivators were customarily deep in debt, for they were dependent on advances made by the landowner or *inquilino* and had to pay steep interest rates. Principal and interest accumulated rapidly, becoming an impossible burden. It was estimated in 1924 that the average tenant family would have to labor uninterrupted for 163 years to pay off debts and acquire title to the land they worked. The *kasama* system created what was in fact a class of peons or serfs; children inherited the debts of their fathers, and over the generations families were tied in bondage to their estates. Contracts were usually unwritten, and landowners could change them to their advantage.

Two factors led to a worsening of the cultivators' position. One was the rapid increase in population brought about through improvements in public health (from 7.6 million in 1905 to 16 million in 1939). This put added pressure on the land, lowered the standard of living, and created a labor surplus. Closely tied to this was the erosion of traditional patron-client ties. The landlord-tenant relationship was becoming more impersonal. The landlord's interest in his tenants' welfare was waning. Important landlord services ceased; surpluses were being withdrawn to support his urban style of life or for investment in other kinds of enterprises. Cultivators accused landowners of being "shameless" and forgetting the principle of *utang na loob;* they would demand services from tenants without pay but would do nothing in return. According to one tenant quoted by historian Benedict Kerkvliet commenting about conditions in the 1930s: "Tinio [a landlord] and others like him in those days no longer upheld their end of the relationship between the tenant and his landlord. They were being unfair to the peasants;

it was unjust. Besides that, we had no protection anymore, and not enough to eat."

Although the area under cultivation increased from 1.3 million hectares in 1903 to 4 million hectares in 1935—stimulated by American demand for cash crops and the growing population—tenancy increased during the United States period. In 1918 there were roughly 2 million farms, of which 1.5 million were operated by their owners; by 1939 these figures had declined to 1.6 million and 800,000, respectively, as individual proprietors became tenants or migrant laborers. Disparities in the distribution of wealth grew. By 1939 the wealthiest 10 percent of the population received 40 percent of the islands' income. Elite and cultivators were separated culturally and geographically, as well as economically; as new urban centers rose, often with an Americanized culture, the former left the countryside to become absentee landlords, leaving estate management in the hands of frequently abusive overseers. The PC played a central role in suppressing antilandlord resistance.

Resistance Movements

The tradition of rural revolt, often with messianic overtones, continued through the American period. Colorum sects, derived from the Cofradía de San José established by Apolinario de la Cruz in 1839-40, had spread throughout the Christian regions of the archipelago in competition with the Catholic establishment and the missionaries of Gregorio Aglipay by the early 1920s. A Colorum-led revolt broke out in northeastern Mindanao in January-February 1924, sparked by a sect leader's predictions of an imminent Judgment Day. The next year a shopkeeper of Jaro on the island of Panay, Florencio Entrencherado, proclaimed himself Florencio I, "Emperor of the Philippines," somewhat paradoxically running for the office of provincial governor of Iloilo that same year on a platform of tax reduction, measures against Chinese and Japanese merchants, and immediate independence. Although he lost the election, the campaign made him a prominent figure in the western Visayan Islands and won him the sympathies of the poor of the sugar provinces of Panay and Negros. Claiming semidivine attributes (that he could control the elements and that his charisma had been granted him by the Holy Ghost and the spirits of Father Burgos and Rizal), Florencio had a following of some 10,000 peasants on Negros and Panay by late 1926; in May 1927 his supporters, heeding his call that "the hour will come when the poor will be ordered to kill all the rich," launched an abortive insurrection.

Tensions were highest, however, in central Luzon, where tenancy was most widespread and population pressures were the greatest. Although the 1931 Tayug insurrection was connected with a Colorum sect and had religious overtones, it was on Luzon that traditional messianic movements gave way to secular, and at times revolutionary, ones. One of the first was the Association of the Worthy Kabola (Kapisanan Makabola Makasinag), a secret society that by 1925 had some

12,000 followers, largely in Nueva Ecija Province. Its leader, Pedro Kabola, called for liberation of the Philippines and promised the aid of the Japanese. The 1931 Tangulan (Kapatiran Tangulang Malayang Mamamayang—Association for an Offensive for Our Future Freedom) movement was both urban and rural based and had as many as 40,000 followers. The most important movement, however, was that of the Sakdalistas. Founded in 1933 by Benigno Ramos, former Nacionalista Party member and associate of Quezon who broke with him over the issue of collaboration, the Sakdal ("To Accuse") Party ran candidates in the 1934 elections on a platform of complete independence by the end of 1935, redistribution of land, and an end to caciquism. Sakdalistas were elected to a number of seats in the legislature and to provincial posts, and by early 1935 the party may have had as many as 200,000 members. Insurrection broke out in May 1935 but, as in the case of other movements, was quickly suppressed by the PC.

Through the decade of the 1930s, tenant movements in central Luzon became more active, articulate, and better organized. In 1938 the Socialist Party joined in a united front with the Philippine Communist Party (PKP). This united front was prominent in supporting the demands of tenants for better contracts and working conditions. As the depression wore on and prices for cash crops collapsed, tenant strikes and violent confrontations with landlords, their overseers, and the PC escalated.

In response to deteriorating conditions, commonwealth president Quezon launched the "Social Justice" program, which included regulation of rents but achieved only meager results. There were insufficient funds to carry it out, and implementation was sabotaged on the local level by landlords and municipal officials. In 1939 and 1940 thousands of cultivators were evicted by landlords because they insisted on enforcement of the 1933 Rice Share Tenancy Act, which guaranteed larger shares for tenants.

The Commonwealth and the Japanese Occupation

The constellation of political forces in the United States that assisted in the resolution of the independence question formed an odd community of interests with the Filipino nationalists. Principal among these were agricultural interests. Sugar beet, tobacco, and dairy farmers feared the competition of low-tariff insular products, and the hardships suffered in a deepening depression in the early 1930s led them to seek protection through a severance of the colonial relationship. In this they had the support of Cuban sugar interests, who feared loss of markets to Philippine sugarcane. United States labor unions, particularly on the West Coast, wanted exclusion of Filipino labor. A number of American observers saw the Philippines as a potential flash point with an expansive Japan and argued for a withdrawal across the Pacific to Hawaii.

In the climate generated by these considerations, Osmeña and Manual Roxas, a rising star in the Nacionalista Party and Osmeña's successor as Speaker of the House, successfully campaigned in Washington for passage of the Hare-Hawes-Cutting Independence bill, which Congress approved over President Herbert Hoover's veto in January 1933. Quezon opposed it, however, on the grounds that clauses relating to trade and the exclusion of Filipino immigrants were too stringent and that guarantees of United States bases on Philippine soil and the powers granted an American high commissioner compromised independence. After the bill was defeated in the Philippine legislature, Quezon himself went to Washington and negotiated the passage of a revised independence act, the Tydings-McDuffie Act, in March 1934.

The Tydings-McDuffie Act provided for a 10-year transition period to independence, during which there would be established the Commonwealth of the Philippines. The commonwealth would have its own constitution and would be self-governing, though foreign policy would be the responsibility of the United States, and laws passed by the legislature affecting immigration, foreign trade, or the currency system had to be approved by the United States president.

If the Tydings-McDuffie Act marked a new stage in Filipino-American partnership, it remained a highly unequal one. Although only 50 Filipino immigrants were allowed into the United States per year under the arrangement, American entry and residence in the islands were unrestricted. Its trade provisions allowed for five years' free entry of Philippine goods during the transition period and five years of gradually steepening tariff duties thereafter, reaching 100 percent in 1946, while United States goods during the full 10 years could enter the islands unrestricted and duty free. Quezon, in getting his revised act, had managed to obtain more favorable terms on bases; the United States would retain only a naval reservation and fueling stations. The United States would, moreover, negotiate with foreign governments for the neutralization of the islands.

The country's first constitution was framed by a constitutional convention that assembled in July 1934. Overwhelmingly approved by plebiscite in May 1935, this document established the political institutions for the 10-year commonwealth period and after July 1946 became the constitution of the independent Republic of the Philippines. The first commonwealth election was held in September 1935. Quezon and Osmeña, reconciled after their disagreements over the independence act, ran on a Coalition Party ticket and were elected president and vice president, respectively.

Commonwealth Government, 1935-41

The first act passed by the new National Assembly, on December 31, 1935, provided for a system of national defense in which military service was obligatory for all citizens. The commonwealth had renounced war as an instrument of national policy, and the new capability was accordingly envisaged for defensive use only. President Quezon obtained the services of General Douglas MacArthur, who had retired from the United States Army; MacArthur was made field marshal of the Army of the Philippines to plan its organization. He developed a 10-year plan for a regular force of 10,000 men, including the PC, which was deactivated and most of its men transferred to the new army. The plan provided for an eventual trained reserve of 400,000 men. Financial difficulties made achievement of these goals impossible; thus, at the time of the Japanese attack in December 1941, the strength of the regular army was about 4,000 and there were 132,000 in the reserves.

The termination at independence of existing trade preferences for Philippine exports to the United States under the Tydings-McDuffie Act had caused considerable Filipino concern. The matter was taken up in 1937 by a joint congressional committee, whose recommendations for amendment of certain trade preferences in the 1941-46 period were adopted in the Tydings-Koscialkowski Act of 1939 and approved by the Philippine assembly and by a plebiscite. The recommendations dealing with the post-1946 period were not acted on. In 1938 the United States high commissioner proposed reconsideration of the economic provisions of the Tydings-McDuffie Act that would have resulted in indefinite retention by the United States of controls over Philippine public finance, tariffs, and immigration. This was to Filipino politicians an unacceptable compromise of full independence and was also not acted upon, leaving the trade preference question unresolved at the outbreak of World War II.

World War II, 1941-45

The Japanese attack on the Philippines started on December 8, 1941, 10 hours after the attack on Pearl Harbor. Initial aerial bombardment was followed by landings of ground troops both north and south of Manila. The defending Filipino and United States troops were under the command of MacArthur, who had been recalled to active duty in the United States Army earlier in the year and designated commander of the United States armed forces in the Far East. The aircraft of his command were destroyed; the naval forces were ordered to leave; and because of the circumstances in the Pacific region, reinforcement and resupply of his ground forces were impossible. Under the pressure of superior numbers, the defending forces withdrew to the Bataan peninsula and to the island of Corregidor at the entrance to Manila Bay. Manila, declared an open city to prevent its destruction, was occupied by the Japanese on January 2, 1942.

Philippine defense continued until the final surrender of United States-Filipino forces on the Bataan peninsula in April 1942 and on Corregidor in May. Most of the 80,000 prisoners of war captured by the Japanese at Bataan were forced to undertake the infamous "death march" to a prison camp 65 miles to the north; it is estimated that as many as 10,000 men, weakened by disease and malnutrition and treated harshly by their captors, died before reaching their destination. Quezon and Osmeña had accompanied the troops to Corregidor and later left for the United States, where they set up a government in exile. MacArthur was ordered to Australia, where he started to plan for a return to the Philippines.

The Japanese military authorities immediately began organizing a new government structure in the Philippines. Although the Japanese had promised independence for the islands after occupation, they initially organized a Council of State through which they directed civil affairs until October 1943, when they declared the Philippines an independent republic.

Most of the Filipino elite, with a few notable exceptions, served under the Japanese. Filipino collaboration in Japanese-sponsored political institutions—which later became a major domestic political issue—was motivated by several considerations. Among them was the effort to protect the people from the harshness of Japanese rule (an effort that Quezon himself had advocated); protection of family and personal interests; and for some a belief that Philippine nationalism would be advanced by solidarity with fellow Asians. Not a few used the device of collaboration to pass information to the Allies. The Japanese-sponsored republic headed by President Jose P. Laurel proved to be unpopular.

Japanese occupation of the Philippines was opposed by increasingly effective underground and guerrilla activity that ultimately reached large-scale proportions; postwar investigations showed that about 260,000 men were in guerrilla organizations and that members of the anti-Japanese underground were even more numerous. Their effectiveness was such that by the end of the war, Japanese control extended to only 12 of the 48 provinces at that time. The major element of resistance in the central Luzon area was furnished by the People's Anti-Japanese Army (Hukbalahap, commonly called Huks—see Glossary), organized in early 1942 under the leadership of Luis Taruc, a communist since 1939. The Huks came to arm some 30,000 men and extended their control over much of Luzon. Other guerrilla units were attached to the United States Armed Forces Far East (USAFFE).

MacArthur's Allied forces landed on the island of Leyte on October 20, 1944, accompanied by Osmeña, who had succeeded to the commonwealth presidency upon the death of Quezon on August 1, 1944. Landings then followed on the island of Mindoro and Lingayen Gulf on Luzon, and the push toward Manila was initiated. Fighting was fierce, particularly in the mountains of northern Luzon where Japanese troops had retreated and in Manila, where they put up a last-ditch resistance. Guerrilla forces rose up everywhere for the final offensive. Fighting continued until Japan's formal surrender on September 22, 1945. The Philippines had suffered great loss of life and tremendous physical destruction by the time the war was over. An estimated 1 million Filipinos had been killed, a large proportion during the last months. The final fighting for Manila left the city one of the most extensively damaged of any major city in the world.

Independence and Constitutional Government, 1945-72

Demoralized by the war and suffering rampant inflation and short-ages of food and other goods, the Philippine people prepared for the transition to independence, which had been scheduled for July 4, 1946. A number of issues remained unresolved, principally those concerned with trade relations between the islands and the United States and security arrangements. Yet in the months following the Japanese sur-render, collaboration became a virulent issue that split the country and poisoned political life. Most of the commonwealth legislature and leading men, such as Laurel, Claro Recto, and Roxas, had served in the Japanese-sponsored government. While the war was still going on, Allied leaders had stated that such "quislings" and their counterparts on the provincial and local levels would be severely punished. Harold Ickes, who as United States secretary of the interior had civil authority over the islands, had suggested that all officials above the rank of schoolteacher who had cooperated with the Japanese be purged and denied the right to vote in the first postwar elections, while Osmeña had countered that each case should be tried on its own merits.

Resolution of the problem posed serious moral questions that struck at the heart of the political system. Collaborators argued that they had gone along with the occupiers in order to shield the people from the harshest aspects of their rule. Before leaving Corregidor in March 1942, Quezon had told Laurel and Jose Vargas, mayor of Manila, that they should stay behind to deal with the Japanese but refuse to take an oath of allegiance. Although the president of a "puppet" republic, Laurel had faced down the Japanese several times and made it clear that his loyalty was first to the Philippines and second to the Japanese-spon-sored "Greater East Asia Co-Prosperity Sphere."

Critics accused the collaborators of opportunism, of getting rich while the people starved. Anticollaborationist feeling, moreover, was fueled by the people's resentment of the elite. On both the local and the national levels, it had been primarily landlords, important officials, and the political establishment who had supported the Japanese, largely because the latter, with their own troops and those of a reestablished PC, preserved their property and forcibly maintained the rural status quo. Tenants felt the harshest aspects of Japanese rule. Guerrillas, particularly those associated with the Huks, came from the ranks of the cultivators, who organized to defend themselves against PC and Japanese depredations.

The issue of collaboration centered on Roxas, prewar Nacionalista Speaker of the House, who had served as minister without portfolio and was responsible for rice procurement and economic policy in the wartime Laurel government. A close prewar associate of MacArthur, he maintained contact with Allied intelligence during the war and in 1944 had unsuccessfully attempted to escape to Allied territory. This exonerated him in the general's eyes, and MacArthur supported him in his ambitions for the presidency when he announced himself a candidate of the newly formed Liberal Party (the liberal wing of the Nacionalista Party) in January 1946. MacArthur's favoritism aroused much criticism, particularly because other collaborationist leaders were held in jail, awaiting trial. A presidential campaign of great vindictiveness ensued, in which the wartime role of Roxas was a central issue, and Roxas outspent and outspoke his Nacionalista opponent, the aging and ailing Osmeña. In the April 23, 1946 election, Roxas won 54 percent of the vote, and the Liberal Party won a majority in the legislature.

On July 4, 1946, Roxas became the first president of the independent Republic of the Philippines. In 1948 he declared an amnesty for arrested collaborators—only one of whom had been indicted—except for those who had committed violent crimes. The resiliency of the prewar elite, although remarkable, nevertheless had left a bitter residue in the popular mind. In the first years of the republic, the issue of collaboration would become closely entwined with old agrarian grievances, producing violent results.

Economic Relations with the United States after Independence

If the inauguration of the Commonwealth of the Philippines in November 1935 marked the high point of Philippine-American good feeling, the actual achievement of independence was in many ways a disillusioning anticlimax. Economic relations remained the most salient issue. The Philippine economy remained highly dependent on American markets—more dependent, according to United States High Commissioner Paul McNutt, than any single state was dependent on the rest of the country. Thus a severance of special relations at independence was unthinkable, and large landowners, particularly those in sugar, campaigned for an extension of free trade. The Philippine Trade Act, passed by the United States Congress in 1946 and commonly known as the Bell Act, stipulated that free trade would be continued until 1954; thereafter, tariffs would be increased 5 percent annually until full amounts were reached in 1974. Quotas were established for Philippine products for both free trade and tariff periods. At the same time, there could be no restrictions on the entry of United States products, nor would there be Philippine import duties. The Philippine peso was tied at a fixed rate to the United States dollar. The most controversial provision of the Bell Act was the "parity" clause—that United States citizens would be granted equal economic rights with Filipinos, for example, in the exploitation of natural resources. If parity privileges of individuals or corporations were infringed upon, the president of the United States had the authority to revoke any aspect of the trade agreement. Payment of war damages amounting to US$620 million, as stipulated in the Philippine Rehabilitation Act of 1946, was made contingent on Philippine acceptance of the parity clause.

The Bell Act was approved by the Philippine legislature on July 2, two days before independence. The parity clause, however, required an amendment relating to the 1935 constitution's thirteenth article, which reserved the exploitation of natural resources for Philippine citizens. This could be obtained only with the approval of three-quarters of the members of the House and Senate and a plebiscite. The denial of seats in the House to six members of the leftist Democratic Alliance and three Nacionalistas on grounds of fraud and violent campaign tactics during the April 1946 election enabled Roxas to gain legislative approval on September 18. The definition of "three-quarters" became an issue because three-quarters of the sitting members, not the full House and Senate, had approved the amendment, but the Supreme Court ruled in favor of the administration's interpretation. In March 1947 a plebiscite on the amendment was held; only 40 percent of the electorate participated, but the majority of those approved the amendment. The Bell Act, particularly the parity clause, was seen by critics as an inexcusable surrender of national sovereignty; the pressure of the "sugar barons," particularly those of Roxas' home region of the western Visayan Islands, and other landowner interests, however, was irresistible.

In the 1946-49 period, inflation and unemployment rose steadily, while production remained below prewar levels. The inability, or unwillingness, of the government to collect taxes contributed to budget shortfalls; and poor prices for export commodities, overvaluation of the peso, and the irresponsible importation of luxury items contributed to a large balance of payments deficit by 1950. The Huk rebellion in central Luzon and the general atmosphere of demoralization and corruption contributed to worsening conditions. The United States Economic Survey Mission sent to the islands in 1950 recommended reform of the land tenure system, further United States aid, and a revision of the Philippine Trade Act.

Security Agreements

The Philippines became an integral part of emerging United States security arrangements in the western Pacific upon approval of the Military Bases Agreement in March 1947. The United States retained control of 23 military installations, including the extensive navy facilities at Subic Bay and Clark Air Base, for a lease period of 99 years. United States rather than Philippine authorities retained full jurisdiction over their territories, including the collection of taxes and the trying of offenders, including Filipinos, in cases involving United States service personnel. Base rights remained a controversial issue in relations between the two countries.

The Military Assistance Agreement was also signed in March 1947. This established a Joint United States Military Advisory Group (JUSMAG) to advise and train the Philippine armed forces and authorized the transfer of aid and matériel—some US$169 million worth by 1957. Much United States aid was used in the support and reorganization of the PC in late 1947 in the face of growing internal unrest. A contingent of Philippine troops was sent to Korea in 1950, and in August 1951 the Philippines and the United States signed the Mutual Defense

Treaty Between the Republic of the Philippines and the United States of America.

The Huk Rebellion

At the end of the war the rural areas, particularly in central Luzon, were a tinderbox on the point of incineration. The Japanese occupation had only postponed the farmers' movement for better conditions. Tensions grew as landlords who had fled to urban areas during the fighting returned to the villages in late 1945 to demand back rent and employed military police and their own armed contingents to enforce these demands. Food and other goods were in short supply. The war had sharpened animosities. The elite, who in large numbers had supported the Japanese, and those tenants who had been part of the guerrilla resistance found themselves on different sides, in contrast to the wars of resistance to Spain and the United States, in which *ilustrados* and farmers had made common cause. Possessing weapons and combat experience and having lost friends and relatives to the Japanese and the wartime PC, guerrilla veterans and those close to them were not as willing to step down in the face of the customary landlord intimidations as they had been before 1942.

MacArthur had put Taruc and Casto Alejandrino, both Huk leaders, in jail in 1945, and United States forces were ordered to disarm and disband Huk guerrillas. Many, however, concealed their weapons or went up into the mountains. The Huks were closely identified with the emerging National Peasant Union (Pambansang Kaisahan ng mga Magbubukid—PKM), which was strongest in the provinces of Pampanga, Bulacan, Nueva Ecija, and Tarlac and had as many as 500,000 members. As part of the left-wing Democratic Alliance, which also included urban left-wing groups and labor unions, the PKM supported Osmeña and the Nacionalistas against Roxas in the 1946 election campaign; they did so not only because Roxas had been a collaborator but also because Osmeña had promised a new law giving tenants 60 percent of the harvest (rather than the 50 percent or less that had been customary). Six Democratic Alliance candidates won congressional seats, including Taruc, who had been released from jail along with other leaders, but their exclusion from the legislature on charges of using terrorist methods during the campaign provoked great unrest in the districts that had elected them. Continued landlord- and police-instigated violence against peasant activities, including the murder of PKM leader Juan Feleo in August 1946, provoked the Huk veterans to dig up their weapons and incite a rebellion in the central Luzon provinces. The name of the movement was changed from the People's Anti-Japanese Army to the People's Liberation Army (Hukbong Mapagpalaya ng Bayan).

President Roxas' policy toward the People's Liberation Army alternated between gestures of negotiation and harsh suppression. His administration established an Agrarian Commission and passed a law giving tenants 70 percent of the harvest, although this was extremely

43

difficult to enforce in the countryside. The Huks in turn demanded reinstatement of the Democratic Alliance congressmen, disbandment of the military police (which in the 1945-48 period had been the equivalent of the old PC), and a general amnesty. They also refused to give up their arms. In March 1948 Roxas declared the People's Liberation Army an illegal and subversive organization and stepped up counterinsurgency activities.

Following Roxas' death from a heart attack in April 1948, his successor, Elpidio Quirino, opened negotiations with People's Liberation Army leader Taruc, but nothing was accomplished. That same year the PKP decided to support the rebellion, overcoming its reluctance to rely on peasant movements. Although it lacked a peasant following, the PKP declared that it would lead the Huks on all levels and in 1950 described the People's Liberation Army as the "military arm" of the revolutionary movement to overthrow the government. From the very beginning the government considered the Huk movement to have been communist instigated, an extension onto the Luzon Plain of the international revolutionary strategy of the Cominform in Moscow. Yet the rebellion's main impetus was peasant grievances, not Leninist designs. The principal factors were continuous tenant-landlord conflicts (in which the government actively took the part of the latter), the dislocations caused by the war, and perhaps as well an insurrectionist tradition going back several centuries. According to Kerkvliet, "the PKP did not inspire or control the peasant movement. . ... What appears closer to the truth is that the PKP, as an organization, moved back and forth between alliance and nonalliance with the peasant movement in Central Luzon." Most farmers had little interest or knowledge of socialism. Most wanted not redistribution of land or collectivization but simply better conditions; the landlord-tenant relationship itself was not challenged, just its more exploitive and impersonal character in the contemporary period.

People's Liberation Army fortunes reached their peak in the 1949-51 period. Violence associated with the November 1949 presidential election, in which Quirino was reelected on the Liberal Party ticket, led many farmers to support the People's Liberation Army, and after that date there were between 11,000 and 15,000 armed Huks. Although the core of the rebellion remained in the area of central Luzon, regional committees ("recos") of the People's Liberation Army were also established in the provinces of what is now the Southern Tagalog Region, in northern Luzon, in the Visayan Islands, and on Mindanao, and antigovernment activities spread to areas outside the movement's heartland. Beginning in 1951, however, the momentum began to slow. This was in part the result of poor training and the atrocities perpetrated by individual Huks. Their mistreatment of Negrito peoples, for instance, made it almost impossible for them to use the mountain areas where these tribespeople lived, and the assassination of Aurora Quezon, President Quezon's widow, and of her family outraged the nation. Many Huks degenerated into murderers and bank robbers. Moreover, in the words of one guerrilla veteran, the movement was suffering from "battle fatigue." Lacking a hinterland, such as the Democratic Republic of Vietnam (North Vietnam) provided for Viet Cong guerrillas, or the "liberated areas" provided for Chinese Communists before 1949, the Huks were constantly on the run. Other decisive factors were the better quality of United States-trained Philippine armed forces and the more conciliatory policy adopted by the Quirino government toward the peasants.

Limited Reform under Magsaysay

Ramon Magsaysay, congressman from Zambales Province and veteran of a non-Huk guerrilla unit during the war, became secretary of defense in 1950 and initiated a campaign to defeat the insurgents militarily and at the same time win popular support for the government. With United States aid and advisers he was able to improve the quality of the armed forces, whose campaign against the Huks had been largely ineffective and heavy-handed. In 1950 the PC was made part of the armed forces (it had previously been under the secretary of the interior) with its own separate command. All armed forces units were placed under strict discipline; thus their behavior in the villages was visibly more restrained. Peasants felt grateful to Magsaysay for ending forced evacuations and harsh pacification tactics that some claimed had been worse than those of the Japanese occupation. The number of battalion combat teams was doubled from 10 to 20, and antiguerrilla tactics were adopted with considerable success. Magsaysay's popularity grew tremendously following the army's supervision of the November 1951 election for which he was responsible. In great contrast to the 1949 election, this was conducted fairly, and the opposition Nacionalista Party made strong gains. He acquired the reputation of being the one honest man in the Quirino administration, and the Nacionalistas sought him as a presidential candidate.

Nominated as Nacionalista Party presidential candidate in April 1953, Magsaysay won almost two-thirds of the vote over his opponent, Quirino, in November. Often compared to United States president Andrew Jackson, Magsaysay styled himself a man of the people, inviting thousands of peasants and laborers to tour the Malacañang Palace, the presidential residence, and encouraged farmers to send him telegrams—free of charge—telling of their complaints. In the countryside a number of small-scale but highly visible projects had been started, including the building of bridges, roads, irrigation canals, and "liberty wells"; the establishment of special courts for landlord-tenant disputes; agricultural extension services; and credit for farmers. The Economic Development Corps project settled some 950 families on land the government had purchased on Mindanao. The capture and killing of Huk leaders, the dissolution of People's Liberation Army regional committees, and finally the surrender of Taruc in May 1954 marked the waning of the Huk threat.

In a decisive break with the past, Magsaysay in 1955 proposed land redistribution, and that same year the legislature, under his insistence, passed the Land Reform Act, which established the Land Tenure Administration, empowered to acquire private lands through either purchase or expropriation. The administration then would sell the land at reasonable rates to farmers. The reform had naturally aroused the determined opposition of the landowning elite, and its effectiveness was limited by the fact that the administration was not allocated sufficient funds for the purchase of large estates for redistribution to the landless.

Magsaysay vowed to clean up government corruption and encouraged the formation of independent labor unions. These commitments and his land reform legislation aroused considerable public expectations that significant change in the system could be accomplished; thus, it was with great shock that people learned in March 1957 that their popular president had been killed in an airplane accident in Cebu.

In 1954 Manila had been the site of the conference that resulted in the formation of the Southeast Asia Treaty Organization (SEATO), the anticommunist alignment of Western and regional powers that arose as a response to the French withdrawal from Indochina. In 1955 the Revised United States-Philippine Trade Agreement (the Laurel-Langley Agreement) was negotiated as an overall instrument to regulate commercial relations over the next two decades. The new agreement abolished the authority of the United States to control the exchange rate of the peso, made parity privileges reciprocal, extended the sugar quota, and extended the time period for reduction of other quotas and for the progressive application of tariffs on Philippine goods exported to the United States.

The Garcia and Macapagal Administrations, 1957-65

Magsaysay's vice president, Carlos P. Garcia, succeeded to the presidency at the time of Magsaysay's death and was shortly thereafter elected to the office. Garcia emphasized the nationalist themes of "Filipino First" and attainment of "respectable independence." Further discussions with the United States took place in 1959 on the question of the military bases. Early agreement was reached on one of the issues under consideration—United States relinquishment of large land areas initially reserved for bases but no longer required for their operation; as a result the United States turned over to Philippine administration the town of Olongapo on Subic Bay, north of Manila, which previously had been under the jurisdiction of the United States Navy.

The 1957 election had resulted, for the first time, in a vice president of a party different from that of the president. The new vice president, Diosdado Macapagal, ran as the candidate of the Liberal Party, which followers of Magsaysay had joined after unsuccessful efforts to form an effective third party. By the time of the 1961 presidential election, the revived Liberal Party had built enough of a following to win the presidency for Macapagal. In this election the returns from each polling place were reported by observers (who had been placed there by newspapers) as soon as the votes were counted. This system, known as Operation Quick Count, was designed to prevent fraud.

Macapagal's announced objectives were the restoration of economic stability, the alleviation of the plight of the common man, and the establishment of a dynamic basis for future growth. He immediately eliminated some economic controls, those on imports being abolished between 1960 and 1962. The peso was freed from its fixed rate and devalued, which resulted in the disappearance of the black market in dollars. The nationalist trend in Filipino attitudes was demonstrated further during Macapagal's term by his issuance of an executive order in 1962 changing Philippine Independence Day from July 4 to June 12, the day in 1898 when Aguinaldo had read the declaration of independence.

Macapagal's social and economic program included a far-reaching reform of the critical agrarian situation. The resultant Agrarian Land Reform Code, which became law on August 8, 1963, had as its main feature abolition of share tenancy by the institution of an agricultural leasehold system; this was a step toward the eventual goal of ownership by cultivators. The law provided for an administrative apparatus organized with legal, financial, technical, and law enforcement support.

The president designated certain areas, starting with central Luzon, for initial implementation of the program. The first results were encouraging, but the extent of the area affected at the end of Macapagal's term in 1966 was insignificant; it amounted to some 29,150 hectares of about 405,000 hectares of rice and corn cultivated by sharecropping tenants.

The issue of jurisdiction over United States service personnel in the Philippines, which had not been fully settled after the 1959 discussions, continued to be a problem in relations between the two countries. A series of incidents in the 1960-65 period, chiefly associated with Clark Air Base, aroused considerable anti-American feeling and demonstrations. Negotiations took place and resulted in agreement in August 1965 on adoption of provisions similar to the status of forces agreement of the North Atlantic Treaty Organization (NATO) regarding criminal jurisdiction. In the next four years agreements were reached on several other matters relating to the bases, including in 1966 amendment of the 1947 agreement, the expiration date of the lease being moved up to 1991.

Philippine foreign policy under Macapagal turned to closer relations with neighboring Asian peoples. In July 1963 he convened a summit meeting in Manila consisting of the Philippines, Indonesia, and Malaysia. An organization called MAPHILINDO was proposed; much heralded in the local press as a realization of Rizal's dream of bringing together the Malay peoples, MAPHILINDO was described as a regional association that would approach issues of common concern in the spirit of consensus.

MAPHILINDO was quickly shelved, however, in the face of the continuing confrontation between Indonesia and newly established Malaysia and the Philippines' own claim to Sabah, the territory in northeastern Borneo that had become a Malaysian state in 1963. In June 1962 Macapagal's foreign minister had pressed the claim on the British, basing it on the argument that the transfer of Sabah by the sultan of Sulu to the British North Borneo Company in 1878 had been a lease rather than full cession. When the British pointed out that the Philippine government did not recognize the status of the sultan, confirmation of a successor to the royal house of Sulu, Esmail Kiram, was quickly arranged. Bad relations between Malaysia and the Philippines over this issue prevented the latter from taking a more positive role in the region, and resentment of the United States grew as Washington supported Malaysia over the Sabah question.

The Marcos Administration, 1965-72

In the presidential election of 1965, Macapagal lost to Ferdinand E. Marcos, wartime veteran of a USAFFE guerrilla unit and senator from Ilocos Norte Province, who was the Nacionalista Party candidate. Macapagal's agrarian reforms had not achieved their goals, and once again the electorate expressed dissatisfaction with official corruption and high prices. During his first term (1965-69) Marcos tackled, not entirely successfully, the serious problems of smuggling and crime. Considerably more successful were two "impact programs." The first was the substantial support given to the dissemination of new "miracle rice" varieties developed by the International Rice Research Institute (IRRI) as a means of overcoming popular dissatisfaction with the availability and the cost of rice. The second was a massive public works program—roads, bridges, schools, health centers, irrigation facilities, and urban beautification projects. Marcos' personal delivery of public works checks to barrio captains, allocations that helped drain the treasury, reportedly contributed to his reelection in 1969. His early admission that "we are in crisis" and his theme of the "New Filipino"—self-reliant, hardworking, and creative—were addressed to popular cynicism and discouragement. Using his patronage powers to the fullest, he also appointed able technocrats to the government.

Foreign policy responded to increasing nationalist sentiment and to changes in the regional environment following the statement of the Nixon Doctrine in mid-1969 of a reduced United States military presence in Asia. In 1966, after heated debate, the legislature had provided for the commitment of a 2,000-man Philippine Civic Action Group (PHILCAG) to the Republic of Vietnam (South Vietnam), the first contingent being sent in August of that year. In 1969, shortly after Marcos' reelection, withdrawal of the Philippine unit was announced. Marcos espoused greater national independence in foreign policy and closer ties with neighboring countries. The Philippines helped form the Association of Southeast Asian Nations (ASEAN) in 1967, which also included Malaysia; trouble between these countries continued over the Sabah issue. In 1968 a new Philippine map was issued including most of Sabah as national territory.

In November 1969 Marcos became the first president of the independent Philippines to win a second term, defeating Liberal Party candidate Sergio Osmeña, Jr. He obtained 60 percent of the vote, the highest ever save for Magsaysay's 1953 victory, and carried all 10 regions (at that time) of the country, including that containing Osmeña's home province of Cebu. Nacionalista Party representatives were elected at the same time from 90 of the 110 constituencies. Marcos assumed his second term, however, against a background of continuing tension and malaise. The political power of the elite was being challenged, and violent student demonstrations erupted in Manila in early 1970. Insurgency was a growing problem, particularly in the Moro regions of Mindanao, and the issue of agrarian reform remained unresolved. There were, moreover, serious issues revolving around trade relations and base rights that had to be negotiated with the United States during the 1970s.

President Marcos and Martial Law

On September 21, 1972, President Marcos issued Proclamation 1081, declaring martial law over the entire country. In an operation described by one observer as "swift, sufficient, thorough, but not unduly harsh," the military under the president's command arrested oppositionists, including members of Congress and provincial governors, journalists, student and labor activists, and criminal elements. (A total of about 30,000 detainees were kept at military compounds run by the army and the PC.) They confiscated weapons and broke up "private armies" connected with prominent politicians and other figures. Newspapers were shut down and the mass media brought under tight contrJl. With the stroke of a pen, Marcos closed down the Philippine Congress and assumed its lawmaking responsibilities, issuing over a thousand presidential decrees by 1976.

The incident that precipitated martial law was an unsuccessful attempt on September 21, 1972, to assassinate the secretary of national defense, Juan Ponce Enrile. In Proclamation 1081, Marcos attributed a rising tide of lawlessness to "elements who are moved by a common or similar ideological conviction, design, strategy and goal and enjoying the active and material support of a foreign power. . ." who intended to establish a new state and society based on "the Marxist-Leninist-Maoist teachings and beliefs." He alleged the existence of a network of "front organizations" working among "our peasants, laborers, professionals, intellectuals, students, and mass media personnel" that sought to promote violence and overthrow the government. Although a conspiracy of leftists was seen as the principal rationale for martial law, Marcos also mentioned the growth of violence between Muslims and Christians on Mindanao and in the Sulu Archipelago as being encouraged by foreign powers.

Conditions on the Eve of Martial Law

Most observers agree that by 1972 lawlessness and unrest had reached new heights in the Philippines, though the existence of a genuine conspiracy among insurgents, even of the left, is strongly doubted. The government's suppression campaign against the People's Liberation Army in the 1950s left only a remnant under Commander Sumulong (Faustino del Mundo); he was more of a gangster than a revolutionary, deeply involved in gambling and prostitution rackets near Clark Air Base. There was also a small People's Army connected to what was left of the pro-Soviet Communist Party of the Philippines (the organization had been largely broken up during the 1950s). The most troublesome insurgent group was the New People's Army (NPA), the armed force of the pro-Chinese "reestablished" Philippine Communist Party, which designated itself the Communist Party of the Philippines-Marxist Leninist (CPP-ML). The party had been organized in 1968 in Tarlac Province by Bernabe Buscayno, alias Commander Dante, a veteran of Sumulong's rackets who had broken with older communists and adopted the Maoist strategy of "People's Democratic Revolution." By the early 1970s the NPA was in control of large portions of Isabela Province on the northeast coast of Luzon. Buscayno was popular among student activists in the universities of Manila, and some links were established between the NPA and the more radical student organizations.

Violence on Mindanao and in the Sulu Archipelago was based on the centuries-long hostility between the Muslims of the region and the predominant Christian population of the islands. As Christian immigration from the crowded regions of Luzon and the Visayan Islands increased, Moros were finding themselves a minority in their own homeland. Bitterness was compounded by the fact that this immigration was largely government sponsored and was perceived by the Moros as part of a plan to extinguish Muslim identity. Communal violence flared up between armed groups such as the Blackshirts and the Barracudas, Moro gangs that terrorized newly arrived settlers from the north, and the Ilagas, or Rats, a Christian vigilante group.

In July 1971 terrorist gangs killed 70 Muslims in a mosque in the barrio of Manili on Mindanao. In Proclamation 1081 Marcos stated that some 3,000 persons (including 1,000 civilians) had been killed in hostilities on Mindanao and in the Sulu Archipelago by September 1972 and that more than one-half million were "injured, displaced and homeless" as a result of communal violence.

Moro demands for autonomy and the freedom to practice the sharia had been voiced since independence, but the "Corregidor Incident" of March 1968 spurred more active Moro resistance. The incident involved the execution of some 30 mutinous Moro recruits who had been undergoing military training on the island of Corregidor before being sent to Sabah as infiltrators. In May 1968 former Cotabato governor Udtog Matalam, reacting to the Marcos administration's apparent lack of regard for Moro lives, organized the Mindanao Independence Movement, demanding self-determination for Mindanao, the Sulu Archipelago, and Palawan. A year later the Moro National Liberation Front (MNLF), an armed group headed by Nur Misuari, a former teacher of political science, was organized on Malaysian soil. The MNLF began to conduct an insurrection after that with the support of Malaysia and certain Islamic states in the Middle East, particularly Libya.

In urban areas strikes by militant labor unions were on the increase, and strikers were joined by student demonstrators calling for an end to "feudalism, bureaucratic capitalism, and American imperialism." In February 1971 the Manila police were mobilized to clear students out of the campus of the University of the Philippines, which they had taken over. In May 1972 police fired on students demonstrating in front of the American embassy. As demonstrations increased up to the proclamation of martial law, hundreds were wounded and dozens killed in violent confrontations with the police. Following a grenade attack on a Liberal Party rally on August 21, 1971, in which nine people were killed and eight Liberal Party senatorial candidates wounded, Marcos suspended the writ of habeas corpus and arrested a number of leftist figures.

The idea of rewriting the Philippine constitution as the basis of a thorough reform of the political system had been considered for some time; in 1967 a bill was passed providing for a constitutional convention, and three years later delegates to the convention were elected. It first met in June 1971, but delegates could not agree on the establishment of a parliamentary system to replace the presidential system of the original 1935 document. The commonwealth constitution had limited the president to a maximum of two terms of four years, and the delegates feared that Marcos might use the parliamentary system to maintain himself in power indefinitely. In September 1971 the convention adopted a clause banning Marcos and members of his family from holding the position of head of state or government under whatever arrangement was finally established. By the summer of 1972 Marcos was able to pressure delegates into reversing their stance, but a constitution was not approved until after the proclamation of martial law.

The New Society

Although martial law was established ostensibly to stem a left-wing takeover of the government, a central theme of government writings after September 1972 was the contrast between the "Old Society," with its corruption and extreme inequalities, and a "New Society" in which not only the institutions but also the basic values of Philippine society would be transformed. Certain aspects of personal behavior, attributed to a "colonial mentality," were regarded as obstacles to effective modernization. These included the primacy of personalistic connections, as reflected in the ethic of *utang na loob*, and the importance of maintaining in-group harmony and coherence, even at the cost to the wider, national community. Fatalism and excessive concern for *amor proprio* (self-esteem) were also regarded by New Society ideologues as contributing to the prevalence of corruption, favoritism, indolence, and explosive violence in the old political system. Much New Society literature reflected Marcos' earlier preoccupations with creating a New Filipino who would be self-reliant, public-spirited, and disciplined. In the president's words: "Our populist, personalist and individualist culture must give way not only to collective responsibility, but beyond that to our historical responsibility."

The old political system, with its parties, rough-and-tumble election campaigns, and a press so uninhibited in its vituperative and libelous nature that it was called the "freest in the world," had been boss ridden and dominated by the elite since the colonial days of the Philippine Commission. The elite, however, had never been a homogenous group; its feuds and tensions, fueled as often by assaults on *amor proprio* as by disagreement over ideology or issues, had made for a pluralistic system in which different interests could compete through the electoral process. Marcos' self-proclaimed "revolution from the top" deprived significant portions of the old elite of power and patronage. The media were tamed, parties dissolved, and elections suspended until they could be held under tightly controlled conditions in 1978. Especially significant during the 1972-81 martial law period was the concentration of power and patronage in a single elite headed by Marcos and his wife, Imelda Romualdez Marcos; she became an increasingly formidable political force upon her assumption of the offices of governor of Metro Manila (see Glossary) and minister of human settlements.

Although Marcos reiterated in Proclamation 1081 that martial law did not mean military government, the military played the central role in closing down constitutional institutions and was a principal source of support for the continuation of martial law rule. Marcos' stated commitment to discipline and rational modernization was cited as a reason for the military's support; according to one administration spokesman, Adrian Cristobal, "since we...have adopted *discipline* as a necessary element of national progress, and since discipline has long been associated in our minds with the military way of life, it is but natural that the military now looms so vividly in our thinking."

The minister of national defense and top military officers played a central role in decisionmaking and enjoyed a close relationship with the president. Budget allocations for the armed forces increased 500 percent in the 1972-76 period, from ₱800 million to ₱4 billion (for value of the peso—see Glossary), and officers and men enjoyed new privileges and power.

New Society Institutions

Because political power was centralized and enforced through the support of the military, the boisterous pre-1972 pluralism was replaced by a more "rational" arrangement in which interest groups were not only coordinated but also controlled by the center. Without such a "corporatist" system, it was argued, programs to foster development from the top down would be blocked by sectional political interests.

To promote harmony on the economic front, the government established the National Tripartite Congress of Labor, Management, and Government, which approved a new labor code providing for compulsory arbitration of labor-management disputes and a limited measure of bargaining over wages. The multifarious labor movement was "restructured" through the establishment of a Trade Union Congress of the Philippines (TUCP), which promoted organization by enterprise rather than by trade. The media were controlled through the Print Media Council and the Broadcast Media Council, which were responsible for policing the communications industry. Youth were organized in April 1975 under the Kabataang Barangay (Youth Association), a hierarchy of youth groups extending from the barrio (renamed *barangay*) level to the center whose leaders underwent special government training programs.

A bewildering array of new political institutions was set up to mobilize mass support for Marcos' presidential decrees and to strengthen central government control on the regional, provincial, and local levels. In line with the spirit of "revolution from the top," they possessed in common a hierarchical structure. Advertised as promoting local initiative and self-government, they, in fact, aided in the control of grassroots political forces, both elite and nonelite. In December 1972 Marcos ordered the creation of citizens' assemblies (*barangays*) in some of the nation's barrios in order to hold a referendum on the new parliamentary constitution (which the convention had drafted after the imposition of martial law). Staged in January 1973, the plebiscite showed 90 percent popular approval, by a show of hands rather than by secret ballot, for the new document. Between 1973 and 1977 Marcos would employ plebiscites five times to show popular support for martial law and pass important amendments to the constitution.

Barangay assemblies replaced pre-martial law barrio councils. Whereas the councils had been elective and thus subject to local political pressures, presumably the appointive assemblies were at the bottom of a hierarchy of similarly structured organs that culminated in the Katipunan ng mga Barangay, or Society of Barangays. A similar structure was imposed on town and municipal government; municipal councils, called Sangguniang Bayan, were established in 1975-76 in cities and municipalities to replace the elective town assemblies. At the top of the town council hierarchy was the National Legislative Advisory Council, which included *barangay*, youth group, labor, agricultural, employer, and other sectoral representatives and acted as a kind of consultative body to the president.

Marcos had made land reform a central goal of New Society policies. In September 1973, on the first anniversary of martial law, he stated that "the land reform program is the only gauge for the success or failure of the New Society. If land reform fails, there is no New Society." What were described as "family-sized plots" (three hectares of irrigated or five hectares of unirrigated land) were to be distributed to tenants who would pay for them over a 15-year period. To receive a Certificate of Land Transfer, tenants had to join associations known as Samahang Nayons (see Glossary). By 1975 almost one-half the nation's barrios had Samahang Nayons, and these were subordinated to municipal-, provincial-, and regional-level bodies, surmounted by a national-level Association of Samahang Nayons. Although in principle based on local initiatives and self-reliance, they remained firmly under central government control (see Land Use and Tenure, ch. 3).

Relations with the United States

Relations with the United States remained most important for the Philippines in the 1970s, although the special relationship between the former colonizing power and colony was greatly modified as trade, investment, and defense ties were redefined. The Laurel-Langley Agreement defining preferential United States tariffs for Philippine exports and parity privileges for United States investors expired on July 4, 1974, and trade relations were governed thereafter in accordance with the generalized preferences of the international General Agreement on Tariffs and Trade (see Relations with the United States, ch. 4). Although the parity privileges of United States citizens in the Philippines were ended, a series of presidential decrees issued by Marcos allowed for gradual transfer to local control over a period of time and attractive "lease-back" arrangements for United States firms. During the martial law years, foreign investment terms were substantially liberalized, and an export development policy was initiated (see Foreign Economic Relations, ch. 3). During the 1970s Japan became an increasingly significant market for Philippine exports.

The status of United States military bases was redefined when an agreement was signed on January 6, 1979. Under the new terms, Philippine sovereignty over the bases was reaffirmed, a Philippine commander appointed to each base, and their total area significantly reduced (see Foreign Military Relations, ch. 5). The United States was guaranteed "unhampered military operations involving its forces in the Philippines," and both sides agreed to review the bases agreement every five years. A United States commitment to supply significant military and economic assistance over the 1979-83 period paralleled the bases agreement.

Developments to the End of Martial Law

On April 7, 1978, the first elections were held under martial law to select members of the interim National Assembly, a legislative body having very limited powers, which had been ratified by the plebiscite of December 1977. Its 200 members included 165 popularly elected representatives, 14 chosen by labor, youth, agricultural, and other sectoral groups; and 21 others, consisting of the prime minister, Marcos (who retained as well his title as president), and his cabinet. Marcos retained the power of issuing presidential decrees, as well as the power to dissolve the National Assembly. Before the election he had organized a political grouping, the New Society Movement (Kilusang Bagong Lipunan—KBL), which won most assembly seats, though it was opposed in Metro Manila by People's Power (Lakas ng Bayan—LABAN), led by former senator Benigno "Ninoy" Aquino, Jr. During the late 1970s the Roman Catholic Church came to represent the most important nonrevolutionary opposition to the martial law government. As the single remaining institution having its own base of support and a large measure of independence in the highly centralized New Society system, the church pursued a policy of "critical collaboration" as defined by its titular head in the islands, Jaime Cardinal Sin, stressing the observance of human rights and preservation of the democratic process. By 1980 church-state relations had become severely strained.

On January 17, 1981, President Marcos issued Proclamation 2045, formally ending martial law. Amendments to the 1973 Constitution passed by plebiscite in April 1981 changed the structure of the government to one headed by a strong, popularly elected president. Marcos retained strong, personal control over the government, and the "New Republic" proved in essence to be essentially a somewhat liberalized extension of the New Society.

* * *

David Joel Steinberg's *The Philippines: A Singular and a Plural Place* provides a good general introduction to the country and pays considerable attention to historic background. Gregorio Zaide's two-volume *The Pageant of Philippine History* is thorough, often engrossing, but stresses specific personalities and events at the expense of a broader analysis. For good discussions of the Spanish period, see John L. Phelan's *The Hispanization of the Philippines* and Robert R. Reed's *Colonial Manila* in the series University of California Publications in Geography. Austin Coates' *Rizal: Philippine Nationalist and Martyr* provides a well-written account of one of the most extraordinary lives of modern times. On American annexation of the islands, Leon Wolff's *Little Brown Brother* and Stuart C. Miller's *Benevolent Assimilation* are highly readable, although the former at times reduces the grim Philippine-American guerrilla war to the status of entertainment. Glenn A. May's *Social Engineering in the Philippines*, Peter W. Stanley's *A Nation in the Making*, and Theodore Friend's *Between Two Empires* are good studies of the American colonial period, while Teodoro Agoncillo, in his two-volume *The Fateful Years*, deals with the Japanese occupation.

Carl H. Landé's *Leaders, Factions, and Parties: The Structure of Philippine Politics* deals with both the preindependence and the postindependence political systems, while Benedict J. Kerkvliet's *The Huk*

Rebellion and Eduardo Lachica's *The Huks: Philippine Agrarian Society in Revolt* provide good, if somewhat differing, accounts of peasant movements both during and after the war. For a broader historical perspective, see David R. Sturtevant's *Popular Uprisings in the Philippines, 1840-1940*. The collection of essays edited by David A. Rosenberg, entitled *Marcos and Martial Law in the Philippines*, provides perspectives on developments up to and after 1972. (For further information and complete citations, see Bibliography).

Chapter 2. The Society and Its Environment

Locally available materials are effectively used for housing in outlying areas.

THE PHILIPPINES CONTINUES to be primarily a rural society in which the family is the prime unit of social awareness. Ritual kin relations and associations of a patron-client nature are still the basis for social groupings beyond the nuclear family, rather than horizontal ties forged among members of economically based social classes. Owing in large part to the existence of a common religious tradition and to the spread of Pilipino as a widely used, if not thoroughly accepted, national language, Filipinos are a relatively homogeneous population, with the important exceptions of the Muslim minority on Mindanao and in Sulu and southern Palawan provinces, as well as upland tribal minorities sprinkled throughout the islands. Filipinos share, for the most part, a common set of values emphasizing social acceptance as a primary virtue and a common world view in which education is emphasized as a principal avenue for upward social mobility and in which success is measured primarily in terms of income and material comforts. Cleavages in the society are not based primarily on ethnic or racial considerations but rather on religious (in the case of Muslims versus the Lowland Christian population), sociocultural (in the case of upland tribes versus lowland coastal Filipinos), and urban-rural differences.

Since 1972, actions by the government have resulted in a number of significant changes or new trends. For example, because of improvements in the national transportation system and in mass communications (including greater availability of radios and television sets) in most parts of the archipelago, ethnolinguistic and regional divisions among lowland Filipinos, who make up over 90 percent of the population, appear to be diminishing. The Philippines appears to be a more integrated and less fragmented nation that it was in 1972, but this accelerated integration of the Lowland Christian population resulted in serious separatist tendencies among the Muslim minority (see Regional Autonomy, ch. 4).

Although the rate of population increase has slowed owing to government family-planning outreach efforts, large numbers of rural migrants continued to flow into the huge metropolitan areas, especially Metro Manila (see Glossary). Filipinos, rapidly becoming a highly mobile population, have also migrated in substantial numbers to the United States and other countries. This has presumably exerted new pressures on the strength of traditional family bonds.

There has been a significant shift in the composition of the elite as a result of political and economic policies followed by the Marcos administration. Families enjoying power, privilege, and prestige in the early 1980s were not always the same as those enjoying similar status a decade earlier. Similarly, the avenues to wealth and power have changed, the military offering the single best example. Owing to the halting of regular elections after 1972, military officers have replaced many old and politically powerful families as local and regional conduits for national government patronage. Traditional patron-client relationships have not ended since the imposition of martial law; they have just shifted to include military personnel as well as wealthy civilians. Because of close contacts between the central government and the new economic elite as well as the military, the newly powerful are less dependent on local power bases than were pre-martial law political and economic leaders. This may result in a long-term weakening of traditional patron-client relationships in favor of ties forged among persons within the same social classes.

Upland tribal people have been threatened and dislocated, and the country's rich rain forests have suffered as a result of economic policies that have permitted fruit and logging companies to expand their holdings of hitherto agricultural land and to push farther and farther into the mountains to exploit timber resources. The office of the Presidential Assistant for National Minorities has succeeded in persuading many Filipinos to respect the cultural diversity manifested by their tribal minorities. It remains to be seen, however, whether these minorities and the ecosystem they share will survive the onslaught of powerful economic forces that include the migration of thousands of lowland Filipinos to frontier areas on Mindanao, as well as the intrusion of corporate extractive industries.

The principal social problems faced by Filipinos in mid-1983, in addition to conflict between Christians and Muslims and between settlers and upland tribes, could be traced in large part to the continued high rate of population growth. Many farm families have moved to the cities, where they have swelled the slum and squatter population, placed extreme pressure on the capacity of city governments to provide jobs, and effected a rise in the urban crime rate. The steady increase in population density has forced other farmers to migrate to frontier areas in search of open land, and this in turn has increased tension between Lowland Christians and minorities. Accordingly, the administration has placed a high priority on limiting population growth through a vigorous program to involve more Filipinos in family planning.

Not all of the problems facing the society have to do with population growth. Although the central government has initiated a number of important improvements, widespread cynicism and even despair have grown as the result of its personal favoritism, its dependence on an expanded military to deal with problems of peace and order, and its failure to stop corruption in the highest ranks of decisionmaking. Government promises of a new society when weighed against the evidence that the "old society" still prevails—in terms of corruption if not always inefficiency—may not persuade most Filipinos to join the New People's Army or another revolutionary group. But the cynicism evident in many sectors of society suggests that the Philippines is in the midst of a transition that might not end without an increase in violence first.

Physical Setting

The Philippine archipelago lies in Southeast Asia in a position that has led to its being influenced historically by both China and India. Even more than most other countries in the area, the Philippines represents a cultural crossroads, a place where Malays, Chinese, Spaniards, Americans, and others have interacted to forge that unique cultural and racial blend known to the world as "Filipino."

The archipelago numbers some 7,100 islands spread over approximately 496,400 square nautical miles of its claimed Exclusive Economic Zone (EEZ—see Glossary) and occupying an area that stretches for 1,850 kilometers from about the fifth to the twentieth parallels north latitude. The total land area is about 300,000 square kilometers. Only a thousand or so of its islands are populated, and fewer than one-half of these are larger than 2.5 square kilometers. Eleven islands make up 94 percent of the Philippine landmass, and two of these—Luzon and Mindanao—measure 105,000 and 95,000 square kilometers, respectively. They, together with the cluster of the Visayan Islands that separates them, represent the three principal regions of the archipelago that are identified by the three stars on the Philippine flag.

Topographically, the Philippines is broken up by the sea, which gives it one of the longest coastlines of any nation in the world (see fig. 2). Most Filipinos live on or near the coast, where they can easily supplement their diet with fish, which abound in 2,000 local species. The fishing industry employs some 600,000 people, and the annual catch reaches some 1.4 million tons.

Off the coast of eastern Mindanao is the Philippine Trough, which descends to a depth of 10,430 meters. The topography above sea level is not quite so impressive, but the Philippines is part of a western Pacific arc system that is characterized by active volcanoes. Among the most notable of its peaks are Mount Mayon near Legazpi, Taal Volcano south of Manila, and Mount Apo on Mindanao. The northern Luzon highlands, or Cordillera Central, rise to between 2,500 and 2,750 meters. They, together with the Sierra Madre in the northeastern portion of Luzon and the mountains of Mindanao, boast rain forests that provide refuge for numerous upland tribal groups, of which the Tasaday on Mindanao are the most primitive and most widely known. The rain forests also offer prime habitat for more than 500 species of birds, including the Philippine eagle (or monkey-eating eagle), some 800 species of orchids, and some 8,500 species of flowering plants.

Like other Southeast Asian nations, the Philippines has a rainy season and a dry season that dominate the cycle of life. The summer monsoon brings heavy rains to Manila from June to November, while the winter monsoon brings cooler and drier air from December to February. In between the two, Manila is hot and dusty from March to May. Even at this time, however, temperatures rarely rise above 37°C. Annual rainfall measures as much as 5,000 millimeters in parts of the country but less than 1,000 millimeters elsewhere.

Figure 2. Geographic Setting, 1983

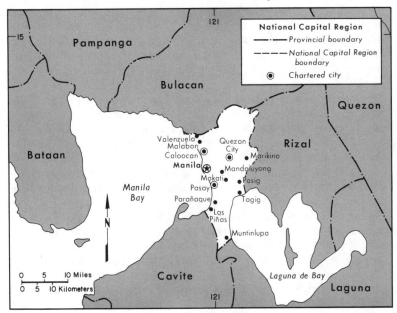

Figure 2. Continued.

Monsoon rains, though hard and drenching, are not normally associated with high winds and waves. But the Philippines does sit astride the typhoon belt, and it suffers an annual onslaught of dangerous storms from July through October. These are especially hazardous for northern and eastern Luzon and Bicol and Eastern Visayas regions, but Manila gets devastated periodically as well. The sea also rears up occasionally to inundate coastal areas with tidal waves as it did the southwestern coast of Mindanao in 1981. Natural disasters come in other forms as well. Mindanao and the Visayan Islands were hit by severe drought in early 1983.

The country's most extensive river systems are the Pulangi (Rio Grande) and Agusan of Mindanao, the Cagayan in northern Luzon, and the Pampanga, which flows south into Manila Bay. Lying to the southeast of the bay is the largest freshwater lake in the Philippines, Laguna de Bay. A number of rivers have been harnessed for hydroelectric power; the Pulangi and Agus (which flows north from Lake Lanao in Mindanao) are two of the more recent examples in this regard.

Whereas wet-rice cultivation is common throughout the lowland areas (and in exceptional upland cases like the Ifugao rice terraces), it is along the rivers and alluvial plains of Central Luzon Region, where irrigation systems make double- and even triple-cropping possible, that yields have been the highest. In the early 1980s only about one-half of the country's rice lands were irrigated, but their yields of 3.3 tons per hectare prompted the government to make vigorous efforts to expand the irrigated hectarage in hopes of attaining permanent self-sufficiency in rice for the country (see Agriculture, Forestry, and Fishing, ch. 3). Since the 1960s these efforts have been supplemented by the development of new, faster growing, disease-resistant hybrid strains of "miracle rice" by the International Rice Research Institute (IRRI) near the University of the Philippines' School of Agriculture in Los Banos, Laguna Province.

Principal crops include rice (grown on about 3.6 million hectares), corn (about 3.3 million hectares), coconuts (about 2.3 million hectares), and sugarcane. Other important products include abaca, tobacco, ramie, pineapples, bananas, timber and paper products, and fish. Development of these industries has not always been beneficial for all concerned. For example, as hardwood forests of Philippine mahogany, narra, and molave have been commercially exploited, the water table has been altered, and many Philippine rivers have become flood hazards for downstream rice lands during the rainy season, only to dry up during the winter monsoon and the hot season that follow. By cutting roads deep into the interior of Mindanao and Luzon, logging companies have opened these new "frontiers" to thousands of settlers who have promptly turned the cutover forest into agricultural land. This, in turn, has accelerated both the erosion of upland soils and the displacement of tribal minorities.

Finally, resources include some major extractive minerals. Among the most important of these are chromite, gold, nickel, iron, manganese, and copper (see Mining and Energy, ch. 3). An especially rich mineral area in northeastern Mindanao and the provinces of Surigao del Norte and Surigao del Sur. Other mineral-rich areas include Marinduque Province, the mountains of northern Luzon, and Cebu Province.

Population

Despite government efforts to limit family size, the population growth rate continues to be a concern. According to the preliminary report of the 1980 census, Filipinos numbered 47,914,017 in that year, up from 42,070,660 in 1975. This represents an annual growth rate of 2.6 percent, down from 2.8 percent in 1970-75, and from more than 3 percent in the 1960s, but more than the 2.4 percent predicted by the official Commission on Population (Popcom). Even at the lower growth rate, the Philippine population will increase to an estimated 77 million by the turn of the century. Moreover, the population is still a youthful one, with 57 percent under the age of 20. And although the birth rate has slowed from 50 to 31 per 1,000, so has the death rate. Population density has increased from 139 per square kilometer in 1973 to 160 in the early 1980s.

The trend of migration from village to city continues to put extra stress on urban areas. As of the early 1980s there were 30 cities having 100,000 or more residents, up from 21 in 1970. Metro Manila's population was 5,924,563, up from 4,970,006 in 1975, marking an annual growth rate far above the nation's at 3.6 percent. Within Metro Manila, the city of Manila itself was growing—more slowly, at a rate of only

1.9 percent per annum—but two other cities within this complex, Quezon City and Caloocan, were booming at rates of 4 percent and 3.5 percent, respectively. When Metro Manila is combined with adjacent Southern Tagalog Region, the two together have more than 12 million residents, or approximately one-fourth of the population of the entire country.

A National Housing Authority report revealed that in the early 1980s one out of four Metro Manila residents was a squatter. This represented a 150-percent increase in a decade in the number of persons living in shantytown communities, evidence of continuing, virtually uncontrolled rural-urban migration. The city of Manila had more than 500,000 inhabitants and Quezon City 371,000 inhabitants in such neighborhoods. Moreover, rural-urban migrants responding to better employment opportunities in peripheral metropolitan cities like Navotas had boosted the squatter element of that city's total population from 4 to 43 percent since 1978.

The burgeoning shantytown communities of Metro Manila and its environs were not the only manifestations of population pressures; a second major migration pattern consisted of resettlement from the more densely to the less densely populated regions. As a result of a population-land ratio that has declined from 1.2 cultivated hectares per agricultural worker in 1960 to less than a hectare by the early 1980s, thousands of Filipinos had migrated to the agricultural frontier on Mindanao. According to the preliminary report of the 1980 census, six of the 12 fastest growing provinces were in Western, Northern, or Southern Mindanao regions, and a seventh was the frontier province of Palawan. Sulu, South Cotabato, Misamis Oriental, Surigao del Norte, Agusan del Norte, and Agusan del Sur provinces all had population growth rates of 4 percent or more, a remarkable statistic given the uncertain peace-and-order situation on Mindanao. Among the fastest growing cities in the late 1970s were General Santos (10 percent growth rate), Iligan (6.9), Cagayan de Oro (6.7), Cotabato (5.7), Zamboanga (5.4), Butuan (5.4), and Dipolog (5.1), all on Mindanao.

By the early 1980s the Mindanao frontier had ceased to offer a safety valve for land-hungry settlers. Hitherto peaceful provinces had become dangerous tinderboxes in which mounting numbers of Philippine army troops and New People's Army insurgents carried on a sporadic shooting war with each other and with bandits, "lost commands," millenarian religious groups, upland tribes, loggers, and Muslims (see The Insurgent Challenge, ch. 5). And because of the large-scale migration into these frontier regions, the spread of shifting cultivation (see Glossary) combined with indiscriminate logging to produce permanent damage to the rain forests of central Mindanao.

Popcom bore primary responsibility for controlling population growth. It set 1985 as its target for reducing the growth rate to 2 percent, with a goal of 1 percent by 2000. Popcom recommended a family size of three children in the 1980s and two for the following decade, birth spacing (average interval between births) of two years in the 1980s and three in the 1990s, and delayed marriage for women (age 23) and for men (age 25).

According to its own records, the agency (created in 1971) has had some success in its first decade of work. In addition to having helped reduce the overall growth rate from 3 to 2.6 percent and the crude birth rate from 39 to 31 per 1,000, its educational effort has succeeded in persuading many Filipinos to marry later, as witnessed by the increase in average age at marriage from 22.8 in 1970 to 24.4 in 1977.

Nevertheless, Popcom has been criticized for overemphasizing information and educational activities to the extent that resources have not been devoted sufficiently to direct service delivery in the form of staffing clinics and moving contraceptive supplies to the rural population. Despite its greater infusion of United States Agency for International Development funds, the Philippines has lagged behind Singapore, the Republic of Korea (South Korea), Taiwan, Malaysia, and Thailand in reducing its birth rate. Popcom has responded by emphasizing outreach activities more since 1978. But, according to sociologist Gayl D. Ness, the Philippines lags behind other regional nations with a program that is "the least efficient and least effective national population program in Asia."

Part of the problem can be traced to the continued opposition of the Roman Catholic Church to the use of new contraceptive technology in birth control. Despite its support for the Responsible Parenthood Council, which involves local priests in a grass-roots program based in part on the rhythm method for contraception, the religious hierarchy continued to be perceived as at least partly responsible for peasant apathy concerning the national need for birth control. Nevertheless, the principal cause for failures in the program seemed to reside not in the ideological stance of the church but in the government's slowness to translate policy into an efficient and widespread program that made fuller use of local clinics to induce rural Filipinos to adopt birth control devices. Perhaps Popcom's growing emphasis on outreach, in which it employed thousands of full-time outreach workers and local government officials, would succeed in this. But even should Popcom meet its goals for 1985 and 2000, the consequences of the high birth rates of the 1960s and 1970s were likely to create economic pressures. There would be a steady increase in the labor force, with attendant demands for jobs and high unemployment levels if those opportunities were not provided.

Ethnicity, Regionalism, and Language

Philippine society is relatively homogeneous, especially considering its distribution over some 7,100 islands. Muslims and upland tribal peoples represent the most obvious exceptions, while approximately 90 percent of the society remains united by a common cultural and religious background. Among Lowland Christian Filipinos, language is the main point of internal differentiation, but this majority interacts and intermarries regularly across linguistic lines. Because of political centralization, urbanization, and extensive internal migration, linguistic barriers are eroding, and government emphasis on Pilipino and English (at the expense of local dialects) has also reduced these divisions. Nevertheless, national integration remains incomplete in the Philippines, which continues in many ways to be a "plural society." As President Ferdinand E. Marcos has said, the Philippines stands as "a nation divided against itself—divided between urban and rural, rich and poor, majorities and minorities, privileged and underprivileged." One cannot begin to understand Philippine society without taking note of this diversity.

Filipinos are among the peoples of the world who have been most exposed historically to interaction between varying ethnic groups, some of this interaction marked by racial considerations. Through centuries of intermarriage, they have become a unique blend principally of Malay, Chinese, Spanish, Negrito, and American. Among the earliest inhabitants were Negritos, followed by Malays, who deserve most of the credit for developing lowland Philippine agricultural life as it is known in the modern period. As these Malays spread throughout the archipelago, two things happened. First, they absorbed through intermarriage most of the Negrito population, although a minority of Negritos remained distinct by retreating to the mountains. Second, they dispersed into separate groups, some of which became relatively isolated in pockets on Mindanao, northern Luzon, and some of the other large islands. Comparative linguistic analysis suggests that most groups may once have spoken a form of "Proto-Manobo" but that each developed a distinct vernacular that can be traced to its contact over the centuries with certain groups and its isolation from others (see fig. 3).

In the absence of any central political power, the Philippines before the advent of Islam became a mosaic of different linguistic groups that exhibited a considerable cultural homogeneity. Both in the mountains and along the coasts, people lived in *barangays* (see Glossary) and were ruled by *datu* (chiefs; sing., *datu*) chosen on the basis of their ability to settle disputes and to fight bravely in defense of the group against other *barangays*. In time, the "Indianized" kingdoms of Sumatra and Java brought the archipelago into their trading orbit, and Chinese traders succeeded in tying many coastal *barangays* into their trading world (see Early History, ch. 1).

With the advent of Islam in the southern Philippines during the fourteenth century, there arose separate sultanates on Mindanao and in the Sulu Archipelago. By the sixteenth century, Islam had spread all the way to Manila Bay; thus when Spanish conquistadores arrived there in the late 1500s they had to wrest it from a Muslim chieftain. Between 1571 and 1898 the Spanish succeeded in providing the necessary environment for development of a Filipino national identity. But they never completely vitiated Muslim autonomy on Mindanao and in the Sulu Archipelago, where the separate Muslim sultanates of Sulu, Maguindanao, and Maranao remained impervious to Christian

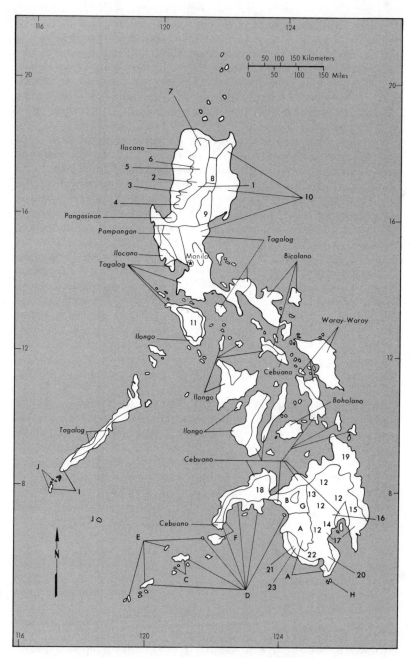

Figure 3. Cultural-Linguistic Groups, 1983

Muslim groups

A	Maguindanao
B	Maranao
C	Tausug
D	Samal
E	Bajau
F	Yakan
G	Ilanon
H	Sangir
I	Melabugnan
J	Jama Mapun

Upland tribal groups—Luzon

1	Ifugao
2	Bontoc
3	Kankanay
4	Ibaloi
5	Kalinga
6	Tinguian
7	Isneg
8	Gaddang
9	Ilongot
10	Negrito

Upland tribal groups—Mindoro and Mindanao

11	Mangyan
12	Manobo
13	Bukidnon
14	Bagobo
15	Mandaya
16	Ata
17	Mansaka
18	Subanun
19	Mamanua
20	Bila-an
21	Tiruray
22	T'Boli
23	Tasaday

Source: Based on information from Gabriel Casal et al., *The People and Art of the Philippines*, Los Angeles, 1981.

conversion. Likewise, the Spanish never succeeded in converting upland tribal groups, particularly on Luzon and Mindanao. Their presence carried greatest weight among lowland groups in concentric circles of influence emanating from Manila. Even among these peoples, however, linguistic differences continued to outweigh unifying factors until a nationalist movement emerged to question Spanish rule in the nineteenth century.

Spanish fear of Chinese economic competition provided the rationale for periodic massacres of the Chinese population in Manila. In the nineteenth century, however, when they badly wanted to find ways to make their colony self-supporting, the Spanish liberalized immigration rules and commercial and residential restrictions. Chinese residents quickly became the middlemen who gathered Philippine raw materials and distributed imported goods throughout the islands, forging a vital link between the domestic economy and the export sector. Many of them also converted to Roman Catholicism and married *indias* (indigenous women). Their offspring enjoyed acceptance both in Chinese trading circles and in the extended kinship networks of their mothers. Thus did Chinese mestizos (see Glossary), who by mid-century represented about one-sixteenth of a population numbering 4 million, emerge as a leading social, economic, and political group in a nascent Philippine national society. The term *mestizo*, whether referring to this group or to persons of mixed Spanish and *indias* descent, carries with it no pejorative meaning. Rather, it refers to a group recognized for its leading role in the Philippine independence movement that enjoys high status in the contemporary social fabric.

On the one hand, then, Philippine national identity emerged as a blend of diverse ethnic and linguistic groups. But on the other hand, as Lowland Christian *indios* began referring to themselves as "Filipinos," they also started to define those who failed to fit this category—namely, Muslims, upland tribal groups, and ethnic Chinese who had not been assimilated by intermarriage. In the very process of defining a national identity, the majority was also drawing attention to a basic societal cleavage.

During the campaign for independence, directed first against Spain and then the United States, these lines were temporarily ignored. In revolting against Spanish rule and then fighting United States troops, the indigenous people became increasingly conscious of a national unity transcending local and regional identities. A public school system that brought at least elementary-level education to all but the most remote barrios and *sitios* (small clusters of homes) during the early twentieth century also served to dilute religious, ethnic, and linguistic or regional differences, as did improvements in transportation and communications systems. United States efforts also served to bring more Muslim and tribal peoples into the mainstream of society. Finally, the diffusion of a cash economy, growth of urban centers, and emergence of a vital national mass media all contributed to this process as well. As a result, during World War II, Muslims, Lowland Christians, and upland tribal

Filipinos joined together in a common effort to free the Philippines from Japanese military control.

Fault lines that were temporarily obscured in the dedication and sacrifice that marked the Philippine nationalist movement soon became evident once again after 1946. This was particularly so in the relationship between lowlanders on the one hand and Muslims and upland tribes on the other. Government policies toward what have come to be known as "cultural minorities" have changed in recent years. Whereas in the 1960s the Commission on National Integration emphasized the need for integrating minorities into the mainstream—a policy that angered and intimidated tribal groups and Muslims alike—in the 1970s this approach was scrapped in favor of efforts to encourage minority cultures to take pride in their separate and unique ways of life. The office of the Presidential Assistant for National Minorities (PANAMIN) was created specifically to protect unassimilated upland tribes from the onslaught of lowland settlers searching out new lands for agriculture. Its director, Manuel Elizalde, Jr., won international attention in 1971 when the tiny Stone Age Tasaday tribe was discovered in southwestern Mindanao. Perhaps partly as a result of this discovery and the fascination it held for many Filipinos, acceptance of diversity rather than acculturation came to characterize the government's efforts on behalf of minorities.

The new policy of accepting cultural diversity has been put to the test by Philippine Muslims who have organized the militant Moro National Liberation Front (MNLF) and other groups to voice their demand for autonomy vis-à-vis Lowland Christian Filipinos who dominate the central government. In the early 1980s, however, the central government seemed most unlikely to equate recognition of cultural diversity with political, economic, or military autonomy for any cultural or religious minority.

Language divisions continue to be important, and these were nowhere more apparent than in the persistent public debate over what the national language should be. The government in 1974 initiated a policy of bilingualism, having the purpose of gradually phasing out English in schools, business, and government and fostering the use of Pilipino in its place. Pilipino, which has been called "the greater Manila lingua franca," has spread throughout the nation, the mass media, and the school system and is expected to be in general use over the archipelago by the end of the century. By that time it may have enough grass-roots support in non-Tagalog-speaking regions to become a national language. This was not the case in mid-1983, however. Filipinos have not quietly accepted one national language at the expense of their regional languages. In fact, the policy promoting Pilipino has come under attack and, as an alternative, English was being stressed in the public school system once again.

Successful Filipinos were likely to continue to be at least trilingual, unless they happened to come from a Tagalog-speaking area, such as Manila. Those who grew up speaking another regional language would probably continue to use that language at home, Pilipino as a medium of ordinary conversation in the cities, and English as the language of commerce, government, and international relations. Both Pilipino, which was gaining use in the media, and English would continue to serve as languages of education.

Some 70 languages were spoken in the Philippines in the early 1980s. Eight of these—Tagalog, Cebuano, Ilocano, Hiligaynon, Bicol, Waray-Waray, Pampango, and Pangasinan—were native tongues for about 90 percent of the population. All eight belong to the Malayo-Polynesian language family and hence are related to Indonesian and Malay, but no two are mutually comprehensible. Each has a number of dialects, and all have impressive literary traditions, especially Tagalog, Cebuano, and Ilocano. Some of the languages have closer affinity than others. Thus it is easier for Ilocanos and Pangasinans to learn each other's language than to learn any of the other six. Likewise, speakers of major Visayan Islands languages—Cebuano, Ilongo, and Waray-Waray—find it easier to communicate with each other than with Tagalogs, Ilocanos, or others.

Commonwealth president Manuel Quezon predicted that after independence "we shall have strife such as that which existed when we were students . . . when the Tagalogs used to fight with the Ilocanos, the Pampangos with Visayans, the Visayans with the Tagalogs, etc." As of the early 1980s his prediction had not come true, but many Filipinos continued to hold stereotypic perceptions of many of their countrymen.

The Lowland Christian Population

Among this great majority of Filipinos, the main source of differentiation has not been race, religion, or custom, but language and geographical separatism, and both of these sources of separate identity have been seriously eroded by migration and urbanization in the twentieth century. Although Lowland Christians maintained stylistic differences in dress until this century and have always taken pride in their unique culinary specialties, whether Tagalog, Ilocano, Cebuano, or another, they have been and continue to be a remarkably homogeneous core population of the Philippines.

Because of their regional base in Metro Manila and adjacent provinces to the north, east, and south, Tagalogs have tended to be more visible than other groups. At the turn of the century, for example, some Americans described the Philippine Revolution as a Tagalog revolt. In the early 1980s many non-Tagalogs remained sensitive about the mere possibility that Pilipino might evolve as the national language because Tagalog so dominates Pilipino that it is not easy to distinguish between the two. At the time of the 1973 constitutional convention in Manila, Tagalog delegates came under attack from speakers of other languages for "high-handedness" in assuming that business would be carried out in Pilipino, and they spoke in their own languages when they took the floor. Tagalogs made up about 24 percent of the population in the early 1980s.

Other important Filipino groups include the Cebuanos, whose language is the principal one in the Visayan Islands area—Cebu, Bohol, Siquijor, Negros Oriental, Leyte, and Southern Leyte provinces—and on parts of Mindanao. The influence of the Ilocanos significantly outweighed their numbers (they were far less numerous than Tagalogs or Cebuanos) because Marcos himself was an Ilocano, and he had appointed fellow Ilocanos to many important civilian and military positions. Ilocanos have a reputation for being ready migrants, leaving their rocky northern Luzon homeland not just for more fertile parts of the archipelago but for the United States as well. Their expansion into the Central Luzon Plain over the past century has led to some friction between them and the Tagalogs.

Other major Lowland Christian groups include the Ilongos (speakers of Hiligaynon), the Bicolanos, the Waray-Waray, the Pampangans (or Kapampangans), and the Pangasinans. The home region of the Ilongos includes most of Panay, Negros Occidental Province, and the southern end of Mindoro. They count among their number many *sacadas* (sugarcane-workers). Their migration in large numbers to the Cotabato and Lanao areas of Mindanao led to intense friction between them and the local Muslim inhabitants and the outbreak of fighting between the two groups in the 1970s. The homeland of the Bicolanos, or "Bicolandia," is the southeastern portion of Luzon together with the islands of Catanduanes, Burias, and Ticao, and adjacent parts of Masbate. The Waray-Waray live mostly in eastern Leyte and Samar in Eastern Visayas Region. The Pampangan homeland is the Central Luzon Plain and especially Pampanga Province. Speakers of Pangasinan are especially numerous in the Lingayen Gulf region of Luzon, but they have also spread to the Central Luzon Plain where they are interspersed with Tagalogs, Ilocanos, and Pampangans.

As migrants to the city, these Lowland Christians have not clustered together in neighborhoods made up exclusively of persons from their own region. Multilingualism generally characterizes these neighborhoods; the language of the local area is used, as a rule, for communicating with neighbors, and English or Pilipino is used as a supplement. Migrants to cities and also to agricultural frontiers have been remarkably ready and willing to learn the language of their new neighborhood while retaining use of their mother tongue within the home. This was perhaps as good an indicator as any of the essential homogeneity manifested by the Lowland Christian majority of Filipinos.

The continued use of regional languages in the Philippines has not implied a failure of nationhood. Filipinos have built their nation and their sense of a national identity despite the lack of a common indigenous language. They have been able to do this because they share a host of common social values and cultural assumptions, a common cultural history, and a strong national consciousness tempered by years of struggle for independence. For 90 percent of the population, such national assumptions and experiences have come to transcend their separate linguistic affinities.

Muslim Filipinos (Moros)

Muslims are the most significant minority in an otherwise quite homogeneous society. Although undifferentiated racially from other Filipinos, they remain outside the mainstream of national life, possessing a separate identity in which their religion and way of life set them apart. During the past decade, in reaction to consolidation of central government power under martial law, Moros have increasingly identified with the worldwide Islamic community, particularly in Malaysia, Indonesia, Libya, and Middle Eastern countries. The more they feel pressured by the central government, the more they react by seeking to consolidate a separate Moro community. Long-standing economic grievances stemming from years of governmental neglect and resentment of popular prejudice against them contribute to the roots of Muslim insurgency (see The Insurgent Challenge, ch. 5).

Moros were confined almost entirely to the southern part of the country—southern and western Mindanao, southern Palawan, and the Sulu Archipelago. Ten subgroups can be identified on the basis of language. Three of these groups—the Maguindanao of North Cotabato, Sultan Kudarat, and Maguindanao provinces; the Maranao of the two Lanao provinces; and the Tausug, who are principally of Jolo Island— make up the great majority of Moros. Lesser groups are the Samal and Bajau, principally of the Sulu Archipelago; the Yakan of Zamboanga del Sur Province; the Ilanon and Sangir of Southern Mindanao Region; the Melabugnan of southern Palawan; and the Jama Mapun of the tiny Cagayan Islands. These groups made up about 5 percent of the Philippine population.

Muslim Filipinos have not traditionally been a closely knit or even allied group. Maranao, Maguindanao, Tausug, Yakan, and others have all been fiercely proud of their separate identities, and conflict between them was endemic for centuries. While divided primarily by different languages and political structures, the separate groups have also differed in their degree of Islamic orthodoxy. For example, the Tausug, as the first group to adopt Islam, have criticized the more recently Islamicized Yakan and Bajau for being less zealous than they in observing Islamic tenets and practices. Internal differences among Moros in the 1980s were outweighed by commonalities of historical experience vis-à-vis non-Muslims and by shared cultural, social, and legal traditions.

Moros shared a strongly separatist viewpoint toward Christian Filipinos that could be traced to the first years of Spanish conquest. Of importance in this context was the circumstance that when Miguel López de Legazpi arrived in Manila Bay in 1571, war with the Moros was still going on. To the Spanish, Moros were no different than Moors, and their extermination was just part of a continuing worldwide struggle between Cross and Crescent. Thanks to their possession of superior firearms, Spaniards succeeded in militantly spreading their faith at the expense of Islam on Luzon and the Visayan Islands. Most of Mindanao, however, did not come within their political or religious orbit until the nineteenth century. Again and again they launched military expeditions against Sulu, Mindanao, and the Brunei sultanate in Borneo, and the Spanish armies that consisted largely of Christian Filipinos. In response, the Sulu and Maguindanao sultanates declared a holy war against Spain. These Moro states marked the frontier of Islam in Southeast Asia; encroachment onto their turf represented a setback not only for Philippine Muslims but also for Islam throughout insular Southeast Asia.

Moros added greatly to the animosity between themselves and non-Muslim Filipinos by raiding the Visayan Islands and Luzon in search of slaves to labor in collecting forest products for their extensive trade with China and Southeast Asia. To Christian Filipinos living along the coasts, the word *Moro* evoked hatred and terror. And as these Filipinos looked more and more to Spain for protection from this dreaded enemy, Moros turned more and more to each other and to their Muslim counterparts of modern Indonesia and Malaysia.

When the Spanish finally crushed Moro independence in the nineteenth century, individual Muslims carried on the holy war on their own. Warriors would prepare themselves through prayer and ritual and then hurl themselves against Christians as *juramentados* ("those who have sworn an oath," i.e., to conduct holy war against the infidel).

Not long after the successful pacification of the Muslim Philippines, Spanish rule was replaced by that of the United States, led by generals Leonard Wood and John Pershing, who brought Moros into submission first in the Sulu zone and then in the Maranao region. Occupation authorities subsequently outlawed slavery, imposed their own laws and notions of justice, and introduced public schools and other public services. It helped little that the new rulers promised not to interfere with Islamic religious practices, for the very notion of separation of church and state was to Muslims a foreign import associated with Christian colonialism. Education, law, and government might be secular matters to Americans and Christian Filipinos, but they were not so to Muslims.

Throughout the American colonial period, Muslim leaders asked to be granted separate independence. Aware that they would be outnumbered nine to one in the new Philippine polity, they worried that they would have little to gain and much to lose in the new national government. Their fears and suspicions were confirmed by national government policies (which followed those adopted by the colonial government) that encouraged migration of Filipinos from densely settled areas like central Luzon to the "open" frontier of Mindanao. By the 1950s hundreds of thousands of Ilongos, Ilocanos, Tagalogs, and others were settling in Cotabato and Lanao provinces, where their influx inflamed Moro hostility. The crux of the problem lay in land disputes; Christian migrants to Cotabato, for example, complained that they bought land from one Muslim only to have his relatives refuse to recognize the sale and demand more money. Muslims claimed that Christians would title land through government agencies unknown to Muslim residents, for whom land titling was a new institution. Distrust and resentment spread to the public school system, regarded by most Muslims as an agency for the propagation of Christian teachings. By 1970 a terrorist organization of Christians called the Ilagas (Rats) began operating in Cotabato, and Muslim armed bands called Blackshirts appeared in response. The same thing happened in Lanao, where the Muslim Barracudas began fighting the Ilagas. Philippine army troops sent in to restore peace and order were accused by Muslims of siding with the Christians. At the time that martial law was declared in 1972, Muslim Mindanao was in turmoil (see The Marcos Administration, 1965-72, ch. 1).

Some Moros have traditionally found a place and role within the Philippine national political and economic structure, gaining both wealth and power as officeholders at the local and national level. But the great majority, especially of rural Muslims, had come by 1972 to believe that the national government, being controlled by Christians, would never give them a fair share of the revenues allocated for economic development. Among the Filipino majority, Moros were widely regarded as second-class citizens in a Catholic country. Thus, Philippines scholar Stuart Schlegel concludes that, in a very real sense, Christian and Muslim Filipinos "belong to different worlds. Each is oriented toward a different wider community from which they draw their religion, their law, their values, and their sense of history."

Despite this mutual distrust and misunderstanding, the Marcos administration has succeeded in slowing the Moro separatist movement's momentum since 1977. The war that had raged between Philippine military forces and the MNLF since the late 1960s, leaving some 50,000 dead, tying down over one-half of the Philippine combat forces, and driving over 100,000 Moros to Sabah, was reduced to skirmishes after the 1976-77 cease-fire. Marcos has used various political methods to enlist Moro cooperation. One strategy was to defuse Moro nationalism by granting "autonomy" to some provinces on Mindanao.

Talks had been held in Tripoli in 1976 between Imelda Romualdez Marcos, Nur Misuari, officially representing the MNLF, and representatives of the Islamic Conference that eventuated in a cease-fire and tentative terms for a peace agreement. The terms spoke of "autonomy for the Muslims" in 13 provinces. By this it was meant that Moros would have autonomy in certain areas (see Local Government, ch. 4). They would also have the right to a "reasonable percentage" from the revenues of mines in their region. In return the central government would retain responsibility for foreign policy and national defense throughout the Philippines. Marcos subsequently declared the 13 provinces to be an autonomous region. But in the referendum that followed, voters in the 13 (eight of which had Christian majorities) overwhelmingly rejected the merger of their provinces into one region and approved a proposal that "administration of the 'autonomy' be under the general supervision and control of the Philippine government." Declaring that Marcos had not acted in good faith in promising autonomy, the MNLF broke off negotiations in 1977.

As of late 1983 there were three overlapping political forces competing for authority in two separate "autonomous regions" encompassing southern and western Mindanao. The first was an "offical" government dominated by Muslims who had been persuaded to join forces with Marcos. The second was the Philippine military establishment, still stationed in the regions, obviously limiting the "autonomy." The third consisted of armed rebel bands, some but not all affiliated with the MNLF, that claimed to be struggling for nothing less than full independence for a Muslim nation to be called the Bangsa Moro Republic (see The Insurgent Challenge, ch. 5).

In an effort to show that the Moro autonomous regions would have some substantive meaning, the Marcos administration has touted a number of social and economic projects. Since 1982 Marcos has indicated, through his minister of education and culture, readiness to grant government recognition to *madrasahs* (Muslim religious schools) on a case-by-case basis. Thus, the government seemed ready to grant a degree of Muslim distinctiveness if not actual autonomy in the education system. Also in an effort to demonstrate the high priority being given to economic development of the Moro regions, Marcos appointed his wife to head the Southern Philippine Development Authority (SPDA).

The question of autonomy for Moros cut across an important division within Muslim society between social conservatives and reformers. Among the latter, autonomy was looked upon with considerable ambivalence. Some feared that, if taken seriously, it might encourage the resurgence of traditional practices and the revitalization of a traditional authority structure seen as less desirable than that developing after modern education and outside sources of income and legal sanction opened up Moro society in the twentieth century. This traditional structure focused on a sultan who was both a secular and a religious leader and whose authority was sanctioned by the Quran. The *datu* were communal leaders who measured power not by their holdings in landed wealth but by the numbers of their followers. In return for their tribute and labor, the *datu* provided aid in emergencies and advocacy in disputes arising between the followers of a *datu* and those of another chief. Thus did a *datu*, through his *agama* court (actually an informal dispute-settling session), become basic to the smooth functioning of Moro society. He was a powerful authority figure who might have as many as four wives and who might enslave other Muslims in raids on their villages or in debt bondage. He might also demand revenge for the death of a follower or upon injury to his pride or honor (*maratabat*).

The *datu* continued to play a central role in Moro society in the 1980s. In many parts of Muslim Mindanao they still administered the sharia (sacred Islamic law) through their *agama* courts. They could no longer expand their circle of followers by raiding other villages, but they achieved the same end by accumulating wealth and then using it to provide aid, employment, and/or protection for less fortunate neighbors. Although a *datu* rarely had more than one wife, polygamy was permitted so long as his wealth was sufficient to provide for more than one. Depending on whether their support had been solicited, *datu* could make or break a government program in their barrios. In short, through their personalistic and paternalistic mode of leadership, they marked Moro society as still basically hierarchical and familial, at least in rural areas.

For Muslim reformers, who often came from urban, educated, and middle-class homes, such authority figures were a source of deep uneasiness. Although they recognized the important role played by *datu* in maintaining cultural continuity for their people, they tended to agree with non-Muslim Filipinos that religious authority should remain separate from civil authority. Tasks like interpreting the law, they believed, could usually be carried out better by trained professionals than by *datu*, who succeeded to their posts primarily by inheritance. To turn the clock back by curtailing freedom and equality, especially as these concerned freedom from old customs and equality between men and women, would in the view of Muslim liberals be perhaps too high a price to pay for autonomy. Thus, the staightforward provision of full autonomy for Philippine Muslims involved important social as well as political implications and considerations.

Upland Tribal Groups

As lowland Filipinos, both Muslim and Christian, have grown in numbers and expanded into the interiors of Luzon, Mindoro, Mindanao, and other islands, they have isolated upland tribal communities in pockets. Over the centuries these isolated tribes have developed their own unique identities. As a result, the Philippines has become the homeland of over 100 tribal groups whose folk arts, apparel, and oral traditions have become a major selling point for the nation's tourist industry. More important, their arts were, in a sense, the last remnants of an indigenous artistic tradition that flourished everywhere before Spanish and Islamic contact.

Ethnically, the upland tribal groups are a blend just like other Filipinos, although they have not as a rule had as much contact with the outside world. They display great variety in social organization, cultural expression, and artistic skills that show a high degree of creativity usually employed to embellish utilitarian objects, such as bowls, baskets, clothing, weapons, and even spoons. Technologically, these groups range from highly sophisticated, like the Bontoc and Ifugao, who engineered the extraordinary rice terraces, to primitive groups such as the Stone Age Tasaday. They also cover a wide spectrum in terms of their integration and acculturation with Lowland Christian Filipinos. Some, like the Bukidnons of Mindanao, have been known to intermarry with lowlanders for almost a century, while others, like the Kalinga, have remained more isolated from lowland influences.

There are 10 principal cultural groups living in the Cordillera Central of Luzon. The name Igorot, the Tagalog word for mountaineer, has often been used with reference to all. At one time it was employed by lowland Filipinos in a pejorative sense, but in recent years it has come to be used with pride by youths in the mountains as a positive expression of their separate ethnic identity vis-à-vis lowlanders. Of the 10 groups, the Ifugao (Ifugao Province), Bontoc (Mountain Province and Kalinga-Apayao Province), and Kankanay and Ibaloi (Benguet Province, north and south of the city of Baguio) are all wet-rice farmers who work the elaborate rice terraces that they have constructed over the centuries. The Kankanay and Ibaloi are among those Igorots who have been the most influenced by Spanish and American colonialism and lowland Filipino culture, owing to the extensive gold mines in Benguet, the proximity of Baguio, good roads and schools, and a consumer industry in search of folk art objects. Other mountain peoples of Luzon are the Kalinga of Kalinga-Apayao Province and the Tinguian of Abra Province, who employ both wet- and dry-rice-growing techniques. The Isneg of northern Kalinga-Apayao Province, Gaddang of the border between Kalinga-Apayao and Isabela provinces, and Ilongot of Nueva Vizcaya Province all practice shifting cultivation (see Glossary). Negritos complete the picture for Luzon; although at one time they dominated the highlands, by the early 1980s they were reduced to small groups living in widely scattered locations primarily along the eastern ranges of the mountains.

South of Luzon, upland tribal groups are concentrated on Mindanao, although there is an important population of mountain peoples, having the generic name Mangyan, living on Mindoro. Among the most important groups on Mindanao are the Manobo (a general name for many tribal groups in southern Bukidnon and Agusan del Sur provinces); the Bukidnon (of Bukidnon Province); the Bagobo, Mandaya, Ata, and Mansaka, who inhabit mountains bordering the Davao Gulf; the Subanun (of upland areas in the Zamboanga provinces); the Mamanua of the Agusan-Surigao border region; and the Bila-an, Tiruray, T'Boli, and Tasaday of the area of the Cotabato provinces. Whereas tribal groups on Luzon are widely known for their carving of wooden figures, their baskets, and their weaving, Mindanao tribes are renowned for their elaborate embroidery, appliqué, and bead work.

PANAMIN has succeeded in establishing a number of protected reservations for tribal groups. Residents are expected to speak their tribal language, dress in their traditional tribal clothing, live in houses constructed of natural materials using traditional architectural designs, and celebrate their traditional ceremonies of propitiation of spirits believed to be inhabiting their environment. They are also encouraged to reestablish their traditional authority structure in which, as in Moro society, tribal *datu* are the key figures. These men, chosen on the basis of their bravery and their ability to settle disputes, are usually, but not always, the sons of former *datu*. Often they are also the ones who remember the ancient oral epics of their people. These they sing once again in an effort to reawaken in tribal youth an appreciation for the unique and semisacred history of their tribal group.

The tribal minorities thus have been caught in the middle of opposing forces for change. After decades of government efforts to integrate them into the mainstream of lowland society, they have more recently been urged to reestablish their cultural separatism. At the same time, social and economic forces for acculturation and modernization were working against this effort, and it was unlikely that PANAMIN would succeed in more than temporarily slowing the process.

The Chinese

In the early 1980s it was unofficially estimated that there were more than 700,000 ethnic Chinese living in the Philippines. Ethnic Chinese, particularly those without Philippine citizenship, held an ambiguous position within the society. Chinese mestizos—the offspring of Chinese-Filipino marriages—have always been willingly accepted into the national society. Intermarriage between the two groups, most often between Chinese men and Philippine women, has been frequent throughout the long history of Chinese presence in the Philippines. Unmixed and unassimilated Chinese, however, have experienced considerable difficulties with respect to citizenship and are frequently the object of prejudice and discrimination.

The Chinese population has increased slowly over the centuries, but it was not until the last decades of Spanish rule that a marked increase occurred. The estimated Chinese population of Manila in 1896 was 100,000. The United States applied the Exclusion Act of 1894 to the Philippines, limiting Chinese immigration to teachers, students, clergy, traders and, most significantly, dependents of residents. The last category precluded any stemming of Chinese immigration, and during the first six years of American rule the Chinese population in the Philippines tripled. Concomitant with increasing nationalism, legal strictures against Chinese steadily increased, causing many to enter illegally and to fail to register as aliens.

The Chinese population is segmented along lines determined by lineage, language, and region of origin in China. Those sharing these features are bound into groups in which preferential treatment is given co-members. Related to them are voluntary associations having elected officers and prescribed duties. These groups and associations have implicit functions as well as explicit duties. They help maintain Chinese culture and govern themselves by Chinese laws, philosophy, and customs; members are given aid, and internal disputes are settled. Through this cultural separatism, Chinese have unwittingly encouraged discrimination against themselves. Chinese schools, of which there were more than 120 in the early 1980s, fostered the maintenance of separate linguistic traditions. Chinese dialects were taught in the schools, and many Chinese spoke their native tongue at home. In these and other ways Chinese have set themselves apart from other Filipinos, leaving the impression, whether true or false, that they disparage Philippine culture.

Actions of the Philippine government in regard to the Chinese before the advent of Marcos had been generally restrictive. Legislation lim-, iting foreign commercial enterprises was aimed at supporting non-Chinese in retail trade. Since 1972 the problems of the Chinese have been somewhat alleviated, and many Chinese feel better off under Marcos' rule than before. One of the principal issues that concerned them was the question of citizenship for alien Chinese who had not been born in the Philippines. From 1975 onward such persons could become naturalized citizens, and although it was not easy to attain this status, many have sought to do so. Economically, the Chinese in the early 1980s were faring rather well. They once again dominated retail trade, were leaders in rice milling, and had shown strength in banking. In return for these benefits, many Chinese became strong Marcos supporters and contributed heavily to his party. Their strong support resulted not so much from specific policies, however, as from their desire for stability and their belief that the present administration continued to offer greater hope for economic stability than any other discernible political alternative. None wanted a return to the anti-Chinese sentiment that infused Philippine politics in the pre-1972 period. Nonetheless, considerable animosity against the Chinese role in the nation's economy still lingered; efforts to defuse it perhaps lay behind the announcement in 1982 that Chinese schools had been persuaded to admit a larger proportion of non-Chinese students. A former governor was quoted in 1982 as asserting that "our country will be run by the Chinese if the present administration continues to give privileges to Chinese businessmen rather than to their Filipino competitors. The Chinese do not only control the country's economy but also its cultural outlets, such as radio, newspapers, schools, television, civic organizations, and others."

The Social System

The great majority of the Philippine population is bound together by common values and a common religion. Social organization generally follows a single pattern as well, although variations do occur on this pattern, reflecting the influence of local traditions. Among Lowland Christian Filipinos, social organization continues to be marked primarily by personal alliance systems, i.e., groupings composed of kin (real and ritual), grantors and recipients of favors, friends, and regular exchange partners. In the interweaving of these social relationships, Filipinos develop and expand their alliances. These relationships have traditionally cut across class lines, and this continued to be the case in the early 1980s. In the Philippines the principal class division was traditionally between what social scientist Frank Lynch termed the "big and little people," and this remained true in most *barangays*. In pre-Hispanic Philippines, and continuing among some upland tribes in the late twentieth century, the division was between *datu* (chief) and *sakop* (follower). Over 400 years of history, the relationship melded into one between landlord and tenant, or patron and client. Joining the landlords as "big people," and usually having ownership to land themselves, were local political leaders, doctors, teachers and other professionals, most of the store owners, rice and corn millers and brokers, middlemen to fishermen and cottage industry artisans, and others with a steady source of income. In contrast to these were the small owners, tenants, and landless workers who made up the great majority of the Philippine population and who depended on the "big people" in constructing their personal alliance systems.

This dichotomy was useful as a broad description of the basic framework of Philippine society, but it could be further refined to highlight the existence among the "big people" of a higher class of the extremely wealthy and nationally powerful owners of great estates, corporations, executives, financiers, high-level military officers, and national political figures. According to government estimates in the third quarter of 1980, the top income group of households earning more than ₱40,000 (for value of the peso—see Glossary) per year represented only 4.2 percent of the total of 8 million households nationwide. Some 48 percent of this group lived in Metro Manila. Those earning from ₱ 20,000 to ₱40,000 per year represented 10.1 percent of all households,| and 31 percent of these lived in Metro Manila. Some 15.5 percent of all households earned from ₱12,000 to ₱ 20,000 per year. The remainder of the population was relatively poor (see Labor and Income, ch. 3).

The disparity in income level between the upper class and the poor was placing mounting pressure on traditional ties that linked persons in different income groups. It was perhaps too early to say whether personal alliance systems were being replaced by more class-oriented ties, but this was something to watch in the immediate future. For the moment it would suffice to note that peasant families, when in need no longer always went to their landlord or to another person of recognized wealth, power, or influence. More and more they looked to their cooperatives or, in the case of urban laborers and *sacadas*, to their labor unions for support.

Personal alliance systems can extend far beyond the local arena, becoming pyramidal structures going all the way to Manila, where members of the national political elite represent the tops of numerous personal alliance pyramids. Since 1972 these national leaders have operated in a comparatively less than open political environment. This has not meant a breakdown in the system of personal alliances, only that new ones have developed to take the place of those that operated before martial law. In particular, the military hierarchy, with its own alliance network, has moved into the space left vacant by opposition political factions. Concomitant with this shift has been a change in the composition of the national economic elite, and new names have suddenly emerged as multimillionaires, owing to their membership in the powerful alliance system constructed by President and Imelda Marcos.

Social Values

Whether in the *barangay* or urban provincial center, social acceptance continues to be the central Philippine value. Stress is placed on skills that will enhance smooth interpersonal relations by helping one get along with others with a minimum of conflict. Filipinos place a high degree of emphasis on *amor proprio* (self-esteem). They are sensitive to attacks on their own *amor proprio* and cultivate a sensitivity to the *amor proprio* of others as well. Anything that might hurt another's *amor proprio* is to be avoided, or else one takes the chance of terminating the relationship. One who is sensitive to others will be said to possess *hiya*, or a sense of shame and embarrassment, the principal sanction against improper behavior. To be considered insensitive or thoughtless is to be thought of as *walang hiya* (having no shame), and this is a serious accusation for any Filipino. *Hiya*, in the words of Philippine scholar Jamie Bulatao, is "a fear of being left exposed, unprotected, unaccepted." Insofar as one possesses a strong sense of this fear, one is likely to develop with great care smooth interpersonal relations, always being careful to treat others' *amor proprio* with respect.

One other basic ingredient to social acceptance involves *tiwala* (trust in another). This is the basis for Philippine camaraderie. It is expected of close kin and friends but not of all acquaintances.

Skills valued in enhancing smooth interpersonal relations and developing awareness of others' *amor proprio* include *pakikisama*, use of go-betweens, and euphemism. Concerning the first of these, Robert Morais, a student of Philippine social relations, gives the following example from one of his informants in the town of Tanay. "I was working at a job in the city and had to stay overnight there. Almost every night, my coworkers wanted me to join them for a few drinks. Even though I knew if I did so, I would save no money, I joined them because of *pakikisama*." *Pakikisama* thus involves pleasing others by conformity. In Tanay, at least, this aspect of *pakikisama* tends to be more prevalent among men and among lower class men more than others. The term, however, may also refer more generally to being kind, "considerate, warm, and affable not only with persons one knows well but also with casual acquaintances," thereby seeking to make public relationships personal. *Pakikisama* is closely related to euphemism, i.e., indirect speech, or even flattery used to avoid conflict in one's relationships and to develop *tiwala* by showing awareness of *amor proprio*. Likewise, use of a go-between in order to avoid direct confrontation is a common practice.

A Filipino possessed of a strong sense of *hiya, amor proprio,* and *tiwala* and expert in the skills of *pakikisama*, euphemism, and use of a go-between in potentially tense situations will be successful in developing smooth interpersonal relations and hence in gaining social acceptance. He will be successful in developing strong personal alliance systems.

Social Organization

According to Morais, personal alliance systems represent an interweaving of social relationships that include some or all of the following components: real kinship, ritual kinship, special debts of gratitude, market exchange partnerships, patron-client bonds, and friendship. These components are not exclusive; each individual interweaves some or all of them to expand his circle and widen his network of social alliances. In the mosaic of interwoven personal alliance systems that characterizes Lowland Christian Filipino society, each Filipino finds a place and develops an individual social environment.

The core of each alliance system is anchored by kinship, of which the primary economic and educational unit is the nuclear family. A Filipino's loyalty is still first and foremost to the immediate family; identity is deeply embedded in the web of kinship. It remains normative that one owes support, loyalty, and trust to one's close kin, and because kinship is structured bilaterally, with kindred including affinal as well as consanguineal relatives, one's kin can include quite a large number of people. Still, beyond the nuclear family, Filipinos do not assume the same degree of support, loyalty, and trust that they assume for immediate family members for whom loyalty is nothing less than a social imperative. With respect to kin beyond this nuclear family, closeness in relationship depends very much on physical proximity.

Bonds of ritual kinship, sealed on any of three ceremonial occasions—baptism, confirmation, and marriage—intensify and extend personal alliances. Called *compadrazgo* or *compadrinazgo*, this mutual kinship system dates back at least to the introduction of Roman Catholicism and perhaps even earlier. It is a primary method of extending the group from which one can expect help in the way of favors, such as jobs, loans, or just simple gifts on special occasions. But in asking a friend to become godparent to his child, a Filipino is also asking that person to become a closer friend. Thus it is common to ask acquaintances who are of higher economic or social status than oneself to be sponsors. Such ritual kinship cannot be depended on in moments of crisis to the extent that real kinship can, but it still functions normatively for small and regular acts of support such as gift giving.

A bond of dyadic character—one involving two individuals—may be formed between two persons based on the concept of *utang na loob* (repayment of debts). Although it is expected that the debtor will attempt repayment, it is widely recognized that the debt (as in the case of one's obligation to a parent) can never be fully repaid, and the obligation can last for generations. Saving another's life, providing employment, or making it possible for another to become educated—these "gifts" incur *utang na loob*. More to the point, such gifts initiate a long-term reciprocal interdependency in which the grantor of the favor can expect help from the debtor whenever the need arises, and the debtor can, in turn, ask other favors. A dyad is thus formed that provides a form of insurance for both parties. Such reciprocal personal alliances have had obvious implications for the society in general and the political system in particular. Under the Marcos regime, they have applied just as readily as in the innumerable cases where the President and Imelda Marcos have granted favors in a highly visible and per-sonalistic manner to individuals, families, communities, and special-interest groups. It may be said, without exaggeration, that many Fi lipinos are caught in a political *utang no loob* relationship as clients of the president, who stands as their principal patron. Morais has noted, however, that educated Filipinos are less apt to feel obligated to extend help (thereby not initiating an *utang na loob* relationship) than are farmers, among whom traditional values remain strong. Perhaps as Philippine society becomes more modernized and urban in orientation, *utang na loob* will become less important in the political and social systems.

In the commercial context, *suki* relationships (market exchange part-nerships) may develop between two people who agree to become, respectively, regular customer and supplier. In the marketplace Fili-pinos will regularly buy given foodstuffs from certain specific suppliers who will give them, in return, reduced prices, good quality, and often credit. Perceived as being operative in such relationships is the idea of personal friendship and mutual trust. *Suki* relationships often apply in other contexts as well, as in restaurants patronized regularly by peo-ple who receive in return special treatment, in small neighborhood retail shops and, perhaps most commonly, in tailoring shops. *Suki* does more than help develop economic exchange relationships. Because trust is such a vital aspect, it creates a platform for personal relationships that can blossom into genuine friendship between individuals.

Also still very much a part of prescribed patterns of appropriate be-havior are patron-client bonds. These may be formed between tenant farmers and their landlords or between any patron who provides re-sources and influence in return for the client's personal services and general support. The reciprocal arrangement may typically involve the giving by the patron of a means of earning a living, or of help, protec-tion, and influence and the giving by the client of labor and personal favors ranging from household tasks to political support. These relation-ships often evolve into ritual kinship ties, as the tenant or worker may ask his landlord to sponsor the baptism of one of his children. Similarly, when favors are extended, they tend to bind patron and client together in a network of mutual obligation or a long-term interdependency.

One last method of extending one's circle of social alliances concerns friendship. Morais suggests that friendship belongs in a category with kinship as the most central of Filipino relationships. Together, these two are the core, which is supplemented by other ties. Certainly ties among those within one's *barkada* (group of friends) are an important factor in the development of personal alliance systems. And here, as in other categories, a willingness to help one another provides the prime rationale for the relationship.

These categories—real kinship, ritual kinship, *utang na loob* relationships, *suki* relationships, patron-client bonds, and friendship—are not exclusive. They are all interrelated components of the Filipino's personal alliance system. Thus two individuals may be cousins, then become friends, and then cement their friendship through the ceremony of godparenthood. Each of their social networks will typically include kin (near and far, affinal and consanguineal), ritual kin, one or two patron-client relationships, one or more other close friends (and a larger number of social friends), and a dozen or more market exchange partners. *Utang na loob* may infuse any or all of these relationships. One's network of social allies may approach 80 or so persons, who more or less will compose one's integrated and interwoven personal alliance system.

The Role and Status of the Filipina

Women have always enjoyed greater equality in Philippine society than is common in other parts of Southeast Asia. Since pre-Spanish times Filipinos have traced kinship bilaterally, and a woman's rights to legal equality and to inherit family property have not been questioned. Education and literacy levels in the early 1980s were as high for women as for men.

Within the family circle in the early 1980s the wife had great power. The home and its care were her domain. She monitored the family finances and often decided on family investments. A woman had almost total say in child rearing, which was generally accepted as her responsibility. She could represent the family in interfamily bargaining, but more often she shaped decisions behind the scenes.

Marriage among Lowland Christian Filipinos was monogamous and usually lifelong because divorce was not legally recognized in the Philippines. Although the legal code permitted separation in cases of adultery and in cases of attempted murder by one spouse of another, it was much more common for couples to separate informally without going through the legal process. In this situation of informal separation, the husband could set up another household with another woman, but there were strong informal social sanctions against women doing the same thing. Such a double standard continued to operate against women's equality wherever sexual mores were concerned. It was, for example, widely accepted that men would have extramarital affairs, while such affairs were not condoned for women.

It was a woman's first responsibility to keep the home and raise the children. Nevertheless, many Filipinas brought home a second income as teachers, clerks, secretaries, and storekeepers. It has long been regarded as acceptable for women to work in such jobs, and many have been able to rise to the top of their profession. Women like First Lady Imelda Marcos and former senator Eva Estrada Kalaw stand as examples of women who have attained national and even international prominence (see Urban Social Patterns, this ch.).

Rural Social Patterns

In mid-1983 nearly seven out of every 10 Filipinos lived in villages, or *barangays*. Each of these consisted of a number of *sitios* (neighborhoods), clusters of households that were the basic building blocks of society above the family units themselves. Most *barangays* numbered from 150 to 200 households, and each *sitio* comprised 15 to 30 households. As a rule, *barangays* also contained an elementary school, one or more small retail stores, and a small Roman Catholic chapel. They were combined administratively into municipalities. In the larger centers one could find a much more substantial church and convent for the resident priest, other non-Roman Catholic churches, a number of retail stores and the weekly marketplace, a full six-year elementary school and probably a high school as well, a rice and corn mill, a cockpit, and the homes of most landowners and middle-class teachers and professionals living in the municipality. This urban concentration was thus not only the administrative center but also the social, economic, educational, and recreational locus. This was particularly so where the center was itself a full-scale town, complete with restaurants, cinemas, banks, specialty stores, gas stations, repair shops, bowling alleys, a rural health clinic, and perhaps a hospital and hotel or two. It was also here that one could find television sets to be common in most homes, whereas some *barangays* in remote areas did not have electrical power.

In the rural Philippines traditional values remained the rule. Here the family remained central to a Filipino's identity, and many *sitios* were composed mainly of kin. Where this was the case, kin ties formed the basis for most friendships and supra-nuclear family relationships. When work needed to be done, whether in the fields or in preparation for a special occasion, neighbors, i.e., kin, pitched in. But even where *sitios* were not made up of relatives, these neighborhoods joined together in order to get a job done for one of their members. Filipinos continued to feel a strong obligation to help their neighbors. All through the year they helped each other in little ways, whether in granting a small loan or providing jobs for neighborhood children, and they expected to be included in neighborhood work projects, such as rebuilding or reroofing a house and clearing new land. The recipient of the help was expected to provide tools and food. Membership in the *tagnawa* (cooperative work group) sometimes continued even after a member left the neighborhood. Likewise, the recipient's siblings joined the group even if they lived outside the *sitio*. In this way, familial and residential ties were intermixed.

In the past, when landlords and tenants normally lived in close proximity, patron-client relationships often grew out of close residential contact. Patron-client reciprocal ties, often infused with mutual affection, continue to characterize relations between tenants and landlords where the latter have stayed down on the farm. Ever since World War II, however, landlords have been leaving the barrios, as *barangays* were then called, and moving to the larger towns and cities or even to one of the huge metropolitan centers like Manila or Cebu, Davao or Caloocan. There, in an urban environment, they have the advantages of more sophisticated entertainment and education and more convenient access to banking and business opportunities. The price paid for this elite exodus from the *barangays* has been the erosion of landlord-tenant, patron-client ties. The exodus of the wealthiest families has also caused patronage of local programs and charities to suffer. By the early 1980s most large landowners had moved to Manila or another metropolis, although as a rule they also maintained a residence in their provincial center. Landowners who remained in the municipality itself were usually schoolteachers, lawyers, and small entrepreneurs who were neither long-standing large landowners (*hacenderos*) nor owners of more than a few hectares of farmland.

Where patron-client ties have eroded, they have been replaced by a variety of new vertical alliances with *barangay* leaders, local leaders of the Marcos political organization, and the local commanders of the Philippine Constabulary, who have become common sources for patronage since 1972. It has been suggested that success of an authoritarian religious organization like the Iglesia ni Kristo (Church of Christ) may also be due in part to the need among farmers for new sources of communal security.

The strength of dyadic patterns in Philippine life has probably caused farmers to continue to seek new patron-client relationships within their *barangays* or municipalities. Their personal alliance systems have continued to stress the vertical dimension more than the horizontal. Likewise, they have sought noninstitutional means for settling disputes, rarely going to court except as a very last resort. Just as the local landlord used to be the arbiter of serious disputes, so the *barangay* head could be called on to perform this function.

In the face of the departure of many landlords for the cities, rural society has retained a surprising degree of continuity. There were, nevertheless, some indicators that this may be changing. Owing in part to a government-sponsored cooperative movement—the Samahang Nayon (see Glossary)—that teaches farmers to pool their assets, some farmers have become more interested in developing horizontal reciprocal alliances with their *barangay* peers. An independent cooperative movement, the Federation of Free Farmers, has also worked to raise awareness of common interests among farmers, although the movement has suffered from government opposition and has so far attracted only a small minority of peasants. Potential organizing strength was most evident among the poorest rural inhabitants, especially the migrant sugarcane field-workers of Negros and Panay. The National Federation of Sugar Workers had gained both members and power in the 1970s, lending force to its demands for better wages and better working and living conditions. The conspicuous consumption of the wealthy landowners and their managers, compounded by improvements in communications that have increased awareness of the gap between rich and poor, has resulted in rising resentment, anger, and alienation, and this has contributed to the growth of an increasingly powerful labor movement in Western Visayas Region.

Urban Social Patterns

The Philippines, like other Southeast Asian nations, has one dominant city that is so much larger and so much more central to the political, economic, and cultural life than other urban areas that it deserves to be placed in a category all by itself as a "primate city." In mid-1983 Metro Manila produced roughly half of the gross national product (GNP—see Glossary) of the Philippines. Manila residents and their neighbors owned two-thirds of the nation's vehicles. With its plethora of wholesale and retail business establishments, insurance companies, advertising companies, and banks of every description, the region has become the unchallenged hub of business and finance. Because of its extraordinary choice of colleges and universities (among which were some, like the University of the Philippines, Ateneo de Manila University, and De La Salle University, that were as good as any in Southeast Asia), it was a magnet for the best minds of the nation. In addition to being the political and judicial capital, Manila was the entertainment and arts capital, with all the glamour of first-class international hotels and restaurants. Owing to a communications and media industry dominated by Manila, Filipinos everywhere were constantly made aware of Manila events: cultural, political, economic, and otherwise. It was little wonder that the city was bursting with the influx of rural Filipinos on whom Manila's glamorous opportunities are no longer lost. More than one-half of the residents of this great, noisy, sprawling urban area had been born elsewhere.

Manila has a modern superstructure of hotels and banks, supermarkets, malls, art galleries, and museums. When one looks beyond this, however, one discovers a substructure of traditional small neighborhoods and a wide spectrum of life-styles ranging from traditional to modern, from those of the inordinately wealthy to those of the abjectly poor. When attending performances at the bayside cultural center or living in walled and guarded enclaves like Forbes Park, one moves in a different world from that experienced by Manila's legions of shantytown dwellers. The difference between a business executive jogging along Roxas Boulevard and the broom-wielding Metro Manila aide he passes encompasses much more than differentials in income. Their life-styles are so different that they might as well be living in two separate cultures.

Both in the case of poverty—visible in thousands of squatters' flimsy shacks—and in the case of wealth—most evident in the elegant, guarded suburbs with their expensive homes and private clubs—Metro Manila offered greater extremes than other urban areas. But in Manila, as in all other urban centers, these economic divisions were not paralleled by racial or linguistic residential patterns. The Philippine city, unlike cities in many other cultures, was truly a melting pot, in which wealth was the only determinant for residence. By contrast the Spanish had required Chinese, *indios*, mestizos, and *peninsulares* (Spanish born in Spain) to live each in their own quarters, where they established their own governing councils.

Different life-styles do not always suggest different values. In fact, whether in poor squatter and slum communities or in middle-class sections of the cities, values associated primarily with rural *barangays* have continued to be important in determining expectations, if not always actions. According to one observer, available evidence suggests "that while *barangay* organization changes with increase in population and urban development, expectations do not." Even when it is clearly impossible to create a warm and personal community in a city neighborhood, Filipinos nevertheless feel that traditional patterns of behavior conducive to such a community should be followed. Thus, although there are distinctive changes in social skills that enhance the principal value of social acceptance, this value is just as important for the urban Filipino, whether poor or middle class, as it is for his rural cousin. Hospitality, interdependence, patron-client bonds, and real kinship all continue to be of importance for urban Filipinos.

Still another indicator of how traditional Philippine values have remained functional for city dwellers is that average household size in the 1980s has been greater in urban than in rural areas. Observers speculated that as Filipinos have moved to the city they have had fewer children but more extended family members and nonrelatives in their households. This may be owing to the availability of more work opportunities in the city, to the fact that urban Filipinos tended to marry later so that there were more singles there, to the housing industry's inability to keep pace with urbanization, or to the high urban unemployment rates that caused families to supplement their incomes by taking in boarders. Whatever the reason, it seems clear that kinship and possibly other personal alliance system ties were no weaker for most urban Filipinos than for their rural kin.

The Marcos administration has repeatedly expressed its concern for the poor. Imelda Marcos, as governor of Metro Manila, head of the Ministry of Human Settlements, secretary general of the National Livelihood Program (KKK—see Glossary), and director of the Bagong Lipunan Improved Sites and Services program (BLISS), has been especially visible in this regard. According to the president, the KKK will ·be instrumental in developing a stronger Filipino middle-class society by combating poverty and unemployment. The KKK was to spend upwards of US$1.5 billion between 1981 and 1987, primarily in loans and subsidies to small- and medium-scale businesses for projects that are intended to improve the quality of life, especially in rural areas, such as cottage and light industries, livestock raising, and agriculture.

Among the most important efforts by Imelda Marcos to date has been the Tondo Foreshore Development Project, a major government housing effort that seeks to improve housing conditions for the 200,000 residents in Manila's biggest slum, but given the sheer numbers of poor, the impact would be slight at best. A new BLISS program promised to focus on the needs of the poorest neighborhoods of 1,700 towns and cities, including 270 in Manila alone. BLISS projects, however, had so far often proved too expensive for the poorest households.

Members of the New Elite

In 1983 the Philippine elite was composed of wealthy landlords, financiers, businessmen, high military officers, and national political figures. A tiny minority of the population, it controlled an extremely high percentage of the nation's wealth. The marked distortion in income distribution favoring a relatively small number of families—between 25 and 90 by some estimates—was reflected in the generally lavish life-styles of members of this group, which usually included owning at least two homes (one in Manila and one in the province where the family originated), patronizing expensive shops and restaurants, belonging to exclusive clubs, and directing a retinue of servants. Many counted among their social acquaintances a number of foreigners, especially Americans and Spaniards and other Europeans. Children attended exclusive private schools in Manila and were often sent abroad, usually to the United States, for higher education.

Among the consequences of the imposition of martial law and continuing authoritarian rule by Marcos was a change in the composition of the national elite. According to one interpretation, this change reflected the gradual concentration of economic power within a small, closely knit group whose members, through an interlocking management network, effectively controlled the modern sector of the economy. In this interpretation, Marcos and his wife were seen as exercising a firm hold at the top, buttressed by relatives and friends who had been placed in charge of key economic and financial institutions. The inner circle of the group was made up of the Marcos and Romualdez families and others, such as Robert Benedicto and Ricardo Silverio, who had particularly close ties with them. Many of its members had neither belonged to the traditional elite nor had been wealthy before 1972. In a more peripheral but still favored position within this modern elite were families, such as the Elizaldes, whose elite status was clearly rooted in traditional society but whose continued social positon and economic prosperity seemed assured, supported as it was by the inner circle. Occupying a marginal position was a third group of families, such as the Zobel-Ayala and Sorianos, who, although clearly set apart from the inner circle and rarely benefiting from its councils, nevertheless had managed to retain control of their vast business interests.

On that basis it was clear that the new national elite was less independent that the pre-martial law landed elite had been. This is not to say that the sugar barons of earlier days had scorned favors from those in power. Their long-standing landed wealth, however, had made them less dependent on any one administration than the new elite of the 1980s tended to be. In the contemporary period no family enjoyed as much autonomy as was typical before 1972; all remained indebted to Marcos in greater or lesser degree. Because of this indebtedness, Philippine elite politics will remain highly centralized until Marcos steps down. His successor will not have the benefit of such personalized reciprocal obligations. That will be the time for a major shifting of loyalties, at which point the Philippine economic elite may return to pre-martial law patterns of decentralism.

Another major change that has occurred in the composition of the Philippine upper class has been the rise of military officers into political and economic prominence for the first time as a group. The declaration of martial law and suspension of regular elections has caused local notables in towns throughout the country to experience a loss of political clout, while local Philippine Constabulary commanders, hitherto unnoticed participants in politics, suddenly became important conduits for national government patronage. These officers began to receive invitations to join local clubs, attend local festivities as honored guests, and accept favors from highly placed local families. Meanwhile, at the national level, generals of the Philippine Air Force watched their power expand as their budgets for men and equipment grew. They provided substantial help to both civilian and junior military officers, who regularly called on them to secure assistance in getting jobs, dealing with family problems, processing applications, supporting community development projects or removing inept government officials. Thus, traditional patron-client relationships have shifted, but not necessarily weakened, under Marcos' leadership. Here again, though, military leaders have depended heavily on Marcos.

In between the urban poor and the affluent and powerful economic, political, and military components of the national elite were those increasing numbers of Filipinos who counted themselves as members of the middle class. These individuals tended to live in urban rather than rural areas, although there was a vital segment of the middle class living in municipalities throughout the country. They included in their number small entrepreneurs, civil servants, teachers, merchants, small property owners, and clerks. In many middle-class families, both spouses worked in different occupations. They tended to place great value on higher education, and most had at least a high school diploma. Though not as cohesive as the economic, political, or military components of the elite group, they shared a sense of commmon identity deriving from similar educational experiences, facility in using English, common participation in service clubs like the Rotary, and similar economic standing. Of all the urban groups, they seemed to be both the most nationalistic in the sense of possessing pride as Filipinos and the most interested in emigrating. Their profound discontent was owing primarily to the drop in real income that civil servants have suffered perhaps more severely than others since 1972. This, combined with their awareness of corruption, has led many to seek new, non-Philippine avenues for their determination to use education, talent, and hard work in gaining greater socioeconomic upward mobility.

Religious Life

For most Filipinos, religion has little to do with church hierarchy or imported theology. Religion is that which one experiences in the local church or mosque; the clergy are those priests, ministers, or the imam with whom one associates in the *barangay*; and orthodoxy is something for which one has neither much time nor interest. Whether one's faith is Islam, Roman Catholicism, Protestantism, or one of the indigenous forms of Christianity, religion holds a central place in the life of a Filipino. But it is central not as an abstract belief system, but rather as a host of experiences, rituals, ceremonies, and adjurations that provide continuity in life, cohesion in community, and moral purpose for existence.

Just as it serves to reinforce community and give shape and meaning to life, so religion is, in turn, influenced and modified by local social customs and institutions. Filipinos seek to extend their personal alliance systems by constructing ritual kinship ties, patron-client bonds, and other linkages with people outside their nuclear family. They do the same thing with religious figures. In an intensely personal way, God is worshiped as a father figure, the Virgin as a compassionate mother, and Jesus as the loving son who died for the sins of each individual. In the words of Philippines scholar David Joel Steinberg, "This framework established a cosmic *compadrazgo*, and an *utang no loob* to Christ, for his sacrifice transcended any possible repayment. . . . To the devout Filipino, Christ died to save him; there could be no limit to an individual's thanks-giving."

Acceptance of Catholicism and Islam has been selective; these world religions have been superimposed on ancient traditions and acculturated. The unique religious blends that have resulted, when combined with intense Philippine religious personalism, have given rise to numerous and diverse revivalist movements. Generally characterized by millenarian goals, antimodern bias, supernaturalism, and authoritarianism in the person of a charismatic messiah figure, these movements have attracted thousands of Filipinos in recent decades, especially in areas like Mindanao, which have been subjected to extreme pressures of change over a short period of time. The farmers who become swept up in these movements, who sing songs, learn secret rituals, wear charms, and buy sacred oil, do so primarily because the movements themselves provide a sense of fraternity and renewed power in an environment where all sense of community has waned. Like the highly visible examples of flagellation and reenacted crucifixion in the Philippines, these movements may seem to have little in common with organized Christianity or Islam. But in the intensely personalistic Philippine religious context, they are not aberrations so much as extreme examples of how religion retains its central role in society.

In mid-1983 approximately 85 percent of the population was Roman Catholic. Muslims accounted for only 5 percent, about equal in number to members of the less well-known Iglesia Filipina Independiente, or

Philippine Independent Church. But whereas Catholics and Aglipay-ans (as Independent Church members are commonly called) could be found all through the archipelago, Muslims remained largely confined to the south. Because of their physical separateness, they have become integrated much less than other religious minorities into the main-stream of Philippine culture. They remained not just a religious mi-nority but a very distinct cultural minority as well.

The remaining 5 percent of the population adhered to other beliefs. For example, there were many Protestant denominations, the mis-sionaries of which have been successful in converting animistic hill tribal peoples and also a significant number of urban middle-class professionals. The Iglesia ni Kristo was the fastest growing church in the 1970s. By the early 1980s its distinctive church structure had become common in central and southern Luzon and was appearing in more and more Visayan communities. Animistic tribal groups, on Lu-zon and Mindanao especially, continued to adhere to indigenous beliefs and practices that predated Muslim and Spanish influence. Many, however, converted to Islam or Christianity over the years.

Historical Background

From its inception in 1571 following the arrival of Miguel López de Legazpi, Spanish colonialism had as its principal raison d'être the con-version of Muslims and other island inhabitants to Christianity. Al-though the Spanish crown also hoped to profit financially from its new colony, it served in the sixteenth century primarily as a vehicle for spreading the faith on behalf of the Roman Catholic Church with which it entered into a complex interrelationship. In return for transporting priests without charge to the Philippines and paying their annual sa-laries, the crown won the right to collect tithes and approve or dis-approve proposed clergy. The crown thus became principal patron of the church.

When Legazpi embarked on his conversion efforts, most Filipinos were still practicing a form of polytheism, although some as far north as Manila had converted to Islam. For the majority, religion still con-sisted of sacrifices and incantations to spirits believed to be inhabiting field and sky, home and garden, and other dwelling places both human and natural. Malevolent spirits could bring harm in the form of illness or accident, while benevolent spirits, such as those of one's ancestors, could bring prosperity in the form of good weather and bountiful crops. Shamans *(baylans)* were called upon to communicate with these spirits on behalf of village and family, and propitiation ceremonies were a common part of village life and ritual. Such beliefs continued to inform the religious practices of many upland tribal groups in the modern period.

The religious system that conquistadores and priests imported in the sixteenth and seventeenth centuries was superimposed on this polyth-eistic base. Filipinos who converted to Catholicism did not simply shed their earlier beliefs. Rather, they superimposed the new on the old.

Saints took primacy over spirits, the mass over propitiation ceremonies, and priests over shamans. But in no case was the substitution complete. This mixing of different religious beliefs and practices was not exactly what the Spaniards had in mind, but it marked Philippine Catholicism from the start.

Also from its inception Catholicism was deeply influenced by the prejudices, strategies, and policies of the Catholic religious orders. Known collectively as friars and individually as Augustinians, Dominicans, Franciscans, Jesuits, and others, these missionaries turned out to be just about the only Caucasians willing to dedicate their lives to converting and ministering to Spain's subject population in the Philippines. They divided the archipelago into distinct territories, learned the vernaculars appropriate to each region, and put down roots in the rural Philippines where they quickly became founts of wisdom for uneducated and unsophisticated local inhabitants. Because most secular colonial officials had no intention of living so far from home any longer than it took to turn a handsome profit, friars took on the roles of protectors of Philippine peasants and interpreters of government policies in the islands. Without them, the crown could not have proselytized the faith successfully. But with them, the crown lost control over colonial policy in practice. If friars chose to ignore an order, the king, who could not expect a reply from them in less than two years anyway, had little choice but to console himself with the thought that at least they were better than nothing at all. In any case, it was assumed that eventually they would be replaced in parish work by secular priests appointed by the archbishop, who, in turn, was appointed by the crown. But a dearth of parish priests willing to live so far away from Spain diminished this threat to friar control. After 200 years of colonial rule, only one-fourth of the 569 parishes were ministered to by non-friars. It was clear by the mid-seventeenth century that only secular priests drawn from the population of the archipelago could be trained in sufficient numbers to erode friar control. As soon as authorities attempted to replace Spanish friars with Filipinos, the question of church leadership became the focal point in an emerging Filipino national consensus against friar colonialism.

Despite the fact that friars took vows of poverty, religious orders accumulated tremendous landed wealth over the three centuries of Spanish colonial rule. Through *obras pias* (charitable foundations) the Roman Catholic Church made extensive loans using its landed estates as collateral and thereby developed into one of the principal financial institutions in the islands. The church thus came to have a vested interest in Spanish colonialism that ultimately transcended the division between friars and secular clergy. But this became apparent only after policies formulated by crown and ecclesiastical authorities opened the door temporarily to Filipino clerics in the late eighteenth and early nineteenth centuries.

In 1767 the Jesuits were expelled from the Spanish Empire. Thus the ranks of the religious clergy were reduced, opening up parishes for indigenous secular, or diocesan, clergy—Chinese and Spanish mestizos and *indio* priests. An outcry by the friars, combined with a number of Filipino revolts and some cases where *indio* priests did not administer their new parishes effectively, led to Jesuit reinstatement in 1859. Thereafter, few Filipinos were permitted more than a minor role in ministering to their own people. In the late nineteenth century the Catholic church in the Philippines was rapidly becoming united against Filipino participation in the priesthood. When the priests José Burgos, Mariano Gómez, and Jacinto Zamora, all leading advocates of Filipino equality in the clergy, were executed in 1872, this confirmed Filipinos in their belief that the church had become an obscenely wealthy and powerful arm of foreign rule (see The Later Period of Spanish Rule, 1762-1898, ch. 1). The revolution that followed against Spain was for many Filipino leaders first and foremost a revolution against Caucasian domination of the church.

In the twentieth century the church has made a remarkable comeback in the Philippines. This has been owing primarily to Vatican willingness first to divest itself of massive church estates and then to encourage Filipino participation in the clergy. In the 1980s the clergy was overwhelmingly Filipino. It had also gained support through its extensive network of parochial schools. So successful was this resurgence that Protestant mission efforts, led by large numbers of American missionaries during the period of American colonial rule, made little headway.

Catholicism as practiced in the Philippines in the mid-1980s blended official doctrine with folk observances. Just as in other Roman Catholic countries, Filipinos attended official church services (men usually not as regularly as women), such as masses, novenas, baptisms, weddings, and funerals. But they supplemented these official services with a number of folk-religious ceremonies that involved just about everyone in the community and have become basic to the community's social and religious calendar.

Perhaps the single event most conducive to community solidarity each year is the fiesta. Celebrated on the day of the town's or barrio's patron saint, this is a time for general feasting. Houses are opened to guests, and food is served in abundance. The fiesta always includes a mass, but its purpose is unabashedly social, with the biggest events being a parade, dance, basketball tournament, cockfights and other contests, and perhaps a carnival, in addition to lots of visiting and feasting.

Christmas is celebrated in a manner that blends Catholic, Chinese, Philippine, and American customs. For nine days people attend *misas de gallo* (early morning Christmas mass). They hang Chinese lanterns and other decorations in their homes, and they join with friends in caroling. On Christmas Eve everyone attends midnight mass, the climax of the *misas de gallo* and the year's high point of church attendance. After the service it is traditional to return home for a grand family meal. The remaining days of the Christmas season are spent visiting

Views of St. Augustine Church and the partially restored inner area of the old walled city, dating from the late sixteenth century
Courtesy J. Lohmann

kin, especially on New Year's Day and Three Kings Day, January 6. The Christmas season is a time of visiting and receiving guests. It is also a time for reunion with all types of kin—blood, affinal, and ceremonial. Children especially are urged to visit godparents.

During the Lenten season most communities do a reading of the Passion narrative and a performance of the *sinakulo* (popular passion play). The custom of reading or chanting of the Passion is unique to the Philippines and could have originated in the pre-Spanish practice of chanting lengthy epics. Its continuing importance in Philippine life, however, may have more to do with popular conceptions of personal indebtedness to Christ for his supreme sacrifice. As at least one observer has suggested, Filipinos have, through the Passion, experienced a feeling of redemption that has been the basis for both millennial dreams and historical revolutionary movements for independence.

According to early 1983 sources, the church was organized into 14 archdioceses and 34 dioceses, attended by two cardinals (Julio Cardinal Rosales died in June 1983, leaving only one), 14 archbishops, 68 bishops, nearly 5,000 priests, 7,000 nuns, and smaller numbers of seminarians and others. (Of the priests, 2,800 were secular clergy, 2,200 religious clergy.) Church and state remained separate, but religious instruction could, at the option of parents, be provided in public schools. Likewise, the state continued to accept the Catholic position on divorce, which remained illegal. Church-state separation was perhaps most obvious over the issue of family planning, where the government's policy of widespread dissemination of contraceptive devices came into conflict with the church's opposition to all but natural methods of birth control.

During the martial law period, the church had become deeply involved in community action programs to assist in alleviating the socioeconomic ills of its many impoverished adherents and had gradually moved into the forefront of vocal opposition to the government. Even before martial law was declared, the church had begun to reassess its role in politics. The social encyclicals of popes John XXIII and Paul VI, the Second Vatican Council, and the second and third synods of bishops had all affirmed that the Roman Catholic Church should become more active in upholding social justice and in opposing economic inequities. In response to these urgings, the Catholic Bishops Conference of the Philippines (CBCP) and the Association of Major Religious Superiors of the Philippines (AMRSP) both spoke out in defense of justice and equality for the poor and powerless. The CBCP set up the National Secretariat for Social Action (NASSA), under the jurisdiction of the Episcopal Commission on Social Action, which together with the government subsequently participated in the formation of the Church-Military Liaison Committee. The committee was disbanded in early 1983 at the behest of the church, however (see Civic Action and Military-Civilian Relations, ch. 5). NASSA had been organized for the purpose of establishing social action centers in each diocese and by early 1981 had organized three regional secretariats of social action—on Mindanao and in the Sulu Archipelago, in the Visayan Islands, and on Luzon—and a large number of social action centers at the diocese level. It also helped to establish a network of Citizen Committees for Justice and Peace at the diocesan level to look into allegations of human rights violations. The AMRSP, meanwhile, in 1974 established the Task Force Detainees to monitor alleged human rights violations.

NASSA and the AMRSP have also given attention to consciousness-raising as part of the church's social action program. NASSA's Basic Christian Community-Community Organization (BCC-CO) sought ultimately to make the rural and urban poor less dependent on patron-client ties by encouraging them to participate in their own community action projects and by educating them concerning the root causes of their poverty. The AMRSP set up an urban and a rural Task Force on Conscientization of Others. It also gave financial support to a number of squatter and labor organizations, such as Zone One Tondo Organization (ZOTO) and the National Federation of Sugar Workers; sponsored a study of living conditions for the *sacadas;* and began "exposure" programs to inform church workers and particularly foreigners of conditions in the Philippines. Both of these church organizations also provided legal aid to detainees.

Under the leadership of the archbishop of Manila, Jaime Cardinal Sin, the church in the late 1970s emphasized a policy of "critical collaboration." This changed, however, to open and forceful criticism in 1983. Throughout, Sin has urged caution, prudence, and restraint in pastoral letters and open statements to the press and president, in order to accommodate a growing rift within the ranks of the church hierarchy between activist and nonactivist clergy. According to one estimate, the activist group (strongest on Mindanao) included some 15 to 20 members of the 86-member CBCP (headed in 1983 by Archbishop Antonio Mabutas) and was well represented in the AMRSP. Criticizing military abuses against civilians, human rights violations in prisons, and "fraud, deceit and connivance" in elections, the group further called for a major restructuring of society, a redistribution of wealth, and an end to government efforts to attract foreign investment, perceived as being at the expense of the Filipino worker. Most, but not all activist clergy rejected violence and dissociated themselves from the New People's Army (NPA). Skeptical of social activist programs were conservative church leaders, such as the late Cardinal Rosales of Cebu, who had opposed major church involvement in politics as a general principle and argued that the church should oppose the government only when it interfered in the religious or financial affairs of the church.

Indigenous Christian Churches

Despite the Roman Catholic Church's twentieth-century resurgence, many Filipinos have joined one of a number of nationalistic and politico-religious movements. In the first decade of this century, Aglipayanism attracted more than 1 million followers. Then, after World War II, the Iglesia ni Kristo became the fastest growing church in the archipelago. In the early 1980s a number of Rizalian groups (centered on the national hero, José Rizal) were also receiving popular attention.

Aglipayanism

The Iglesia Filipina Independiente, led by Gregorio Aglipay, received the patronage of revolutionary leader Emilio Aguinaldo during the revolt against Spain and subsequent conflict with American forces and rode the tide of antifriar nationalism in absorbing Filipino Roman Catholic clergy and forcibly seizing church property before 1906. One out of every 16 diocesan priests and one out of four Philippine Catholics converted to Aglipayanism in those years of violent national and religious catharsis. It was not until decisions by the United States governor general and the Philippine Supreme Court restored church property to Catholics that the tide began to reverse itself. Then, too, the temporary decline of Philippine nationalism hurt Aglipayanism. United States colonial policies that encouraged Philippine participation in the governing process tended to take the punch out of the nationalist movement. To Aglipayans, for whom fervent nationalism was both heart and soul of their appeal, this proved critical. The Iglesia Filipina Independiente, formally organized in 1902, thus enjoyed less than five years of growth before it began a precipitous decline to its present minority status.

Whereas Aglipay was head of the church, another Filipino, Isabelo de los Reyes, was responsible for early church doctrine and organization. Members were instructed to worship the one true God as a universal force and principle and to reject the doctrine of the Trinity and the possibility of miracles. They were to accent only the gospel according to Mark among the New Testament books and to deny prophecy and revelation. Good works were stressed over the efficacy of prayer, and no mention was made of rewards or punishments in the hereafter.

For many Aglipayans who had lost faith in the Roman Catholic Church, but not in its dogma, such ideas were shocking. Many returned to the Catholic fold, especially after Americans and then Filipinos replaced Spanish priests. Among those who remained, a crippling schism emerged over doctrinal interpretation, especially after 1919 when members were suddenly instructed to discard earlier church statements concerning the divinity of Christ.

To some extent the schism was due to Aglipay himself, who shifted his theological views between 1902 and 1919. At first he de-emphasized doctrinal differences between his church and Roman Catholicism, and most Aglipayan priests followed Roman Catholic ritual, saying mass, hearing confession, and presiding over folk-Catholic ceremonies just as always. Later he moved closer and closer to Unitarianism, causing de los Reyes to revert to Catholicism. In 1938 the church formally split, the faction opposing Aglipay later winning a court decision giving it the right to both name and property of the Aglipayan church. Followers of Aglipay continued to argue that they represented true Aglipayanism. In the early 1980s those who rejected the Unitarian stance and adhered to the concept of the Trinity were associated with the Protestant Episcopal church of the United States.

Iglesia ni Kristo

In mid-1983 all over Luzon, the Visayan Islands, and even northern Mindanao, unmistakable Iglesia ni Kristo places of worship, all similar in design and architecture, were being constructed for a rapidly growing membership. Founded by Felix Manalo Ysagun in 1914, the Iglesia ni Kristo did not attract much notice until after World War II, when its highly authoritarian organization and evangelical style began to fill a need for urban and rural families displaced by rapid changes in Philippine society. The church requires attendance in twice-weekly services, where guards take attendance and forbid entrance to nonmembers. Membership dues based on ability to pay are mandatory. Members are expected to be disciplined, clean, and God-fearing. Gamblers and drunks face the possibility of being expelled, and the church also forbids (on penalty of expulsion) marriage to someone of another faith and membership in a labor union. Thus does the Iglesia ni Kristo intrude deeply into the lives of its members. Before martial law it even told them how to vote, and its discipline in this respect was so effective that it quickly became known and respected for its ability to get out the vote for candidates of its choice.

There are a number of reasons why so many Filipinos have joined such an authoritarian church, not the least of which is the institution's ability to stay the decline of traditional Philippine vertical patron-client relationships, especially in urban areas. The church has also been successful in attracting potential converts through its use of mass rallies not unlike Protestant revival meetings in the United States, in which participants are encouraged to become emotionally carried away in a highly charged atmosphere of religious communalism. The message is always simple and straightforward: listeners are told that the Iglesia ni Kristo is the mystical body of Christ, outside of which there can be no salvation. Roman Catholicism is denounced; only through membership in the Iglesia ni Kristo can one hope for redemption.

But perhaps the principal reason for the success of this church concerns the more worldly benefits it bestows on members. The church has embarked on its own effort to ensure that members are literate. It provides socioeconomic welfare programs, jobs, and a powerful sense of community for believers, who now include a growing number of former tenants invited to work on its agricultural development projects. Thus the Iglesia ni Kristo has become for its members a government within a government, one that looks out for the interests of its supporters in a world viewed by many as becoming more and more hostile and insecure.

Rizalian and Other Cults

The pressures and insecurities that have impelled some Filipinos to join the Iglesia ni Kristo have persuaded others to join highly emotional and apocalyptic movements usually centering on the persona of one charismatic leader who promises followers the realization of a new utopia. Such millennial movements are nothing new in Philippine history; they are the modern embodiment of the *cofradia* of 1839-41, the Guardia de Honor, the Santa Iglesia, and many different Colorums (see Glossary; The Later Period of Spanish Rule, 1762-1898, ch. 1). Still, it is disconcerting to Filipinos when such a movement attacks the Manila police headquarters as the Lapiang Malaya did in 1967. As an actual attack it failed horribly when 33 members were shot down on the street. But as a symbolic attack on westernization and urbanization, it succeeded in demonstrating both the intensity of despair of those caught in the modernization crucible and the motivating power of their millennial dream. Fortified by sacred oil, amulets (which are often laminated matchbox covers bearing a picture of Rizal, whom they have deified), and sacred incantations, other sects have also attacked constabulary units in remote rural areas like Bukidnon. They have been especially successful in attracting upland tribal groups and poor slash-and-burn farmers caught in the squeeze caused by the migration of land-hungry farmers. Such victims of the population boom have found a new sense of fraternity in these religious communities. Although there were many different and competing groups, the major ones in mid-1983 were variants of Rizalianism, i.e., the belief that Rizal, known to believers as Papa Rizal, will redeem the faithful from their life of suffering in a world where they have lost all power and place.

Protestantism

From the start, Protestant churches in the Philippines have been plagued by disunity and schisms. At one point after World War II, there were over 200 denominations representing less than 3 percent of the populace. Successful unions of some denominations and the formation of the National Council of Churches in the Philippines (NCCP) have brought a degree of order. There remains a deep gulf and considerable antagonism, however, between middle-class-oriented NCCP churches and the scores of more evangelical denominations sprinkled throughout the islands.

Protestantism has always been associated with United States influence in the Philippines. Beginning with President William McKinley's inspiration in 1898 that Filipinos must be Christianized (when in fact most were already Roman Catholic), Protestant evangelizing became an unofficial part of the general mission to make Filipinos over in the American image. All major denominations in the United States, and most minor ones, sent missions to the colony, where they found the most fertile ground for conversions to be among upland tribes not yet reached by Catholic priests and among the urban middle class. Most American schoolteachers who pioneered in the new Philippine public school system were also Protestants, and they laid the groundwork for Protestant churches in many lowland barrios as well. Filipinos who converted to Protestantism often experienced significant upward social mobility in the American colonial period. Most were middle-level bureaucrats, servants, lawyers, or small entrepreneurs, but some became nationally prominent despite their minority religious adherence.

The schismatic tendency of Philippine Protestantism arose in part from the high visibility of Americans as the churches were being organized. So long as American "mother" churches provided most of the financial underpinnings for Philippine congregations, few Filipinos were allowed into top church leadership positions. This ran counter to Philippine nationalism before World War II and prompted some Filipinos to break away and set up their own denominations. Since 1946 this point of tension has been minimized by strong Filipino participation in church leadership and by a reduction of church dependency on American donations. In the 1980s almost all member churches of the NCCP, for example, were led by Filipinos.

In common with Protestant mission efforts elsewhere in Asia, Protestantism in the Philippines has made its major contributions in the fields of education and medicine. Throughout the islands, Protestant churches have set up clinics and hospitals that employ American as well as Filipino doctors and nurses. They have also constructed private schools, including a number of outstanding institutions of higher education like Silliman University, Central Philippine University, Philippine Christian College, and Dansalan Junior College in Marawi.

Under Marcos, Protestant churches have become, if anything, even less united than before. As is true within the Roman Catholic hierarchy, Protestant leaders are divided regarding whether or not they should engage in the politics of opposition. A few NCCP members have done so, but most have taken an apolitical point of view, emphasizing the power of faith and efficacy of prayer regardless of sources of economic and social grievance.

Islam

Filipino Muslims were firmly rooted in their Islamic faith, and this generalization has never been more accurate than it was in the 1980s. Every year hundreds go on the hajj (pilgrimage) to the holy city of Mecca and return wearing white caps, to be addressed thereafter by the honorific, hajji. In most Muslim communities there is at least one mosque from which the muezzin calls the faithful to prayer several times a day. Those who go will remove their shoes before entering, then pray in straight rows before the *mihrab* (niche) in the direction of Mecca. An imam, or prayer leader, will lead the recitation in Arabic of verses from the Quran, following the Shafi'ite practices of Sunni Islam. Like Muslims everywhere, the Moros often neglect to perform the ritual prayer *(salat)* five times a day, but they do celebrate the great festivals of Islam, including that marking the end of Ramadan, the ninth month of the Muslim calendar and a period of obligatory fasting; Muhammad's birthday; the night of his ascension to heaven; and the New Year, the first day of the month of Muharram. Also as in other Muslim societies, there are believers who do not always keep the fast (going without food and drink in daylight hours) during Ramadan or perform the duty of almsgiving *(zakat)*. At the same time, other rituals and practices may be scrupulously observed. In short, according to observer Peter Gowing, "The Moros are identifiably and unmistakably Muslim and they are right to be somewhat annoyed when outsiders suggest, on the basis of observed blending of pre-Islamic and Islamic elements [found in different degrees everywhere in the Islamic World], that 'they are not true Muslims'."

Islam, as observed in the Philippines, has absorbed indigenous elements, much as has Roman Catholicism. Moros thus make offerings to spirits *(diwatas)*, whether malevolent or benign, believing that such spirits can and will have an effect on the well-being of one's crops, one's family, and oneself. They include pre-Islamic customs in ceremonies marking their rites of passage, birth, baptism *(pag-gunting)*, marriage, and death. And although Muslim Filipino women are required to stay at the back of the mosque for prayers (or otherwise out of the sight of the men), they are, thanks to their Filipino roots, much

103

freer to do what they please and go where they want than are women in many other Islamic societies. Although specific practices vary from one Moro group to another, with some like the Tausug being generally more orthodox than others, these differences are less significant than are the essentials of Islam that they all share.

Thanks to a general resurgence of Islam since World War II, Muslims in the Philippines have a stronger sense of their unity as a religious community than they had in the past. Since the early 1970s more Muslim teachers have visited and more Philippine Muslims have gone abroad—either on the hajj or on scholarships—to Islamic centers than ever before. They have returned revitalized in their faith and determined to strengthen the ties of their fellow Moros with the international Islamic community. As a result, Muslims have built hundreds of new mosques and many new religious schools, where students (male and female) learn to read the Quran in Arabic and where they also learn the basic rituals and principles of Islam. A number of Muslim institutions of higher learning have also been opened. Like the Jamiatul Philippine al-Islamia in Marawi, they offer advanced courses in Islamic studies.

Divisions along generational lines have emerged among Moros. Many young Muslims who are dissatisfied with their old leaders assert that *datu* and sultans are unnecessary to the modern Islamic society they hope to build. Among themselves, such young reformers were divided between moderates working within the system for their political goals and militants engaging in guerrilla-style warfare. Although the administration has managed to some degree to isolate the militants, it is important to remember that Muslim reformers, whether moderates or militants, are united in their strong religious adherence. To the extent that they feel threatened by the continued expansion of Christians into southern Mindanao and by the continued presence of Philippine army troops in their homeland, this bond would be significant. To quote Gowing: "One cannot stay in the Muslim region of this country, and come to know Muslims intimately in their own homes, without sensing how central Islam is for them as an organizing principle of everyday living." During the past decade Islam has given Philippine Muslims, whether Tausug or Maranao, urbanites or farmers, men or women, educated or uneducated, a strong basis for unity.

Education

As of mid-1983 the educational system was reaching a relatively large part of the population at least at the elementary level. According to government figures, which count as literate everyone who has completed four years of elementary school, the claimed overall literacy rate had reached 89.4 percent by 1981, up from 82.6 percent in 1970. Literacy rates were virtually the same for women and men. Enrollment at the elementary level also was high, representing a participation rate of about 90 percent of the relevant age-group. Elementary education was free, and in the 1980-81 academic year it was provided to some 8.3 million schoolchildren, an increase of more than 1 million over the figure for 1970-71. About 40 percent of the secondary-level age-group was attending school on a fee-paying basis; in 1978-79 students numbered nearly 3 million. High-school enrollment rates were lower on Mindanao and in Eastern Visayas Region than elsewhere. Enrollments in institutions of higher learning exceeded 1 million.

Religious and secular private schools educated many other students. There were about 300,000 attending 1,200 Roman Catholic parochial schools, not to mention 52,000 attending 122 Chinese schools. A growing number of Muslim children were pursuing Islamic and Arabic studies in over 1,000 *madrasahs* (Muslim schools).

Filipinos have a deep regard for education, which they understand to be a primary avenue for upward social and economic mobility. From the outset of United States colonial rule, with its heavy emphasis on mass public education, Filipinos internalized the American ideal of a democratic society open for individuals to get ahead through attainment of a good education. Middle-class parents make tremendous sacrifices in order to provide secondary and higher education for their children. For most Filipinos, educational aspirations are tied closely to economic goals.

Despite the high value Philippine society placed on education, central government expenditures for education were moderate. Estimated expenditures for education in 1982 amounted to only 2.1 percent of GNP, low in comparison with many other developing countries. Educational expenditures on a per capita basis in 1979 amounted to the equivalent of US$8, but the trend was in the direction of proportionately more spending, and various programs to improve educational quality and availability were in progress. For example, with the help of two World Bank (see Glossary) loans in the amount of US$150 million, the government has been able to purchase additional instructional materials. In more than half the schools, the supply of textbooks had increased to the point that one book had to be shared by only two students rather than 10. Nonetheless, many Filipino educators were reportedly concerned about eroding overall quality in the system and the impact that it could have on national well-being in a competitive global economy.

Historical Background

Filipinos who led the revolution against Spain in the 1890s were known as *ilustrados* ("enlightened ones"). *Ilustrados*, almost without exception, came from wealthy Filipino families that could afford to send them to the limited number of secondary schools *(colegios)* open for non-Spaniards. Some of them went on to the University of Santo Tomás in Manila or to Spain for their higher education. Despite their importance in articulating Filipino goals and grievances, they were never more than a tiny minority, and they spoke and wrote in the language of their colonial oppressors in seeking to reach the non-

Spanish-educated Filipino masses.

While *ilustrados* set an example for other Filipinos concerning the importance of education, those who sought to follow their lead did not have available a mass public education system. By 1863, however, the Spanish government had subscribed to the principle of free and compulsory primary education, and by 1898 enrollment in schools at all levels exceeded 200,000 students. Between 1901 and 1902 over 1,000 American teachers, known as "Thomasites" for the S.S. *Thomas*, which transported the original group to the Philippines, fanned out across the archipelago to open up barrio schools and begin the work of making Filipinos over in the American image. They taught in English, and although they did not succeed in Americanizing their wards, they did instill in them their deep faith in the general value of education. Almost immediately, enrollments began to mushroom from a total of only 150,000 in 1900-1901 to just under 1 million in elementary schools two decades later. After independence in 1946 the government picked up this emphasis on education and opened thousands more schools in even the remotest areas of the archipelago during the 1950s and 1960s.

Education in the Modern Period

This expansion in quantity was not always accompanied by qualitative improvements; therefore, quality became a major concern in the 1970s and early 1980s. Data for the 1970s showed significant differences in literacy for different regions of the country and between rural and urban areas. Western Mindanao Region, for example, had a literacy rate of 65 percent as compared with 90 percent for Central Luzon Region and 95 percent for Metro Manila. A survey of elementary-school graduates taken in the mid-1970s indicated that many of the respondents had failed to absorb much of the required course work, revealing major deficiencies in reading, mathematics, and language. Performance was poorest among respondents from Mindanao, only somewhat better for those from the Visayan Islands, while the best performance was in Central Luzon and Southern Tagalog regions. Other data revealed an important association between low literacy levels and a high incidence of poverty. In fact, throughout the school system there was a direct relationship between levels of income and of educational attainment. As a rule, families with incomes below the poverty line could not afford to educate their children beyond elementary school. Programs aimed at improving productivity and income could alleviate some of the problems in education, such as high dropout rates that reflected, at least in part, family and work needs. Other problems, such as poor teacher performance, reflected overcrowded classrooms, lack of particular language skills, and low wages, which manifested themselves in turn in poor student performance and high repeater rates; direct action was required.

Vocational education was being given greater emphasis. Traditionally, Filipinos have tended to equate the attainment of education directly with escape from manual labor. Thus it has not been easy to win general popular support for vocational training. There was also greater stress on education for nationbuilding purposes, and the central government has made no secret of the fact that it regards support for nationbuilding and for its programs as one and the same. The new emphasis on developing national consciousness in the schools represented a major shift away from the old educational focus on developing individualism and democratic principles. Under the modern system, public-school teachers were encouraged to be "cadres" for national government programs. In an already highly centralized educational system, the schools and their teachers were coming more directly under central government control.

In mid-1983 the educational system offered six years of elementary instruction followed by four years of high school. A seventh year of elementary school was being implemented, but many small *barangays* still had only a four-year primary school. Children entered primary school at the age of seven and were instructed in either their local vernacular or Pilipino. English was the medium of instruction in most schools after the third year, and it remained the language of instruction in high schools. Only 21.7 percent of Filipinos who were 25 years or older in 1975 had completed elementary school. These figures substantiated the high dropout rate; less than one out of six Filipinos went beyond the elementary level. Nonetheless, there continued to be a shortage of secondary schools in many rural areas.

One of the most serious problems in the Philippines in the 1980s concerned the large number of students who completed college but then could not find a job commensurate with their educational skills. Owing to the availability of higher education in hundreds of privately run colleges (many of which are diploma mills run mainly for profit), the country was turning out hundreds of thousands of college graduates each year. Manila, where students attend the University of Santo Tomás, the University of the Philippines, Ateneo de Manila University, and many other educational institutions, had such a large student population that the government, fearing massive student demonstrations during the presidential inauguration ceremonies in 1981, postponed the opening of the 1981 school year until the ceremonies were over. Many students have stayed in Manila after graduation, whether or not they have been lucky enough to obtain white-collar employment. Not only have they swelled the rolls of the unemployed but also they have given rise to greater urban discontent. Because parents paid significant sums in tuition for their children to attend a four-year university like the University of the Philippines, there was bound to be widespread discontent if they could not cash in on this investment with a decent job. This white-collar unemployment problem, together with the massive problem of urban in-migration and housing insufficiency in Manila, may account for the upsurge of crime and violence in the metropolis that began in the early 1970s.

Health and Living Standards

Living conditions throughout the country reflected the great disparities in income distribution between the poorest and the wealthiest households and the concentration of the latter in urban metropolitan areas, especially Manila (see Income Distribution and Living Conditions, ch. 3). Access to health, welfare, and related services varied accordingly.

Surveys conducted by the Food and Nutrition Research Institute of the Philippines in the mid-1970s found that the average Filipino diet lacked sufficient nutrients, such as calories, protein, vitamin A, thiamine, riboflavin, calcium, iron, and ascorbic acid. Operation Timbang, a program of weighing 5 million preschool children, revealed that 5.8 percent suffered from severe (third-degree) malnutrition, another 24.8 percent from second-degree malnutrition, and 45 percent from mild undernourishment. Pregnant and nursing mothers were also found to be malnourished in many instances. Statistics from the government-run Disease Intelligence Center showed that "of the 10 leading causes of death among infants, eight are due to various infections and nutritional deficiencies like avitaminosis." The Food and Nutrition Research Institute of the Philippines has estimated that up to 40 percent of all deaths in recent years have been caused by malnutrition.

In recognition of the seriousness of this situation, the administration in 1981 inaugurated the National Livelihood Program (KKK) under the aegis of the Ministry of Human Settlements, which is headed by Imelda Marcos.

The government has also initiated a massive campaign to improve nutrition in the Philippines. It has built "nutri-huts" staffed by paramedics, produced and distributed millions of "nutri-pak" food supplements, and advertised good nutrition through the use of "nutri-buses" that traveled throughout the nation. As of 1979, according to the Asian Development Bank, average daily caloric intake had risen from 1,671 in 1974 to 1,804. Although this was still well below the United Nation's 2,210-calorie minimum daily requirement, it placed the Philippines eighth out of 25 Asian countries on the nutrition scale, up from last in the mid-1970s. Imelda Marcos was quoted in 1982 as saying that the Philippines had overcome the "protein gap."

Another health problem concerns the dearth of doctors, nurses, and medical facilities, especially in rural areas, a state of affairs owing not only to doctors' preferences for urban living but also to the "brain drain" of medical personnel to the United States. The World Health Organization's Primary Health Care project in the western Pacific reported in the late 1970s that 73 percent of the Philippine people do not benefit from doctors, that the average doctor-population ratio is one to 3,222, and that only 3 percent of the 15,000 doctors in the Philippines are involved in public health.

In an effort to make medical care more easily available to its people, the government has implemented a program of training hundreds of "village-chosen health workers," or paramedics, who will provide not only basic, low-level health care but also information on disease control and sanitation. As of 1981 there were 4,555 *barangay* health stations and 1,991 rural health units serving municipalities and settlement areas. Staffed by these paramedics, they sought to bridge the gap between urban services (about one-third of all physicians in the country lived in Manila) and rural needs. The government has also supported the training of thousands of midwives in an effort to help alleviate the serious shortage of trained medical personnel in rural areas of the country. Through the Ministry of Health, it operated 353 hospitals with 32,255 hospital beds, an increase of 69 percent over the number of hospitals in 1974.

The government's active involvement in improving health and welfare services and hence living standards represents a principal part of its commitment to establishing what it had termed in the past a New Society. But until the trend toward uncontrolled urbanization is reversed by diminishing the gap between urban and rural health, sanitation, nutrition, education, and employment conditions—that is, until living conditions in the *barangay* are greatly improved—the establishment of the New Society will remain more a declaration of objectives than a statement of reality in the Philippines.

* * *

In recent years there have been a number of excellent new accounts of the Philippine people and their society. *The Philippines: A Singular and a Plural Place*, by David Joel Steinberg, is a good starting place, full of insights as well as information. Eric S. Casino's *The Philippines: Land and Peoples, A Cultural Geography* is an important companion volume to *The Filipino Nation: A Concise History of the Philippines*, by Helen R. Tubangui et al. More specifically on Philippine society and culture is Mary Racelis Hollnsteiner's collection of articles entitled *Society, Culture, and the Filipino* in three volumes. One might also consult Gilda Cordero-Fernando's *Being Filipino* and *Rediscovery: Essays in Philippine Life and Culture*, edited by Cynthia Nograles Lumbera and Teresita Gimenez-Maceda. *The People and Art of the Philippines*, written by Gabriel Casal et al., was published in 1981. The best travel guide, which is full of social and cultural information, is *Philippines*, by Hans Johannes Hoefer et al. For much more in-depth research on Philippine society and the environment, there are a number of indispensable research guides: *Philippine Studies: Geography, Archaeology, Psychology, and Literature: Present Knowledge and Research Trends*, by Frederick Wernstedt et al.; *Philippine Studies: History, Sociology, Mass Media, and Bibliography*, edited by Donn

V. Hart; and Kit Machado, Richard Hooley, and Lawrence Reid, *Philippine Studies: Political Science, Economics, and Linguistics*.

For information on the physical setting of the Philippines, the central work is still Frederick L. Wernstedt and J.E. Spencer's *The Philippine Island World: A Physical, Cultural, and Regional Geography*. A number of excellent studies have been written over the last few years pertaining to ethnicity, regionalism, and language. Among the best are Andrew B. Gonzalez' *Language and Nationalism: The Philippine Experience Thus Far*, Renato Rosaldo's *Ilongot Headhunting: A Study in Society and History*, and Peter G. Gowing's *Muslim Filipinos: Heritage and Horizon*. Concerning Philippine values and their social system, see Emma Porio, Mary Racelis Hollnsteiner, and Frank Lynch's *The Filipino Family, Community, and Nation*, Robert J. Morais' *Social Relations in a Philippine Town*, and Irene Ortigas and Felix Regalado's *Society and Culture in the Rural Philippines*. (For further information and complete citations, see Bibliography.)

Chapter 3. The Economy

Modern hi-rise buildings of Makati business district overlook residential area of Manila.

HAVING A PER CAPITA gross national product equivalent to US$792 in 1982, the Philippines was one of the lower middle-income developing economies of the world. Although industrial and service enterpises contributed the lion's share of production, a disproportionately large share of the labor force was in the agricultural sector, which remained the foundation of the economy. Over a third of all manufacturing production was based on the processing of food and other agricultural commodities, especially rice, corn, and coconuts. Small farms and enterprises predominated, but there were several large mining and manufacturing conglomerates. Most enterprises were owned by private individuals, and in general the economy was open to free enterprise and trade.

During the 1970-81 period the economy grew more rapidly than the average of other countries in the same income category. The average return on new investment, however, was extremely low compared with that achieved by economies growing as quickly from a similar resource base. Given the general underemployment of labor in the Philippines and the mounting foreign debt, this level of inefficiency could not be permitted to continue in the 1980s without serious repercussions. The principal culprit was manufacturing, which failed to expand as rapidly as the government had planned.

The most intractable problems facing the economy in the early 1980s concerned the distribution of wealth, which was a source of popular unrest. Wealth was concentrated among owners and managers of a relatively few well-organized and productive enterprises and landholdings, while the majority of the work force was engaged in small-scale business and farming. Although the quality of life has improved for most people, the incomes of over 40 percent of the population continued to be at or below the margin of subsistence. Some regions of the country were substantially poorer than others—particularly areas in the Visayan Islands and on Mindanao.

The economy also lacked some key resources. Although the country had plentiful nonenergy mineral resources and the potential to develop substantial hydroelectric and geothermal capacities, it depended heavily on imported oil. Labor was the most abundant resource, but the exodus of skilled workers overseas—though contributing to foreign exchange earnings—created bottlenecks at home. Above all, the economy was short of capital and had to borrow heavily from abroad.

The government's strategy to remedy these problems, launched in the early 1980s, entailed a complete reform of its fiscal, monetary, and trade policies to foster efficiency and competition, to increase manufactured exports, and to promote small-scale, labor-intensive, and regionally dispersed industries. Although by no means promising the formation of a welfare state, President Ferdinand E. Marcos has also emphasized expenditures on education, health, and other social services and devoted a large share of public funds to infrastructure development. By implementing land reform, at least on rice and corn farms, the government was ameliorating some of the inequalities in rural areas. A comprehensive energy program for the 1980s was intended to reduce the dependence on foreign oil.

The worldwide recession of the early 1980s jeopardized this trade- and market-oriented strategy and caused considerable public dissension. Some businesspeople complained about official waste and corruption, while others clamored for financial assistance. Farmers and consumers placed contradictory demands on the government over the prices of agricultural products. The technocratic prime minister was under fire for bending to the demands of the nation's international creditors that the government tighten its belt and eliminate many subsidies. The 1980s would test the political strength of Marcos as he walked the tightrope between popular unrest at home and international financial insolvency.

Patterns of Development

The economy inherited by the newly independent Republic of the Philippines in 1946 was the legacy of successive colonial administrations that had brought commercial success to only a small elite of absentee landowners and foreign immigrants who resided in Manila and the larger towns. There was a nascent urban middle class of small-scale entrepreneurs, civil servants, and skilled workers, but the overwhelming majority of the population formed an impoverished group of smallholder, tenant, and landless farmers. Working small plots of land, these farmers grew rice and corn for subsistence and various cash crops for sale to the urban traders and exporters. After World War II, which disrupted domestic commerce and destroyed the industry centered in Manila, the government was required not only to rehabilitate the preexisting economy but also to build modern and equitable linkages between the diffuse and undeveloped rural sector and the more dynamic urban commercial sector.

During the last half-century of colonial rule, the principal stimulus for economic modernization was United States investment. Although the free-trade regime enforced in commerce led to the development of industries processing minerals, timber, sugar, and abaca (a kind of hemp) for export, American sources provided most of the capital investment and absorbed much of the income. There was little incentive to develop local manufacturing to compete with American products that entered the economy duty-free. As a result, popular preoccupation with the colonialist aspects of the postwar relationship with the United States demanded that economic nationalism find at least rhetorical expression in government policy.

United States aid sustained the economy in the immediate postwar period, although total reconstruction assistance was less than one-tenth of wartime property damages as estimated by the Philippine government. Persistent budgetary and balance of payments deficits, however, produced financial chaos in 1949, and the government responded by setting up import and foreign exchange controls. Together with other incentives for "new and necessary" industries, these measures inaugurated an industrialization strategy based on the substitution of domestic manufactures for imported consumer goods.

Import substitution motivated the rapid expansion of industry, especially in the 1950s and 1960s. Between 1950 and 1956 manufacturing value added (see Glossary) grew by nearly 13 percent per year on average. By the end of the 1950s, this growth rate slowed by about one-half because of inefficiencies in production and limited demand. Domestic industry, moreover, remained overwhelmingly dependent on imports of capital goods and raw materials from the United States, the high cost of which caused intermittent balance of payments crises.

In 1962 the government abandoned import and foreign exchange controls in favor of free-market trade mechanisms and enacted a major devaluation of the currency. It left in place, however, extremely high tariff barriers for most industrial imports, continuing the process of import substitution. As a result, although industry—including mining, manufacturing, construction, and utilities—had expanded to produce 23 percent of the gross domestic product (GDP—see Glossary) in 1960, the growth rate was only 5.6 percent per year from 1960 to 1971 (see table 2; table 3, Appendix).

The industrial bias of the import substitution strategy left the agricultural sector to develop basically as it had during the colonial period and to carry the burden of paying for imports. With the major exception of sugar, however, productivity declined during the 1950s, and food crop production barely kept pace with the growth of the population. The situation was especially grim for tenant farmers, who constituted some 40 percent of all farmers in 1960. Plagued by small farm size, a lack of credit, and high rental payments, the nation's farmers were able to increase the average product per farm-worker by less than 2 percent per year.

The expansion of the area under cultivation, which was the principal source of agricultural growth in the 1950s, decelerated in the next decade, and the government became increasingly aware of the need to improve productivity. The development and introduction of high-yielding varieties of rice seed in the mid-1960s boosted productivity, particularly in well-irrigated Central Luzon Region. Even in this favorable environment, however, the 5-percent increase in yield was less than one-twentieth of that achieved experimentally under optimal cropping conditions. The scarcity of knowledge concerning appropriate cropping patterns and the requirement for expensive chemical fertilizers and pesticides hampered the modernization efforts of the government. By 1971 some 50 percent of the working population was employed in agriculture, forestry, and fishing activities—down from

61 percent in 1960—and the value added per worker had increased by just under 3 percent annually from 1960 to 1971.

In the late 1960s the government of President Marcos concluded that the import substitution strategy had failed to create enough new jobs in industry to absorb the large numbers of rural inhabitants who were migrating to Manila and the major cities, agriculture having failed to absorb the additional labor force. More and more people were turning to employment in the less productive services sector and to casual labor that offered only meager remuneration. Officially reported unemployment fluctuated between 5 and 10 percent during the 1950-70 period. Underemployment, however, taking into account the number of workers employed in marginal pursuits, may have affected as much as one-fourth of the population.

To redress this situation, the nation's economic planners altered their strategy. Following advice from the World Bank (see Glossary) and other aid donors, the government decided to promote the labor-intensive export industries that had proved so successful in other Southeast Asian countries. Especially after the imposition of martial law in 1972, this strategy became a part of Marcos' plans for the New Society (see President Marcos and Martial Law, ch. 1). Along with this went a major effort to ameliorate urban and rural poverty through expenditures on public works and agrarian reforms.

The steep devaluation of the currency in 1970, followed by the elimination of tariffs on selected raw materials imports and other incentives, stimulated the rapid growth of manufactured exports throughout the 1970s and into the next decade. Exports of garments, electronic components, handicrafts, and other labor-intensive items increased by about 27 percent per year from 1972 to 1981 (see Trade Patterns, this ch.). The manufacturing sector expanded by 6.8 percent per year from 1971 to 1981 and industry as a whole by 7.3 percent per annum. Industrial employment grew by about 4 percent per year from 1970 to 1978—about twice the rate of the 1960s. By 1980 the World Bank estimated that 17 percent of the labor force could be classified as industrial, compared with 15 percent in 1960.

Agriculture progressed during the 1970s as the introduction of new farm technologies spread and the government implemented a land reform program. Value added from the agricultural sector expanded by about 5 percent per year from 1972 to 1981, and the nation began exporting a small rice surplus in 1977. The increased use of better varieties of rice and fertilizers was responsible for most of the gains in production. Some stimulus to productivity may also have resulted from the transfer of land ownership to some 370,000 grain farmers who had been tenants. Continued population pressure in the rural areas, however, prevented the average value added per worker from rising more than 1 percent per year. By 1980 some 46 percent of the labor force was estimated to be in the agricultural sector.

The overall performance of the economy in the 1970s was respectable if unspectacular. The nation's gross national product (GNP—see Glossary) grew by about 6.2 percent per year from 1971 to 1980—about 1 percent higher than in the 1960s and twice the rate of population growth (see fig. 4). This performance wás better than the average for most developing countries but disappointing in view of the nation's substantial natural and human resources. Unemployment and poverty continued to plague a large portion of the populace. The recorded unemployment rate was only 5 percent at the end of the 1970s, but there was no evidence to suggest that the problem of underemployment had diminished. In fact, the real wages of unskilled day laborers in Manila declined by some 7 percent per year compared with the consumer price index, indicating that the urban labor market was overcrowded. The fact that 37 percent of the labor force was relegated to the services sector in 1980, compared with only 24 percent in 1960, also showed that the opportunities for productive labor were negligible.

External economic developments caused considerable problems for the economy in the 1970s. Chief among these were the sudden increases in the international price of petroleum in 1973 and 1979, each round of increases importing inflation into the Philippine economy. When the international prices of the nation's own exports were favorable, as during the 1971-73 period, the effect of the increased import costs on the balance of payments and price level was muted. After 1973, however, the prices of the primary export commodities—sugar, coconut oil, copper, and timber—generally declined, except for a brief reprieve at the turn of the decade.

Constraining forces from outside the economy intensified in the early 1980s because of the worldwide recession and skyrocketing international interest rates. Since 1973 the Philippines has relied on foreign loans to raise the level of fixed investment and to cover the chronic current account deficits, and by 1982 the total outstanding medium- and long-term debt owed to foreign lenders reached the equivalent of US$13 billion. Because of rising interest rates and poor export prices, the payments needed to service this debt alone took up one-fourth of all export earnings.

To reduce this debt burden, the government embarked on a structural adjustment program in 1980, supported by loans from the World Bank. The program sought to liberalize further foreign trade and to restructure investments and production in some 14 manufacturing industries. The government also borrowed heavily from the International Monetary Fund (IMF—see Glossary) to support the balance of payments in the short term. The IMF, however, has been generally less tolerant than the World Bank of large budget deficits and has set strict conditions on its loans, causing some consternation among the government's economic planners (see Capital Flows, this ch.).

The IMF was especially critical of the government's increasing involvement in corporate bailouts and takeovers in the private sector. Especially in the aftermath of a major financial scandal in 1981 involving an industrialist who defaulted on a large number of unsecured debts, the government has earmarked special funds to assist ailing enterprises.

117

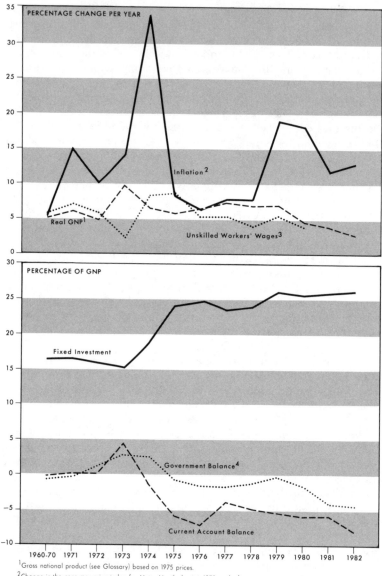

PERCENTAGE CHANGE PER YEAR

Inflation[2]

Real GNP[1]

Unskilled Workers' Wages[3]

PERCENTAGE OF GNP

Fixed Investment

Government Balance[4]

Current Account Balance

[1] Gross national product (see Glossary) based on 1975 prices.

[2] Change in the consumer price index for Metro Manila, having 1972 as the base year.

[3] Change in the index for average daily wages of unskilled workers in the Manila area and suburbs, having 1972 as the base year. Data not available after 1980.

[4] Consolidated accounts of central and local governments and some, but not all, government-owned enterprises.

Source: Based on information from *International Financial Statistics Yearbook, 1982,* Washington, 1982, 372-75; "Philippines," *International Financial Statistics,* 36, No. 3, August 1983, 348-49; and "Philippines: Stand-By Arrangement and Compensatory Financing Facility," *IMF Survey,* 12, No. 5, March 7, 1983, 72.

Figure 4. Major Economic Indicators, 1960-82

The continuing recession, however, has made these funds inadequate, and some government-owned banks have converted much of the overdue debt into government-owned stock in the debtor companies (see Banking and Finance, this ch.).

Prime Minister and Finance Minister Cesar Virata has criticized the conditions imposed by the IMF and other lenders. Virata sees the problems as brought on either by uncontrollable external events or by structural deficiencies that can only be remedied in the long run. In the interim, the government contends, economic aid and loans to the Philippines must be free-flowing to enable the country to meet its long-term objectives. The latter include exploiting agriculture for food, exports, and energy supplies; developing labor-intensive industry and selected capital-intensive industries based on domestic supplies of raw materials; improving the transportation and communications infrastructure, particularly in rural areas; reducing the reliance on imported energy; and increasing domestic savings by reforming the financial system.

Although the government has committed itself to an economic development strategy for the 1980s that favors private enterprise, free trade, and market-determined pricing mechanisms, it was sensitive to criticisms from at least four distinct interest groups: first, avowedly nationalistic business interests—some connected to the president himself—that lobbied for special government support and protection; second, vocal and sometimes violent opposition groups that clamored for far-reaching land reform, better wages and working conditions, labor union freedoms, diminished foreign intervention, and regional autonomy; third, business groups that supported the government's expressed policies but wished to ensure that they were cleanly and equitably implemented; and finally, foreign interests on which the economy depended for long-term finance, investment, and technological assistance.

Critics of the government's economic policies included both supporters and opponents of Marcos. Almost everyone agreed that corruption at all levels of government has sometimes jeopardized the most well-intentioned government projects and programs. Particularly irksome to some members of the business community was the government rescue of failing enterprises on the basis of personal favoritism rather than economic rationalism. Other businesspeople criticized the lack of local participation in economic decisionmaking, the inequitable distribution of wealth by region and class, the limited scope of the current land reform, and the weak competitive position of export industry. Opponents of Marcos argued that the nation's business elite and the government have conspired with foreign interests, spearheaded by the IMF and World Bank, to exploit the nation's natural resources and cheap supply of capable labor. There were probably many nonrevolutionary businesspeople who agreed with the opposition forces that the antiprotectionist strategy of the government was causing unnecessary hardship for the domestic economy. Addressing these criticisms and placating the many powerful interest groups while improving the lot of the average citizen was the formidable task of the government in the critical decade of the 1980s.

Labor and Income

The "equitable distribution of the fruits of development" is a major goal of Philippine public policy, but progress toward this objective has been slow. Estimates of combined unemployment and underemployment run as high as one-third of the labor force, and the proportion of all households living in absolute poverty may be as much as 45 percent. Ever mindful of these stark realities, the government has initiated a number of programs to generate employment opportunities, ensure job security and safety, and subsidize the cost of living for low-income groups. In general, however, it followed the "trickle-down" theory of development, believing that employment would develop primarily through the expansion of private investment and profits. Wages were low, reflecting the abundance of labor. The deterioration of the employment and income situation in the early 1980s has caused considerable dissatisfaction, and organized labor groups have challenged the wisdom of government strategy. The unorganized majority of the labor force, however, has had little recourse but to bear the brunt of continued poverty.

Employment and Labor Relations

Generating sufficient employment for the rapidly expanding labor force of some 19 million persons in 1983 was the single most important economic task. The working-age population was growing by about 3.1 percent annually during the early 1980s—about 0.6 percent faster than the population growth rate—as the children of the 1960s population boom matured. Also, because the proportion of female job seekers was increasing, the government expected the labor force to expand by some 3.7 percent per year during the 1980-87 period. Just to keep unemployment at the 5-percent rate recorded during the early 1980s, some 700,000 additional jobs would be required each year, and the GDP would have to grow by 6 or 7 percent yearly.

A recession in the 1980-82 period made this goal all the more difficult to attain and cast doubt on the official unemployment statistics. Given the sharp downturn in economic growth rates, it seemed unlikely that unemployment had not grown, despite official data to the contrary. Unofficial estimates ran as high as 9 percent. Statistics on the labor force have been deficient for a number of purely technical reasons, and it was practically impossible to be accurate about the levels of employment.

Moreover, government unemployment statistics do not count the so-called underemployed, who, according to two Filipino scholars, comprised 10.7 percent of the labor force in the 1976-78 period. The same researchers noted that another 8.2 percent of the work force were full-time laborers seeking additional work. Both of these rates were sharply higher than similar rates estimated for the early 1970s, and it was unlikely that they had improved by 1983.

Metro Manila (see Glossary) had a much higher unemployment rate than the rest of the country. In the fourth quarter of 1981, for example, the government calculated that 12.9 percent of the labor force in this region was unemployed. Some 70 or 80 percent of all industrial employment was located in the area, and the high level of unemployment reflected the poor performance of the factory sector during the recession.

A detailed breakdown of employment by economic activity was unavailable beyond the fourth quarter of 1978, when 16.7 million persons were employed. Some 52 percent of this total were engaged in agriculture, forestry, and fishing activities; about 0.4 percent in mining; 11.5 percent in manufacturing; 0.2 percent in utilities; 2.9 percent in construction; 10.5 percent in commerce; 4.1 percent in transportation, commmunications, and storage; and the remainder in other services and unreported industries.

Although the tentativeness of the data cannot be overemphasized, statistics suggest that during the 1970s only in the agriculture, forestry, and fishing and the services sector—which included government, domestic, and other services—did employment growth equal or exceed the growth of production. This shows that production in those sectors was relatively labor intensive but not necessarily remunerative. By contrast to the performance of the 1960s, however, the manufacturing and mining industries had become somewhat more labor intensive, while the construction, commerce, and transportation sectors had become dramatically less so. The changes in the latter indicated the increasing use of capital and sophisticated technologies.

One response of the government to these employment problems has been to encourage within limits the export of skilled Filipino laborers, about 70 percent of whom were sent to the Middle East. The Ministry of Labor and Employment (MOLE) created the Philippine Overseas Employment Administration in 1982 to consolidate the functions of three separate government agencies that processed applicants for overseas work. In 1981 government agencies hired some 26,800 workers on the basis of direct government-to-government negotiations, recruited 15,200 workers through local employment agencies, and found placement for 55,300 seamen. The bulk of recruitment—200,400 workers—came from private agencies.

Overall, for the January 1975 to mid-1981 period some 823,000 workers were contracted for overseas employment: some 42 percent were production, transportation, and construction workers; 31 percent were seamen; service and professional/technical staff accounted for about 11 percent each; while the rest were clerical, managerial, sales, or agricultural workers. In 1980 the MOLE boasted that 1.7 million Filipinos were employed overseas in more than 100 countries, and the plans for the 1983-87 period were to process 300,000 contracts a year. The worldwide recession and declining oil prices, however, threatened the program in 1982 and 1983 and limited the value of remittances received by the economy (see Trade Patterns, this ch.).

One unaccounted cost of the overseas employment program was the loss of skilled and technical laborers to domestic construction, utilities, and manufacturing firms. In September 1982 the government issued a controversial directive requiring all recruitment agencies to get clearances from an applicant's present employer before allowing the worker to go abroad, a measure that labor groups denounced as unconstitutional. The MOLE also found it necessary to take steps against recruitment fraud and the reported harsh treatment of some Filipino seamen.

Apart from this unique recruitment system for overseas labor, the purpose of government policy has been to encourage industrial expansion, particularly in those sectors that could employ the nation's competitively priced labor. Although the government has set minimum wages since 1970, the increase for the entire 1972-81 period was less than 3 percent for the highest and less than 2 percent for the lowest minimum-wage category, after accounting for consumer-price inflation. The government has exempted export-oriented and labor-intensive industries from many of the minimum-wage provisions, and some 60 percent of the employed work force were self-employed or unpaid family workers beyond the pale of any regulation. The inflation-adjusted wage rates of both skilled and unskilled laborers in Metro Manila declined dramatically during the 1970s (see Income Distribution and Living Conditions, this ch.).

Nonetheless, the setting of minimum wages was the focus of national attention, and the National Wage Council, made up of MOLE, labor, and industry representatives, was directly attached to the Office of the President. Presidential decrees set the wage rates depending on the size, location, and activity of economic enterprises. Since 1972, decrees have established a cost-of-living allowance, a thirteenth-month pay bonus, and an employees compensation fund, in addition to annual pay increases for all wages subject to government supervision.

The government's control over wages suited its policy of "tripartism," which placed it in a mediating position between labor and industry. After the declaration of martial law in 1972, the government began to control the union movement, which it thought to be dangerously disorganized. The government outlawed strikes in "vital" industries—virtually any it chose—and announced its intention to reorganize the movement. The government reduced the number of unions and supported the expansion of a moderate labor federation, the Trade Union Congress of the Philippines (TUCP), which claimed a membership of 1.3 million out of 2.3 million organized workers in 1982. Unionized workers, however, represented only one-quarter of the nonagricultural labor force. The ultimate objective of the government was to have one labor organization for each industry to conduct collective bargaining on an industrywide basis. The major forums for wage settlements since 1975 have been nationwide tripartite conferences held two or three times a year with participants from the TUCP, other unions, the MOLE, and employers' associations.

After the termination of martial law in early 1981, the government responded to growing public pressure to eliminate the ban on strikes. The revision of the 1974 Labor Code in August 1981 permitted strikes and lockouts to be declared when collective bargaining became deadlocked or in protest of unfair labor practices. Both instances, however, required prior notification to the government, and the MOLE retained the right to transfer cases affecting the "national interest" to the National Labor Relations Commission for compulsory arbitration. A sharp increase in the number of strikes during 1981 and the first five months of 1982 prompted further legislation to clarify the amended labor code. In June the legislature declared labor disputes in public utilities, power corporations, banks, hospitals, and export-oriented industries to be in the "national interest" and under the discretionary control of the MOLE, which could force laborers back to work and into compulsory arbitration.

Regardless of the government's back-stepping to control the outbreak of labor unrest in the post-martial law period, debilitating strikes continued into 1983. In the relatively unrestrained atmosphere of 1981 there were 260 strikes involving 98,585 workers and the loss of some 1.8 million worker-hours. According to the government the incidence of strikes decreased by 40 percent in 1982 but because of their prolonged duration resulted in roughly twice the number of lost worker-hours. Most strikes were declared because employers failed to comply with minimum wages or other government-mandated labor standards. Often, in fact, the unions were posturing for increased wage settlements, a procedure that was illegal. Many employers have found that they could force arbitrations and successfully argue for exemptions to government regulations on the basis of economic duress. Some strikes had political overtones and led to confrontations with the police and security forces (see Other Dissident Actors, ch. 5).

Income Distribution and Living Conditions

Information concerning the distribution of income or other assets is the hardest to obtain and the least reliable economic data for most countries, and the Philippines is no exception. In mid-1983, however, the available data and popular perceptions left little doubt that incomes were highly skewed toward a wealthy elite. A 1982 World Bank publication reported that in the 1970-71 period the wealthiest quintile of all the nation's households earned 54 percent of the total income generated in the economy, while the bottom 40 percent received only 14.2 percent of the total. Despite government attempts to redress the situation, official statistics for the third quarter of 1980 showed that the top quintile had increased its share to 59.2 percent, while the bottom 40 percent had risen to only 14.6 percent.

Household income surveys—last conducted in 1975—have provided the raw data for the only detailed estimates of Philippine poverty. The

World Bank staff has conducted the most thorough and sensitive analysis of these data, calculating separate rural and urban poverty lines based on assumptions about the per person costs of meeting a household's basic needs. The study found that the incidence of poverty increased from 38 percent of all households in 1971 to 45 percent in 1975. The most dramatic increase occurred in urban areas, where the percentage of poor households in the total rose from 24 to 40 percent in just four years. Rural poverty, however, remained more severe than urban poverty—some 48 percent of all rural households in 1975 compared with 41 percent in 1971 (see fig. 5).

The World Bank report conjectured that conditions improved in the late 1970s because of an increase in food production. Data showing that real wages in the Manila area dropped by more than 12 percent for skilled workers and by nearly 27 percent for unskilled workers from 1975 to 1980, however, suggested a deterioration. A University of the Philippines study conducted in 1980 in Metro Manila determined that 76 percent of all household heads earned less than the P1,500 (for value of the peso—see Glossary) of monthly income needed to maintain the average family of six persons. Household income surveys demonstrated that although the average incomes may have risen, the median incomes have decreased, suggesting a larger percentage of poor households in 1980 than in 1975.

Earnings data for the fourth quarter of 1978, based on individual rather than household income, suggested that agricultural and service-workers continued to be the poorest. There were perhaps 4 million poor households—some 1.5 million in lowland rice farming, 1 million in upland farming, 550,000 in wage-labor agriculture, 300,000 in coastal fishing, and 600,000 in urban services.

The overwhelming regional income gap was between Metro Manila and the rest of the country. In 1980 the average household income for this area was three times the average for other areas. Metro Manila and adjacent Southern Tagalog Region together accounted for about 46 percent of GDP, compared with their 22 percent share of the population. Four other regions—Central Luzon, Western Visayas, Central Visayas, and Southern Mindanao—producing 30 percent of GDP and representing 34 percent of the total population, formed a middle-income category. The remaining seven regions were the poorest. The incidence of poverty within the regions varied enormously from the worst case of Northern Mindanao Region to the best case in Central Luzon Region.

In 1978 the government established what became the Ministry of Human Settlements—the bailiwick of the president's powerful wife, Imelda Romualdez Marcos—to coordinate government programs to reduce poverty. The ministry itself provided low-cost housing services through its subsidiaries. One of its efforts dealt with slum improvement in Metro Manila, of which Imelda Marcos was also governor, and in other urban areas. Almost all Philippine cities have large squatter and slum areas housing between 20 and 35 percent of the population. By

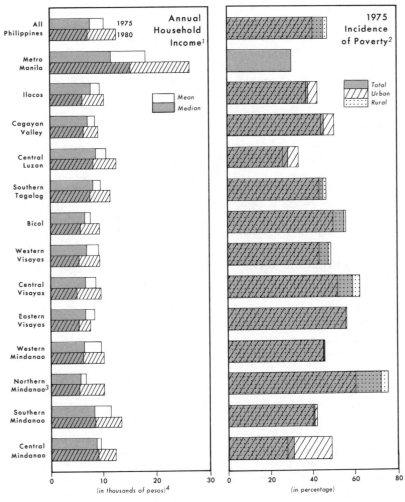

[1]Average household income expressed in 1980 prices as adjusted by regional consumer price indexes; not adjusted for number of persons per household, which is about six people. The data for 1980 are based upon a survey for the third quarter of that year.

[2]Percentage of all households falling below separate urban and rural poverty lines estimated by the World Bank (see Glossary), calculated on a per capita basis. Figures are likely to be biased upward because of the miscalculation of low-income household expenditures. Similar data were unavailable for 1980, but attempts to adjust the poverty lines to 1980 suggested that the incidence of poverty had increased for all regions.

[3]Excluding Bukidnon Province, which was not surveyed.   [4]For value of the peso-see Glossary.

Source: Based on information from Philippines, National Economic and Development Authority, National Census and Statistics Office, *Philippine Statistical Yearbook, 1981*, Manila, 1981, 92-107; and Philip Bowring, "The Poverty Puzzle," *Far Eastern Economic Review*, Hong Kong, March 27, 1981, 126.

Figure 5. Annual Household Income, 1975 and 1980, and Incidence of Poverty, by Region, 1975

1983 improvement projects were in progress at five sites in Metro Manila and in the cities of Baguio, Cebu, Bacolod, Cagayan de Oro, Iloilo, and Davao. Although preferred by residents to earlier efforts that literally destroyed their neighborhoods, the Ministry of Human Settlements programs have continued to encounter resistance from slum dwellers and have suffered contract delays, cost overruns, and delinquent repayments from the beneficiaries. Many of the beneficiaries, moreover, have been middle-income rather than low-income families.

The most publicized campaign to combat poverty and unemployment in the post-martial law period was the National Livelihood Program (KKK—see Glossary), launched by the Ministry of Human Settlements in 1981. Its purpose was to provide groups of five or more individuals with cheap, unsecured loans to set up crop and livestock farming, forestry, fishing, warehousing, and marketing enterprises in the countryside and in regional towns and cities. As of January 1983 some 200,000 individuals had received a total of P900 million out of a planned fund of 9 billion to be expended by 1988. Early criticism of the lending program centered on the large amount of paperwork required of the largely ill-educated applicants, widespread graft, and poor repayment records. A reform of the program in December 1982 decentralized accounting procedures to the local authorities, established a special fund for provincial and municipal government heads having a good management record, and allowed the local managers to retain the repaid interest for relending.

The National Economic and Development Authority (NEDA) has urged government ministries, agencies, and corporations to consider the regional distribution of their expenditure programs (see Government Planning and Policy, this ch.). As a result, the per capita expenditures on economic infrastructure, such as transportation, communications, irrigation, and power facilities, have risen appreciably in the middle- and low-income regions and have accelerated the pace of economic growth in these areas since the late 1970s. The government paid particularly close attention to the development of Mindanao, where Muslim insurgents have been fighting for autonomy. The average annual growth of the per capita GDP on Mindanao during the 1972-80 period, however, was just shy of the national average.

Marcos stated publicly to a visiting military delegation in December 1982 that he opposed the creation of a "welfare state" in the Philippines because it would be too costly, undermine the work ethic, and lead to corruption. Nevertheless, in most of his speeches the president has been committed to the promotion of the general welfare and sensitive to public concern and unrest over the plight of the poor. Although limited in scope, numerous public welfare programs—including land reform, nutrition and health, subsidies on basic commodities, social security, and primary education—have appreciably improved the overall living standards of even the poorest groups (see Health and Living Standards, ch. 2).

Private and Public Enterprise

Marcos reiterated his commitment to private ownership and control of the economy in November 1982, stating that the overall thrust of government policy was "to strengthen the hand of the private sector and the [sic] private enterprise in the total national development effort." The government reserved the right, however, to regulate business and to set up public enterprises where private initiative was lacking. Certain policies and projects have caused dissension within the business community. Controversy typically resulted from alleged political favoritism and the encroachment of some public enterprises and agencies on private entrepreneurial activity. The dire need for corporate financing, moreover, intensified the competition for bank credit and placed small-scale businesses at a disadvantage. Many businesspeople were also alarmed at government policies that opened the economy to foreign competitors. The more important members of the business community, however, appeared united in their reluctance to share their wealth with broader segments of the population.

Ownership and Management

The popular perception that some 90 families owned controlling shares of the country's most important economic enterprises persisted into 1983. The most important of the 45,000 or so corporations and partnerships in existence in 1982 were formed by a small number of individuals, often related, and only 200 firms were listed on the two stock exchanges. In 1978 there were 6,000 closely held stock corporations, having five or fewer stockholders in possession of more than 50 percent of the total equity. Only 105 had gone public by 1982, despite government encouragement. The legal definition of a public stock corporation, moreover, was quite narrow, merely requiring more than 20 stockholders.

The major corporations were controlled by four groups of business interests: the so-called crony capitalists linked to the Marcos family, domestic entrepreneurs having no clear links to the government, foreign businesses, and government or semigovernment agencies. Of the top 50 corporations (ranked by their 1981 net sales), 11 firms, representing more than 33 percent of the total net sales for all 50 companies, have been linked by opposition political groups to the small elite circle of Marcos' family and friends. Another 22 domestic firms in the top 50 generated some 31 percent of the total net sales; firms controlled by foreign companies numbered 12 and produced some 25 percent of the total sales. The remaining companies were government controlled.

The ethnic Chinese formed a special subset of the Filipino business community. In most years during the 1970s, the registered investments of alien Chinese citizens—including those from single proprietorships and partnerships, as well as corporations—were twice as large as those of alien United States citizens, who formed the second most important category. The popular impression, moreover, was that many more investments went unrecorded and that the ethnic Chinese controlled most wholesale trade and the underground economy of smuggling and moneylending. It was also alleged that they have flourished under the rule of Marcos. Persons of mixed Chinese and Filipino descent, called Chinese mestizo, were considered part of the mainstream business community and even joined the government (see The Chinese, ch. 2).

During the recession of the 1980-82 period, the government sharply increased its presence in the economy. Government agencies—primarily banks—controlled 92 companies having more than 100 subsidiaries in 1981. Many of these had been acquired during the financial crisis of 1981 from private entrepreneurs associated with Marcos (see Banking and Finance, this ch.). Altogether from 1978 to 1981 the government poured P14.3 billion into corporate equity. Some P2 billion of fresh equity in 1981 came from the National Development Company, a government-owned conglomerate set up to manage the reorganization of distressed enterprises taken over by the government and to fund special priority projects (see Manufacturing, this ch.). The value of government corporate equity reached 5 percent of the GNP in 1981, compared with 3 percent in 1978. The government asserted that many of these enterprises would be merged and resold to the private sector as soon as possible.

Private contact between businesspeople and government officials was the major means of communication between the private and public sectors, but there were other, more public forums as well. The Philippines Chamber of Commerce and Industry was the most influential business lobby and sponsored periodic government-business conferences that were attended by Marcos and most of his cabinet. Specific industries also had their own business or employer's associations.

The organization and management of corporations was modeled on United States businesses, reflecting the colonial past and the American education of many of the nation's key businesspeople. The major difference between the two business systems, however, lay in the realm of finance. Philippine firms relied on short-term credit from commercial banks rather than long-term credit from the stock or bond markets, which were poorly developed. According to a Philippine business journal, many managers tended to exhibit a "lack of discipline or credit consciousness," and their "unscrupulous moral make-up" led to high levels of fraud.

Banking and Finance

During the 1970s the financial sector progressed rapidly, spearheaded by increases in the share capital of commercial banks, the development of a money market, the strengthening of Central Bank powers, the creation of specialized investment houses and offshore banks (see Glossary), and the improvement of banking technology. As a result, after the oil shock of 1973 the total assets of the financial system grew at about 11 percent per year in real terms through 1980.

The system received a devastating shock in January 1981, when a textile manufacturer, Dewey Dee, fled the country leaving behind P635 million in unsecured debts. Government financial technocrats, who already had planned a sweeping reform of the system, were able to turn the disaster to their own purposes, however, and implement a program for the 1980s. The reform was supposed to lengthen the maturities for many financial instruments and to narrow the persistent gap between domestic savings and investment.

The premier banking institutions were the commercial banks, including many small private commercial banks, two government-owned banks, and four branch offices of foreign banks (see table 4, Appendix). The 1981 financial crisis forced the government to take over the operations of five private commercial banks. Many of the private banks were small, family-run institutions and often owned by Chinese mestizos. The two largest commercial banks—the government-owned Philippine National Bank (PNB) and Citibank of the United States—accounted for over 20 percent of all financial assets in 1982. The PNB acquired 40 percent of the equity of the nation's largest construction firm in 1983 in return for the cancellation of that company's delinquent debt, which in turn threatened the profitability of the bank.

There were three specialized government banks. Development Bank of the Philippines (DBP) specialized in long-term loans, Land Bank of the Philippines financed the agrarian reform program, and Philippine Amanah Bank provided loans to the Muslim community on Mindanao. The financial position of the DBP was precarious in early 1983 after it had amassed some 87 delinquent accounts, making up half of its assets. The weak accounts included that of the fourth largest firm in the country, Marinduque Mining and Industrial Corporation. The government appointed a talented and respected businessman as chairman of the bank in late 1981 to restore the solvency of the bank.

Savings banks and savings and loan associations extended credit for less than a year or invested in bonds and home mortgages. Private development banks provided modest amounts of credit to small- and medium-sized businesses for longer than a year at a time. Many of these loans were funded indirectly from the DBP, and because the private development banks were located all over the country, they were vehicles for promoting regional development.

The premier nonbank financial institutions were the Government Service Insurance and the Social Security systems. Private insurance agencies invested primarily in government bonds and mortgages, finance companies provided short-term loans to consumers, and investment companies functioned like merchant banks in other countries. Other financial intermediaries included trust companies, mutual building and loan societies, credit unions, and pawnbrokers.

The short-term money market grew especially rapidly in the early 1970s and has dominated interactions in the financial system. So-called deposit substitutes—special certificates and promissory notes issued by investment companies and businesses outside the interest-rate control of the government—caused most of the increase and actually exceeded the value of time and savings deposits in 1975. Government tax measures restrained the growth of deposit substitutes in the late 1970s, and by 1981 they were equivalent to 40 percent of the value of bank deposits.

The long-term capital market, by contrast, remained undeveloped. The Manila Stock Exchange and Makati Stock Exchange traded shares from only 85 of the 270 corporations listed in 1982. Even the active over-the-counter market was sluggish, barely averaging ₱50 million of trading each day. The economic recession, depressed international prices for minerals, and resulting low stock dividends accounted for some of the market's problems, but there seemed also to be a strong structural bias against the market for corporate securities.

In response to the structural weaknesses pointed out in a major World Bank study in 1979, the government embarked on a series of institutional reforms in 1980. Under the reform program, a commercial bank having sufficiently large resources could become a universal bank or "unibank," which was allowed to engage in investment banking. A unibank could own a maximum of 35 percent of the equity of any commercial enterprise, and total equity holdings could not exceed 50 percent of the bank's net worth. To compensate for the increased competition from unibanks, investment houses were permitted to manage trust and foreign exchange operations and could borrow from the Central Bank. Thrift banks and rural banks were allowed to act as full-service domestic banks and could graduate into higher banking categories as their resources grew. The overall purpose of the reform was to stimulate healthy competition in the banking community and to improve the efficiency of all financial institutions through the achievement of greater economies of scale. In conjunction with the institutional reforms, the government also adjusted interest rates and set up new systems of monetary control by the Central Bank (see Monetary Policy and Price Control, this ch.).

After one year under the new system, which was completely implemented only in late 1981 after the shock of the Dewey Dee scandal, five unibanks were in operation, and most banks seemed to be operating profitably. There were complaints from small banks about the new system of preference for large institutions and from borrowers over the general lack of domestic credit. Many foreign banks that had set up offshore banking units in the Philippines, moreover, complained that they were still being excluded from domestic operations (see Capital Flows, this ch.).

Government Planning and Policy

Philippine economic planning is indicative and not at all binding on business. Nonetheless, by employing various fiscal and monetary controls and incentives, the government does have the power to move

Ayala Avenue, main thoroughfare of the Makati business district
Courtesy Tourist Research and Planning

the economy in specified directions. The chief institutions involved in this process of friendly arm-twisting are the various economic ministries, especially the Ministry of Finance, NEDA, the Central Bank, and the Board of Investments (BOI).

The drafting of economic plans is the responsibility of NEDA, whose National Census and Statistics Office is the principal source of economic data. NEDA was founded in 1972 to replace and centralize the planning operations of several previous agencies. Its plans are typically of four or five years in duration, but NEDA monitors their progress annually and modifies its projections according to actual economic circumstances. The development plans for the 1974-77, 1978-82, and 1983-87 periods contained similar objectives, such as the expansion of employment, maximization of growth, equitable distribution of incomes, development of social services and amenities, and achievement of monetary stability.

The 1983-87 economic development plan focused on three broad objectives: sustainable economic growth, equitable income distribution, and development of human resources. The policies designed to meet the first objective involved a change in the interest rates, tariffs, and fiscal incentives to encourage efficient, labor-intensive, and export-oriented industries and to foster competition and the efficient use of energy and other scarce economic resources. The continuation of the

131

agrarian reform program, attention to regional development, and improved delivery of basic social services were intended to achieve the second major goal. Expanded education, health, nutrition, housing, social security, and other social services were also designed to fulfill the third development objective. The GNP growth rate calculated to meet these targets was 6.5 percent per year.

In order to facilitate regional economic development, NEDA has established regional offices to work in conjunction with regional development councils mandated by the government in 1972. It was not until 1978, however, that the councils each had drafted a five-year plan to fit in with the national program, as well as a list of local projects to be considered by the relevant economic ministry or agency. The regional councils, however, lacked any formal budgetary responsibility, and their annual proposals have rarely been incorporated into ministry programs at the national level.

The coordination between economic planning, project selection, and actual implementation, moreover, has been inadequate even at the national level. Although NEDA maintained close contact with the cabinet ministries, there was much jockeying for access to the scarce investment funds. Actual spending seldom achieved NEDA's targets or even the authorizations of the Office of the Budget and Management. Coordination was especially lacking between NEDA and many important public enterprises. Although the sectoral distribution of expenditures did not correspond exactly to the planned allocations, the public expenditure program and other fiscal incentives nonetheless influenced the pattern of economic activity.

Fiscal Policy and Incentives

The economic development plan for the 1978-82 period projected that total national and local government expenditures would average about 21.5 percent of the nation's GNP, excluding the expenditures of public enterprises. Because of insufficient financial resources, however, the actual average was only about 14.5 percent, about 3.5 percentage points higher than in the 1960s. Consolidated public expenditures—including those of public enterprises—rose to approximately 18.5 percent of GNP in 1982 (see table 5, Appendix).

The increase in public expenditures during the 1978-82 period was primarily the result of expanded investments by public enterprises. Central government contributions to public enterprises producing petroleum products and electric power were especially large, increasing from less than 4 percent of all public sector expenditures in 1978 to more than 5 percent in 1982. Equity contributions to distressed enterprises in other industries, channeled through the National Development Company, grew to over 3 percent of the total expenditures in 1981. At the same time, the government provided extensive support to public enterprises in charge of irrigation, water supply, housing, and other infrastructure projects. Because of the poor performance of the government-owned banks, the budget has also allocated significant resources to these institutions.

Determining the sectoral distribution of public expenditures is complicated by the fact that central government data are available only on an obligation basis, i.e., that authorized by the Office of the Budget and Management, and that there is no sectoral breakdown of local government expenditures. Excluding local government expenditures, financial investments, and debt-service payments, during the 1978-82 period the leading categories of expenditure were energy and power (18 percent of the total); transportation (14 percent); defense (13 percent); education (12 percent); agriculture, forestry, and fishing (11 percent); and general administration (10 percent). Some 9 percent of all expenditure went toward housing, community development, health, and other social services; about 4 percent to improving the water supply; and the remainder to various other sectors. Because comparable data were unavailable for earlier periods, few clear trends emerged except for the obvious expansion of expenditures on energy and other utilities. The draft budget for the 1983 fiscal year (FY—see Glossary) displayed no major changes other than a relative decrease in expenditures on energy and an increase in the share allocated to transportation and communications.

One trend that emerged during the 1970s was the rising proportion of capital expenditures in the public sector budget. From less than 15 percent of the value of current expenditures in FY 1972, capital expenditures steadily increased until they equaled current expenditures in FY 1981 before falling slightly in the following year. In 1981 government capital expenditures represented some 38 percent of all investment in the economy. Some critics have argued that the expansion of public sector investment has been at the expense of the maintenance of previous investments, and the FY 1983 and future budgets planned to allow a larger share to be allocated to this purpose.

Despite constant modifications in the tax schedule throughout the late 1970s, the government was unable to achieve its objective of increasing central and local government tax revenues from about 12.5 percent of GNP in the mid-1970s to an average of 14.6 percent of GNP during the 1978-82 period. In fact, because of the recession in 1981, tax revenues barely exceeded 11 percent of GNP. To offset these shortfalls, the government imposed an across-the-board 3-percent ad valorem import duty in early 1983. Reforms of the fiscal incentive and tariff system, however, which were developed to improve economic efficiency, also seemed to be reducing government tax revenues. Corruption and the mismanagement of public funds cost the government some P10 billion each year, according to an estimate by the Manila *Times Journal*, or a sum equivalent to 23 percent of all public sector revenues in 1981.

Public enterprises, moreover, have been unable to generate sufficient funds from their own operations to finance their vastly expanded investment needs. In 1980 the operating surplus of public enterprises was equivalent to only 11 percent of their capital expenditures and had increased only slightly by 1982. The difference had to be financed from government and private banks and added substantially to the public sector deficit. One reason for the poor revenue performance of some corporations has been the government's decision to reduce the charges to consumers of items such as electric power. In effect, the low fees represented subsidies that had to be supported indirectly from government coffers. The government's objective for the 1983-87 period—to revise the charges of government corporations frequently in line with rising investment and operating costs—was not popular within the private business community and the general public (see Utilities and Construction, this ch.).

The public sector deficit rose precipitously from less than 2 percent of GNP in the mid-1970s to well over 4 percent in 1982. Part of the increasing deficit represented the government's attempts to counter the business recession of the early 1980s. By 1983, however, this counter-cyclical policy came under criticism from the nation's international creditors, who financed an important part of the public sector's debt. In response to this pressure, the government announced a "drastic cutback" in expenditures for 1983 and 1984 in order to reduce the overall public sector deficit to 2 percent of GNP and maintain its creditworthiness. The government applied the brakes to fiscal expansion in late 1982, causing some complaints from Imelda Marcos over the slow release of funds for her KKK program. The harsh cure for fiscal overspending was also denounced by many members of the private business community (see Capital Flows, this ch.).

The fiscal incentives system remained an important means of stimulating economic activity in preferred industries. The system became regularized in 1967 after the passage of the Investment Incentives Act and the creation of the BOI and was strengthened under the Export Incentives Act of 1970. The BOI had the power to authorize accelerated depreciation allowances and various other tax measures and legal guarantees to investors, according to an annual plan of priorities. The BOI has effectively controlled competition in both preferred and nonpreferred industries by administering licenses to import machinery and equipment.

During the 1970s about one-third of industrial investment—some 10 percent of all investment in the economy— came under the control of the BOI. The weak performance of manufacturing, however, pointed out several problems with the incentive system. Rather than consider the economy's comparative advantages, the BOI satisfied itself with protecting the market shares of domestic producers. Because most of the incentive measures cheapened the cost of capital relative to labor, they limited the absorption of labor into new enterprises. Registration with the BOI, moreover, involved a massive amount of red tape. Despite efforts to correct some of these biases and inefficiencies, similar problems remained until 1982.

In April 1983 Marcos signed a comprehensive revision of the incentive law, reducing the total number of incentives from 20 to eight and simplifying their administration. The new incentives were based on the actual performance of the applicants, rather than the capacity of the domestic market, and were calculated on the basis of total value added, including labor, in the production process. So-called pioneer industries were to receive extra incentives as in the past, but their number was substantially reduced. New procedures allowed industries not specified in the priorities plan to import capital equipment at will. Together with enhanced incentives for exporters and tariff rate changes, the new program was to move the economy closer to a system of free trade (see Trade Patterns, this ch.). Furthermore, the role of the BOI in industrial planning was to be strengthened, and investment priorities were to be calculated on the basis of the long-run comparative advantages of the economy (see Manufacturing, this ch.).

Monetary Policy and Price Control

The importance of monetary policy in the Philippines was reflected in the career of Cesar Virata, longtime minister of finance and concurrently the prime minister and head of NEDA in mid-1983. Together with the governor of the Central Bank, the main implementing agency of monetary policy, the minister of finance dominated policymaking on the Monetary Board, the architect of monetary policy. The main goals of monetary policy were to promote savings and investment, control inflation, and stabilize the balance of payments. Monetary control consisted of three principal components: regulating the banking system, financing the public debt, and controlling the prices of selected commodities.

During the 1978-82 period domestic savings averaged about 22.5 percent of GNP, virtually unchanged from the early part of the 1970s and about average for an economy having resources similar to the Philippines. The level of investment, however, was typically 5 or 6 percentage points higher, necessitating imports of financial capital. To reduce this resource gap, the government introduced a number of monetary measures at the start of the 1980s to correspond to institutional changes in the banking system (see Banking and Finance, this ch.).

The deregulation of bank deposit and loan interest rates was the major focus of monetary reform. Until July 1, 1981, the Central Bank administered all interest rates except those for commercial paper; thereafter all rates for deposits and for loans maturing after one year were allowed to charge freely according to market conditions. In January 1983 all interest rate ceilings were abolished, and a 90-day prime rate system of market-determined interest rates was initiated. As a result of these measures, interest rates on deposits and loans have risen to a level higher than the rate of inflation for the first time since 1978, providing incentives for savers.

The availability of credit from financial institutions was based primarily on the reserve requirements stipulated by the Central Bank. Until 1982 the reserve requirement for general deposits was 20 percent, meaning that 80 percent of these liabilities could be loaned out to borrowers. In January 1983 the requirement was reduced to 18 percent, and the Central Bank was planning to lower it further to make more credit available to industry. Banks were required to retain only 3 percent of the value of their long-term deposits. Banks could also receive loan funds from special discounting facilities at the Central Bank. The lending rates were set to ensure a profit for the recipient banks in the case of loans for preferred economic activities but carried a substantial penalty if the banks were selling previously contracted loans in order to improve their liquidity.

The Central Bank also conducted open market operations, handling sales of treasury bills, Central Bank Certificates of Indebtedness (CBCI), and other government securities. The CBCI was developed in the aftermath of the Dewey Dee scandal in order to finance advances made to failing investment houses and other institutions (see Banking and Finance, this ch.). Immediately following the financial crisis, the Central Bank assumed greater powers for regulating the money market for commercial paper as well.

The net effect of discounting, open market operations, and changing the reserve requirements was to regulate the supply of money and credit in the economy. From 1978 to 1982 the supply of domestic credit grew at an average of nearly 24 percent per year, while the money supply (see Glossary) expanded at a rate of over 19 percent per year. The rapid expansion of these funds contributed to the annual inflation rate of about 14 percent experienced during this period as measured by the Manila consumer price index. The Central Bank announced its intention of restraining the growth of domestic credit and the money supply to 16.4 percent and 14.4 percent, respectively, during 1983.

Before 1970 authority to control prices was restricted to temporary action in times of emergency. In an effort to curb inflation, however, the government created a national council empowered to prevent hoarding and speculation by fixing the prices of specified commodities. In 1983 its successor, the Price Stabilization Council, controlled the prices of rice, corn grits, milk, sugar, cooking oil, pork, chicken, eggs, canned fish, and school supplies. The producers of many of these commodities, however, have lobbied vigorously for the removal of all controls, and the government was studying the effects of complying with this request. Other agencies regulated the prices of public transportation, utilities, fertilizers, and petroleum products. The fund to control petroleum products was abolished in July 1983 as part of the austerity program to eliminate subsidies.

Agriculture, Forestry, and Fishing

The agricultural sector was the foundation of the traditional economy and remained so for the modernizing economy of the 1980s. Agriculture was the principal source of income and employment and supplied surplus earnings that could be invested elsewhere in the economy. Exports such as coconut products, sugar, pineapples, and timber earned precious foreign exchange. Until the late 1960s, however, the country did little to develop or realize its varied agricultural potential. Since then, efforts to improve agricultural productivity have met with some success, especially in the important food crop sector. Agrarian reform and the expansion of rural finance and extension services, moreover, have partly ameliorated the uneven distribution of wealth that burdened the smallholder and tenant farmers who made up the majority of the rural population.

Although the physical setting of the archipelago defies typification, for the purpose of agriculture, variations in rainfall and topography form some important distinctions. Annual rainfall of from 1,500 to 2,000 millimeters and a distinct, seven-month dry season beginning in October characterize the climate of the Ilocos, Central Luzon, and Western Visayas regions and the western part of Southern Tagalog Region. A second climatic pattern—characterized by the same amount of rainfall but a five-month dry season starting in December—is prevalent in western and northern Mindanao and in the western half of Cagayan Valley Region. Considerably more rainfall, on the order of 2,500 to 4,000 millimeters per year, and a wet season from October to March typify the climate in Southern Mindanao, Bicol, and Eastern Visayas regions. A fourth type of climate, having a short dry period from January through March, a wet season from April to December, and rainfall averaging from 2,000 to 3,500 millimeters each year, is found in the eastern portion of Southern Tagalog Region and in southwestern Mindanao. Temperature variations are slight (see Physical Setting, ch. 2).

The principal topographical distinction is between the lowland and upland areas. The soils of the plains and valleys contain deep, alluvial deposits often mixed with volcanic ash that are amenable to irrigated rice cultivation. The higher ground also has good, loamy soil but has been subject to some erosion from the deterioration of the forest cover. Although there are some notable exceptions, upland areas are generally devoted to rainfed farming and dryland crops.

Land Use and Tenure

The precise pattern of land use was impossible to determine in 1983 because estimates were based on surveys conducted in the 1960s. The country's officially reported 30-million-hectare land area included some 12.7 million hectares of forests, 7.1 million hectares of cultivated croplands, and 7.5 million hectares of so-called plantation uplands. Relative to their share of the total land area, Luzon and the Visayan Islands were more intensively cropped than Mindanao and Palawan. The ratio of plantation upland to cultivated cropland was highest in the Visayan

Islands, where there were 1.3 hectares of the former for every hectare of the latter, and lowest in Palawan, where the latter outnumbered the former by two to one. The upland area was slightly larger than the lowland area on Luzon, and the opposite was the case on Mindanao.

The Food and Agriculture Organization (FAO) estimated that in 1980 the area under temporary crops was about 7.1 million hectares, that under permanent crops 2.9 million hectares, and that under forest cover about 12.3 million hectares. The FAO classified some 6.6 million hectares as other unused agricultural land, over three and a half times the government estimate. The divergent estimates obscure trends in land use over time. Government estimates suggest that the area under crops grew rapidly during the 1970s by about 4.5 percent per year, while the FAO projections show the average growth to be barely positive, most of the expansion occurring in the upland areas. Government data on the total area harvested, which also include areas that are double-cropped, are more complete and systematic than land use estimates. The area harvested expanded by 2.8 percent per year from 1969 to 1980, the most rapid increases occurring for coconuts, root crops, and other chiefly upland crops. In general, there seemed to be little room for the extensive development of new farmlands in the 1980s, except on Mindanao and Palawan.

As of mid-1983 there had been no agricultural census since 1971. According to the census, the average farm size was 2.7 hectares for rice and 2.9 hectares for corn—the two principal food crops. The largest farms were concentrated in commercial agriculture; about 80 percent of sugarcane, 89 percent of livestock and poultry, 44 percent of abaca, and 42 percent of coconut farms were larger than 10 hectares. Over three-quarters of the livestock and two-thirds of the sugarcane farms were over 50 hectares in size. Some 29 percent of all farm households were tenants, while another 11 percent were only part owners of the fields they tilled.

Land tenure patterns are the result of a number of historical, political, and cultural influences and the cause of considerable social tension. The Spanish introduced sharecropping patterns into what had been a communal society having quasi-egalitarian forms of landownership. During the twentieth century the rate of tenancy increased, and landlord-tenant relations deteriorated as more and more landlords moved to the urban areas and neglected their tenants. Throughout this history, militant political movements have drawn on peasant dissatisfaction with the inequalities of the tenure system for support (see The Insurgent Challenge, ch. 5). In response to actual or potential peasant unrest, Philippine governments since the turn of the twentieth century have promised some kind of agrarian reform. Not until Marcos ruled under martial law, however, did the government deliver in any significant manner on its promises.

The land reform program initiated in 1972 by presidential decree was limited to rice and corn farms and consisted of two types of landholding arrangements. Tenants on farms larger than seven hectares

Traditional methods retain significance even as modernization of agriculture spreads.
Courtesy Tourist Research and Planning Organization

could become full owners, while those on smaller plots were eligible to become permanent leaseholders, working the land at a fixed, contractual rent. After several surveys the government concluded that some 397,000 people on 731,000 hectares qualified for the ownership program, and 609,000 people on 732,000 hectares were eligible for the leasehold program. As of early 1982 certificates of land transfer had been issued to 105 percent of the targeted recipients in the first group. They had 15 years to amortize the assessed value of the land in payments to the Land Bank of the Philippines, which purchased the land from the original landowners. As of early 1982 only 1,800 people had prepaid these property loans and received full title. About 90 percent of the targeted beneficiaries in the leasehold program had signed contracts with their landlords under the supervision of the Ministry of Agrarian Reform as of early 1982.

The reform program ran into several obstacles at first, including administrative inefficiency and red tape, the conversion of eligible lands to other uses, and the slow formation of pre-cooperatives (Samahang Nayons—see Glossary), to which all tenants affected by the reform were required to become contributing members. Under martial law, moreover, the courts of agrarian relations became less effective in promoting the rights of tenants, and many of the new institutions set up at the local level continued to be dominated by landlords and other powerful interests. The courts were abolished in 1982. After a slow start, however, many of these obstacles were overcome, despite reports that abuses of the system persisted into the 1980s. Sharecropping remained, however, and some observers noted that leasehold arrangements could be less beneficial than sharecropping arrangements in some cases.

The restriction of the land reform program to tenants on rice and corn farms severely limited its effect on the agricultural sector as a whole. Landless agricultural workers, comprising between 500,000 and 700,000 six-person households in 1978—were totally untouched by the reform. About one-half of this number was engaged in rice farming, one-third worked in the sugarcane fields, and the remainder tended coconut trees. There were also many households or individuals who found employment in the services sector but who, given the opportunity to farm their own land, would return to agricultural production. As population pressures increased, the plight of these families became more pronounced.

Irrigation and Farm Modernization

The basic distinction in agriculture is between irrigated and rainfed farms, the former occupying 1.2 million hectares of some 3.5 million hectares of potentially irrigable lands in 1981. The earliest irrigation systems, such as the magnificent rice terraces of northern Luzon, date back to the precolonial era, but the bulk of the existing systems were built in the twentieth century. Virtually all the irrigated land is devoted to rice farming. Government programs to modernize farming have concentrated on the expansion and improvement of irrigation systems and the development of high-yielding farm technologies associated with these systems. By contrast, the development of rainfed agriculture was just beginning in the 1980s but promised the best results for the greatest number of farmers.

National irrigation systems covered some 470,000 hectares in 1980, ranging in size from 100 hectares to 80,000 hectares, and were constructed and managed by the National Irrigation Administration (NIA), a semiautonomous government agency. Communal systems were owned and operated by groups of farmers themselves, and there were about 5,700 systems covering some 550,000 hectares in 1980. About 2,000 of these systems, covering some 340,000 hectares, had received assistance from the government for construction and maintenance. There were about 190,000 hectares of irrigated land served by privately owned pump and other types of systems that drew water from lakes and reservoirs. These estimates of irrigated land referred to the total service area, including land covered by roads and service facilities, as well as fields that received insufficient amounts of water even in the wet season.

Compared with the 1960s, when the area under irrigation actually decreased, in the 1970s the area grew by more than 5 percent per year. The number of personnel at the NIA quadrupled to 35,000 employees from 1970 to 1979. By 1980 some 205,000 hectares of the existing national systems had been completely rehabilitated, and 330,000 hectares of new systems or extensions to old facilities were under construction.

The government planned to extend the service area of the national systems by about 630,000 hectares from 1982 to 1991 and to rehabilitate another 300,000 hectares. Rehabilitation was expected to become more important because irrigation works already under construction seemed sufficient to ensure an adequate supply of rice for domestic consumption. Moreover, there was little room for expansion beyond the construction already under way in 1983 outside of Central Luzon Region and Mindanao, where less than half the potentially irrigable lands had been developed. Security problems imperiled the development of irrigation works on Mindanao, as they have impeded the progress on the Chico River systems of Cagayan Valley Region (see The Insurgent Challenge, ch.5).

Other problems plagued the irrigation program. The NIA was unable to recover more than 10 percent of its operation costs from fees charged to farmers using its facilities. Even in its best collection year in 1981 the administration collected only half of all fees due. Despite government support, the irrigation authorities were chronically short of funds to maintain the systems. In response to these and other problems, the NIA has been setting up irrigators' associations among the farmers on the national systems in blocks of 50 hectares. In 1982 some 2,300 such associations covering 60,000 farmers had been formed, and the ultimate objective was to turn over the operation and maintenance of the facilities to these groups.

The delivery of support services to the farming community is the responsibility of many private and public institutions. Government agencies are concerned with the development of new technologies and their promotion through the extension service, the provision of credit, and occasionally the production and marketing of agricultural commodities. The private sector produces, imports, and distributes inputs such as fertilizers, pesticides, herbicides, and veterinary medicines. Some of these dealers provide credit and technical advice to go along with their products. Private entrepreneurs, moreover, purchase, process, and market the bulk of all farm production, even acting as intermediaries for government purchasing agencies. Private rural banks provided about 6 percent of all farm credit in 1980.

The chief institution promoting agricultural development is the Ministry of Agriculture, which had some 22,000 employees in 1982. Some 8,600 technical staff—about 90 percent having college degrees or certificates—were assigned to 12 regional offices. These offices were established in 1980 to take over the local functions of the ministry's six technical bureaus: plant industry, animal industry, soils, agricultural extension, cooperatives development, and agricultural economics.

Some 15 government agencies provide extension services for various crops and kinds of farms, but the Ministry of Agriculture's extension bureau is by far the most important. In 1983 there were about 9,300 field extension agents in the provinces—about one agent for every 270 rice and corn farmers. The total force was expected to reach 12,500 by the mid-1980s. Although this ratio was favorable by Asian standards, the field staff lacked the necessary salaries, training, equipment, and support from the regional technical experts to perform their duties adequately. A major project begun in 1979 was designed to ameliorate some of these problems by the mid-1980s. Most of the extension agents devoted their efforts to rice and corn farming. Other agencies, specializing in extension services for commercial crops, were understaffed and poorly financed.

The quality of agricultural research has been good by any standard. There were four national research centers, five commodity-specific research institutes, nine regional research institutes, and over 100 field stations affiliated with the nation's colleges and universities. The College of Agriculture at the University of the Philippines and the International Rice Research Institute, both located at Los Banos, are renowned worldwide for the quality of their research and training programs. In addition, the technical bureaus of the Ministry of Agriculture maintained their own experimental facilities, and the regional offices were developing one integrated agricultural research station in each of their areas.

The main thrust of the government's research and extension efforts has been to promote the use of modern inputs. The Bureau of Plant Industry facilitated the use of modern seed, especially high-yielding rice, hybrid corn, and hybrid vegetable seed. At the start of the 1980s more and more private firms were becoming involved in the development of new seeds, and farmers showed an increased awareness of and interest in procuring improved seed from registered growers. The unbalanced development of programs for different kinds of crops, the lack of storage and handling facilities, and insufficient extension and control, however, inhibited the progress of these promotional efforts. Moreover, the average seeding rate was still high because of the possibility of flood damage, damage to the seeds, and insufficient knowledge about planting methods.

Fertilizer consumption increased from an average of 35 kilograms per hectare of harvested rice and corn land in 1971 to about 49 kilograms in 1980, based on the nutrient content of fertilizers—chiefly nitrogen from urea. Despite subsidies on the price of fertilizer ranging from 30 to 60 percent of the final cost and high tariffs on imported fertilizers, only 20 percent of the fertilizer used came from domestic sources (see Manufacturing, this ch.). The government has been trying to reduce the subsidy element to promote efficient farming but remained unsure of the political wisdom of such a measure in 1983. The application rate of fertilizers was often less than half of the recommended dosage. A similar situation prevailed in the use of agrochemicals—primarily biocides—that nonetheless have become quite common.

Agricultural credit programs have been the major means of promoting the use of modern inputs and methods. In 1980 there were 28 supervised credit programs in operation, under which the participating farmers were required to accept a package of farm technology, extension, marketing, and other services from government agents. In addition, there were 24 special financing programs for integrated farming operations and 20 other programs that were subject only to the scrutiny of banking officials. Government-owned banks supplied the majority of the preferential credit for these programs. Private rural banks, cooperative banks, savings and loan associations, and development banks received government assistance to implement programs in their areas.

Although successful at first, the agricultural credit programs encountered severe problems in the late 1970s as arrears mounted in many accounts, and some 400 rural banks became ineligible for further loans from the Central Bank. The government banks were suffering heavy losses on their agricultural as well as other kinds of loan accounts (see Banking and Finance, this ch.). The volume of credit extended to agricultural producers nonetheless increased from ₱678 per hectare of area cultivated in 1975 to ₱1,303 per hectare in 1980—the latter expressed in 1975 pesos to adjust for inflation. Overall agricultural credit from financial institutions—including loans for processing and marketing—declined slightly on a per hectare basis. This level of credit was insufficient, and some surveys suggested that informal lines of credit from family, friends, and moneylenders made up as much as three-quarters of all credit available in the late 1970s, compared with about a third in the mid-1970s. The government reacted negatively to a report from the World Bank in 1982 suggesting that interest rate subsidies be removed from the various agricultural loan programs.

One problem of the agricultural credit and modernization programs has been the concentration on single commodities rather than integrated farming of several crops and livestock. Sophisticated forms of crop rotation were needed to maximize production, especially on rainfed farms. Beginning in 1975 the government experimented with integrated area development projects, of which there were 13 in 1983. The most significant experiment was taking place in Iloilo Province under a loan from the World Bank. The Ministry of Agriculture has also established so-called integrated estates and compact farms, where production credit and extension services were made available for total cropping systems. The objective of the government was to shift its single-commodity programs to integrated farming programs as rapidly as possible in the 1980s.

Agricultural cooperatives have also had a modernizing influence on the farming community by enhancing the commercial capabilities of farmers. Although the establishment of cooperative farms dates back to the early twentieth century, those in existence in 1983 grew out of the Samahang Nayons created after 1973. The Samahang Nayon was originally a preliminary form of cooperative but in the 1980s has been recognized by the government as a legally constituted organization having the right to engage in commercial activities. At the beginning of 1982 there were more than 22,000 Samahang Nayons at the *barangay* (see Glossary) level connected by federations at the municipal, provincial, regional, and national levels. Most of these groups were marketing organizations that purchased inputs and sold produce in bulk form to reduce costs. In addition to the Samahang Nayons, or organized in conjunction with such organizations, there were credit union, rural bank, consumer, marketing, and service cooperatives. In 1979 there were 1,516 such registered cooperatives, of which more than half were credit institutions and most of the rest, marketing organizations.

Farm Production and Marketing

Rice is the staple crop and has been the focus of the government's major agricultural development effort, the Masagana 99 program, so named for its goal of producing 99 *cavans* (one *cavan* equals 50 kilograms) of rice per hectare, begun in 1973. Although the number of farmers receiving credit under the program declined from a peak of 800,000 in 1975 to some 180,000 by 1980, the effect of the support services accompanying the credit allocation was to increase yields from 1.72 tons of unmilled rice per hectare in 1971 to 2.14 tons in 1980 (see table 6, Appendix). High-yielding and quick-maturing varieties of rice accounted for 82 percent of the total production in 1979 and covered 72 percent of the area harvested—over 90 percent of the area on irrigated rice farms.

Rice yields were greatest on irrigated farms, where they averaged 2.8 tons per hectare in 1981. Yields on national irrigation systems were as high as 3.7 tons per hectare but were less than the potential of over 6 tons per hectare on well-irrigated land. Yields from lowland and upland areas having no irrigation were less than two tons per hectare. Regional statistics available for 1979 showed that yields were highest in Central Luzon Region—the rice basket of the country. Western Mindanao and Southern Mindanao regions also obtained better-than-average yields, while productivity in Eastern Visayas Region was the lowest in the country (see table 7, Appendix).

The National Food Authority (NFA) purchased 579,000 tons of milled rice in 1981—about 12 percent of the total production—to support farm prices, maintain a buffer stock, and export overseas. The support price for rice increased by 55 percent from 1978 to 1982 but rose by only two-thirds of the rate of inflation. The support price was available only on government purchases, and the average price prevailing in the marketplace was usually 10 to 25 percent less. Some unscrupulous middlemen purchased rice from the farmers at as much as 50 percent less than the official support price and then resold it to the NFA at a profit. The NFA maintained over 260 warehouses around the country in 1981, having a storage capacity of 1.3 million tons, and kept a buffer stock equivalent to at least a 90-day supply of rice for the nation. Although the NFA has exported some rice since the nation reached self-sufficiency in 1977, the high percentage of broken rice reduced its attractiveness to most international buyers.

Corn is the second most important food crop, and the harvested area for this crop actually surpassed that for rice in 1981. During the 1970s production increased by over 5 percent per year, chiefly as a result of the expansion of the area harvested. The average yields of less than one ton per hectare were among the lowest in Asia. Corn is the primary product in the upland areas of Mindanao and the Visayan Islands, which together accounted for three-quarters of all corn lands. The nation was self-sufficient in the production of white corn for human consumption, but the NFA has had to import more than 200,000 tons of yellow corn each year since 1980 to feed the growing livestock industry. The aim of the corn loan program, Maisagana, was to produce enough yellow corn to satisfy domestic demand and even to export by the mid-1980s. Only 35,000 out of a targeted 500,000 hectares of corn land came under the Maisagana program in early 1983.

Cassava, sweet potatoes, beans, peas, citrus fruits, vegetables, and nuts are important supplements to the staple diet. Vegetable farming located near the urban centers is also an important source of cash income for many farmers. Pineapple and banana plantations, set up on the Visayan Islands and on Mindanao, produce for export as well as for domestic consumption (see fig. 6). Altogether, production of food crops other than grains grew by over 15 percent per year during the 1970s. The value added of banana production alone rose from less than 4 percent to almost 8 percent of the total value added in agriculture from 1972 to 1980, surpassing the value of coconut products. Reduced demand from Japan in the early 1980s, however, probably ended the

145

production boom. The major banana and pineapple producers were foreign companies.

Coconut production dominates commercial farming, providing income directly or indirectly to some 14 million people. In 1980 the nation harvested 16 billion nuts and exported three-quarters of the total world demand for coconut imports. Coconut production was carried out on both large plantations and smallholder farms. The government claimed that 95 percent of all coconut holdings were less than five hectares in size in 1980 and that tenancy was therefore not a problem. Production was concentrated in the upland areas of Mindanao and Southern Tagalog Region, where there were from 13 to 21 trees per person. The government considered the average yield of 46 nuts per tree to be too low and since the 1960s has been replacing the large number of aging trees. It was not until the 1970s, however, that "miracle" hybrids were introduced. Developed from seed nuts imported from Malaysia, the hybrids could produce five times the yield of the old trees. By 1980, however, the government had distributed only 1.7 million seed nuts on 6,914 hectares of land—less than 1 percent of the 3.1 million hectares devoted to coconuts. The maturation of the hybrid plants would take at least five years, and they would begin to affect production only at the end of the 1980s.

Considerable controversy racked the coconut industry in the early 1980s. The issue was the government levy on copra and coconut-oil exports. The levy financed investments by the Philippine Coconut Authority, which since its establishment in 1973 had set up a number of public enterprises to take over most of the processing and marketing of coconuts. The debate over the levy was especially troublesome because two of its supporters—Minister of National Defense Juan Ponce Enrile and business mogul Eduardo Cojuangco—were close associates of Marcos and controlled the leading enterprises in the coconut industry. These included the United Coconut Planters Bank (UCPB), one of the largest commercial banks in the nation, and United Coconut Mills, which owned 93 percent of the coconut-oil milling capacity in 1982. The purpose of the UCPB, which received much of its equity from the levy, was to make investments on behalf of all coconut producers and to establish insurance and education funds.

Critics argued that the large landowners, traders, and millers have passed the burden of the levy onto the majority of smallholders, tenants, and field-workers, whose incomes have decreased. Some observers even blamed the increase in antigovernment activities on Samar in Bicol Region on the coconut levy. After reneging on a pledge to end the levy earlier, Marcos abolished the tax in August 1982. The levy would probably be reassessed after international prices recovered from their abysmal lows in the early 1980s. In the interim, the government was supporting the domestic price of coconut and had earmarked ₱ 50 million to promote multiple cropping of cash crops on coconut lands.

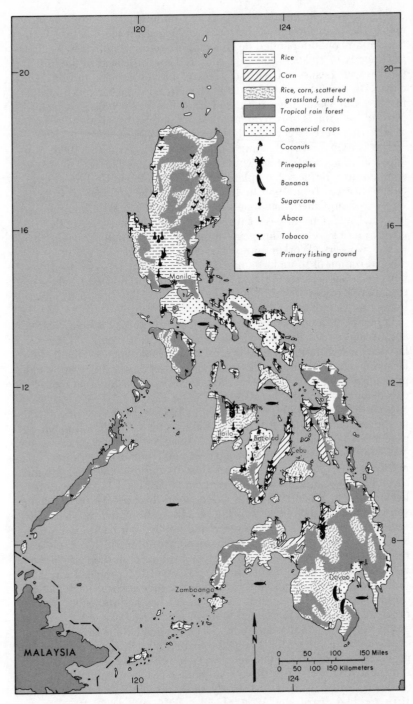

Figure 6. Agricultural Activity, 1982

Sugarcane is the next most important commercial crop after coconuts and is the basis for one of the oldest industries in the country. Some 5 million people depended on this crop directly or indirectly for their livelihoods in 1980. Production centered on the island of Negros, in the Visayan Islands, in parts of Central Luzon Region, and on Mindanao. The area harvested in 1982 was virtually unchanged from that in 1970, but yields have increased from five to six tons per hectare. Most of the crop is grown on large estates and farms; about 80 percent of all farms were larger than 10 hectares in 1982.

The National Sugar Trading Corporation, established in 1978, marketed all the country's sugar at controlled prices but was unable to compensate producers completely for the 67-percent decline in international prices from 1980 to 1982. Many of the 400,000 or so fieldworkers complained that wages were below the legal minimum and less than sufficient for basic subsistence. They were also upset that the government gave more financial support to the plantation owners than to the workers. Worker unrest has also occurred as a result of the mechanization of some farm operations. The sugar crisis of the 1980s, however, was less severe than that of the 1975-78 period, when international prices fell rapidly from all-time highs, and prices were beginning to increase in 1983.

Other commercial crops included tobacco, abaca, rubber, coffee, cotton, and cacao. Production was expanding most rapidly on the rubber and coffee farms, which were either plantations or smallholder farms clustered around larger estates and possessing facilities. Although producing from a small base in 1983, there was considerable room for expansion, particularly on Mindanao.

Livestock production generated about 12 percent of the value added in the agriculture, forestry, and fishing sector in 1980. Although 80 percent of all production took place as a backyard activity, there were over 100 commercial farms engaged in poultry and pig farming, primarily in the Manila environs. Another 100 large-scale farms around the country were cattle ranches, ranging in size from 10,000 to 15,000 hectares each. Since 1976, after a decline in the early 1970s, the livestock population has been growing steadily. The nation was virtually self-sufficient in the supply of swine and poultry but had to import up to half of its beef requirements. The rising cost of feeds, however, was reducing the profits of most commercial producers in the early 1980s.

Cattle and carabao (water buffalo) remained the principal forms of draft power. The nation's herd had still not recovered from its depletion during World War II, and the government has had difficulty getting ranchers to invest in larger and more productive stocks. A supervised credit program for cattle fattening aimed at smallholder farmers, however, has been successful. Launched in 1977, the program covered 68 provinces and over 134,000 borrowers by 1982 and had distributed some 242,500 head of cattle to smallholder farms. A similar program for goats, which were in extremely short supply, was introduced in 1979 and had distributed 17,400 head to 62 provinces by 1982.

Coconuts and sugarcane are the leading commercial crops. Less important but still valuable are tobacco, rubber, coffee, cotton, cacao, and abaca, dyed fibers of which are shown here.
Courtesy Tourist Research and Planning Organization

Milk production from cattle and carabao has been negligible, and efforts by the Ministry of Agriculture and other agencies to promote smallholder production have proved uneconomical. Some larger commercial producers have established dairy farms for specialized markets in Manila, but the dairy industry as a whole was as yet undeveloped.

The prospects for livestock and dairy farming were good. Veterinary supplies were generally available, and private and public vaccination programs had reduced substantially the risks from disease. Although the cost of feeds has risen, there were a number of unconventional feeds that showed promise; including rice bran, sugarcane tops, the leafy and fast-growing *ipil-ipil* shrub, and cassava chips. Three international development loans, the latest beginning in 1980, were helping the Bureau of Animal Industry expand its development programs rapidly. In particular, the loans were funding the procurement of quality cattle stock for crossbreeding at the bureau's stock farm and the cattle-fattening program.

Forestry

Until the late 1970s the trade-off between the use of forestland for commercial and farming purposes, on the one hand, and for protecting the nation's valuable watersheds, on the other, was settled in favor of the former. In the late 1960s forestry production accounted for some 17 percent of the total value added from the agriculture, forestry, and fishing sector and for over a quarter of the value of all exports. Over 170,000 hectares of forestland were deforested each year, while less than 10,000 hectares were reforested (see table 8, Appendix). One of the major achievements of the martial law period was the reversal of this trend so that more area was reforested each year than was destroyed. This has resulted in the reduction of forestry's contribution to less than 9 percent of agricultural value added in 1980 and to slightly over 7 percent of the value of exports. The problems of flooding and siltation on the major irrigation schemes, however, have made this shift necessary.

According to estimates by the FAO, in 1980 forestlands covered 13.0 million hectares. Of this total, some 3.5 million hectares were fallow, 1.9 million hectares were unproductive because of the harshness of the terrain, and 690,000 hectares were legally protected reserves. Based on data for 1979 broken down by major geographical areas, Mindanao contained 85 percent of the area classified as commercial forest. In 1981 eastern and northern Mindanao were estimated to have 3.5 million hectares of forest reserves. About 94 percent of the total forest area consisted of dipterocarps, generally known as Philippine mahogany. The remainder consisted of pine, mangrove, mossy, or montane growth.

Most timberland was licensed to concessionaires for exploitation and development. But from 1975 to 1981 log production steadily decreased, and the total number of concessionaires declined from 461 to 250 firms, covering 7.7 million hectares of forest. The Bureau of Forestry De-

Timber awaits export at Manila's harbor.
Courtesy Tourist Research and Planning Organization

velopment (BFD) of the Ministry of Natural Resources prescribed an annual allowable cut for each producer, although licenses were issued for periods as long as 25 years. The staff conducted periodic field surveys to ensure that the concessionaires were following the proper allowable cut and using correct selection and replanting techniques. In 1982 the BFD reduced the allowable cuts for most firms by about half, implemented a partial ban on log exports, and took special measures to control log smuggling. Not only were these measures designed to conserve forest resources, but they were also to stimulate the domestic wood-processing industry (see Manufacturing, this ch.).

The main reason for the loss of forest area is the expansion of the population and its incursion into forested areas. Shifting cultivators (*kaingineros*—see Glossary) are responsible for most of the illegal destruction; they include two distinct groups of people. First are upland tribal groups, who farm open areas deep in the forests and whose number is diminishing (see Upland Tribal Groups, ch. 2). Far more destructive are the lowlanders who have migrated in increasing numbers to the forest areas, often following the swath of commercial foresters. In 1978 and 1979 nearly all of the reported area that was deforested

151

was attributed to the activities of shifting cultivators. According to government statistics, their destructiveness was reduced to a level of about 5,000 or 6,000 hectares in 1981 and 1982.

The reported success in reducing the degradation of forestlands was somewhat surprising because the BFD had only 3,560 forest guards. The agency has therefore enlisted the support of *barangay* officials and logging companies to protect the territory under their jurisdiction. The government has also initiated an innovative forestry management program that enlisted *kaingineros* themselves as active participants in the planting of tree crops and forests. As of 1981 the BFD had issued some 9,700 permits to *kaingineros* living on 121,000 hectares as part of this program.

Reforestation efforts are many and varied. The BFD itself managed projects covering 245,000 hectares of forest plantations in 1981. Special targets of the government's efforts were 15 of the 39 watersheds critical to the national irrigation systems. Other government agencies, private logging companies, citizens' groups, and individual families reforested about 316,000 hectares during the 1975-81 period. The BFD estimated in 1980, however, that 1 million hectares of land was in need of immediate reforestation and that more than 2 million hectares of brushland required attention in the long run.

Fishing

The archipelago contains extensive fishing grounds. The Exclusive Economic Zone (see Glossary) encompasses about 496,400 square nautical miles of marine and coastal waters, and the land territory contains another 5,570 square kilometers of freshwater and brackish-water areas. Although marine waters deeper than 200 meters account for about 99 percent of this area, fishing activities have concentrated on the shallower coastal grounds that were easily accessible to small vessels. The concentration of fishing in coastal areas has caused the serious depletion of fishing stocks in some grounds, while fishing in the marine grounds has often been left to foreigners.

The total catch in 1980 was nearly 1.7 million tons and amounted to about 31.4 kilograms per capita—some 4 percent short of the government's objective (see table 9, Appendix).Estimates of the annual sustainable yield from saltwater sources alone, however, run as high as 2.5 million tons. Tuna, scrod, mackerel, sardines, anchovies, bream, slipmouth, snapper, and perch accounted for about three-quarters of the marine catch in 1979. Milkfish, tilapia, and brackish-water shrimp were the principal inland and aquiculture species.

The municipal fisheries produced 1.1 million tons of fish in 1980. Some 600,000 people were employed in these coastal operations, using about 250,000 *bancas* (wooden-hulled vessels). Most of these vessels were outriggers, and about 45 percent of the fleet was motorized in 1980. The *banca* operators used hand lines, casting nets, and other low-cost gear. Municipal fishing has been hampered by the low productivity of coastal waters, inadequate onshore facilities, and poor prices.

More than half a million Filipinos are employed in coastal fishing operations, using mainly wooden-hulled outriggers.
Courtesy Tourist Research and Planning Organization

The households deriving their income from this fishery were among the poorest in the nation (see Income Distribution and Living Conditions, this ch.). Production on some of the major grounds—especially Manila Bay and San Miguel Bay—has suffered from overfishing, on the part of both subsistence operators and encroaching commercial vessels. Although the overall production of municipal fishing operations increased in the 1970s, the catch per vessel declined by over 20 percent.

Some 3,000 licensed commercial vessels, averaging 49 gross registered tons each, operated in coastal and marine waters in 1980. About 31 percent of the commercial catch of 448,000 tons was handled at the Navotas Fish Landing and Market Authority in Manila, while the remainder was landed at 200 commercial ports around the country. The major fishing grounds were the Sulu Sea, Manila Bay, and the Visayan Sea. The Bureau of Fisheries and Aquatic Resources (BFAR) of the Ministry of Natural Resources had installed 19 ice and cold storage plants around the country as of 1980, but a majority of these were not operating, and many were located too far from the landing sites.

Inland production came chiefly from some 176,000 freshwater and brackish-water fish ponds and fish pens that were in operation in 1980. Although the aquiculture area increased by only 5 percent from 1970 to 1980, the average yield per hectare rose by 34 percent to 772 kilograms. This productivity, however, was quite low by international standards. Many fish pens were located in the massive Laguna de Bay, southeast of Manila, which encompassed 95,000 hectares. Although the government had restricted the construction of fish pens to some 18,000 hectares in the center of the lake, a survey in 1982 showed that some 6,000 fish pens were located in prohibited areas. The 60,000 persons who depended on the lake for their subsistence protested loudly in early 1983 that wealthy individuals and companies had used their influence to establish illegal facilities, and the government responded by sending the navy to destroy the illegal pens.

In 1981 the BFAR's staff of 3,300 provided extension services to 14,000 municipal and 381 commercial operators. In addition, government banks had provided loans to 5,700 individuals and companies for the acquisition of vessels, gear, and fish pond feeds. The BFAR had also supervised the formation and management of 142 fishing associations having 5,000 members altogether by 1981. In the first half of the same year, the BFAR produced and distributed 45 million fingerlings and oyster seedlings. Under a loan from the World Bank, the Philippine Fisheries Development Authority was constructing or improving landing sites, ice plants, and storage facilities at seven ports in Bicol and Western Visayas regions—two of the poorest in the country.

Fisheries training and research were generally disorganized until 1979, when the government gave chief responsibility to the University of the Philippines. Seven regional colleges or fishery schools having an adjacent training center were given the primary task of implementing government-supported programs. The BFAR maintained 25 freshwater, 20 brackish-water, and 14 marine fish farms for research and the production of fish stock. Several important international research centers located in the country included the Southeast Asia Fisheries Development Center and the International Center for Living Aquatic Resources Management. The ability of the government to manage its own resources, however, was limited by the poor coverage of marine surveys and the small enforcement force (see Organization and Training, ch. 5).

Industry and Services

Since independence, the government's economic policies have stressed industrialization. Industry's reliance on imported capital equipment and intermediate goods and its poor export performance, however, have been burdens to the rest of the economy. Although some industries increased their exports significantly during the 1970s, they generally had weak linkages to the domestic economy. The growth of industrial output, moreover, did not keep pace with the expansion of industrial investment, and about 85 percent of the new entrants into the labor force each year had to find jobs in agriculture and services.

In response to these problems, the government has initiated a program of structural adjustment and reform aimed at the comprehensive overhaul of most industry. While specific programs for the service sector have not been developed, strong government support was being granted to automotive, tourism, and financial services. Furthermore, infrastructure services, such as construction, transportation, communications, and public utilities, were integral to the government's programs.

Manufacturing

The manufacturing sector shows the best promise for productively employing the growing labor force. This sector accounted for about a quarter of GDP in 1981 and had been growing by about 7 percent per year since 1970. The structure of manufacturing was dualistic; the so-called informal or unorganized sector, composed of establishments having fewer than five workers, employed about two-thirds of the manufacturing labor force but produced less than 5 percent of its value added in 1978, when estimates were last available. At the other extreme was the minority of large producers that generated the most income. Some 80 percent of all manufacturing was oriented toward the domestic market—chiefly urban and middle-class markets. Almost all the manufacturing of modern consumer products took place in Metro Manila.

The structure of manufacturing was skewed toward light industry, the production of consumer goods, and the processing of agricultural and mineral products. Food, beverage, and tobacco products accounted for 40 percent of the value of manufacturing output in 1980, and this industry had the largest number of small producers and was the most regionally dispersed (see fig. 7; table 10, Appendix). The petroleum-refining industry was the second largest manufacturing subsector in terms of value, but the three refineries were operating at less than 70 percent of capacity in the early 1980s. The important chemical industry produced only 27 percent of the fertilizer nutrients consumed in 1979 and almost none of the chemicals needed for the rapidly growing plastics and synthetic textile industries. The machinery industries were based on the assembly of imported components. During the 1972-80 period the most rapidly expanding industries produced electrical and nonelectrical machinery, metal products, processed foods, and furniture. Some of these were important in the drive to increase the exports from nontraditional manufacturing industries (see Trade Patterns, this ch.).

The most important measures of the structural adjustment program for manufacturing concerned reforms of the fiscal incentive and tariff systems (see Fiscal Policy and Incentives, this ch.). Several specific industrial projects and policies have also been initiated. First, the government planned to invest in 11 so-called major industrial projects that would be focal points for the development of capital- and intermediate-goods industries. Second, the Ministry of Trade and Industry was developing sectoral programs for each major industry. Third, special programs to promote medium- and small-scale industry were to be enhanced. Finally, new investment was to be encouraged on sites located outside of Metro Manila.

The 11 major industrial projects to develop the basic industries centered on the chemical, smelting, metal products, and machinery industries (see table A). The total cost of the investment program was the equivalent of nearly US$5 billion. These funds were to come from suppliers' credits and joint venture capital from overseas, as well as from the National Development Company and private domestic investors. Because of the weak state of the nation's international finances and the unattractiveness of several of the key projects to foreign investors, four of the projects and part of a fifth were shelved indefinitely in June 1983. The program had come under attack from a number of prominent industrialists and economists in the Philippines. The government was nonetheless forging ahead with as many of the projects as it could reasonably afford.

The Ministry of Trade and Industry, which was created in 1981 by the merger of two previous ministries, itself had six bureaus and 17 affiliated agencies to monitor the progress of these projects and to implement its sectoral plans for manufacturing. The most important of these were the National Development Company and the Board of Investments (BOI). Agencies were also created to draft or implement rationalization plans for particular industries. In 1981 there were special agencies overseeing the heavy engineering, textiles, iron and steel, cement, and copper industries. The two most developed industrial rationalization plans were for textiles and cement. The latter was one of the major industrial projects, and the former was supported by a loan from the World Bank.

The government promoted regional and small-scale industrial development through a variety of programs. Another affiliate of the Ministry of Trade and Industry launched a fund of| ₱800 million for small-scale and cottage industries in 1981, and the ministry's own Bureau of Small and Medium Industry provided counseling services to over 1,000 businesses that year. Special financing facilities from the Development Bank of the Philippines (DBP) and Central Bank had committed ₱1 billion to promoting small-scale industry, and the KKK included small-scale industries in its lending programs (see Income Distribution and Living Conditions, this ch.). The government has also established three export-processing zones and five industrial estates located outside of Metro Manila and was expanding these sites in the 1980s (see Trade Patterns, this ch.).

Mining and Energy

The mining industry produced only 3.2 percent of GDP in 1981 and had expanded at a rate of about 5.7 percent per year since 1972. In spite of the small share of the sector in the whole economy, it was an important source of raw materials for manufacturing and a major contributor to foreign exchange earnings. Because of adverse international prices, lagging technological development, and a cutback in exploration

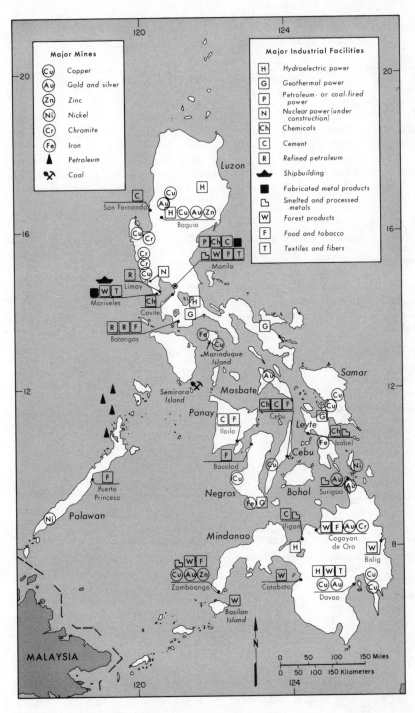

Figure 7. Industrial Activity, 1982

Table A. The 11 Major Industrial Projects, 1983[1]

Project	Cost	Location	Proposed Annual Output	Status
Copper smelter	US$250 million	Isabel industrial estate, Leyte Province	138,000 tons of copper cathodes and 442,000 tons of sulfuric acid from local copper	Construction complete; official inauguration in July 1983
Phosphatic fertilizer plant	US$350 million	Isabel industrial estate, Leyte Province	1.1 million tons using sulfuric acid from smelter	On stream, scheduled for mid-1984 start
Diesel engine plants	US$60 million and US$30 million, respectively	Dasmariñas, Cavite Province; and Parañaque, Rizal Province	Unspecified number of low- and high-range engines, respectively	Dasmariñas low-range plant on stream, scheduled for 1983 start; Parañaque high-range plant shelved indefinitely
Cement industry expansion	US$40 million	Seventeen existing plants, on Semirara Island and at other sites	7.5 million tons from existing sites converted to coal power; up to four new plants of 1 million tons each	Nine existing sites converted to coal; negotiations with Soviet Union on Semirara joint venture
Integrated steel mill	US$1 billion	Iligan, Lanao del Norte Province	1.2 million tons of rolled and sheet steel products from direct-reduction process using iron-ore tailings and local coal	Negotiations for construction bids in progress; output may be cut in half to reduce costs
Heavy engineering complex	US$100 million	Bataan, Batangas Province	3,500 tons of machinery and 12,000 tons of steel products	Negotiations under way on financing and equipment supply; output may be cut
Coconut chemical complex	US$100 million	Bauan, Batangas Province	30,000 tons of fatty alcohol, 29,000 tons of fatty acids, and 8,000 tons of glycerin from 69,400 tons of coconut oil	Under construction and scheduled for operation in 1985
Petro-chemical complex	US$1.2 billion	Limay, Bataan Province	350,000 tons of ethylene	Shelved indefinitely
Aluminum smelter	US$650 million	Tagaloan, Misamis Oriental Province	140,000 tons of billets, ingots, and slabs	Shelved indefinitely
Pulp and paper mill	US$250 million	Bislig, Surigao del Sur Province	Expansion of existing plant from 146,000 to 329,000 tons	Shelved indefinitely
Alcogas distilleries	US$640 million	Twelve major distilleries located throughout country	137 million liters of anhydrous alcohol from molasses to be mixed with gasoline	Shelved indefinitely

[1]Projects announced in 1979. Information, including substantial changes from original plans, as of mid-1983.

efforts by many producers, mining activities were expected to decrease in importance during the 1980s. Many firms were diversifying into other lines of business. Domestic supplies of energy, moreover, were based less on mineral resources than on hydroelectric and geothermal sources.

The major metals produced in the Philippines are copper, gold, nickel, and chromium. In 1979 the nation's shares in the total world production of these commodities were 4 percent, 2 percent, 5 percent, and 6 percent, respectively. The Philippines was among the top 10 exporters for all of these minerals. In addition, silver, cobalt, lead, manganese, molybdenum, and zinc are mined, as well as low grades of iron ore (see table 11, Appendix). The Bureau of Mines and Geosciences of the Ministry of Natural Resources has also identified significant deposits of bauxite. The major nonmetals include the raw materials for cement, dolomite, phosphatic rock, and silicon.

The total commercial energy consumed in the country in 1981 was estimated to be equivalent to 86 million barrels of crude oil, but domestic sources of petroleum accounted for less than 2 percent of this demand (see table 12, Appendix). Three oil fields located off Palawan were in production in 1983. The oldest site, the Nido field, suffered from the incursion of water into its wells and produced only about 4,000 barrels per day in 1983, compared with a high of 40,000 barrels after its discovery in 1979. Similar problems plagued the Cadlao field, opened in 1981, which produced about 6,000 barrels per day in 1982. In February 1983 the first wells at the Matinloc-Pandan-Libro complex began producing at a rate of 9,000 barrels per day. As of mid–1982 the estimated recoverable reserves at these three sites were 643,000 barrels, 1.8 million barrels, and 1.2 million barrels, respectively.

The government has had to offer attractive terms to foreign oil companies to maintain their interest in what has been a difficult area of exploration. Whereas in the 1950s and 1960s the government insisted on majority participation in all projects, in the 1970s and 1980s it relied on production-sharing contracts that had favorable rates of return for the foreign companies, who assumed most of the risks involved in exploration. As a result, some 90 operating contracts were awarded in the 1973-81 period. These contractors drilled 112 wells and conducted 125,000 kilometers of seismic surveys during the period. An additional 17 wells were drilled in 1982, and the Bureau of Energy Development of the Ministry of Energy authorized funds for drilling 15 wells in 1983. The World Bank committed a loan of US$37.5 million in 1983 to make seismic and aeromagnetic surveys in unexplored areas. The survey program was to concentrate on seven of the 15 sedimentary basins identified in the archipelago—in particular, the area around Cotabato on Mindanao, all of the Visayan Islands except Panay, and in Bicol, Southern Tagalog, Central Luzon, and Ilocos regions. Some possible oil fields were located in disputed waters (see External Defense, ch. 5).

Prospects for these exploratory efforts were not promising, given the complex geophysical structure of the archipelago (see Physical Setting, ch. 2). One major discovery in the early 1980s, the Galoc field near the other sites off Palawan, was located in deep water and would require as much as US$1 billion to develop. Some foreign investors have let their exploration leases expire, and others have pulled out of the country altogether despite favorable contracts. If the exploration trends continued, it was not likely that the country could produce more than 15,000 barrels per day through the mid-1980s. This amount would suffice to meet about 4 or 5 percent of the nation's commercial energy requirements.

Coal figured prominently in the government's energy program for the 1980s. The revised six-year energy plan for the 1981-87 period expected coal to increase its share of commercial energy consumption from 1 to 19 percent—some two-thirds from domestic mines. Most of the demand would come from the conversion of oil-fired industrial and power plants to coal-fired facilities. The conversion of the cement factories alone was expected to increase demand to 1.2 million tons per year. Domestic production in 1981 was about 700,000 tons—double the amount produced in 1980. The government hoped to double production again in 1983. As of 1980 the total domestic reserves were about 180 million tons, of which as much as 130 million tons was located on Semirara Island.

Other forms of commercial energy were associated with the power utilities (see Utilities and Construction, this ch.). These included geothermal, hydroelectric, bagasse, wood-burning, and other sources. The only mineral-based source was nuclear power, and the government was receiving assistance from Australia to find domestic supplies of uranium for its new reactor. Accounts of commercial energy production did not include the fuel wood, bagasse, and other materials collected and burned by individual farming households for their own use, which were equivalent to perhaps a third of all primary energy consumed in 1981.

Utilities and Construction

Although the electric power and water utilities produced only about 1 percent of GDP in 1981, they were vital sources of energy and convenience for a large portion of the population. Of more than 7 million households nationwide, in 1980 some 2 million households outside the Manila area were connected to electric power systems of some sort, while nearly all households in Metro Manila had access to electric power. Public water supply facilities reached about 82 percent of households in Metro Manila, about 55 percent of households in the smaller urban areas, and some 33 percent of those in the rural areas. About half of the power generated each year went to industrial users, and irrigation and flood control were essential to agricultural production.

The total installed capacity of the National Power Corporation (NPC), the state-owned utility that controlled the major power grids, was 4.2 billion watts in mid-1982. About 115 rural electric cooperatives and various captive power plants at industrial facilities provided an additional capacity of more than 620 million watts. Production estimates for 1981 suggested that 65 percent of all power generated came from oil-fired plants, about 20 percent from hydroelectric facilities, some 1 percent from coal-fired plants, and the remaining 14 percent from geothermal facilities. The government planned to increase the shares to 32 percent from geothermal, 14 percent from coal, 29 percent from hydroelectric, and 3 percent from other non-oil sources by 1987.

In mid-1983 the Philippines was the second largest producer of geothermal power in the world after the United States. If it exploited the estimated 200 billion watts of geothermal capacity located at 15 major sites, the country could become the largest producer. Three sites, having facilities totaling 560 million watts of capacity, were already producing in 1982, and two more, averaging over 100 million watts each, were to become operational in 1983 and 1984. These facilities were being developed by either a subsidiary of the Philippine National Oil Company (PNOC) or foreign contractors under the same kind of agreements as for oil exploration.

Many major hydroelectric facilities were associated with irrigation projects. Two large networks scheduled to be completed in the mid-1980s would add about 300 million watts each to the capacity of the Luzon grid. The National Electrification Administration, which supervised power outside of the main network, also planned to construct some 250 mini-hydroelectric facilities to supply the countryside with an additional 300 million watts of total capacity by 1987. In early 1982 three of these plants were in operation, and equipment had been ordered for 25 others.

The major coal and nuclear power facilities were not operational in 1983. The Bataan nuclear reactor, which has been delayed in order to install additional safety equipment, was scheduled to begin production in 1984, having a capacity of 620 million watts. The coal plants would be located at the site of major mines, but construction had yet to begin as of mid-1983.

The plan of the NPC was to complete the basic power grids on Luzon, Leyte, Cebu, Bohol, Negros, and Panay by the end of 1985. Until the present construction projects were completed, however, brownouts would continue. A major drought on Mindanao was seriously disrupting the power supply in 1983. Because of the decline in international oil prices, however, the NPC was considering the delay of some of its projects. The proposed underwater cable to link the geothermal power plant in Leyte to the Luzon grid, for example, was shelved in 1983 as uneconomical.

The government was forcing the NPC to rely less on contributions from the national budget and more on the collection of fees to finance its operations and investments. Beginning in late 1982 the NPC completely restructured its schedule of power tariffs and was gradually raising its rates by about 22 percent through 1983. The unpopular price increases were the result of agreements with the World Bank and the IMF.

Agencies affiliated with the Ministry of Public Works and Highways, Ministry of Human Settlements, Ministry of Health, and Ministry of Local Government were working together in 1983 to implement an integrated program to improve the water supply and sewerage systems, especially in the rural areas. The ambitous goal of the program was to serve 37 percent of the population outside of Metro Manila with piped water from communal faucets, about 29 percent with piped water from household connections, and 27 percent with water from protected wells by 1990. As of 1980 there were some 400 communal faucet systems and 10,000 well systems throughout the country.

The government was setting up rural waterworks and sanitation associations in each *barangay*, which received technical and financial assistance from the central government. In addition to engineering water supply facilities, these agencies were constructing sanitary toilet facilities at the rate of about 200,000 units per year. As of 1982, however, 2 million households had unsanitary toilets, and another 1.3 million had no facilities whatsoever. By 1990 the government planned to construct 1.5 million new toilets and to rehabilitate 2.5 million units.

Construction was the leading industry of the 1970s, growing by about 15 percent per year from 1972 to 1981 and reaching 8.5 percent of GDP. The share of government construction works rose steadily from 16 percent in 1970 to 44 percent in 1980, and this trend was expected to continue into the next decade.

Based only on housing permit data, which did not include the activities of informal builders, the residential construction industry produced from 25,000 to 30,000 new dwellings each year—chiefly for middle- and upper middle-class families. In 1981 two government housing agencies produced 15,000 new units for low-income and middle-income households. As many as 300,000 new units were constructed by informal producers, using primarily lightweight materials. A reform of the housing finance system in the early 1980s was expected to increase the number of units built for middle-income households, but government agencies would continue to be the only major producers of adequate low-income facilities, including sites-and-services projects built by the members of the households (see Income Distribution and Living Conditions, this ch.).

The overseas construction industry expanded rapidly during the second half of the 1970s. As of the end of 1981 Philippine construction firms had US$2.4 billion in outstanding contracts that employed 57,000 laborers abroad, mostly in the Middle East (see Trade Patterns, this ch.).

Transportation and Communications

During the 1970s the transportation system improved markedly, while the government undertook to reorganize the extremely fragmented communications industry. Public expenditures on transportation in the 1978-81 period represented more than 2 percent of GNP—about twice the level of the 1960s. Projections showing that the road systems would carry some 78 percent of all passengers and 47 percent of all cargo by the mid-1980s caused the government to focus initially on the expansion of this network. In the late 1970s, however, the government began to concentrate more on the rehabilitation and maintenance of the highway network and investment in port facilities for the transportation of bulk cargoes. Most investment in communications came from the private sector, but public funds were becoming increasingly important.

The total road network expanded at a rate of about 8 percent per year during the 1970s, reaching a length of about 155,000 kilometers by 1981 (see fig. 8). According to statistics for the previous year, only 18 percent of these roads could be used in all kinds of weather; the rest were susceptible to flooding. The all-weather facilities were concentrated in the national highway system, which made up 17 percent of the total road length in 1980. The number of four-wheeled vehicles increased by 6.5 percent per year during the 1970s to 937,000 vehicles in 1982. In addition, there were probably more than 250,000 motorcycles in operation. The vehicle fleet included some 81,000 colorful jeep jitneys ("jeepneys") available to taxi large numbers of people.

Because of competition from the highway system, the conditions of the government-owned Philippine National Railroad deteriorated during the 1970s. As of 1979 only 740 kilometers of main-line track and 80 kilometers of branch lines were operating out of a total network of 1,060 kilometers on Luzon. Since 1979 the government has been rehabilitating about 450 kilometers of track running from Manila to Legazpi under a loan from the Asian Development Bank (ADB). Another railroad system consisted of 117 kilometers of track on the island of Panay. The privately owned system, regarded as unsafe, was scheduled for rehabilitation and limited operation in the early 1980s.

The government was building an overhead light rapid transit system in Metro Manila, scheduled to operate on 15 kilometers of track starting in 1984. In 1983 there were an estimated 950,000 registered motor vehicles in the region, and the rapid transit system would relieve this traffic by accommodating 40,000 passengers an hour.

The Philippine Port Authority regulated the operations of 34 ports. of entry, 54 subports of entry, and 12 other national ports in 1980.. There were 219 municipal ports and 286 private ports, piers, and wharves, used primarily for exports. During the 1970s the facilities at the major ports were rehabilitated or expanded, and expansion projects continued in 1983 at Cebu, Zamboanga, Cagayan de Oro, and Iloilo. The second phase of the international container terminal at Manila, the largest port in the country, was under construction and expected to handle almost 500,000 20-foot-equivalent units of container traffic per year by 1986. Another container port was planned for Cebu.

In 1980 the overseas merchant marine fleet totaled 183 vessels, each vessel averaging over 10,000 deadweight tons. The interisland fleet, including fishing vessels, consisted of 10,500 vessels, averaging 314 deadweight tons each. The coastal liner service, operating on regular schedules, had 1,964 ships averaging about 85 deadweight tons. Most of the domestic fleet was built before 1969 and needed to be replaced. In 1980 there were 163 shipping repair and construction companies in the country, having shipyards that accommodated 794,460 gross tons of vessels. A major new yard, in the town of Subic, was to add 300,000 tons to the shipyard capacity in 1982. Half of the shipyard capacity, however, was not in use in 1980. The replacement needs of the fleet were being met primarily through the importation of second-hand vessels rather than new construction.

The government-owned Philippine Airlines, the only scheduled domestic airline and the international flag carrier, expanded its international passenger service by 22 percent per year during the 1970s and its domestic service by 2.7 percent per year but operated at a loss. The airline flew 13 wide-bodied jets on its international lines and served domestic airports with 12 small jets and 15 turboprops in 1983. A new international airport in Manila was completed in 1982, and the old facility was being converted to a major domestic terminal. There were 39 secondary airports outside of Manila, of which five occasionally handled international flights.

In 1981 there were 62 local telephone companies, nine domestic telegraph and telex companies, and three data communications firms. The Bureau of Telecommunications of the Ministry of Transportation and Communications, which operated its own limited telephone and telegraph services, planned to integrate the systems over the next two decades. Relying as much as possible on private enterprises, the government hoped to create one or two corporate institutions for each kind of telecommunication service. In 1981 there were only 422,000 main telephone stations nationwide, of which 282,000 were in Metro Manila. Telegraph and telex services reached 1,223 of 1,561 municipalities. The government was just beginning to develop a backbone network for data transmission.

The postal system has long been the subject of public ridicule, but the appointment of a new director in 1981 brought a genuine improvement in the system's efficiency. One year later, mail that had often taken two weeks to travel from one part of Metro Manila to another was being delivered within one day of mailing some 80 percent of the time. The Bureau of Posts promised to deliver mail on the main routes on Luzon within two days beginning in 1983.

Five television networks operated 38 broadcasting stations and 55 transmission facilities around the country in 1980. There were approximately 1 million television sets in 1979, chiefly in Metro Manila.

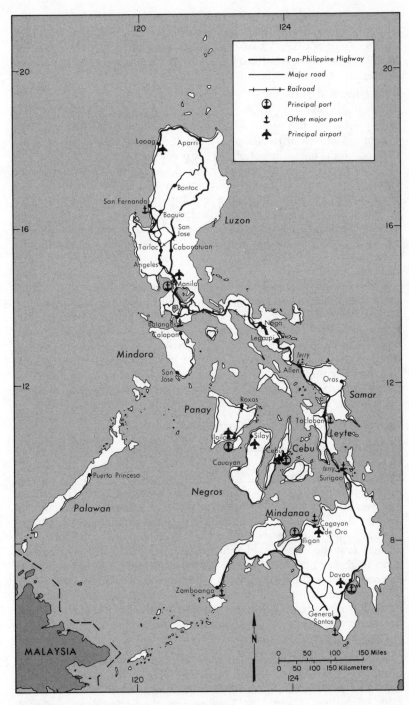

Figure 8. Transportation System, 1982

Eleven major radio networks and some 313 radiobroadcast stations were in operation in 1980, and there were an estimated 2 million radios in use in 1979. A survey of urban areas throughout the country in 1980 found that two-thirds of all adult respondents had a radio at home, and 19 percent had a television set.

Marketing and Services

Retail and wholesale trade, which by law was restricted to Filipino enterprises, run the gamut from large-scale department stores in Manila to a plethora of *tiendas de sari-sari* (general stores) that sell individual items normally sold in larger packages. Almost all retail trade is in the hands of private entrepreneurs. During the 1970s, however, the government became more involved in the marketing of rice and corn, and in 1983 the National Food Authority was granted the right to buy and sell all foodstuffs, including poultry and livestock. This agency continued to work with private millers and processors but had set up 281 retail marketing centers by 1981. The commercial activities of the nation's retailers and wholesalers produced 23.6 percent of GDP in 1981.

Government, financial, real estate, accounting, engineering, entertainment, hotel, restaurant, household, and other services produced 10.3 percent of GDP in 1981—a decrease from the 13.4 percent contribution in 1972. As in the commerce sector, most of these enterprises were small-scale and family-run or consisted of even a single individual hired out as a domestic servant or other kind of laborer. Metro Manila had the full complement of modern services, including many first-class hotels and a major international convention center. Several of these enterprises, however, were having trouble turning a profit.

Foreign Economic Relations

Although less dependent on international trade than several other Asian countries, the Philippines relied on foreign financial capital and, above all, on the export of a variety of products to finance the imports needed to run the economy. Like most developing countries, the nation has usually been unable to export as much as it imports. The current account deficit, which includes transfers in the form of foreign grants, became especially burdensome after a second round of oil price increases launched the world into recession in 1979. The subsequent drop in the prices of Philippine exports and escalating international interest rates pushed the deficit to 8.5 percent of GNP in 1982. After financing this deficit with capital flows, the Central Bank still had to draw down its foreign reserves by US$1.14 billion to meet the overall balance of payments deficit (see table 13, Appendix).

Capital Flows

As the current account deficit widened, managing the external debt became a major constraint on economic policy. The total debt rose from 22.7 percent of GNP in 1972 to 34.5 percent of GNP in 1982, or US$17.1 billion. About US$13 billion was fixed-term debt, some 93

*Jeepneys are assembled mainly from imported parts on assembly
lines tailor-made for the Philippines.
Courtesy Tourist Research and Planning*

percent of which had a maturity of five years or more. The remainder
consisted of so-called revolving credits—short-term loans that basically
liquidated themselves in the normal course of trade. Servicing this
debt cost another US$1.8 billion in interest payments in 1982, which
added to the current account deficit. The debt-service ratio (see Glossary) reached some 25 percent of all foreign exchange earnings in
1982—above the 20-percent level usually considered prudent by international bankers.

There was some concern on the part of international bankers about
the government's reckoning of the reported official reserves at the end
of 1982, which as the result of the balance of payments gap dropped
to US$2.5 billion—equivalent to 117 days of imports. These critics
pointed out that many of the so-called reserves were themselves obligations to foreign banks. The Central Bank privately acknowledged
that US$2 billion of its reserves came from deposits, loans, and currency
swaps from foreign banks, which, theoretically at least, did not belong
to the government.

Fearing a potential debt crisis such as that in Mexico during 1982,
the government moved quickly to make some important arrangements

with international lenders in early 1983. Foremost was a US$510 million arrangement with the IMF, which alone would liquidate the planned payments gap in 1983. The Central Bank also concluded negotiations for a second structural adjustment loan from the World Bank, valued at US$302 million. A consortium of international banks committed a loan for US$300 million in January. Overall, the Central Bank announced that it was reducing its ceiling on foreign borrowing for the public sector from US$2.4 billion in 1982 to US$2 billion in 1983. Only half of this total would be allowed to come from commercial sources.

The dependency on foreign credit has caused some concern and controversy both within and outside the government. Publicly, the government has argued that the conditions imposed by the IMF loan were too harsh, including tight restrictions on the expansion of the government deficit. Some opponents have charged that through its two structural adjustment loans, which required broad policy changes aimed at removing obstacles to foreign trade, the World Bank has had undue influence on Philippine affairs. The government remained committed, nonetheless, to the policy reforms approved by the World Bank, believing that they were in the public interest. The short-term measures of the IMF, however, were problematic but necessary to maintain the confidence of other commercial lenders and investors.

The concessional elements of most of these long-term loans, moreover, could not be ignored. Because the Philippines is classified by the World Bank as a middle-income country, it has not qualified for much aid in the form of grants. In 1981 the country received only $142 million in grants, of which Japan and the United States—the two most important bilateral donors—provided US$45 million and US$33 million, respectively. The United States also offered military assistance (see Foreign Military Relations, ch. 5). Loans and financial assistance amounted to over US$1 billion, of which the World Bank and other multilateral sources accounted for over one-half. The total grant element (see Glossary) of all these concessional loans and export credits was about 74 percent in 1981.

The most controversial kind of foreign influence in the economy has been direct foreign investment. From 1958 to 1981, based on balance of payments data, the net inflow of foreign investment averaged only 0.3 percent of GNP, while the outflow of income from these investments averaged 1.1 percent of GNP. This excluded the many important investments made before 1958 and did not show the amount of employment and income generated for the domestic economy, which otherwise might not have been available. In the decade before the establishment of martial law in 1972 there had been a net outflow of investment funds. Thereafter, the inflow averaged about 0.5 percent of GNP and reached over 1 percent of GNP in 1981 before falling in 1982 to 0.8 percent. Of the US$2.2 billion invested in the Philippines from 1970 to 1982, the United States accounted for 48 percent and Japan for 18 percent. The principal investments were in the energy, electronics, automotive, and other manufacturing industries, although there were some important foreign plantations in agriculture.

Despite various government measures to stimulate foreign investment since 1972, a number of restrictions and regulations deterred many investors. Remembering the political controversy over the issue of so-called parity rights for United States investors, the government severely limited the property ownership rights of foreigners. In addition, all expatriate staff were issued licenses that had to be reviewed frequently. Ten years after the start of a foreign-owned venture, the government reserved the right to make the company sell shares to the Philippine public. The government has also not allowed the offshore banking units of foreign banks to open up operations in local currency.

In an effort to ameliorate some of the concerns of foreign investors, the government streamlined the operations of the BOI in 1982, setting up a one-stop office for investors. The government also authorized the Central Bank to set up a subsidiary to sign long-term property leases on behalf of foreign investors, who would pay for the property in one lump sum and receive the profits from the sale of the property upon their withdrawal. Representatives of United States, Japanese, and West European businesses, however, continued to seek broader assurances that their investments would be protected in the event of political changes. In negotiations on a bilateral investment agreement between the United States and the Philippines in 1982, the United States side reportedly sought guarantees that rules in force at the start of an investment enterprise would remain in force throughout the life of the project. No agreement was reached, and the Philippine side characterized such assurances as essentially the same as parity rights.

Trade Patterns

The Ministry of Trade and Industry has embarked on a major campaign to promote the sale of so-called nontraditional exports: electronic equipment, garments, gifts and housewares, fresh and processed foods, leather goods and footwear, and furniture. Already these items had grown in importance from less than 9 percent of the value of merchandise exports in 1972 to about 57 percent of the total in 1982. The ministry included the promotion of overseas construction contracts in its export program and had set up a special committee to coordinate the development of these industries.

The most important manufactured exports were electronics, garments, and processed foods. The electronics export industry expanded its sales from the equivalent of US$2 million in 1972 to over US$1 billion in 1982, surpassing within the space of a decade traditional items, such as sugar, copper, and coconut oil, as the leading foreign exchange earner. The 31 semiconductor firms in operation in 1981 reportedly assembled about one-fifth of all production in the world; 13 of these firms were foreign subsidiaries. The garment export industry suffered a slump in 1982 as the result of tighter quota restrictions from its importers and failed to reach the government's target of US$1 billion. Despite the 12.6 percent decline in sales registered in 1982, the roughly US$540 million of products exported was nearly 300 times the value exported 10 years earlier. The export of fresh and processed food and beverage products nearly doubled from 1977 to 1981, reaching about US$675 million. About one-third of this total came from the export of two traditional items, bananas and desiccated coconut, and the rest from a wide variety of nontraditional items, such as canned and frozen tuna, coffee, cocoa, mango, papaya, and processed fruits.

The overseas construction industry produced revenues that were difficult to calculate because many workers found ways to skirt the formal banking system to remit their earnings back home. The Central Bank estimated that about US$1.6 billion of remittances entered the economy in 1982, of which only one-half went through the banking system. This sum represented about one-fifth of all foreign exchange earnings, but only US$700-US$800 million could be used for balance of payments purposes. In early 1983 the Central Bank announced the tight enforcement of remittance regulations and began a special raffle that distributed a lottery ticket for each US$100 remitted through local banks.

The Ministry of Trade and Industry favored the expansion of contracts by Philippine construction companies more than the export of individual laborers to other foreign companies. At the end of 1981 there were 148 registered contractors working overseas, and in the first seven months of 1982 Philippine construction firms picked up an additional US$646 million in contracts, compared with US$782 million in 1981 and only US$358 million in 1978. About 80 percent of these contracts were for projects in the Middle East—nearly half in Saudi Arabia alone. Declining international oil prices, however, were jeopardizing contracts that were already negotiated, as well as new projects in 1983. Both the minister of labor and employment and the minister of trade and industry made trips to the Middle East early in the year to save as many contracts as possible for Philippine firms. Several Middle Eastern countries, moreover, wanted to discuss complaints about the behavior and treatment of Filipino laborers in their countries.

One reason for the increasing share of nontraditional exports in the value of all export trade has been the poor performance of traditional items. Depressed international prices for sugar, copper, and coconut products caused most of the decrease. Government requirements that some products be reserved for domestic consumers and producers or conserved to protect the environment also affected the performance of coconut-oil and log exports. The value of traditional exports decreased by 22.6 percent from 1981 to US$2.1 billion in 1982. It would have dropped further had not the government been exporting sugar under long-term contracts that would last until the mid-1980s, by which time a recovery of prices was likely.

Foreign exchange earnings from the sale of services other than construction or from remittances and other transfers totaled about US$2 billion in 1981. Tourist receipts contributed US$344 million, and transportation services generated US$144 million. The promotional efforts of the Ministry of Tourism through its 11 overseas offices helped increase the number of tourist arrivals by 22 percent per year from 1970 to 1981, to more than a million persons.

Trade policy and the restructuring of the fiscal incentive system have improved the opportunities for exporters substantially in the 1980s. Although the expressed policy in the previous decade was similar, the incentive structure ultimately favored domestic producers and some importers. In early 1981 the government reduced the tariffs charged on imports of raw materials and intermediate goods used by exporters. In 1983 the government restructured the fiscal incentives of the BOI to promote exports; eight special tax measures were made available variously to new and existing exporters. Only one general incentive remained for new or expanded investments regardless of market orientation. To encourage the use of resources available locally, including labor, the government also gave a tax incentive based on the local content (value added from local sources) of exported goods.

The Ministry of Trade and Industry also announced in 1980 that it would expand the number of export-processing zones, which gave special incentives to exporters located at these sites. After further research, however, the government decided to scale down this program and to combine the export-processing zones with planned industrial estates for domestic manufactures. Only half of the 16 zones planned for 1988 were likely to be started. As of December 1982 there were 54 companies located at the export-processing zone in Mariveles, seven companies at Mactan, and five in Baguio. The proposed sites were the provinces of Pampanga, Albay, and La Union and the cities of Iloilo, Bacolod, Cagayan de Oro, Davao, and Cavite; only the latter would be exclusively for export companies.

The exchange rate also affects the attractiveness of exports to foreign buyers. Since 1980 the flexible government policy that allowed the peso to devalue by 34 percent as of mid-1983 has aided the nation's exporters. But because the exchange rate was quoted in terms of the United States dollar, which appreciated in value during much of this period, the effective depreciation relative to the currencies of other trading partners was slight. In an unusual move, in late June 1983 the government devalued the peso by a further 7.3 percent in one fell swoop to boost exports and reduce imports. The major markets for Philippine products are the United States, Japan, the Netherlands, the Federal Republic of Germany (West Germany), Hong Kong, Indonesia, Britain, Taiwan, and Australia (see table 14, Appendix).

The country's major imports were mineral fuels, raw materials and components for industry, and capital goods and equipment. In 1981 petroleum imports accounted for 26 percent of the total of US$7.8 billion of imported merchandise, compared with 21 percent in 1975. Almost all these imports came from Saudi Arabia. Chemicals, including fertilizer, accounted for 11 percent of imports, materials for electronic manufacturing for 8 percent, and other raw materials and intermediate goods for 17 percent. Capital goods—primarily manufacturing, transportation, and energy-related equipment—made up 24 percent of all imports. Imports of consumer goods decreased from a 10-percent share of the total in 1975 to about 8.5 percent in 1981. The principal sources of Philippine imports were the United States, Japan, Saudi Arabia, Kuwait, Hong Kong, Australia, and Indonesia.

Tariff changes begun in 1981 were intended to reduce the average import tariff rate from 43 percent that year to 28 percent by 1985. Most of the change would be accounted for in the reduction of extremely high tariffs on consumer goods. This category of imports, however, would remain the most protected. The government was also gradually eliminating quantitative restrictions on imports. Despite the decrease in the value of imports by 1.8 percent in 1982 to US$7.8 billion, the export shortfall prompted the government to impose a 3-percent ad valorem duty on all imports in 1983. Since the additional tariff was levied across the board on all goods, it left intact the restructuring of tariffs that were to improve the efficiency of the domestic and export industries.

Not only did the government levy an additional tariff in 1983, but it also required that importers make payments of taxes and duties in advance of the arrival of goods at customs. The advance payments were to eliminate so-called technical smuggling whereby importers falsified customs documents to undervalue shipments of goods. This form of tax evasion was often accomplished in collusion with dishonest customs agents. The weakness of the government's fiscal position in the early 1980s has caused a major campaign to rid the customs system of this kind of corruption.

* * *

Book-length studies of the Philippine economy are few and out-of-date, the most comprehensive being that compiled by the World Bank team of Russell J. Cheetham et al., *The Philippines: Priorities and Prospects for Development*. Other World Bank studies, such as Barend A. de Vries et al., *Philippines: Industrial Development Strategy and Policies* and Edward K. Hawkins et al., *The Philippines: Aspects of the Financial Sector*, together with the Philippine study by Romeo M. Bautista et al., *Industrial Promotion Policies in the Philippines*, give the analytical basis for the policy reforms of the 1980s. Articles in the weekly *Far Eastern Economic Review* and daily *Asian Wall Street Journal* chart current economic events in a readable, journalistic style. *Asia Yearbook*, published by the Far Eastern Economic Review, is a convenient summary of annual economic events. The Joint Publications Research Service reprints numerous articles from the Philippine press in its *Southeast Asia Report* and its *South and East Asia Report* series that provide a useful perspective. Walden Bello, David Kinley, and Elaine Elinson in *Development Debacle: The World Bank in the Philippines* provide a provocative critique of government economic policy that is unfortunately flawed by its conspiratorial tone. Rene E. Ofreneo's *Capitalism in Philippine Agriculture* is an interesting critique of agricultural development policies. (For further information and complete citations, see Bibliography.)

Chapter 4. Government and Politics

Malacañang Palace in Manila is the official residence of the chief executive.

IN 1983 FERDINAND E. MARCOS was in his eighteenth year of rule that had begun with his election in 1965. Limited to two consecutive four-year terms under the constitution of 1935, he was reelected in 1969 but in September 1972 proclaimed martial law and ruled thereafter under presidential emergency powers stipulated in the transitory provisions of a new constitution adopted in 1973. In January 1981, against the backdrop of growing domestic and foreign criticism of alleged political repression and human rights violations, martial law was finally lifted. Several months later Marcos was elected to a term of six years in the first presidential election held under the 1973 Constitution. In that election he faced only a nominal challenge because the opposition, still in a state of disarray after nearly nine years of lethargy under martial law, decided to boycott.

Unlike its predecessor, the Constitution of 1973 sets no limitations on the number of presidential terms. It is unclear whether Marcos, who became 66 years old in September 1983, would seek another term in 1987. Equally unclear is who would succeed him in the event of his disability or death. The question of succession continues to draw speculation if only because the president's wife, Imelda Romualdez Marcos, is reputedly the second most influential personality in the power structure and hence has been widely regarded as almost certain to become a central figure in the politics of succession—as heiress presumptive or kingmaker.

Politics was dominated by the Marcoses and the New Society Movement, the ruling political machine created in 1978 to pave the way for eventual return to political normality, the first phase of which could come as early as mid-1984, coinciding with the elections scheduled for the "regular" National Assembly. The most recent parliamentary elections had been held in 1978, but the legislature elected at that time was called "interim" because of the transitional nature of political and governmental processes until the regular assembly came into being.

The New Society Movement began as a party of bureaucrats, pro-Marcos business elite, and pre-1972 politicians friendly to Marcos. It had little mass following but with generous bureaucratic assistance quickly established itself as the principal vehicle through which the traditional system of patron-client relationships could function. This system of relationships through the New Society Movement doubtless gave the government a strategic advantage over the opposition groups, which had neither organization nor resources to match the ruling party.

Marcos' rule was bolstered further by his firm grip on the armed forces, which comprised the army, navy, air force, and Philippine Constabulary. Despite the lifting of martial law, military involvement in civil affairs diminished only slightly. Unquestionably, the military

177

continued to be a major power base for the Marcos leadership, playing a key role in sustaining the highly centralized government setup in which the preeminence of Marcos' executive and legislative prerogatives was seldom questioned. The only institution that could possibly provide a semblance of countervailing power was the interim National Assembly, but this body was filled almost entirely with pro-Marcos members of the dominant parliamentary group, the New Society Movement.

Voices critical of the government came from broad strata of the society but, aside from the commonality of their opposition to Marcos, they were far from united on such critical matters as organization, leadership, and strategy. The fragmented opposition groups insisted that the rules of partisan politics should be liberalized to permit an orderly and peaceful development of a truly representative and fair political system. In their view the alternatives were the radicalization of the opposition and the worsening of the long-festering communist insurgency.

Most observers believed, in the early 1980s, that none of the organized opposition groups, legal or otherwise, posed any serious threat to the establishment, individually or in coalition. They were, nevertheless, mindful of the possibility of political destabilization coming from the Roman Catholic Church—the only national organization over which the Marcos administration had no direct control. Church-state friction was increasingly manifest after the mid-1970s. The church leadership, divided as it was between activists and nonactivists, viewed its own role as the conscience of the nation and was generally critical of the government's alleged insensitivity to human rights, the plight of the poor and powerless, and abuses and corruption among military and civilian officials. For its part the Marcos administration maintained that church activists were politically intrusive, involving themselves in some instances in subversive activities in violation of the laws. In 1983 efforts were continuing by both government and church leaders to reconcile their differences through open dialogue.

Foreign relations were relatively free of tensions. The Philippines placed special emphasis on promoting mutually beneficial ties with the United States, which continued to operate military installations in the Philippines, the two most important being Clark Air Base and Subic Bay Naval Base. Friendly relations with Southeast Asian countries were also stressed, as were relations with Islamic states of the Middle East that were perceived to bring some moderating influence to bear on the Muslim Filipino (Moro) secessionist rebels at home and abroad.

Government

In 1983 the government was led by Marcos, who was both head of state and chief executive, in addition to being the commander in chief of the armed forces and leader of the New Society Movement (Kilusang Bagong Lipunan—KBL). Despite its parliamentary facade, the government was essentially presidential and was organized as a unitary structure (see fig. 9). Because of constitutional amendments passed in 1976, Marcos held the additional post of prime minister from 1978 to 1981, when the latter post was relinquished to Cesar Virata, the minister of finance and the best known technocrat in the country.

Constitutional Framework

In September 1972 martial law was proclaimed as necessary to protect the integrity of the nation from forces of lawlessness, rebellion, and secession. Marcos announced a series of measures that he said were essential to his efforts to restore law and order and to bring about reforms in the social, economic, and political sectors of the society. Among these measures was the suspension of political party activities. Reforms envisaged by him were to bring an end to social inequities of what he called the "old sick society" and to usher in eventually a "new society."

The constitutional convention, which had been formed on a nonpartisan basis in 1970 to draft a new basic law of the land, continued its work to replace the constitution of 1935. The 1935 charter had been retained in toto at independence in 1946. In November 1972 the convention adopted a draft constitution, and among its major innovations was the adoption of a British-style parliamentary form of government under a prime minister who would in that capacity represent the majority bloc of elected representatives in the national legislature. The draft constitution also provided for a president who would have substantially reduced powers in marked contrast to the strong presidency under the 1935 constitution. In the proposed new constitutional scheme, the president was limited to ceremonial duties.

Evidently, after the declaration of martial law a new section was added to the draft document to accommodate the exigencies of what was to become known as the "crisis government." This addition took the form of Article XVII, entitled "Transitory Provisions," which outlined the procedures through which the parliamentary form of government would eventually come into being. They provided for an interim National Assembly, which would come into existence automatically upon the ratification of the 1973 Constitution and would remain until the regular National Assembly was formed through elections called by the interim legislature. The interim body was to have as its members the incumbent president, the vice president, those members of the existing bicameral legislature who opted to serve therein, and those delegates of the constitutional convention who had voted for Article XVII. Significantly, the transitory provisions allowed—not without strong objections by some delegates to the convention—the incumbent president to continue to exercise his powers under the 1935 constitution as well as the powers vested in the president and the prime minister under the 1973 Constitution. Additionally, they empowered the incumbent president to rule by decree indefinitely; the presidential decrees were to have the effect of law, to be binding even

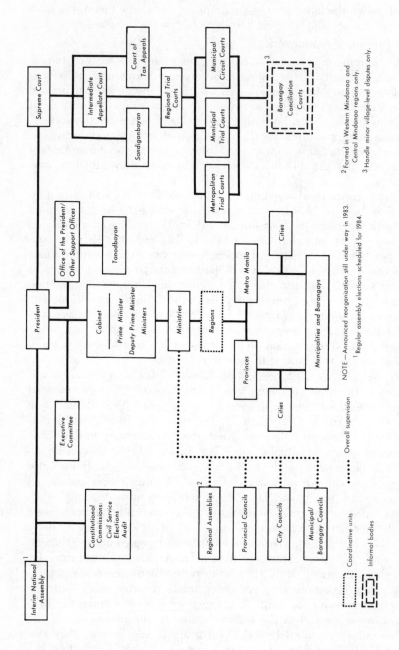

Figure 9. Organization of the Philippine Government, 1983

after the lifting of martial law "unless expressly and explicitly modified or repealed by the regular national assembly."

Originally, the draft was to have been submitted to a popular referendum on January 15, 1973, but this did not happen. On January 7 Marcos called on citizens 15 years old and above to take part in "national consultation" between January 10 and 15. The consultation was to take place through the newly created barangays (called barrios until then; see Glossary), which he said would provide "a real basis of a working, direct, particularly Filipino democracy." In a decree of December 31, 1972, which ordered the creation of the barangays, Marcos had declared that the new institution was "necessary to broaden the base of citizen participation in the democratic process and to afford ample opportunities for the citizenry to express their views on important national issues." Specifically, on January 7 he asked the barangay residents to discuss whether they approved of the New Society program, the reform measures he initiated under martial law, the holding of a plebiscite on the draft constitution, and the convening of the interim National Assembly as provided for in the draft. Additionally, the barangay members were called on to decide whether they should approve of the way Marcos led the country, whether martial law should continue, whether the regularly scheduled national elections should be held in November 1973, and whether the draft basic law should be adopted.

On January 17 Marcos summarily announced the draft constitution ratified, inasmuch as an overwhelming majority of barangay members (who voted by a show of hands and then only in limited parts of the country) had not only approved the new constitution but also expressed that their endorsement should be taken as an official act of ratification. In response to what he called "the wishes of our people expressed so forcefully, so unanimously, so overwhelmingly," he signed a proclamation for continuation of martial law and another to the effect that the interim National Assembly would not be convened at that time. He also announced the suspension of elections for the next seven years. Three days later he denied charges that his regime was dictatorial, stating that it could be more aptly described as one of "constitutional authoritarianism." He let it be known also that the barangays would be called on to voice their views on important issues whenever necessary in the future.

The Constitution declares the Philippines a republican state based on popular sovereignty. In renouncing war as an instrument of national policy, it affirms the supremacy of civilian authority over the military. It directs the state to "establish, maintain, and ensure adequate social services in the field of education, health, housing, employment, welfare and social security." It also ensures "the rights of workers to self-organization, collective bargaining, security of tenure and just and humane conditions of work."

Apart from the preamble, the Constitution contains 17 articles dealing, respectively, with the national territory; declaration of principles and state policies; citizenship; fundamental rights; duties and obligations of citizens; suffrage; the presidency; the National Assembly; the prime minister, the cabinet, and the Executive Committee; the judiciary; local government; the constitutional commissions; accountability of public officers; the national economy and the patrimony of the nation; general provisions; amendments; and transitory provisions. Of these, the Executive Committee was added through an amendment in 1981.

A bill of rights, along the lines of the United States model and as originally written into the 1935 constitution, is retained for the most part in the 1973 Constitution. Expressly guaranteed are basic human rights to life, liberty, and property—rights that are not to be deprived without due process of law; freedom from "unreasonable searches and seizures of whatever nature and for any purpose" except on probable cause established by a judge; the privileges of the writ of habeas corpus (except in cases of invasion, insurrection, or rebellion); freedom of abode and travel; and privacy of communication and correspondence. Among other constitutional guarantees are the freedom of speech and the press, the freedom of assembly, the right to petition the authorities for redress of grievances, the freedom of worship, and the right to form associations. The state is prohibited from enacting ex post facto law. Involuntary servitude and cruel or unusual punishment are outlawed.

The Constitution sanctions a free enterprise system, but it allows the state to regulate or prohibit private monopolies in the public interest. The state may, in the interest of public welfare or national defense, establish and operate industries and means of transportation and communication and, on payment of just compensation, transfer to public ownership utilities and other private enterprises to be operated by the government. In addition, the Constitution calls on the state to implement a land reform program aimed at emancipating the tenants from the bondage of the soil (see Land Use and Tenure, ch. 3). All lands of the public domain and natural resources are declared to belong to the state.

Authority to interpret the articles of the Constitution is vested in the Supreme Court. All cases involving the constitutionality of a treaty, executive agreement, or law are heard and decided by the full bench of the Supreme Court (chief justice and 14 associate justices). Judgment requires the concurrence of at least 10 justices. The procedure for amending the Constitution requires initiatory action either by the legislature on a vote of three-fourths of all its members or by a constitutional convention that is to be convened by the legislature by a vote of two-thirds of all its members. The legislature may also submit the question of calling such a convention to the electorate in an election. An amendment becomes effective when ratified by a majority of the votes cast in a referendum.

The Constitution was amended in 1976 and again in 1981. Generally, the 1976 amendments strengthened Marcos' already formidable executive powers and empowered him to rule by decree at his own discretion until martial law was lifted and even thereafter if, in his judgment, it was required. The 1981 amendments revised the governmental form from the parliamentary to the presidential style and made it possible for Marcos to serve as head of state and chief executive of the government. They also provided for the creation of the Executive Committee, which would serve as a collective caretaker body in the event of the death or incapacitation of the president.

Central Government

Under the Constitution the government divides into the executive, legislative, and judicial branches. The separation of powers is based in theory on the principle of checks and balances, but actually the executive branch remains the dominant force. Its authority, buttressed by the preeminence of the presidency as the single most important seat of political power, extends to all administrative subdivisions of the country.

The Presidency, the Executive Committee, and the Cabinet

The president is popularly elected to an unlimited number of six-year terms and must be a natural-born citizen and at least 50 years of age. Should two or more candidates tie for the highest number of votes, one of them is chosen by a vote of a majority of all the members of the National Assembly. Presidential powers are broad with regard to policymaking, executive prerogatives, appointment and dismissal of senior government officials, and war and peace. The president nominates the prime minister and appoints other cabinet members, addresses the opening session of the interim National Assembly, and exercises legislative initiatives through the prime minister. As commander in chief, the president may call out the armed forces to prevent or suppress lawlessness, invasion, insurrection, or rebellion and in these crises may suspend the privilege of the writ of habeas corpus or declare martial law. Constitutionally, the president is exempt from any lawsuit for official acts or acts performed by authorized officials.

The mode of presidential succession is laid down under the constitutional amendments of 1981. In the event of permanent disability, death, removal from office, or resignation, the president's functions and powers are to be exercised collectively by the Executive Committee until a successor is chosen. The constitutionally fixed 15 members of the committee are chosen by the president; at least half of these members must be members of the interim National Assembly. New elections are held 45 to 60 days from the time a special election is called by the assembly. The call for the election must be issued within 30 days from the time the vacancy occurs unless a regular presidential election is already scheduled within 18 months. If the president-elect dies or fails to meet legal requirements, the Executive Committee, headed by the prime minister, is to serve as caretaker body until a new chief executive is elected. If the National Assembly withdraws its confidence from the prime minister, however, the Speaker of the assembly is called on to preside over the committee.

Apart from its caretaker role, the Executive Committee serves as the highest executive forum available to the presidency. It met for the first time in August 1981 with seven members; in August 1982 four more were added, including Imelda Marcos. In 1983 the 11 members of the committee (four seats were left vacant) were among the most influential public officials in the country. Ordinarily, the committee, chaired by the prime minister, met weekly with the cabinet to discuss a wide range of policies and issues requiring top-level and urgent official attention.

The cabinet is an important advisory and deliberative body, second only to the Executive Committee. It is composed of the prime minister, deputy prime minister, ministers (called secretaries until June 1978) with or without portfolio, and other high-ranking officials. A majority of cabinet officials who are heads of ministries must be elected members of the assembly. The prime minister and the deputy prime minister are both nominated by the president from among the members of the assembly; the election of these two senior officials by the assembly is a virtual certainty. Other cabinet members are nominated by the prime minister for presidential appointment. Cabinet members serve at the pleasure of the president and may resign voluntarily or be removed by the chief executive without affecting their membership in the assembly. Collectively, they are responsible to the legislature, which may withdraw its confidence in the prime minister by a majority vote of its members. If a motion of no confidence is carried, the president must submit a nominee for a new prime minister to be elected by the assembly. Under the principle of checks and balances, the prime minister may advise the president to dissolve the assembly "whenever the need arises for a popular vote of confidence on fundamental issues, but not on a matter involving his own personal integrity."

In the early 1980s there was a continuing effort to reorganize the bureaucracy in order to eliminate red tape and duplication of functions. Under a major change announced in July 1981 concerning the composition of government ministries, there were 18 "line ministries" and seven "support offices" having full ministerial status. The line ministries included the following portfolios: agrarian reform, agriculture, education and culture, energy, finance, foreign affairs, health, human settlements, trade and industry, justice, labor and employment, local government, national defense, natural resources, public works and highways, social services and development, tourism, and transportation and communications. The support agencies included the Office of the President, the Office of the Budget and Management, Office of Media Affairs (formerly Ministry of Public Information), Office of Muslim Affairs, Office of the Solicitor General, National Economic and Development Authority, and National Science Development Board. The heads of all these ministerial-level units were regular participants in the weekly cabinet sessions chaired by Prime Minister Virata. Also regularly taking part were senior presidential assistants with full cabinet rank; the most influential of these was the presidential executive assistant. Special cabinet sessions could be called by the president to consider top national issues.

National Assembly

Until 1972 the legislature was known as Congress, a bicameral body that had functioned in the context of an open, highly spirited partisan political competition (see Independence and Constitutional Government, 1945-72, ch. 1). Under the 1973 Constitution it was renamed the National Assembly (Batasang Pambansa). Under the transitory provisions of this Constitution, the National Assembly was to serve as an interim legislature having as its members the incumbent president and those representatives of the Congress and those delegates of the constitutional convention who had voted for the transitory provisions of the basic law. When the Constitution went into effect in January 1973, the assembly should have been convened by the president as provided for in the Constitution, but this was not done. Marcos explained that the Congress was a major cause of political anarchy and of the inequities perpetuated in the name of democracy. The decision not to convene reflected his distaste for old-style parliamentary politics, which he argued was tainted by corruption and the prohibitive cost of free-for-all electioneering.

When the Constitution was amended in 1976, the original provisions for the interim National Assembly were dropped in favor of new ones with membership to be determined by both election and appointment for a term of six years. The first parliamentary elections under the amended charter took place in April 1978; the next elections were scheduled for May 1984. Of the 200 members, 165 represented regional constituencies, 21 included the president and his cabinet appointees, and 14 were selected from among government-sponsored youth, agricultural, and labor organizations.

The assembly convenes annually on the fourth Monday of July for its regular session, to which the president delivers his "state of the nation" address. Its members, who elect the Speaker from among themselves, are granted parliamentary immunity, subject to some statutory restrictions. Members may not hold any other public office except as members of the cabinet and the Executive Committee or as deputy ministers (called ministers of state). The deputy ministers do not hold cabinet rank and are appointed by the president to serve as liaisons between the assembly and the ministries to which they are assigned.

As part of the legislative checks and balances against the executive branch, the Constitution originally provided for "a question hour at least once a month" or as often as parliamentary rules would allow. The prime minister and his cabinet colleagues may be required to answer questions by members of the assembly. In October 1981, however, rules for the question hour were revised so that it would be, as one legislator put it, "almost futile, if not useless, for assemblymen to propound questions that dig critically into government performance." Under new rules, members are required to submit their questions first to the Speaker of the assembly to determine if the points to be raised are "non-opinionated." Reportedly, Marcos was not in favor of reviving the old practice of "privileged speech hour," where lawmakers could air any topic they chose.

Bills are initiated by both the line ministries and the members of the assembly. Bills on appropriations, revenues, and other major categories originate only in the executive branch. A bill must pass three readings in the appropriate legislative committee on separate days. When passed by the legislature, a bill is sent to the president for assent. If vetoed, the bill must be reconsidered by the legislature, and the presidential objections may be overridden by two-thirds of all of the lawmakers. The assembly shares the treaty-making power with the president; no treaty is valid and effective without parliamentary concurrence. The power to declare a state of war rests, however, solely with the assembly. In times of war or other national crises, the assembly may grant emergency powers to the president; these powers remain valid until the next adjournment of the legislature, unless withdrawn sooner by the latter.

Under the 1981 amendments the Constitution provides the assembly the power to restrain other constitutional entities of the state. Specifically, the legislature may remove the president, justices of the Supreme Court, and members of the three constitutional commissions—the Civil Service Commission, the Commission on Elections, and the Commission on Audit. The grounds for removal are "culpable violation of the Constitution, treason, bribery, other high crimes of graft and corruption." Impeachment must be approved by a vote of at least two-thirds of the assembly.

The Judiciary

The legal system is derived for the most part from Spanish and United States patterns. Civil code procedures on family and property and the absence of jury trial are attributable to Spanish influences, but the bulk of important statutes governing trade and commerce, labor relations, taxation, banking and currency, and governmental operations are of United States derivation, introduced at the turn of the century when the United States had replaced Spain as the colonial power over the Philippines.

In the years after independence the judicial system as evolved earlier was retained intact. It was not until 1980 that the first comprehensive step was taken to revise the system as a part of the nation's continuing process of modernization. In August of that year a presidential committee on judicial reorganization was formed to streamline the court structure, to weed out incompetent and corrupt judges, and to simplify court procedures as a means of administering justice in a more efficient, expeditious, and inexpensive way. After two months of intensive review and investigation, the committee reported to Marcos that "there are problems, both grave and pressing, that call for remedial measures"

*President Marcos addresses the National Assembly
(Batasang Pambansa), 1979.
Courtesy Embassy of the Republic of the Philippines,
Washington*

and in effect confirmed widely held popular views that the judicial system should be given a sweeping overhaul.

A reform bill was subsequently enacted, whereby all civil courts would be abolished except the Supreme Court, the special court handling only graft and corruption cases (Sandiganbayan), and the Court of Tax Appeals. The dissolved courts were to be replaced by newly constituted courts under newly appointed judges.

The judicial reorganization was still under way in 1983. There was a sense of urgency on the part of the Marcos administration about the pressing need to restore public confidence in the court system. In early 1982 Supreme Court justice Juvenal K. Guerrero commented that the prestige of the judiciary had "deteriorated and degenerated to the lowest ebb in public estimation." He called particular attention to the need to have justices and judges "who are fair and impartial, honest and incorruptible, competent and efficient."

In January 1983 Marcos, commenting on the judicial reorganization, stated that the reform in general and the appointment of new judges in particular would be carried out in a fair and nonpolitical manner. This statement was made in connection with a report submitted to him by a specially appointed body to look into the integrity of all judges. That body had recommended that at least half of some 1,600 incumbent judges were unfit, but subsequently almost all of these judges were reappointed.

As of early 1983 the judicial system was headed by the Supreme Court, which had administrative supervision over the judges of all inferior courts. The highest court had a chief justice and 14 justices, who, along with judges of all inferior courts, were appointed by the president and held their offices during good behavior until the age of 70 or until they became incapacitated. The Supreme Court had original jurisdiction over cases affecting ambassadors, other public ministers, and consuls and over petitions for injunctions and writs of habeas corpus. Its appellate jurisdiction covered cases relating to the constitutionality of a treaty, executive agreement, law, ordinance, or executive order; cases involving the legality of any tax, impost, assessment, or toll; cases in which the jurisdiction of any inferior court was at issue; criminal cases in which the penalty of death or life imprisonment was involved; and all cases in which an error or question of law was involved. The highest court could also order a change of venue to avoid a miscarriage of justice. The Constitution empowers the national legislature to define, prescribe, and apportion the jurisdiction of the various courts, but the Supreme Court is exempt from the assembly's purview.

The reform act states that pending the completion of reorganization, the existing courts may continue to function. By mid-1983 for the most part the old courts had been reconstituted. The new structure comprised the Supreme Court at the top and inferior courts established at three levels. The Supreme Court was not affected by reorganization, though it appeared likely that the number of its justices might be increased to expedite the disposition of the growing case load. The 45-member Court of Appeals was replaced by the 50-member Intermediate Appellate Court, below the Supreme Court but above the provincial level. The new appellate court was to hear appeal cases not expressly reserved for the Supreme Court and was given additional jurisdiction over certain cases involving questions of fact.

Provincial-level courts would be replaced by "regional trial courts," which would handle cases previously tried by the courts of first instance, the juvenile and domestic relations courts, the circuit criminal courts, and the Court of Agrarian Relations. Each major population center would be served by a metropolitan trial court. Also at the bottom of the court hierarchy would be a municipal trial court established in each city or municipality (town) and a municipal circuit trial court for a varying number of cities and municipalities.

Local Government

In the years after independence the national government sought to upgrade local government by delegating powers, limited as they were, to local subdivisions and by encouraging broad grass-roots support of and participation in community affairs. Local autonomy had to be balanced, however, against the officially perceived need to ensure effective political and administrative control from Manila, especially in those areas infested with antigovernment insurgency. In any event, the importance of local government as an essential link in the overall scheme of governance was evident in the establishment of a cabinet-level department or ministry in 1972, in the incorporation of a separate article on local government in the 1973 Constitution, and in the reorganization of that ministry into a "more compact and specialized" body in 1981. As reconstituted in that year, the Ministry of Local Government was responsible for training local officials for more efficient implementation of development programs, assisting the president in supervision over local affairs, and assisting in the administration of justice in the *barangays*. After 1981, however, the ministry was no longer responsible for implementing local community development programs; this function was transferred to the Ministry of Human Settlements, headed by Imelda Marcos.

As of mid-1983 the country had a three-tiered structure of local subdivisions—73 provinces and Metro Manila (see Glossary) at the top, 60 cities and 1,534 municipalities in the middle, and more than 41,400 *barangays* at the bottom (see fig. 10). The provinces were grouped into 12 regions plus the National Capital Region, which was coterminous with Metro Manila; this was to enable the national and local governments to pool resources and coordinate their developmental projects more efficiently. The heads of local subdivisions were popularly elected, as were provincial, city, and municipal councillors, to the local representative organs called Sangguniang Bayan.

Inadequate financial resources were frequently singled out as the major reason for lackluster local government performance. The local units, including the *barangays*, had limited power to raise their own revenues, but receipts were barely enough to meet local needs. As a result, dependence on the national treasury for at least 50 percent of local requirements meant national government involvement in local affairs, especially with regard to public works projects and the construction of schools, housing, and roads.

The province is the largest administrative unit, headed by the elective governor, the principal executive agent of the central government, who is aided by the vice governor and a number of senior officials concerned with finance, tax collection, audit, public works, agricultural services, health, and schools. These functionaries are technically subordinate to the governor but are actually responsible to their respective central government ministries that they represent locally. All lower ranking functionaries are on the provincial payroll, having been appointed by the governor.

Metro Manila has a special status because it embraces the national capital, the seat of political and economic power and the center of cultural activity. Its jurisdiction covers four cities, 13 municipalities, and about 1,800 *barangays*. The region has been under the governorship of Imelda Marcos since its reorganization in 1975.

Cities physically within a province but administratively independent have broader taxing powers than municipalities. A city must have a

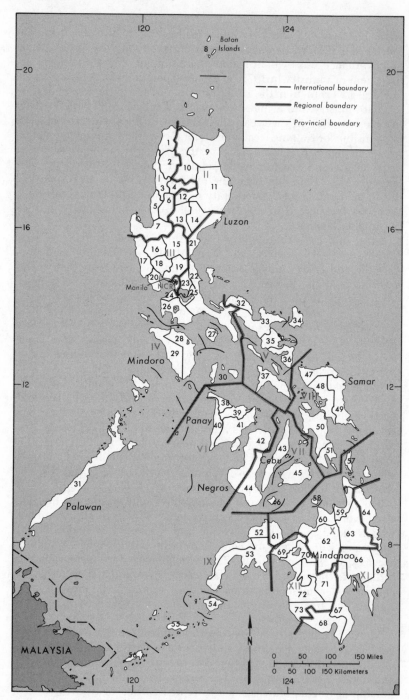

Figure 10. Regions and Provinces, 1983

Classification of Provinces by Geographic Regions

NCR NATIONAL CAPITAL REGION

I ILOCOS
1 Ilocos Norte
2 Abra
3 Ilocos Sur
4 Mountain
5 La Union
6 Benquet
7 Pangasinan

II CAGAYAN VALLEY
8 Batanes
9 Cagayan
10 Kalinga-Apayao
11 Isabela
12 Ifugao
13 Nueva Vizcaya
14 Quirino

III CENTRAL LUZON
15 Nueva Ecija
16 Tarlac
17 Zambales
18 Pampanga
19 Bulacan
20 Bataan

IV SOUTHERN TAGALOG
21 Aurora
22 Quezon
23 Rizal
24 Cavite
25 Laguna
26 Batangas
27 Marinduque
28 Mindoro Oriental
29 Mindoro Occidental
30 Romblon
31 Palawan

V BICOL
32 Camarines Norte
33 Camarines Sur
34 Catanduanes
35 Albay
36 Sorsogon
37 Masbate

VI WESTERN VISAYAS
38 Aklan
39 Capiz
40 Antique
41 Iloilo
42 Negros Occidental

VII CENTRAL VISAYAS
43 Cebu
44 Negros Oriental
45 Bohol
46 Siquijor

VIII EASTERN VISAYAS
47 Northern Samar
48 Samar
49 Eastern Samar
50 Leyte
51 Southern Leyte

IX WESTERN MINDANAO
52 Zamboanga del Norte
53 Zamboanga del Sur
54 Basilan
55 Sulu
56 Tawitawi

X NORTHERN MINDANAO
57 Surigao del Norte
58 Camiguin
59 Agusan del Norte
60 Misamis Oriental
61 Misamis Occidental
62 Bukidnon
63 Agusan del Sur

XI SOUTHERN MINDANAO
64 Surigao del Sur
65 Davao Oriental
66 Davao
67 Davao del Sur
68 South Cotabato

XII CENTRAL MINDANAO
69 Lanao del Norte
70 Lanao del Sur
71 North Cotabato
72 Maguindanao
73 Sultan Kudarat

minimum population of 150,000 persons or a revenue of at least ₱30 million (for value of the peso—see Glossary). The city is headed by a mayor and a vice mayor. The pattern of ministerial representation at the provincial level is also common at the city level. The mayor has some discretionary powers of local appointment.

Unlike the city, the smaller municipality is subordinate to the provincial government, operating under a uniform statute applicable throughout the country. The municipal government, headed by the mayor and situated in a town, is responsible for law and order and operates the public market, agricultural services, health, education, and public works under the supervision of provincial and central government officials.

The lowest and most numerous subdivision is the *barangay*, which was formally reconstituted as a local governing unit in mid-1974. The *barangay* is located in the municipality or even in a semi-urban area and is inhabited by about 200 persons or 35 families. It may levy taxes and may issue ordinances and is run by a six-member council chaired by a captain. *Barangay* officials are popularly elected, are responsible for law and order, and provide limited support services to the central government's community development projects. The government has made use of the traditional, grass-roots methods for settling minor village disputes by establishing *barangay* conciliation courts. Strictly speaking, *barangay* officials are not part of the civil service; they are not on the central or provincial payroll. They receive some stipend, however, and play influential intermediary roles in linking the grass-roots level to higher government authorities.

Regional Autonomy

In 1983 armed resistance to the Marcos administration was still continuing, albeit on a low-key, sporadic level (see The Insurgent Challenge, ch. 5). At issue was the question of autonomy for Moros on the southern islands of Mindanao, the Sulu Archipelago, and Palawan. This problem was to have been resolved in accordance with an agreement reached in December 1976 by representatives of the Philippine government, the Moro National Liberation Front (MNLF), and several Islamic countries (see The New Society, ch. 1; Relations with Other Selected Countries, this ch.). The Tripoli Agreement provided for the creation of an autonomous Muslim region in the southern Philippines, but within the territorial framework of the sovereign Philippines. Specifically, it recognized the Moros' right to a separate judiciary, legislature, administration, and security force, as well as the right to maintain their own schools and economic and financial system and to be represented in all major organs of the state. The agreement stated that the province of foreign policy and national defense was to be under the sole and exclusive jurisdiction of the central government. The relationship between the autonomous region and the central government was an issue to be settled through further negotiations.

Ensuing negotiations proved unproductive, however, as the MNLF and the Marcos administration disagreed on specifics of the agreement. In mid-1979 the government announced the establishment of two autonomous regions as part of what it called "a positive implementation" of the Tripoli accord. In May of that year, elections were held for two regional assemblies (Sangguniang Pampook)—one in Western Mindanao Region and the other in Central Mindanao Region. The principal tasks of these regional authorities were to improve internal security, maintain law and order, and provide employment. The presidential decree for the two regions mentioned the government's readiness to devolve responsibilities for community development activities to the regional authorities and to grant such powers as would be needed for lending substance to local autonomy. In defining the nature of the central-regional relationship, however, the decree left little doubt that the two regional governments could function only within the latitude that the central government was willing to concede. According to the decree, the regional governments were both placed under the presidentially appointed executive councils, which became operational in December 1979.

Despite these measures for autonomy, participants in the Tripoli negotiations of 1976 continued to argue that the Marcos government was reneging on the initial agreement. Apparently, some Islamic countries, notably Saudi Arabia, urged the Philippines to implement the Tripoli Agreement in good faith. Shortly after Marcos' state visit to Saudi Arabia in March 1981, the government announced several new measures: new elections for the two regions, and the establishment of Islamic courts as part of broader efforts to preserve the Islamic cultural heritage for Moros.

Civil Service

Public service comes under the general supervision of the constitutionally independent Civil Service Commission, whose commissioners are appointed by the president to a single nonrenewable term of seven years. The civil service as defined in the Constitution covers "every branch, agency, subdivision, instrumentality of the government, including every government-owned or -controlled corporation." Public officials fall into two categories: competitive and special. The competitive category consists of those officials whose appointments are made "only according to merit and fitness" to be determined "as far as practicable by competitive examination," whereas the other covers positions that are "policy-making, primarily confidential, or highly technical in nature." As many as two-thirds of all public officials are believed to be noncompetitive and are appointed by the president or by the heads of local subdivisions. Career civil servants may not be suspended or dismissed except for cause as provided by law. To ensure nonpartisanship, members of the civil service and of the armed forces are prohibited from engaging in any political activity in whatever manner, but they may stand for election after resignation from their posts.

Candidates who lose in an election may not be appointed or reappointed to any government position within one year of such election.

Government service continues to be one of the more desirable, if not the most respected, occupations because of the opportunities it offers for financial security and mobility. Competition is generally intense, and when applicants exceed the number of positions being filled, political connections become a decisive factor. Once recruited through competitive or noncompetitive means, officials—especially those who are regarded as protégés of national or local leaders—are expected to return favors under the time-honored Filipino pattern of honoring reciprocal obligations, called *utang na loob* (see Social Organization, ch. 2). This emphasis on personal alliances and reciprocal obligations is sometimes blamed for the pervasiveness of graft and corruption in government.

In the early 1980s the government was determined to boost the morale and efficiency of public officials and to restore public confidence in the integrity of the bureaucracy. This was evident in frequent purges of erring officials, especially after the late 1970s. In 1978, for example, a special watchdog agency called Tanodbayan was created to handle the investigation and prosecution of all cases involving public officials, who would be tried by the Sandiganbayan. In 1981 a law against corruption was amended to impose stiffer penalties of 10 to 15 years' imprisonment, forfeiture of properties, and permanent disqualification from public office. For officials charged with corruption, membership in an exclusive club and frequent travel abroad without justifiable reason were listed as prima facie evidence of misbehavior under the amended law. Moreover, in 1982 Marcos created a special high-powered study group to assess the extent, nature, and dimensions of graft and corruption in government and to recommend necessary remedial steps. Additionally, the president publicly called on the news media to help the authorities combat corruption by exposing venal public officials if there was supporting evidence (see Crime, ch. 5).

In welcoming the establishment of the special study group, the *Philippines Sunday Express* commented that for the average citizen "the most common manifestation of corruption which seems to permeate even the lowest levels of the government bureaucracy" was the necessity to shell out what was known as "grease money" to facilitate one's dealings with government officials. To the question "What about big-time graft?" its answer was that "many public servants in the higher echelons consider it a built-in benefit of their positions to exact some form of personal accommodation from private individuals and institutions doing business with the government."

Generally, observers agreed that only drastic measures, such as dismissal, can minimize the problem to a tolerable level, but a senior government official acknowledged that there was no easy solution. In the November 20, 1982, issue of the English-language daily *Times Journal*, the official stated that as an example, many of those holding "sensitive" or much-coveted positions in the Bureau of Internal Rev-

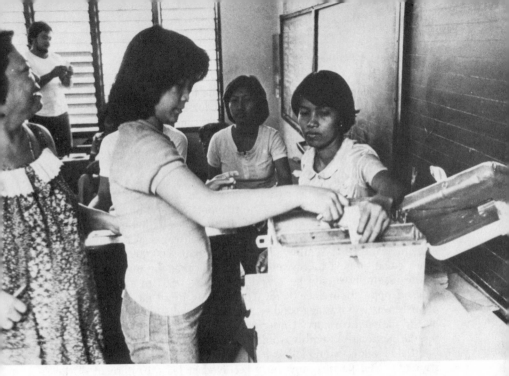

Voter casts ballot in barangay election, 1982.
Courtesy Embassy of the Republic of the Philippines, Washington

enue had "strong and influential backers and firing them would be difficult." A study released by a research team of the University of the Philippines in December 1982 showed that 77 percent of the interviewees described government agencies as corrupt and that the public had very little respect for government officials.

The Electoral System

Elections are under the jurisdiction of the Commission on Elections, an independent constitutional body whose nine commissioners are appointed by the president for a single term of seven years. The commissioners have the powers to administer and enforce electoral laws and to serve as the sole judge of all electoral disputes. They may deputize—with the consent or at the request of the president—law enforcement agencies or the armed forces to ensure free, orderly, and honest elections; register and accredit political parties; and recommend to the legislature necessary measures for minimizing election expenses and for eliminating all forms of fraud and irregularities, political opportunism, or frivolous candidacy. The rulings of the commission on disputed election results may be referred to the Supreme Court for review.

The Constitution enfranchises all citizens over the age of 18 except those disqualified by law. As of mid-1981 the country had about 25.8 million qualified voters. Voting is compulsory, and absence from the polls except for justifiable reasons is liable to prosecution and imprisonment of one to six months. To stand for elective offices from the presidency down to the *barangay* level, candidates must meet requirements relating to age, citizenship, literacy, and residency. There are about 81,000 polling stations throughout the country, 11,800 of them in Metro Manila.

In late 1982 there were public hearings in the interim National Assembly concerning the pros and cons of electoral reform. The debates were focused on issues such as the reapportionment of regional seats in the assembly, synchronization of elections, accreditation of political parties, and shifting of party affiliation. Each regional deputy to the interim National Assembly represented about 200,000 persons in a given constituency; there were suggestions that the number of seats in the assembly should be raised from 165 to 207 to account for increased population since 1978. The holding of all elections simultaneously was widely suggested as a means of reducing expenses borne by the national treasury. Under current projections, elections for the regular National Assembly would be held in 1984; the local and presidential elections would follow in 1986 and 1987, respectively. The law stipulates that parties must have received at least 10 percent of the vote in the preceding national elections to be eligible to contest the next one. This presented a problem in that only one party, the ruling New Society Movement (KBL), could meet that requirement. Therefore, there were legislative maneuvers aimed at modifying that requirement.

Another proposed reform was focused on what was known in the Philippines as "political turncoatism"—the practice of shifting party affiliation. In an effort to stabilize party politics, the Constitution enjoins the elective officials from changing their party allegiance during their term of office. In a similar vein, no candidate to any elective office may shift his or her party identification within six months preceding or after an election, unless otherwise allowed by law. These restrictions were viewed as unrealistic by some politicians. Their argument was that in case of conflict between party loyalty and loyalty to the nation, the latter should prevail if the party to which he or she belonged was judged to be no longer in the best interest of the country.

Politics

In 1983 Marcos' rule was undergoing a trial-and-error period, entailing a political arrangement that he believed would best suit the temperament and needs of Filipinos. This process was underlined by his conviction that the pre-1972 political structure—preempted by a minority of political, bureaucratic, and economic elite—had been saddled with inequities and injustices, to say nothing of incompetence and corruption. Politics under martial law was designed to remedy all the failings of the old society through a new approach—rule by decree, the application of discipline, and the depoliticization of what was believed to have been an overheated, free-for-all political environment.

Yet in the years after the mid-1970s, a widespread sense of futility was manifest in street demonstrations, in a rash of bomb explosions, in armed insurgencies and, significantly, in the activism of Catholic clergy and lay-workers. Dissenters argued that the political scene after 1972 was no better, if not worse, than the old one. In 1983 it was unclear, however, whether the oppositionists could translate their frustrations into a credible alternative, inasmuch as their rhetorical stridency was matched by neither organizational or leadership unity nor the resources necessary to pay for the high costs of partisan politics.

The Politics of Consolidation, 1972-78

Democratic processes and institutions were introduced by the United States after the turn of the century and were retained after independence. Imperfect as they were, the success of these imported political practices gave the Philippines a reputation as "the showcase of democracy in Asia." As political consolidation got under way under martial law, however, it became evident that the political scene would not be what it had been. Before 1972 the constitutional separation of powers was generally observed, each of the three branches jealously guarding its province of power. Political power was centralized in Manila, but it was shared by two equally influential institutions—the presidency and Congress. The checks and balances between them, coupled with the openness of bipartisan competition between the Nacionalista and the Liberal parties, effectively precluded the emergence of one-man or one-party rule. Transfer of power from one party to another was peaceful, effected as it was through popular elections. Furthermore, the mass media served practically as a fourth estate. Although given to sensationalism at times, the press was a fierce critic of public affairs and an effective check on governmental excesses.

Political restructuring was carried out in a cautious, gradualist manner so that the power elite would not be rattled. At the time of martial law the top rung of the power structure consisted of some 200 high-ranking officials, elected and appointed, and a few key provincial governors. The second level was made up of provincial and municipal leaders serving as governors, mayors, provincial and city council members, and others who did not hold government positions but were nonetheless influential because of their wealth or local following. These local leaders constituted the vital links between national politicians and their local constituents. As middlemen they often helped their patrons at the national level by delivering local votes or by raising political funds.

A substantial number of top government officials were allied with or were drawn from a privileged minority of economically powerful families throughout the nation. Numbering several hundred, these families, or oligarchs as they were disparagingly called, controlled the major commercial and banking houses, industrial enterprises, real estate holdings, and sugar plantations. Marcos, a product and beneficiary of the old political order, was aware of the stark reality of political life in the Philippines—that real power emanated from neither the presidency nor Congress but from the economic and political fiefdoms of the prominent families.

In seeking to reshape the power structure, Marcos had the leverage with which to reward loyal supporters with lucrative government contracts and key government positions—not to mention his emergency powers. Among his first moves were extending government authority to all regions by dispatching security forces, ordering the disbanding of armed retainers in the service of some prominent oligarchs, and reviewing the economic and other activities of these families. His aim was to ensure the malleability of these local power holders in government hands, depoliticize them, and make them less independent politically. Under martial law, politics were to begin and end with Marcos. The political connections of these families were weakened considerably when the government dismissed thousands of incompetent and corrupt officials, many of whom had dyadic relationships with powerful economic interests. Most of the vacant government posts were filled with Marcos supporters. Most of the 15,000 officials who had been elected in 1971 and whose four-year terms expired in 1975, moreover, were simply retained in their positions indefinitely. Thousands of village leaders were also co-opted into the power hierarchy through the hastily created *barangays* between 1973 and 1975.

By the mid-1970s political calm had been restored under a structure dominated by a combination of Marcos' associates, senior civil servants, high-ranking army and Philippine Constabulary officers, and a small number of technocrats. Complementing the political elite were a number of traditional entrepreneurs and their managerial technocrats who, for practical reasons, collaborated with the Marcos leadership. They were quickly joined by new families who began to amass fortunes through informal and frequent access to national leadership (see Social Organization, ch. 2; Ownership and Management, ch. 3).

Stability was ensured through continued suspension of partisan political competition and government supervision over the printed and electronic media, which exercised so-called self-censorship under the guidelines enforced by two bodies, the Print Media Council and the Broadcast Media Council, both created in 1974. Under these circumstances it was difficult if not impossible for the opposition to organize. Former senator Benigno "Ninoy" Aquino, Jr., perhaps the most popular rival to Marcos before martial law, languished in jail, charged with crimes allegedly committed before 1972; the opposition lacked a focus of unity. Nevertheless, there were undercurrents of dissatisfaction with the Marcos administration. Former senator Jovito Salonga asserted in late 1975 that after three years of martial law, the country was still plagued with "the same old ills plus all the evils and injustices of one-man rule."

In late 1976 Marcos' grip on the political structure became firmer. Constitutional amendments passed at that time abolished the interim National Assembly mentioned in the 1973 Constitution. That assembly,

As minister of human settlements, Imelda Romualdez Marcos is responsible for a wide range of social service activities, including provision of low-cost housing.
Courtesy Embassy of the Republic of the Philippines, Washington

which was technically composed of many pre-1972 politicians whose loyalty to Marcos was ambivalent, was never convened. The amendments provided for a new interim National Assembly to be filled with both elective and appointive officials who were supposedly more in tune with the politics of the New Society. They also gave Marcos the power to legislate whenever the legislature failed or was unable to act properly on any matter for any reason. His decrees were to become part of the law of the land, the legality of which was not to be questioned by any judicial or other institution.

In 1977 antigovernment voices grew louder in tone, albeit still low-key. Among those protesting were some of the "old society" politicians whose institutional link to the new political order was severed under the 1976 constitutional amendments, as well as educators, lawyers, university students, intellectuals, Catholic priests and nuns, workers, and slum dwellers. Their various reasons included low wages, tuition hikes, government corruption, deteriorating living standards, and alleged brutality on the part of security officials. Of particular interest was the rising tension in the church-state relationship after late 1976 when the government started moving against the so-called Christian Left, some church activists being alleged to have collaborated with subversives. The Catholic Bishops Conference of the Philippines (CBCP)—the ruling body of the church—deplored the government action, reaffirming its policy of "critical collaboration" with the Marcos administration. That policy, first laid down in the early martial law period, contained elements of both cooperation and criticism in relation to the government (see Church-State Relations, this ch.). Protest was also heard from external sources that leveled charges of political repression and human rights violations at the Marcos government.

Steps Toward Political Normality

The government sought to defuse political tensions by announcing in August 1977 a plan for parliamentary elections in 1978 as a first step toward what it called political normality. Normality meant, according to the government, not a return to old processes and institutions, but rather the restoration of the integrity of the democratic processes that were said to have been corrupted in the old society. Earlier, in December 1976, the Marcos administration had achieved limited progress for political stabilization in the southern Philippines by reaching a tentative accord with the Moro insurgents on the question of regional autonomy (see Regional Autonomy; Relations with Other Selected Countries, this ch.; The Insurgent Challenge, ch. 5).

Partisan political activities were allowed to reopen in 1978. At the start of the year, Marcos announced that the KBL would soon be formed as the ruling organization, and the ban on political parties was lifted accordingly. In April of that year, the first elections since November 1971 were held for seats in the interim National Assembly to be formed under the 1976 amendments. The KBL captured 151 of the 165 seats amid reports of widespread election frauds. As many as 26 political parties took part, but the KBL aside, only two other minor parties—both regionally based—returned one or more seats. Most of the nationally known parties boycotted the election (see Political Parties, this ch.)

The KBL's emergence came to provide Marcos with a link to the grass-roots level; more significantly, its overwhelming presence in the interim National Assembly assured Marcos a constitutionally legitimized institutional base for his legislative and political supremacy. The legislature was inaugurated for a six-year term on June 12, 1978, an occasion officially hailed as a major step in the transition from constitutional authoritarianism to liberalism. Marcos announced that he would hand over legislative powers to the assembly, cautioning the assemblymen at the same time that he would reassert himself if they failed in their duties.

At the inauguration Marcos was sworn into the additional post of prime minister, and a new cabinet including all of its previous members was announced. One of the new ministers was Imelda Marcos, who was in charge of the newly created Ministry of Human Settlements, which was to be responsible for the planning, coordination, and development of social services activities. At the time, the First Lady was also governor of Metro Manila, an elected member of the interim National Assembly, and a frequent presidential envoy to foreign capitals.

The question of presidential succession was bound to surface sooner or later in light of the constitutional ambiguities. In August 1978 a presidential decree, dated June 11 of that year, was revealed, stipulating that the Speaker of the assembly would become acting president and the deputy prime minister (still left vacant), acting prime minister, pending the election of a new national leader in the case of the president's death or disability. Within days of the decree the KBL members of the assembly publicly endorsed a proposal to name Imelda Marcos deputy prime minister, thereby placing her in direct line of succession. At that time, the position of the deputy prime minister was widely regarded as more important than the acting president because the latter position would be almost certainly a ceremonial one. In September Marcos rejected the proposal, evidently fearing public charges of what some observers called a "political dynasty."

If public criticisms, muted and oblique as they were, were any indication, the Philippines in the late 1970s seemed to be beset with increasing crime, cynicism, and economic tensions. That public dissatisfaction with the state of the nation was not without factual basis was acknowledged by none other than Marcos, who in August 1978 expressed his own disappointment with the persistence of corruption, dishonesty, and selfishness. Soon afterward, Marcos ordered the creation of special bodies to curb irregularities in government. In addition to efforts to restore political peace in the southern regions by granting limited autonomy to the Moros, in September 1979 Marcos for the first time publicly hinted at the possibility of ending martial law in 18 months. He did so despite earlier pronouncements that martial law was needed to crush the enemies of the state, to overcome economic difficulties, and to prevent the country from retrogressing toward the chaos of the "old society." In mid-December he announced local elections for January 1980; caught unprepared, the opposition groups fared badly in the election, the KBL candidates winning 95 percent of all local executive and legislative seats. Oppositionists accused the government of fraud and interference.

At both the national and the local levels, the balance of political advantages was overwhelmingly in Marcos' favor. His control of the military, bureaucracy, and business elite and his influence over the mass media were greater than ever. In addition, he could always count on his well-financed KBL to lend an appearance of parliamentary democracy. The imbalance was admittedly a source of embarrassment even for Marcos, who at times expressed his disappointment with the absence of a strong, loyal opposition. He maintained that a credible opposition was essential if "democratic dialogue" was to take place between adversaries.

The opposition groups sensed a political opportunity in 1979 and 1980, owing to student unrest, unchecked inflation, rising unemployment, and restiveness among industrial workers and the urban slum dwellers. Official attempts to contain both radical and moderate labor union pressures for higher wages brought the threat of general strikes, which had been banned since 1972. The Catholic church continued to be a thorn in the side of the Marcos administration in its self-arrogated role as the conscience of the state and defender of social justice and human dignity.

In late August 1980 some 70 opposition leaders managed to close ranks and issued a joint manifesto called the Covenant for National Freedom. The manifesto called for, among other things, immediate termination of "the Marcos dictatorship," the unconditional dismantling of martial rule, and the holding of free and honest elections (see Political Parties, this ch.). Government spokesmen dismissed the proclamation as a rhetorical exercise, pointing out at the same time that the signers of the covenant were for the most part members of the "old society" oligarchy. Marcos himself sounded conciliatory, however, in his invitation in September 1980 for a dialogue with the opposition, including the communists and Moro rebels. The invitation drew mixed reactions.

Missing from the covenant signers was Aquino, who had been in the United States for medical attention since his release from prison three months earlier. Aquino continued to speak out against the Marcos government, reneging on his promise not to engage in any partisan political activity while abroad. On August 4, 1980, he stated in New York that, without revealing the source, he had been "told of plans for the launching of a massive urban guerrilla warfare" in Manila and that "Marcos would be well advised to take this warning very seriously." There were conflicting interpretations whether this speech was an advocacy of terrorism or a friendly warning, but whatever the truth, Manila was hit by a spate of bomb explosions between August 22 and October 19, 1980. A group calling itself the April 6 Liberation Movement claimed responsibility, asserting that violence was unavoidable in view of Marcos' refusal to heed reason and to dismantle his "repressive regime." The group also announced support for Aquino's bid to lead a new, democratic Philippines. It acknowledged, however, that the April 6 group had not been formally recognized by Aquino. On October 20 Marcos ordered the arrest of 30 prominent Filipino oppositionists, including seven then residing in the United States, on charges of subversive activities. Among the latter were Aquino and Raul Manglapus, a former senator, who was actively involved with the dissident Movement for a Free Philippines. In November the Philippine government formally requested the United States to arrest and deport the seven suspects.

Political Developments since January 1981

Martial law was lifted on January 17, 1981, with some qualifications. Two days later Marcos told the interim National Assembly that the lifting was voluntary and that the United States had not exerted any pressure. He also outlined a transition period of about two years before the regular National Assembly could be elected. In his speech to the interim legislature the president promised the opposition "liberal leeway" and identified six priority tasks for the government: constitutional amendments, increased food production, government reorganization, energy, industrial projects, and economic programs in general. Also stressed in that speech was his pledge not to exercise emergency decree powers "unless absolutely necessary," noting that there was at the time "no threat that the government could not meet."

The lifting of martial law was welcomed by some, but popular reaction was generally guarded, the prevailing sentiments being that what was removed was the legal facade of martial law but not its reality. Opposition leaders called the lifting "a hollow gesture." Cynicism was fairly widespread because under the 1976 constitutional amendments the president could exercise almost unlimited decree powers even after martial law. Moreover, two presidential decrees, dated September 12, 1980, but not made public until January 11, 1981, gave Marcos open-ended powers to deal with any national crisis. These decrees, the Public Safety Act and the National Security Act, not only empowered the president to order arrests, close the media, and suspend habeas corpus in a grave emergency but also granted Marcos, his cabinet, and other public officials immunity from prosecution for any official acts performed during the martial law period.

From February 17 to 22, 1981, Pope John Paul II visited the Philippines under a somewhat relaxed political climate. During his stay the pope steered a middle course in dealing with a number of problems facing the Marcos leadership and the church as well. On the one side, the pope emphasized the view that the exigencies of national security, no matter how compelling, should not be allowed to take precedence over the dignity of human rights. On the other, he told the Catholic clergy of the country not to take "an exaggerated interest" in political matters.

The Constitution was amended again in 1981, despite strong opposition protests. The new amendments provided for a presidency that would henceforth be filled through direct elections and for a prime minister to be nominated by the president for confirmation by the interim National Assembly. They also provided for the Executive Committee to serve as a collective caretaker body for the purpose of presidential succession and for procedures accrediting political parties. The amendments reaffirmed the legality of the presidential decrees released in January, concerning the granting of immunity to civilian and military officials, thereby assuaging the apprehensions of some public officials about the possibility of criminal liability for past misbehavior.

In the presidential election held on June 16, 1981—the first since 1969—Marcos ran as the KBL standard-bearer. He was opposed by a field of 12 candidates, all but two of them being independents. Aquino, then in self-imposed exile in the United States, was widely regarded as the best bet against Marcos, but he was not among the candidates.

In March he had expressed his readiness to return to the Philippines to campaign for the coalition of moderate opposition groups called the United Democratic Organization (UNIDO), which had been formed by some signers of the Covenant for National Freedom in 1980. He did not have to return because in late April UNIDO decided not to contest the election after the government rejected its demands for changes in election procedures. In any event Aquino, then 48 years of age, would have been ineligible to challenge Marcos, given that the minimum age qualification under the Constitution was 50. In May UNIDO, contending that no free and honest elections were possible, decided to promote a nationwide boycott of the election, a position that a broad national coalition of radical groups promptly espoused as well. This was the first time that conservatives, moderates, liberals, and radicals participated together in a common political action. Marcos warned the boycotters that they would be prosecuted or dismissed from government if they were on the public payroll. The coalition's principal spokesman was Joaquin Roces, former publisher of the *Manila Times*, which had been reputedly the most influential newspaper in the country until it was shut down under martial law.

Of the 12 presidential candidates, only two were identified with political parties—the Nacionalista and the Federalista. Representing the factionally split Nacionalista Party was Alejo Santos, former defense minister and congressman who had long retired from politics and who had decided to run because, according to his campaign manager, "nobody else wanted to run against Mr. Marcos." Santos was associated with a minority faction of the Nacionalista Party that was suspected of playing the role of opposition as part of a government scheme to lend some credence to Marcos' assurance that the June 16 election would be free, honest, clean, and orderly. During the campaign Marcos commended Santos as a worthy opponent and shortly before the election day denied reports that he was surreptitiously financing the Santos campaign. The Federalista Party was represented by Bartolome C. Cabangbang, former congressman who had long championed the cause of statehood for the Philippines—as the fifty-first state of the United States. The 10 other candidates were mostly political unknowns.

The KBL had the distinct advantage in the campaign, if for no other reason than that the coverage in the news media focused mostly on Marcos and little on the opposition. Marcos promised continued commitment to economic development, social justice, fair distribution of wealth, support for private enterprises but not "pure capitalism," greater popular participation in government, stronger and more effective government, and support for the balance of power in Southeast Asia until the United Nations could become viable enough to enforce world peace on its own. For his part Santos declared that he would consider himself "an interim president" if he won, convene a constitutional convention to rewrite the basic law of the land, and call new elections to "choose the best man for the presidency and other positions." He asserted that

Marcos had "ruined our political institutions and systematically manipulatd the constitution to perpetuate himself in power."

Election results were predictable, as were incidents of violence and opposition charges of massive KBL fraud. Marcos received 88 percent of the vote; Santos, 8.2 percent; and Cabangbang, 3.6 percent. Nearly 85 percent of the 25.8 million registered voters went to the polls. Ten independent candidates garnered 0.2 percent.

Marcos was sworn in on June 30 for a term of six years as the president of what he called the "fourth republic." In proclaiming "a new beginning for democracy," he pleaded for unity and unswerving allegiance to his leadership. Within a month, cabinet-level agencies were reshuffled. In his state of the nation address to the interim legislature on July 27, the president set forth seven major national tasks to be carried out during the next six years. These were the further reduction of population growth, elimination of unemployment and underemployment, greater agricultural and industrial productivity, correction of imbalances in regional development, lesser dependence on imported oil, rational allocation of domestic resources, and solution of problems in both public and private sectors of national life. Among his first official acts were the issuing of an executive order separating the powers of the president and of the prime minister and the nomination of Minister of Finance Cesar Virata as prime minister—and as such, chairman of the Executive Committee under the Constitution—and Minister of Local Government Jose A. Rono, a key political strategist for Marcos, as deputy prime minister. At the time, the KBL's first choice for the premiership was reportedly the First Lady. Virata, probably the best know Filipino technocrat and well respected in international financial circles, was also named to the Executive Committee. The initial seven members of the Executive Committee included Virata, Rono, Minister of National Defense Juan Ponce Enrile, Minister of Trade and Industry Roberto Ongpin, Minister of the Budget and Management Manuel Alba, Minister of State for Foreign Affairs and Assemblyman Emmanuel Pelaez, and governor of Cebu Province Eduardo Gallas. By all reckoning these seven were among the most influential confidants of the president.

The fourth republic, also called "new republic," marked renewed interest in improving popular welfare. This was manifest in the start of the National Livelihood Program (KKK—see Glossary), a multifaceted antipoverty program under the direction of Imelda Marcos in her capacity as minister of human settlements. The KKK program gave the First Lady considerable leverage with which to attract grass-roots support for the government, which evidently had become aware that grievances linked to poverty would provide a fertile breeding ground for popular unrest. Indeed, the major challenge facing the government in recent years was the problem of distributive justice. According to tentative indications after the late 1970s, the extent of poverty might not have increased since the early 1970s, but then neither did it decrease. Roughly half of all Filipino families were estimated to have incomes below the subsistence level. Opposition leader Salonga was even more pessimistic; in February 1981 he maintained that 70 percent of all families were below the poverty line set by the World Bank (see Glossary), and the gap between rich and poor was wider than ever (see Income Distribution and Living Conditions, ch. 3).

As part of the continuing effort to ensure domestic tranquillity, the government in August 1981 restored labor's right to strike. In force since September 1972, the ban on strikes had been at the heart of labor-government tension for years. The government was on the defensive after May 1979, when the pro-Marcos Trade Union Congress of the Philippines (TUCP) broke its seven years of silence and joined other militant unions in pressing the government to rescind the restrictions on collective bargaining and strikes. The TUCP contended also that unscrupulous employers had taken advantage of the ban by exploiting workers and by harassing union leaders, not to mention by union-busting activities. In the past, the TUCP leadership usually supported the government line that industrial unrest among low-wage workers had been instigated by subversives.

Two influential business groups, the Philippines Chamber of Commerce and Industry and the Employers Confederation of the Philippines argued that strikes should stay banned to ensure industrial peace. For quid pro quo the government gave the business groups the right to lockout and also assured them of intercession if strikes were threatened in "industries vital to the national interest." The broadly phrased term vital "industries" covered public utilities, banks, factories in export-processing zones, and defense-related establishments. Some labor groups, such as the left-of-center May 1 Movement (Kilusang Mayo Uno—KMU) and other allied federations, opposed the amended labor law of August 1981 as antilabor and promanagement. At first even the progovernment TUCP raised objections, which were later withdrawn on the promise of the government to rectify "certain inadequacies" in that law.

The Marcos administration's stability was further ensured through a reshuffle of the military high command. In July the president appointed General Fabian S. Ver and Lieutenant General Fidel Ramos as the new chief of staff and vice chief of staff, respectively. Both were related to the president and were from Marcos' home region of Ilocos. In August Ver, promoted to full general, pledged to rid the military of corrupt and abusive officers and men (see Political Role, ch. 5).

In 1982 anti-Marcos groups continued to grope for elusive unity, as indicated by the birth of a "grand coalition" in March (see Political Parties, this ch.). In May elections were held for 281,000 positions in some 42,000 *barangay* councils on a supposedly nonpartisan basis. Before the election, as many as 90 percent of the *barangay* officials were believed to be Marcos supporters. In June two regional assemblies for Moros in the southern Philippines were newly elected, the KBL candidates sweeping all 34 seats contested. In August four new members, including Imelda Marcos, were added to the Executive

*President Marcos and the First Lady, Imelda Romualdez Marcos,
welcome a foreign visitor at an official function.*
Courtesy Tourist Research and Planning

Committee. By that time the First Lady had acquired additional responsibilities as the chairperson of the Southern Philippine Development Authority and secretary general of the KKK movement. Another major development was Marcos' much-publicized state visit to the United States in September (see Relations with the United States, this ch.). The warm reception given Marcos by President Ronald Reagan drew Filipino opposition charges that the Marcos government was being propped up by Washington because of the United States strategic interest in Philippine bases.

During the first half of 1983 the political scene was relatively uneventful. The power structure was based on the military, the KBL, the bureaucracy, and the business community. The inner circle of power was evidently cohesive, its key members being, the Marcoses aside, Prime Minister Virata, Minister of National Defense Enrile, Deputy Prime Minister Rono, Presidential Executive Assistant Juan C. Tuvera, General Ver, and General Ramos. This circle was evidently allied with a tightly knit group of new economic oligarchs who controlled, with government blessing, the mass media, agriculture, banking, and major industries.

The government's principal priority was less political than economic, evidencing its growing concern about sluggish economic performance, inflation, and unemployment. Political protests were still staged by students, labor groups, many pre-1972 party politicians, intellectuals, city dwellers, and church activists. The degree of articulation, as well as the strength of conviction, varied considerably among the protesters, but nearly all agreed on the need to restore "democracy." The government blamed their dissent on infiltration by subversives, while expressing the optimism that in time the state of the nation would qualitatively improve through hard work, discipline, and national reconciliation.

The Assassination of Aquino

This period of relative calm was shattered on August 21, 1983, by the slaying of Aquino within minutes of his voluntary return to his homeland after three years of self-imposed exile in the United States. He was killed with a single bullet in the head behind the left ear from within 18 inches while being escorted off a plane by government security guards at Manila International Airport. The alleged assassin, disguised as an airport maintenance worker, was shot and killed on the spot by nearby security guards. Marcos said that the unidentified assassin was a "professional killer" presumably linked to the communist subversive groups. He warned what he called "opportunistic elements" not to try to take advantage of this situation to foment disorder, anarchy, and chaos. The opposition was quick to blame the government for the tragedy, citing the suspicious circumstances in which the killer was able to enter a maximum security area.

In the weeks preceding the assassination, Aquino had been warned "indirectly and directly," as Marcos put it, not to return to the Philippines in light of unspecified "confirmed reports" of plots against his life. In a prepared statement that Aquino had planned to read to his thousands of supporters gathered at the airport, he wrote of his resolve to work for "a genuine national reconciliation" and to join "the ranks of those struggling to restore our rights and freedoms through nonviolence." In a post-assassination interview, Corazon Aquino was quoted as saying that her husband "wanted to talk to the president and persuade him to restore our freedoms before it was too late." Evidently, it was Aquino's conviction that the only way to promote his cause was to return to the Philippines and to work for the revival of moderate, nonviolent opposition by helping broad strata of the politically aware segment of the population to overcome their despair over the lack of alternatives to Marcos.

On August 24, amid growing public suspicions of government complicity in the assassination, Marcos announced the creation of a commission of inquiry for a "free, unlimited, and exhaustive investigation into all aspects of the tragedy." The investigative panel was to be composed of five members appointed by the president and to be chaired by Supreme Court Chief Justice Enrique Fernando, a close confidant of Marcos. The commission's secretariat was placed under the supervision of Marcos' executive assistant, Tuvera. Opposition leaders charged that the panel was stacked with Marcos loyalists. The archbishop of Manila, Jaime Cardinal Sin, was asked by the president to serve on the commission but declined the invitation; his consent would have lent credibility to the integrity and independence of the commission's investigation. In expressing his dissatisfaction with the government explanation of the assassination, Sin stated publicly that a large number of Filipinos held the government responsible for the killing and that "even those who are not ready to pin the blame directly on the military find the government at fault because, whoever did the murder, one fact remains clear and unmistakable: Ninoy was killed while he was in the custody of government security men. And there is no way that the government can wash its hands clean and disclaim total responsibility for the killing." On August 31, more than 2 million people jammed the streets in Manila for the funeral of Aquino; the unprecedented turnout was generally seen as a massive, spontaneous outpouring of popular empathy with Aquino's anti-Marcos cause.

Because of the assassination, the political future of the Philippines grew somewhat more uncertain, as indicated by mounting concern among businesspeople and bankers (Filipino as well as foreign) about the stability of the Marcos leadership. Aquino's death fueled speculation about Marcos' apparent ill health and about the effect this would have on the likely power struggle among Marcos loyalists, split into two rival factions, with support from cliques of the military. Equally uncertain was whether the initial surge of anti-Marcos momentum generated by the shock and grief stemming from the assassination would galvanize the splintered opposition into a solidly unified bloc. Most observers were of the view that the death of Aquino, the most visible symbol of moderate and democratic opposition to Marcos, would probably leave the opposition forces fragmented and leaderless as before. Despite the unremitting clamor for unity among anti-Marcos groups, indications were that personality conflicts of the leading opposition figures were likely to remain unresolved.

Political Parties

In the early 1980s party politics were clearly overshadowed by the single most salient reality of Philippine political life—the dominant personality of Marcos. In popular perception, politics were understood in terms of his personalized rule rather than institutional rule under the KBL. To most Filipinos the appearance of majority rule under the KBL's imprimatur was an abstraction that had no practical meaning. Political parties were peripheral to the center stage of political life, where policies and decisions were made by Marcos together with a small number of confidants to be carried out by the bureaucracy, the KBL, and the military. Difficulties facing anti-Marcos groups were formidable, to say the least, if only because the KBL had enormous resources with which to lure popular support.

In 1983 the state of political parties was far from clear, except for the likelihood that the KBL's one-sided dominance would remain unchanged in the foreseeable future, provided that Marcos would be around to oversee his political empire. It also appeared possible that there would be intense jockeying for advantage among several opposition groups in anticipation of the parliamentary election in 1984 and local elections two years after that. In any event, pitted against the KBL were several parties, all of which were organizationally frail, rent by personal rivalries, financially handicapped, vulnerable to financial and business pressures, and lacking in media exposure. Most opposition leaders regarded unity as essential, but they failed to agree on the question of unified leadership, let alone the question of framing a consistent political strategy.

The KBL was created by Marcos on the structural foundation of the pre-1972 Nacionalista Party, on whose platform he had been first elected in 1965. It opened its door to all those who would support Marcos, regardless of their past political background. The KBL was the only party that had branches in all local subdivisions of the government. Its secretary general was Rono, deputy prime minister, minister of local government, and majority leader in the interim National Assembly. It controlled all legislative committees in the assembly and frequently held party caucuses at which Marcos normally presided. The government's legislative intentions and strategies were almost always conveyed to this caucus, and decisions reached there would become the basis for draft legislation called the "cabinet bill," which would usually be enacted after three readings in the interim legislature. Needless to say, the KBL's role in relation to the government was one of junior partner.

From its inception the KBL benefited from its standing as a government party and as such from its nearly exclusive access to patronage and the pork barrel. This linkage was important if for no other reason than the pervasiveness of patron-client relationships traditionally ingrained as a natural order of the society. Apparently, KBL connections were valued less for the lofty principles or the platform of the party than for the political or material benefits such tie-ins were perceived to yield. On balance, the power of the dyadic pattern helped the well-financed KBL more than it did the opposition. Candidates having greater credibility than others as patrons had the advantage in attracting voter support.

The opposition groups generally agreed on the single goal of replacing the Marcos regime with a new system, but the form and substance of the substitute, let alone tactical matters, was unresolved. Most prominent opposition leaders were those who were intimately involved in the bipartisan politics between the dominant Nacionalista and Liberal parties before 1972. But their organizational bases atrophied, a casualty of martial law restrictions, factional infighting, defections, or Marcos' tactic of co-optation. The process of rebuilding individually or through the politics of alliance-building was under way in the early 1980s, but its outcome was uncertain.

The politics of legal, as distinguished from illegal or clandestine, opposition resumed in 1978 when in response to the formation of the KBL, former senator Lorenzo M. Tañada and Aquino, then in prison,

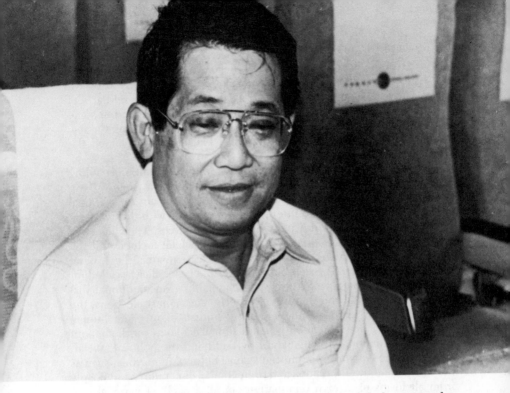

Benigno "Ninoy" Aquino, Jr., aboard flight to Manila,
August 21, 1983
Courtesy United Press International Photo

organized People's Power (Lakas ng Bayan—LABAN) to contest the parliamentary elections of the year. Better known by its acronym LABAN (fight), this principally Manila-based group received 40 percent of the vote in Metro Manila but failed to return a single seat. The former Liberal and Nacionalista parties did not enter the contest because of disagreement within both parties on the merit of taking part in what they claimed were "farcical" elections. Of the 27 parties participating, apart from the KBL, only two other parties—both regionally based—returned one or more seats. One was the Pusyon Bisaya Party from Central Visayas Region, gaining 13 seats and the other, the Mindanao Alliance from Northern Mindanao Region, gaining one seat. Shortly after the election, the Pusyon Bisaya Party split into contending factions.

The next round of tests for partisan politics came in the local elections of 1980, which were contested by the KBL and several moderate-to-conservative opposition groups: the dominant faction within the Nacionalista Party, led by the traditionally powerful Laurel family of Batangas Province; the National Union for Liberation (NUL) formed in December 1979 by former president (1961-65) Diosdado Macapagal;

211

and regional groups, such as the Mindanao Alliance, the Pusyon Bisaya Party, and the Concerned Citizens' Aggrupation. The Liberal Party of the pre-1972 reputation and LABAN boycotted the election, but some of their members ran individually as NUL candidates. Among the few successful opposition candidates was Jose Laurel V, who gained the governorship of Batangas Province.

Oppositionists turned their attention to unity or coalition-building after the KBL's lopsided victory. This was manifest in August 1980, when 72 leading opposition figures signed the Covenant for National Freedom with the declared intention of doing away with the "existing structures of injustice and exploitation" under Marcos. The alliance of these leaders came to be known as UNIDO, which included all the opposition groups taking part in the 1980 election, plus the Liberal and LABAN parties. The five-point manifesto of the alliance called for immediate termination of Marcos' "dictatorship"; unconditional dismantling of "martial rule" and free, orderly, and honest elections; the enhancement of national independence, human dignity and human rights, social justice, and a self-reliant national economy for the benefit of Filipinos; national reconciliation by rectifying the political, social, and economic injustices committed against cultural minorities, such as the Moros; and the "liberation and protection of our country and people from all forms of foreign domination" in all aspects of national life. UNIDO was deliberately ambiguous on the question of unified leadership or tactical matters. Notably missing from UNIDO were two prominent personalities, Tañada and Jose Diokno, former senator and president of the Civil Liberties Union of the Philippines; their absence was glaring because of their active interest in opposition unity.

The lifting of martial law failed to reinvigorate party politics. A critical test for the opposition was whether UNIDO could have a credible performance in the June 1981 presidential election. UNIDO announced its intention to challenge Marcos if the Commission on Elections would extend the campaign period from 55 days to 120 days, purge the electoral roll of fake voters, assure the opposition equal access to the news media, and reconstitute the commission to ensure its political impartiality. When the commission refused to change election rules, UNIDO decided to boycott the election. The Nacionalista Party was the only major "opposition" party in the election, but its nominee, Santos, could speak only for the faction led by Jose J. Roy, a longtime Marcos supporter. Santos received less than 10 percent of the vote.

In January 1982 a new opposition party emerged under the banner of the Social Democratic Party (SDP). Its cofounders were Reuben Canoy, member of the interim National Assembly and leader of the Mindanao Alliance, and Hilbrio Davide, another member of the assembly from Cebu. Canoy split from the Mindanao group as a result of personality clashes with its leader, Homobono Adaza, governor of Misamis Oriental Province. Later, the Mindanao Alliance was reconstituted as Makabayang Alyansa (National Alliance) under Adaza. The SDP's status as an opposition party was suspect in the eyes of many opposition leaders partly because of Canoy's attempts to include Francisco Tatad, minister of information under Marcos until 1980, who had been Santos' campaign manager in the 1981 election.

The politics of party realignment continued in 1982. In February Luis Jose, a political associate of Manglapus, and Aquilino Pimentel, Jr., mayor of Cagayan de Oro and a Mindanao Alliance leader, formed the Philippine Democratic Party (PDP); Tañada was named as its honorary chairman. Then in June the PDP and LABAN merged under the chairmanship of Tañada. At that time the two parties announced their agreement on the principle of "democratic socialism" and on the need for dismantling United States military bases in the Philippines. The PDP-LABAN's political objectives were to establish a federal form of government and a multiparty system. In March 1983 the party announced its decision to participate in the May 1984 parliamentary elections. It claimed a membership of 10,000, the bulk of them based on Mindanao and the Visayan Islands.

The opposition strategy of alliance was tried again in April 1982, when Assemblyman Salvador H. Laurel announced a new "grand coalition" of more than 10 parties called the United National Democratic Organization. The umbrella group retained the acronym UNIDO, used until then by the alliance formed in August 1980. UNIDO was in fact the successor to the previous UNIDO, albeit in a broader form. The new UNIDO had some 20 vice presidents, including Aquino, listed as vice president for external operations, and Manglapus, vice president for foreign affairs. The group's five-point unity charter announced in May 1982 called for the restoration of popular sovereignty, respect for human rights and social justice, economic development and social reconstruction, elimination of graft and corruption, and maintenance of friendly relations with all nations.

UNIDO sought to present a moderate political alternative to Marcos. Its viability seemed problematic, however, apparently because of political rivalries between backers of Aquino and the Laurels, two of the most prominent names in national politics before and after 1972. In any case, in June 1983 UNIDO announced a plan for national reconciliation, offering to open a dialogue with armed rebels and to persuade them to take part in the forthcoming national elections. Signed by 28 opposition figures, the plan proposed general amnesty for all political offenders, including those residing abroad, as a major step toward defusing the current political tension and bringing about reconciliation through peaceful means; repeal of all restrictive laws and decrees so that all political groups could submit their respective programs to the verdict of the electorate; repeal of the presidential commitment order; and discontinuance of the practice of allowing the armed forces to interfere in purely civilian matters, such as elections and court proceedings (see Organization and Training, ch. 5).

Church-State Relations

Developments since 1972 have shown the Roman Catholic Church to be one of the two most salient national institutions of the Philippines—the other being the Marcos administration. Although roughly 85 percent of Filipinos are Catholic, church and state have been separate under the successive constitutions; before 1972 they had a relationship of complementary coexistence with little or no overt signs of conflict between them. In 1983 both institutions continued to profess the common goals of upholding the dignity of human rights and of advancing social justice, but they had divergent views on the propriety of the methods to achieve these goals. In a real sense this divergence is a culmination of forces at work before and since martial law, and both church and state agreed that their common goals could be better served through dialogue than through mutual recrimination.

The church's emergence as a major source of and vehicle for dissenting voices against the Marcos rule is attributable to events after 1972. Until then the church hierarchy had been conservative and generally identified itself with power and privilege, despite its awareness of the need to minister to the problems of social injustice, particularly after 1965 when the Second Vatican Council under Pope John XXIII had redefined the church's primary evangelistic mission (see Religious Life, ch. 2). The church's initial response to martial law was a mix of support and opposition, many church leaders agreeing with Marcos' rationale for wide-ranging reforms, a smaller number objecting to what they believed were portents of a repressive rule.

The church has two major organizations, the Catholic Bishops Conference of the Philippines (CBCP) and the Association of Major Religious Superiors of the Philippines (AMRSP); the former is considered to be more conservative than the latter, and both organizations are known to be divided into activist and nonactivist groups. Neither of these organizations could speak with a single voice, and the united front of all church leaders against the Marcos leadership was not yet evident in the early years of martial law. Nevertheless, the government became increasingly irritated by the activists' concern for the plight of urban squatters, poor farmers, and low-wage earners as evidenced in the church's social action programs. Defensive about the failures of social services programs, the government tended to discredit religious social activists, calling them the Christian Left and collaborators with the communists. Efforts to reconcile church-state differences initially led to the formation of the Church-Military Liaison Committee (CMLC) in November 1973. Also resented by the government were the church activists' protests against the military's alleged disregard for due process of law and human rights. In 1974 the AMRSP set up Task Force Detainees (TDF) to monitor martial law abuses.

The government's first major crackdown in late 1976 on priests, religious and lay-workers, foreign missionaries, and church radio stations and church publications was not taken lightly by the church's leaders, who for the first time spoke against the government in a unified voice. Church-state relations grew tense after 1977, as the church hierarchy, headed by Cardinal Sin (who was archbishop of Manila and then president of the CBCP), frequently voiced its criticism of martial law excesses. In July 1979 Cardinal Sin contended that many people having grievances against officials and the army had turned to their parish priests, inasmuch as they had lost faith in the courts, had no genuine elected representatives to work for them, and did not find the media to be independent and reliable as sources of information. Two months later he publicly claimed that there could be a civil war in the Philippines unless Marcos ended martial law and prepared the way for return to political normality.

The possibility of a church linkup with anti-Marcos political opposition did not seem farfetched in October 1979, when Aquino urged from his prison cell that Cardinal Sin should "provide the necessary leadership" of the country allegedly because politicians have "collectively lost" their credibility. The cardinal denied any interest in such leadership but made it clear that the church would not consign itself to a passive role where the right to uphold social justice was concerned. In April 1980 he promulgated new religious statutes that called for the restoration of labor strikes, students' rights to autonomy, detainees' rights to speedy trial and freedom from torture, rights of urban poor to due process before being evicted from residences, and the lifting of martial law. The new statutes also upheld the right of priests and religious leaders to participate in political action.

The lifting of martial law and Pope John Paul II's visit to the Philippines in January and February 1981, respectively, brought a brief respite to the war of words between church and state, but the rift between the two institutions remained broad. The government continued to arrest priests and nuns found to be "conniving" with subversives. The church leveled charges of religious persecution at the Marcos administration, Cardinal Sin himself saying that government actions were a virtual invitation to a church-led anti-Marcos struggle. Church-state tension peaked in July 1982 when Cardinal Sin was reported to have said that Marcos had lost the respect of the people and thus should resign. A senior government official retorted that the cardinal was suffering from "hallucinations" and had the ambition of becoming a "Filipino Khomeini."

Frayed nerves and tempers then calmed somewhat, with both sides expressing the need for dialogue. In reemphasizing the incompatibility of church with communism, for example, Cardinal Sin stated in October 1982 that some priests and nuns who had embraced communism should be held accountable for their acts. For its part the government reiterated Marcos' policy of church-state unity and reconciliation through mutual cooperation. Against this backdrop was held a high-level dialogue through the vehicle of the CMLC, but to no avail. Indications were that the government used the occasion to press its point that some members of the clergy should be prosecuted for unlawful acts undertaken as "ordinary citizens." Apparently, the CMLC meetings were dominated by Minister of National Defense Enrile, a skilled former trial lawyer, who led the military delegation and whose charges that some church "social action centers" had been infiltrated by communist insurgents were given prominent media coverage. The CBCP decided in January 1983 to withdraw from the CMLC.

The church leadership continued to defend its social action programs, acknowledging, however, that some members of the clergy had sold out to Marxist ideology. It also stressed the view that the real issue facing both church and state was the reason for their sellout, observing that "maybe the situation is such that Marxism is the answer to needed reforms, but Christianity cannot join with Marxism because communism is atheistic." On February 11, 1983, Cardinal Sin stressed the need for a new church-state body for dialogue. On the same day, Marcos expressed the hope for a more active dialogue with the church and ordered the cabinet to formulate specific KKK programs in which all segments of society, including the church, could participate.

The church's response to Marcos was contained in its pastoral letter issued on February 15. Prepared by the CBCP and entitled "A Dialogue for Peace," the letter for the first time expressly clarified the church's position on violence and radical priests. It declared, "Criminal acts can in no way be justified as the way to liberation. If these priests, religious, and lay workers are guilty of these and similar criminal acts of which they are accused, let them suffer the consequences of their acts. We do not exempt them from the ordinary demands of law simply because they work for the Church." At the same time, the bishops of the Philippines spoke forcefully against injustice, corruption, poverty, and maltreatment of persons under detention. They maintained that there were "many aspects of the current political system that invite the dissent of the ordinary citizen," that there were injustices stemming from the government's development program that favored multinational corporations and foreign tourists, and that the country was being increasingly "militarized." Insurgency, according to the bishops, might be the response of some Filipinos who felt that they could not seek redress except through violence. The February 15 pastoral letter, which was read in the more than 3,000 churches in the country, implored the government to "seek out, with all possible objectivity and sincerity, the root causes of the social disturbances of our time and apply genuine remedies to them, not mere promises and palliatives of empty propaganda."

In mid-March 1983 Cardinal Sin proposed the creation of the National Legislative Advisory Council after meeting with Prime Minister Virata, stating that this was in response to Marcos' invitation to the church for cooperation in certain socioeconomic projects. The council would be made up of three cabinet ministers, three church representatives including one Protestant bishop, two members of the opposition, and two from the private sector. The council would address issues such as law and order, national security, business and economic affairs, social and labor affairs, politics, and Muslim affairs. As of mid-1983 discussions were still under way on the council scheme.

Foreign Affairs

The Philippines maintain diplomatic, commercial, and cultural ties with many nations of the world. Particularly stressed are relations with the United States because of mutually beneficial security and economic ties; with Japan for economic reasons; with Southeast Asian countries for neighborly cooperation; and with Middle Eastern countries for oil, for Filipino overseas workers, and for moral support for Manila's effort to restore calm in the southern Philippines. The Philippines maintains an observer status to the Nonaligned Movement (see Glossary).

Relations with the United States

Philippine-United States relations were friendly in 1983, as in the past, and were based on mutual recognition of each other's independent interests. These were especially pronounced in economic and security affairs. Initially, the economic links were established under the Philippine Trade Act of 1946 passed by the United States Congress. This act provided for not only continued duty-free trade with the United States until 1955 but also "parity" rights under which American citizens were granted the same rights as Filipinos with respect to the exploitation of natural resources, landownership, and retail trade. The parity clause was deplored by Filipino nationalists as a residual of neocolonialism. The 1946 trade act was also criticized for its bias against the Philippines. The act was later modified under the 1955 Revised United States-Philippine Trade Agreement (Laurel-Langley Agreement) in order to remove what Filipinos regarded as unequal provisions in the 1946 act (see Economic Relations with the United States after Independence, ch. 1).

The 1955 agreement expired in July 1974, despite intermittent bilateral efforts since the mid-1960s to extend it in a revised form or to conclude a new instrument to govern economic and commercial relations after 1974. In 1979 the two countries signed a commodity-tariff trade agreement within the framework of the General Agreement on Tariffs and Trade, revised and agreed to by 83 nations in Tokyo in September 1973. In the early 1980s there were substantial economic and commercial links between the two nations. In 1982, for example, the United States was the Philippines' largest trading partner with two-way trade valued at US$3.28 billion, or 25.9 percent of Philippine foreign trade for the year. As of mid-1982 the American-owned share of foreign investments in the country was 48 percent of the total. American banks held about half the Philippine foreign commercial debt (see Foreign Economic Relations, ch. 3).

Cooperation in mutual defense was based on three agreements covering military bases, military assistance, and mutual defense (see Foreign Military Relations, ch. 5). Under the first (1947) the Philippines granted the United States the right to retain the use of bases and operate them rent-free for a period of 99 years. The second agreement, amended in 1953, became the basis for security assistance. Under the third—the 1951 Mutual Defense Treaty Between the Republic of the Philippines and the United States of America—the two countries pledged to meet external aggression in accordance with their respective "constitutional processes." This treaty would remain in force indefinitely unless notice was given to the other party one year in advance of termination.

Mutual cooperation was not without an irritant. At issue was the unresolved question of Philippine sovereignty over the American military bases, the Philippine contention being that the United States should not exercise extraterritorial rights to primary court jurisdiction over American military personnel and Filipinos on and off the base areas. Efforts to revise the bases agreement led to a tentative accord in 1959 to revert some bases to the Philippines and to shorten the original lease on the bases from 99 to 25 years. The 1959 accord was not put into effect until 1966, however, when the touchy question of court jurisdiction was finally settled, the United States making limited concessions by giving Philippine courts jurisdiction over "off duty" American servicemen. These concessions came at a time when the Lyndon B. Johnson administration actively sought a Philippine contribution toward the United States war effort in the Republic of Vietnam (South Vietnam) and when the United States bases assumed major military significance.

In 1971 the two countries began a series of discussions on revising the bases accord but did not make much progress. In the spring of 1975 the Philippine government undertook a reassessment of military agreements with the United States in light of what it called "new realities" in Asia. This was occasioned by the collapse of Kampuchea (Cambodia) and South Vietnam and the consequent withdrawal of the United States from Indochina. Minister of Foreign Affairs Carlos Romulo stated in May 1975: "We are inescapably led to the conclusion that the mutual defense treaty is far from being mutual and that it exists solely for the protection of the United States forces stationed in the Philippines." He was alluding to the belief of many Filipinos that the Mutual Defense Treaty had not guaranteed as automatic or as rapid an American response to an external attack on the Philippines as the United States was treaty-bound to do for the member countries of the North Atlantic Treaty Organization.

The bases agreement was amended in January 1979 to meet some of the further Philippine demands for changes. Among other things, it provided for continued "unhampered military operations" of the United States within certain designated areas of the bases. Criminal jurisdiction over offenses committed by American servicemen on and off the bases against local laws and Filipinos was left to further negotiations. Concurrent with the amendment, the United States agreed on a schedule of security assistance to the Philippine government, subject to United States congressional appropriations.

The Marcos administration hailed the amended accord as "fair and substantial" with regard to compensation and also "equal to if not better than the agreements which the United States has with other countries." A senior government official pointed out that the agreement was timely, ensuring the United States presence needed to redress power disequilibrium in Asia and to prevent "a polarization of Asia by the conflicting powers in the continent." United States ambassador to the Philippines Richard Murphy stressed at the time that the American forces in the Philippines "not only underscore our determination to help preserve conditions essential for peace and progress in the region, but they also play an essential role in maintaining unimpeded access to vital sea lanes and air corridors in the western Pacific, Indian Ocean, and adjacent areas."

The 1979 amendment became a target of renewed attacks from anti-Marcos groups, claiming that the American military presence and assistance helped to bolster and in fact prolong Marcos' "dictatorship." In arguing that the only way to bring an end to the continued United States interference in domestic affairs and to recover the Philippines' real sovereignty was to dismantle the bases, they cited the dangers of incidents involving nuclear arsenals alleged to be stored in the bases. They also contended that the unhampered military operations of the bases by the United States would pose a threat of plunging the country into unwanted war with other countries.

Relations between the two nations became more cordial after the inauguration of President Ronald Reagan. In November 1981 an extradition treaty was signed after years of negotiations. The Marcos government had pressed for the treaty in a purported effort to deal with Filipino fugitives in the United States facing criminal charges. In so doing, the Marcos government denied allegations that the treaty would be used against Filipino political oppositionists residing in the United States. As of mid-1983 the treaty had yet to be ratified by either government.

In September 1982 Marcos paid a state visit to Washington, his second in 16 years. President Reagan praised the Philippines under Marcos as "a recognized force for peace and security in Southeast Asia" through its bilateral as well as multilateral efforts in the region. He stressed the point that "the United States deeply values its close friendship and alliance with the Philippines." The two presidents discussed a wide range of bilateral issues and understandings, and agreements were reached, as Marcos put it, "where previously there were doubts, hesitations, misunderstandings and even conflict." These talks produced agreements covering taxes; civil aviation; tourism, agricultural, scientific, and technological cooperation; a United States Export-Import Bank loan for a nuclear power plant; typhoon-tracking and early-warning procedures; and the initiation of annual ministerial-level security consultative conferences. Several American investment missions to the Philippines were also to be organized in 1983.

219

Back in Manila, Marcos assessed his state visit as an "unbelievably phenomenal success," resulting in more Americans becoming aware of the Philippines' "strategic importance" for international stability. He deplored, however, the American media's "unfavorable slant" in reporting on his country, adding that the media did not even know about the lifting of martial law in 1981, let alone the Philippines' success with its agrarian reform program and the doubling of its gross national product (GNP—see Glossary) in recent years. Within days of his return, a Philippine-United States Business Development Council was created to expand trade and investments relations with the United States.

Before and after Marcos' visit, a principal focus of bilateral relations was the bases agreement slated to be reviewed in 1983. The official view in Manila was that the compensation for use of the bases as agreed in 1979 was "sorely inadequate when weighed against the undeniable strategic nature of the bases to the United States" and that it should be substantially increased in the form of "rent, not aid." This distinction was important in that if paid as rent the Marcos administration would have a free hand in spending the money; it would not be subject to stringent United States congressional rules governing annual appropriations.

Beginning April 11, 1983, representatives of the two countries met in Manila to discuss the bases agreement, and on June 1 they announced agreement on issues such as operational use of the bases, access and information, respect for Philippine law, economic and social improvement of areas surrounding the bases, criminal jurisdiction, and labor and taxation (see Foreign Military Relations, ch. 5). In his letter to Marcos, Reagan pledged that the executive branch of the United States would make "its best effort to obtain appropriation of security assistance for the Philippines" during the five fiscal years beginning in 1984. In pledging a total of US$900 million for the period, Reagan pointed out that under the United States constitutional system, "the Congress has sole authority to appropriate funds." He also took the occasion to stress that the bilateral agreement "has again underlined the close and historic ties linking our two countries, and will contribute to further strengthening the peace and security of the western Pacific region."

For his part, Marcos stated that the successful conclusion of the review as evidenced in a memorandum of agreement would not only meet the requirements of the moment but also provide the Philippines with "a stronger sense and substance of security for the future." He expressed his full conviction about "the dependability and sincerity of America as an ally, not only of the Philippines, but as ally of freedom, peace, and stability for the entire region of Asia and of the world." In acknowledging his awareness of "the views of those who advocate the removal of the bases," Marcos made it clear that the bases agreement could not be terminated abruptly without disrupting "the present basis of international relations" bearing on both regional and international stability. This was in reference to the position taken by various anti-Marcos groups that had in February 1983 formed the Anti-Bases Coalition (ABC), under Tañada's chairmanship, to campaign for the immediate removal of all United States bases amd military installations and for the immediate abrogation of the military bases agreement.

Relations with Other Major Powers

In the early 1980s Japan was the second largest trading partner and investor after the United States. It was also a major source of loans for Philippine economic development. Relations with Japan improved steadily, as manifest in the substantial inflow of Japanese goods, investments, technology, and tourists. In 1974 the treaty of friendship, commerce, and navigation that had been signed in 1960 was signed into force by Marcos under his broad emergency powers. The treaty had been left unratified because of the lingering Filipino mistrust stemming from the Japanese occupation of the country during World War II. At the time of signing, visiting Japanese prime minister Tanaka Kakuei assured the Filipinos that Japan had no intention of seeking economic domination anywhere in Asia and promised to take necessary action against Japanese firms suspected of unethical and aggressive business activities in the Philippines. Three years later, Japanese prime minister Fukuda Takeo declared in Manila that Japan would not become a military power.

In May 1979 a revised treaty of friendship, commerce, and navigation was signed with Japan. Under the treaty, Japan promised to correct the trade imbalance that had been unfavorable to the Philippines since 1975. Japan was granted most-favored-nation status under the treaty, with the proviso that the tariff preferences and other advantages the Philippines accorded other members of the Association of Southeast Asian Nations (ASEAN) would not apply to Japan (see Relations with Neighboring Countries, this ch.). The treaty obliged the two countries to cooperate in shipping and the prevention of marine pollution. Despite the treaty, however, trade relations remained in Japan's favor, prompting the Philippines to press for liberalization of Japanese protectionist measures. Japan was also under pressure for increased official development assistance to major Philippine industrial projects.

Relations with China and the Soviet Union were correct and at times cordial. The Philippines avoided taking sides in Sino-Soviet disputes, apprehensive that a policy of supporting one side against the other would antagonize either China or the Soviet Union into extending aid and comfort to the Filipino communist rebels against the·Marcos government. Although long suspicious of both Chinese and Soviet intentions toward their Asian neighbors, the Philippines had come to recognize, by the early 1970s, the need for a modus vivendi with the communist states. This was especially true after the startling revelations of Sino-American moves for détente in 1971 and China's seating in the United Nations later in the year.

In September 1974 the Philippines and China signed a trade agreement under which China would supply 1 million tons of crude oil in 1974 and 1975. Formal relations were finally established in June 1975, at the end of Marcos' visit to Beijing (Peking)—the first state visit by an ASEAN head of state. A trade accord was signed at the time, granting each other most-favored-nation treatment. Shortly after the state visit, it was disclosed in Manila that the Chinese leaders had assured Marcos of their intention not to meddle in the internal affairs of the Philippines and that his government should be "free to deal with any insurgency, subversion or rebellion."

Relations with China expanded under a series of agreements in 1978 and 1979 concerning scientific and technical cooperation, crude oil supply, civil aviation services between Manila and Beijing, hotel construction in China, trade expansion, and agricultural exchanges. The level of bilateral trade was equivalent to US$173 million in 1979 and an estimated US$200 million in 1980.

Politically, the two countries shared similar if not identical views on major regional and international issues. In August 1981, visiting Chinese premier Zhao Ziyang agreed with Marcos that problems of Afghanistan and Kampuchea should be solved according to United Nations resolutions calling for the withdrawal of all foreign troops from these countries. The two leaders also agreed to increase mutual consultations on various international questions and to expand trade and other economic exchanges. Zhao took the occasion to stress the Chinese policy of not seeking hegemony or creating a sphere of influence in Southeast Asia. During Zhao's visit Marcos reportedly sought his assurance that China would keep its hands off the communist insurgency in the Philippines; an official acknowledgment in Manila in September 1981 indicated—without specifying when—that China had withdrawn its support from the communist rebels.

As of 1983 a pending issue concerned conflicting territorial claims by both countries to a cluster of tiny islands that the Philippines called Kalayaan (Freedom Land), which was a part of the larger Spratly Islands lying astride major sea-lanes in the South China Sea about 850 kilometers southwest of Manila. The island group was claimed also by Vietnam, Taiwan, and part of it by Malaysia (see Relations with Neighboring Countries, this ch.). In March 1978 Manila and Beijing agreed to settle the claims peacefully.

In September 1970 the Marcos administration expressed its readiness to normalize relations with the Soviet Union and other socialist countries but not with China. In 1975 the Soviet Union understandably indicated its displeasure with Manila's decision to normalize ties first with China by announcing the postponement of Marcos' scheduled August visit to Moscow—a visit that could have opened diplomatic relations with the Soviets. In any case, formal relations were established in June 1976. The evolution of bilateral cooperation was slow to materialize, however.

The Soviet effort to befriend the Marcos leadership continued into the early 1980s. Generally, Moscow supported Marcos' domestic and foreign policies and refrained from any activity that could be misconstrued as an act of giving aid and comfort to the remnants of the formerly pro-Soviet Filipino communists. Soviet imports from the Philippines amounted to about US$100 million in 1977 as against exports to that country of about US$21 million. Soviet criticism of the United States military bases in the Philippines was directed mainly against Washington and was couched in language designed to arouse anti-bases sentiments among the Filipinos. Even after Manila and Washington agreed on the amendment of the bases agreement in 1979, an official Soviet commentary termed "the present state" of relations with Manila "a good example of mutually advantageous cooperation," adding that "opportunities for this cooperation are by no means exhausted." Later in 1979 the Soviet Union announced the decision to award Imelda Marcos the Order of Friendship among Peoples for her contribution as honorary chairwoman of the Philippines-Soviet Friendship Society.

In June 1982 the Soviet Union proposed several steps for increased trade and economic cooperation. This was followed by the signing of a scientific and technical cooperation agreement and a preliminary accord on a joint venture in a cement plant having an annual capacity of 1 million tons. The cement project was the first major industrial venture to be undertaken between the two countries. A feasibility study was done in September 1982 by Soviet experts, but as of early 1983 the status of the project remained unclear other than Manila's proposal for the Soviet financing of the entire project, costing an equivalent of US$250 million.

In the early 1980s, despite the expressed readiness on both sides to broaden economic links, the Philippines was concerned about increasing Soviet activities in Southeast Asia in general, not to mention the expansion of facilities at Camranh Bay in Vietnam. Such apprehension continued to underline the official view in Manila that the United States presence in the region was all the more essential to offset Soviet influence.

Relations with Neighboring Countries

In the early 1980s the Philippines had friendly ties with its Southeast Asian neighbors, bilaterally and within the context of ASEAN. Its policies rested on the premises that the region should not be allowed to become a cockpit of superpower conflicts, that a credible United States military presence was essential to the maintenance of regional peace, and that ASEAN states should expand economic cooperation.

Bilateral cordiality prevailed in Manila's relations with almost all countries as evidenced in exchanges of high-level goodwill missions. Australia and New Zealand had friendly ties with the Philippines, which sent military officers to Australia for six-month or 12-month training. With Thailand, the Philippines concluded an extradition treaty in September 1980, and the two countries had frequent consultations on the problem of Thai security stemming from the Vietnamese invasion of Kampuchea in December 1978. In May 1980 Marcos was reported to have stated that the Philippines would be willing to allow the United States to use the latter's bases in the Philippines for repulsing aggression against Thailand, should the Thai government request such assistance. Indonesia continued to figure importantly as a supplier of crude oil and as collaborator in the matter of ocean border patrol and crossing. Singapore and the Philippines continued to press for expanded trade among the members of ASEAN and for a more active role for the private sector in an ASEAN plan for complementary industrial development.

On the negative side, there were three sources of potential friction in relations between Manila and its neighbors. First was the Philippine declaration of a 200-nautical-mile Exclusive Economic Zone (EEZ— see Glossary) in 1979, resulting in overlapping claims between the Philippines and Taiwan—and by extension, China. Second was Manila's claim to sovereignty over Kalayaan, which the Philippines began occupying in 1968 and administered as part of the Palawan Province. Its claim was based on the self-proclaimed right of discovery and undisputed possession. The third source of conflict was the territorial dispute with Malaysia over Sabah State in northern Borneo. The dispute led to the deterioration of relations from 1963 to 1969, when the two countries agreed to strengthen regional cooperation through ASEAN, founded two years earlier. The Sabah issue did not fade away, however, as the Philippine government continued to suspect that Sabah was being used by Moro rebels as a major training and supply base for their armed insurgency (see The Insurgent Challenge, ch. 5). Worse, the Philippines suspected that Sabah's powerful leader, Tun Mustapha, was giving material aid to the Moro rebels as part of his alleged ambition to create a separate state for himself.

Malaysia welcomed Marcos' statement at the 1977 ASEAN summit conference in Kuala Lumpur that he was taking "steps to eliminate one of the burdens of ASEAN, the claim of the Philippine Republic to Sabah." In the early 1980s, however, Sabah remained an unresolved if muted issue as much because of internal politics in Manila as because of Malaysia's own lingering suspicion. Anti-Marcos groups strongly objected to the 1977 statement as a formal renunciation of sovereignty over Sabah and demanded full disclosure of the circumstances surrounding Marcos' "unconstitutional" renunciation for public debate. For its part, Malaysia looked on the opposition demand as foreshadowing the possibility that Marcos' statement, which it came to regard as ambiguous at best, might not be binding on his successor government. Thus, some Malaysian politicians publicly argued that Marcos should have the 1973 Constitution amended to lend substance to his 1977 statement. This was rejected in Manila as an affront to the integrity of the Marcos leadership.

In the early 1980s the Philippine security authorities held the view that Moro insurgents still had Sabah connections—a view that the new leadership of Sabah, under Harris Salleh, publicly refuted. In any case, the Philippines did not want the Sabah issue to sour its relations with Malaysia. In late 1981 Marcos expressly banned any public discussion on the matter.

Association of Southeast Asian Nations

For decades the Philippines was an active proponent of regionalism. Its first involvement came in 1954 when the Philippines joined with Australia, Britain, France, New Zealand, Pakistan, Thailand, and the United States in forming an anticommunist alliance called the Southeast Asia Treaty Organization (SEATO). This alliance was phased out in 1977 based on its resolution in 1975 that SEATO was out of step with the post-Vietnam realities in Southeast Asia (see Foreign Military Relations, ch. 5). In 1961 the Association of Southeast Asia (ASA) was formed by the Philippines along with Malaya (became Malaysia in 1963) and Thailand for economic and cultural cooperation. Two years later the Philippines teamed with Indonesia and Malaya to set up a loose nonpolitical federation called MAPHILINDO (for Malaya, the Philippines, Indonesia), but neither of these had any tangible results because of old and new political differences among the participants. Yet in 1966 it became a founding member of the Asian and Pacific Council (ASPAC), whose aim was to promote unity and mutual assistance among Australia, Japan, Malaysia, Nationalist China (now Taiwan), New Zealand, the Philippines, the Republic of Korea (South Korea), South Vietnam, and Thailand. The ASPAC never got off the ground and faded away.

Manila's quest for regional cooperation received a significant boost in the 1965-66 period when the "confrontation" between Indonesia and Malaysia—until then the main obstacle to regionalism in Southeast Asia—gave way to neighborliness. In August 1967 ASEAN was formed by Indonesia, Malaysia, the Philippines, Singapore, and Thailand to seek cooperation in the economic, social, cultural, and technical fields.

In its early years ASEAN was long on rhetoric and short on accomplishments. In 1971 it proclaimed the idea that Southeast Asia, like the Indian Ocean, should be a Zone of Peace, Freedom, and Neutrality, but this concept had no practical significance. It was not until the communist victories in Kampuchea, Vietnam, and Laos in the spring of 1975 that ASEAN members felt the compelling need to bury their petty differences in the face of the disquieting prospect of an expansionist Vietnam backed by its patron, the Soviet Union.

Against this backdrop ASEAN's first summit was held in Bali, Indonesia, in February 1976. The five heads of state signed a treaty of amity and cooperation and agreed on guidelines for multifaceted cooperation, complementary industrial ventures, and preferential trade arrangements within the region. At the second ASEAN summit, in 1977, Marcos announced his new position on the Philippine claim to Sabah.

ASEAN's newfound unity faced a test after Vietnam invaded Kampuchea at the end of 1978 and installed the pro-Hanoi puppet regime of Heng Samrin in place of the Khmer Rouge regime of Pol Pot. The view in Manila was that unless the Vietnamese troops were withdrawn from Kampuchea, the same tragedy could befall other Southeast Asian states. Equally disquieting to Manila was the possibility that the Soviets could use Kampuchea as a springboard for the balkanization of Southeast Asia. The ASEAN states publicly demanded the withdrawal of the 200,000 Vietnamese troops from Kampuchea, refused to recognize the Heng Samrin regime, called for self-determination in Kampuchea, and urged three disparate Kampuchean resistance factions to take joint action against the puppet regime. In June 1982 a tripartite coalition was formed under former head of state Prince Norodom Sihanouk.

As of 1983 the Philippines continued to regard ASEAN as a major focus of its foreign relations and was satisfied with the level of political unity demonstrated by the ASEAN states. At the same time, it continued to press the ASEAN states for the pooling of their economic resources for greater intraregional benefits. Specifically, the Marcos government called on fellow member states to set up a common market for agricultural products, to increase the number of products under the ASEAN preferential trading arrangement, to adopt a tougher stand against the protectionist policies of certain industrialized nations, and to implement the ASEAN industrial complementation plan as early as practicable. The Philippines also wanted a substantial boost in intra-ASEAN trade, which in 1978 had accounted for only 13.8 percent of all ASEAN trade with other regions of the world.

Relations with Other Selected Countries

The Philippines continues to place a special emphasis on the development of amicable ties with other countries, notably the Islamic countries of the Middle East. There are three interrelated reasons: to ensure a stable flow of crude oil, to sell Philippine goods and services to oil-rich Arab countries, and to isolate Moro rebels from their external sources of material support.

Libya and Saudi Arabia have been among the several Islamic states that have showed interest in the status of Moros. After the early 1970s the Philippines' particular concern was to dissuade Libya from giving arms to Moro rebels and to seek Saudi Arabia's mediation for a negotiated settlement to the Moro insurgency. It was through Libyan help, however, that the first major step toward reconciliation was taken in late 1976, when the two antagonists had peace talks in the Libyan capital of Tripoli under the watchful eyes of Libya, Saudi Arabia, Senegal, and Somalia—the four states officially representing the Organization of the Islamic Conference (see Glossary). These talks produced a tentative accord on a cease-fire and a framework for Moro autonomy in the southern Philippines (see The New Society, ch. 1). The Tripoli Agreement notwithstanding, the Moro insurgency continued on a sporadic, low-key level after 1977, causing concern among some Islamic states that sided with the Moro rebels' claim that the Marcos administration was reneging on its promise of full autonomy. Meanwhile, after 1977 Libya stopped its arms delivery to the Moro rebels.

Manila had considerable economic ties with Saudi Arabia—the single largest supplier of oil and largest market for Filipino labor. In 1980 the Saudis briefly cut off their oil delivery over reports that the Marcos regime was tolerating the maltreatment of Moros. In 1980 they denied the claims by some Moro rebels that their secessionist struggle had been supported by Saudi Arabia. In March 1982 Marcos paid a state visit to Saudi Arabia to discuss economic and technical cooperation. At that time the Saudi government reportedly pledged its effort to exert influence on other Islamic states not to support the Moro rebels on the condition that the Marcos government take more steps in good faith to implement the Tripoli Agreement (see Regional Autonomy, this ch.). Soon after the Marcos visit, the two countries agreed on concrete measures for cooperation in trade, civil aviation, irrigation, and labor exchange.

* * *

Among the few readily available and most informative studies on the contemporary politics and government of the Philippines are *Marcos and Martial Law in the Philippines*, edited by David A. Rosenberg; Carl H. Landé's *Leaders, Factions and Parties: The Structure of Philippine Politics*; Stephen Rosskamm Shalom's *The United States and the Philippines*; and *Political Change in the Philippines*, edited by Benedict J. Kerkvliet. Also recommended are *The Politics of Islamic Reassertion*, edited by Mohammed Ayoob, and *Strategies of Survival: The Foreign Policy Dilemmas of Smaller Asian States*, by Charles E. Morrison and Astri Suhrke; these two works contain chapters dealing with the Philippines. A very succinct overview of Philippine politics during the years of martial law is available in a research monograph entitled *The Internal Situation in the Philippines: Current Trends and Future Prospects*, jointly prepared by Larry A. Niksch and Marjorie Niehaus. Also noteworthy is a World Bank memorandum on the political and economic future of the Philippines prepared in 1980 and reprinted as a special pullout supplement to the December 1980 issue of *Asian Record*. For a year-to-year overview of the political scene, the best sources are the annual survey articles appearing in the February issues of *Asian Survey* and in the annual yearbooks published by Far Eastern Economic Review. (For further information and complete citations, see Bibliography.)

Chapter 5. National Security

Main gate of Fort Santiago in Intramuros, Manila

TWO MAIN INSURGENCIES were active in mid-1983, although neither had sufficient strength to destabilize the government. The Communist Party of the Philippines-Marxist Leninist and its military arm, the New People's Army, have been in revolt since the late 1960s. The communist insurgency, apparently unsupported by any foreign power, was concentrated in northern and southeastern Luzon, Samar, and eastern Mindanao—areas where it could capitalize on issues connected with economic deprivation, social disruption, or grievances against local officials or the central government. The group followed a Maoist strategy of waging a "people's war" in the rural areas and trying to build a united front of opposition elsewhere. The insurgency's growth in the early 1980s has required increasing military involvement to keep it under control.

On Mindanao and in the Sulu Archipelago, Muslim Filipinos, commonly known as Moros, have waged a guerrilla war since 1972, alternately pressing for either secession or increased autonomy. The Moro insurgency has declined in intensity since the mid-1970s as a result of military action by the government, official offers of incentives to surrender, internal factionalism, reduced external support, and limited political accommodation by the government. It was still a significant threat to public order in the southern portion of the country, however. As of mid-1983 links between the two insurgencies appeared limited to small-scale joint tactical training on Mindanao, but the potential for their cooperation over the long term was of great danger to the government.

Public order in areas not troubled by insurgency was fairly well established. Under the system of what President Ferdinand E. Marcos called "constitutional authoritarianism," a very powerful central executive has the constitutional mandate to supplement the legislative process by the issuance of presidential decrees. Official emphasis has been placed on instilling order and discipline, in both the governmental process and the population, to permit smooth implementation of social and economic reforms. In practice, this has meant that in the interests of maintaining public order, some traditional avenues of expression for views opposing those of the government have been closed off or restricted by laws and official actions that limit political and civil liberties. In consequence, many who have protested various government policies and programs, including students, workers, clergy, and urban slum dwellers, often have broken laws in so doing and clashed with military or law enforcement officials. Certain opposition politicians have been charged with criminal offenses and their organizations declared illegal. Others in the opposition who appeared to have been radicalized by such actions have been implicated in bombings and other acts of politically inspired violence.

The nation has faced no threat of direct foreign aggression since the Japanese invasion in World War II, and Marcos has expressed his belief that such will continue to be the case until the end of the century. The two ground forces, the army and the paramilitary Philippine Constabulary, formed the dominant elements of the armed forces; both were oriented toward fulfilling an internal security mission. The small navy and air force provided support and limited patrol capabilities. Should a serious external threat develop, the nation was a party to a mutual defense treaty with the United States. An agreement between the two nations provided for the maintenance of several United States military installations in the Philippines.

Since the declaration of martial law in 1972, the armed forces have tripled in size, as has the annual defense budget when measured in real terms. The influence of higher ranking military officers in national decisionmaking has increased significantly, and military officers have taken a larger role in local administration, especially in areas troubled by insurgency. Under Marcos, the armed forces have assumed an important role in national development, and their civic action mission has grown accordingly. Public acceptance of the increased status and expanded role of the armed forces has been marred, however, by periodic reports in the Philippine press in the late 1970s and early 1980s of mistreatment of civilians—most often in areas of insurgent activity—by armed forces and police personnel. International and Philippine human rights groups have also complained of mistreatment of persons detained for political offenses. The government and the armed forces leadership have acknowledged that there have been occasional abuses and have instituted several programs to punish offenders and tighten discipline.

Crime, which dropped off sharply after martial law was imposed, has been steadily rising since 1976 and by the 1979-80 period had surpassed pre-martial law levels. Although rising crime rates remained a sensitive issue—one justification for martial law was to check crime and lawlessness—according to official statistics, crime rates across the nation compared favorably with those of many neighboring countries and the United States.

Public Order and Internal Security

Upon the declaration of martial law in September 1972, the Marcos government took as its major priority the tasks of combating the insurgent threat to national security, removing conditions of internal anarchy it declared to prevail, and restoring peace and order to the nation. These goals were deemed a necessary first step before "structural imbalances" in the society hindering national development could be attacked and a "New Society" created that would ensure the safety of every Filipino and enable each to become a better citizen and improve his economic welfare. In the government's eyes these goals required the use of extraordinary measures, entailing the suspension or restriction of certain legal rights and procedures so that the government could act more efficiently and expeditiously. This was made possible both through the use of martial law powers and through the increased authority accorded the executive branch under the 1973 Constitution (see Constitutional Framework, ch. 4).

After martial law was lifted in January 1981, the exercise of civil and political liberties was gradually allowed to increase, although as of mid-1983 some restrictions remained. The exercise of the right to free assembly has generally been observed, and rallies, demonstrations, and strikes have increased in frequency. These first two required permits, which some applicants were granted and others denied, but taken as a whole, officials have been more permissive in allowing politically inspired public meetings and have at times tolerated those without permits. Filipinos were free to travel throughout the nation, except in certain areas troubled by insurgency. They were also free to go abroad and to emigrate, although some members of the opposition have experienced delays in obtaining necessary travel documents. Freedom of religion was well respected, and since the conflict with the Moros, the government has shown increasing interest in helping the Muslim minority preserve and maintain its religious and cultural heritage.

Official tolerance for media coverage of controversial events had also increased somewhat as of mid-1983, and reporters have shown more assertiveness in pursuing their stories. Topics investigated, for instance, have included alleged incidents of military abuse against civilians, corruption among officials, and press freedom itself. In 1982-83 reporters made public their opposition to the summoning of journalists by military officers and intelligence officials to discuss with them stories considered controversial, as a result of which the solicitor general issued a ruling that the journalists did not have to appear. Although television broadcast facilities and all major newspapers having national circulation were owned by persons sympathetic to the government, elements of the media have become more candid in news coverage. In addition, there were also several opposition newspapers in the hinterlands that regularly published stories criticizing government programs. Reporters and publications of the international press generally were allowed to enter the nation without difficulty.

Members of the news media were aware, however, that government and intelligence officials scrutinized publications for topics printed and how subjects were treated, and it was generally recognized that certain matters remained off limits, although these appeared to be fewer in mid-1983 than in the past. Most agreed that direct criticism of the Marcos family continued to be all but ruled out. In late 1982 a paper published thrice weekly in Manila, *We Forum*, was closed down, the editor and several staff members were arrested, and the printing press was sequestered after publishing a story questioning the war record of the president and his right to many of the medals he held. A government prosecutor charged that the paper had become an "open agitation-propaganda outlet" for opposition figures and organizations based in the Philippines and abroad. According to a government press statement, those charged were involved in a conspiracy to undermine the people's faith in the president and "pave the way for his assassination and the forcible takeover by opposition leaders."

Since the late 1970s the government has gradually increased the scope of permitted political activity, and a number of opposition groups have formed. The transition has not been accomplished without stress, however, and disruptions of public order have occurred. Elections held since 1978 have been marred, as in the pre-1972 years, by violence, accusations of voting irregularities committed by government officials, and charges that the election oversight committee was staffed by persons loyal to Marcos and biased toward the government.

The precise line between legal and illegal opposition activity has been hard to define since 1972, however, and prominent leaders of the opposition have on occasion been charged with subversion. Even after the lifting of martial law, the president retained the right to deal directly with those he determined to present a threat to the national security. Treatment of figures in the opposition appeared to vary according to the degree of political power each could command.

As of early 1983 several organizations and movements operated outside the permitted legal framework of opposition, some seeking only change within the system, others advocating revolution or demanding autonomy. The most serious of these were the communist and Moro insurgencies, which have seriously disrupted peace and order in many areas. Law and order in those locales have also been marred by the violent actions of several independent small armed groups seeking to achieve limited social or political goals, or acting for self-aggrandizement. Outlawed elements of the political opposition have also resorted to violence to press their cases and were treated as subversives by the government. Certain groups from which activist political opposition has emerged in the past, including the Roman Catholic Church, students, and workers, were also viewed by the government as potential sources of subversion or antigovernment violence.

The Insurgent Challenge

There has been a tradition of insurgent movements in the nation, dating back to sustained Moro resistance to conquest by Spain and to repeated uprisings throughout the country against Spanish colonial rule. Conflict associated with resistance to administration by the United States lasted from 1898 until 1913, and anti-Japanese guerrilla activity was widespread and fierce during World War II. Successors to one of those guerrilla forces, the central Luzon People's Liberation Army— identified with the Huk (see Glossary) movement—presented an insurgent challenge to the government during the late 1940s and early 1950s.

During the 1970s and early 1980s the insurgent threat has come from two main sources: Moros in the south seeking autonomy or independence, and communists working throughout the nation to promote revolution. In neither conflict did political settlement or military victory appear imminent as of mid-1983.

The government has used a "carrot and stick" policy to fight insurgency, mixing peaceful tactics with more coercive measures. The carrot took the form of encouragement for Moro insurgents to defect by offering monetary rewards and commissions in the armed forces and paramilitary units. The government has given wide publicity to land reform and development assistance programs, which in large part were designed to cure some of the problems of economic deprivation and social discontent that have helped foster both insurgencies. In addition, it has attempted to accommodate certain Moro political objectives, showing some success in reducing local support for the insurgents and co-opting several Moro leaders.

The government has also negotiated diplomatically with foreign sympathizers or supporters of insurgent causes to preclude rebels from receiving outside support. Maintaining a dialogue with Islamic nations provided an especially productive approach during the Moro conflict in the mid- and late 1970s (see The New Society, ch. 1). Efforts to deny Moro rebels support and sanctuary in Malaysia have been frustrated, however, by the suspicion of some Malaysian officials that despite strong denials by the Philippine government, the Philippines continued to have latent irredentist claims to Sabah State in Malaysia (see External Defense, this ch.). Relations with China and the Soviet Union were also conducted with an eye to precluding the initiation of support for the communist insurgents.

The government has used the stick approach as well, meeting the insurgent challenge with military force, building up the size of the armed forces, and increasing the number of local militias. To make maximum use of available resources, the armed forces have set up unified regional commands to coordinate counterinsurgency operations by all four services. These developments have contributed greatly to the reduction and containment of the Moro insurgency and to the military's capability to mount campaigns against the communist insurgents in regions throughout the nation. In early 1983 the armed forces began undergoing reorganization to develop small-unit, ranger-style capability and to improve mobility.

As might be expected in areas where insurgents were active, conditions of public order were substantially worse than in the rest of the nation. In such locales there existed a confusing mix of rival structures of authority—government, military, and insurgent—which frequently resulted in a situation best described as anarchic. Civilians caught between competing systems of authority at best received fewer services than those in more secure areas. At worst they were caught in a cross fire that was accompanied by property destruction, casualties, and loss of life.

The problem of establishing and maintaining internal order in many areas, and particularly on Mindanao, has been compounded by the existence of several small armed groups other than those of the two main insurgencies. Among a number of Christian bands were several responsible for ritualistic murders and other acts of violence. Included in these groups were members of the Rizalian sect, who were implicated in an assault on constabulary and police officials and Del Monte plantation security guards in January 1979. Armed members of another sect, known as Rock Christ, were responsible for several murders in 1981, which were apparently motivated by disputes over landownership. Another aggressive Christian vigilante gang, known as the Ilagas (Rats), has been identified with anti-Moro violence since the early 1970s. It and other similar groups have sometimes been accused of acting with the condonation of local officials and military officers.

Groups of armed tribal minorities, either obtaining weapons privately or given weapons by the government for self-defense, have been responsible for violence against other minorities, the armed forces, the police, and settlers or corporations perceived to be encroaching on their land. Among these were several groups on Mindanao, as well as the Kalinga and Bontoc tribal people, who have opposed the construction of dams on the Chico River in northern Luzon since the late 1970s. Private security forces licensed by the government to protect certain enterprises from the insurgents and special security units, such as those officially established to police tribal minority areas, have also been implicated in attacks on private citizens and other armed groups.

Another kind of armed group implicated in regional violence and sometimes confused with major insurgent groups were "lost commands" made up of Moro insurgents or armed forces retirees and renegades. Operating outside the mainstream of the Moro insurgent movement or beyond the regular command of the armed forces, they have engaged in extortion, kidnappings, wanton violence, and bombings. The most famous was the lost command of former Philippine army lieutenant colonel Carlos "Charlie" Lademora. His group, sometimes referred to in the press by the sobriquet "Charlie's Angels," operated in eastern Mindanao. The group was reported in the international press to have undertaken anticommunist operations on Mindanao and Samar with the approval of government officials.

The guerrilla war nature of the combat and the difficulty of assigning responsibility for violent acts to any one group has made it extremely difficult for the government to target only insurgents and to distinguish between rebels, sympathizers and supporters, outlaws, and innocent bystanders. In practice, after striking their targets, guerrillas generally retreated, leaving only local residents in the area when the armed forces retaliated. The government was aware that bitterness over having been subjected to violence perpetrated by the armed forces has prompted some to join antigovernment groups. Officials have also publicly acknowledged that abusive behavior by military and police officials in areas troubled by insurgency and elsewhere has not helped the government win civilian cooperation in the battle against insurgency. Emphasis has therefore been increased on preventing such behavior and on limiting the suffering of noncombatants when possible. In early 1982, for instance, the minister of national defense ordered the armed forces to cease the practice of forcing families in parts of Mindanao to abandon their homes and farms and move to "strategic hamlets." The tactic was intended to deny rebels local support but caused great hardship for many and received substantial unfavorable publicity in both the Philippine and the international press.

As of early 1983 government and military officials had indicated that they considered the Moro insurgency to be contained and had identified the communists as the most serious threat to national security. In recognition of this, a new counterinsurgency plan was scheduled to commence in 1983 that concentrated on winning the contest with the communists for the "hearts and minds" of the populace. Called Operation Katatagan, the strategy centered on neutralizing the communist leadership and political structure and denying rebels access to manpower and material resources. Civil relations were deemed to be the most important element in this campaign, which focused on turning the Philippine military into a "well-motivated, people-oriented" force, keeping the people on the government's side, involving them in the fight against insurgents, and preventing insurgency from taking root in threatened areas. The plan also envisioned increasing intelligence and tactical operations capability in order to separate active guerrillas from persons subjected to communist propaganda or coerced into supporting the communist cause.

The Communists

The communist movement in the Philippines consists of two formally outlawed party organizations. The older is the pro-Soviet Philippine Communist Party (Partido Kommunista ng Pilipinas—PKP), established in 1930. Its rival, the Communist Party of the Philippines-Marxist Leninist (CPP-ML), was established on December 26, 1968, as the result of an internal schism in the parent PKP. The CPP-ML, by far the larger and more active, pursued a Maoist-influenced program, while leaning toward China in the Sino-Soviet dispute. Its military arm, the New People's Army (NPA), comprised the nation's only armed communist insurgent force in the early 1980s, the PKP having few, if any, armed units. Relations between the two parties were marked by mutual recriminations, and prospects for reconciliation appeared poor as of mid-1983.

Both communist parties, the NPA, and all affiliated groups have been legally outlawed. The PKP has maintained a more moderate posture toward the Marcos government, however, favoring constitutional rather than violent change, and although its members still exercised their option to criticize the government's policies, they have been able to establish some degree of legitimacy and retain limited freedom of movement. The PKP, which was estimated to number fewer than 200 as of 1981, reportedly had covert sympathizers among intellectuals and in labor groups, but it was not considered a significant insurgent threat by the government.

In contrast, the CPP-ML and the NPA have pursued a policy of armed struggle against the government and have been targets of extensive counterinsurgency and antisubversive measures. The exact size of the movement was unknown, but according to various analysts, as of early 1983 party members numbered 3,000 to 4,000 and NPA regulars anywhere from 6,000 to 10,000. Estimates of supporters and sympathizers ranged from 100,000 to as high as 1 million.

The CPP-ML characterized the Philippines as a semifeudal, semicolonial society that was "ruthlessly exploited" by United States imperialists, the "comprador big bourgeoisie," landlords, and bureaucratic capitalists. Armed revolution was viewed as the only way to overthrow the "U.S.-Marcos clique," free the people from their oppression, and institute a people's democratic revolution. The main weapon in the struggle, the NPA, was committed to waging a protracted guerrilla war in rural areas in order to establish stable bases from which to encircle the cities and eventually take over the nation. A subordinate element in that strategy entailed developing a united front of workers, peasants, ethnic minorities, intellectuals, students, and selected members of the "national bourgeoisie"—all of whom would join the struggle under the leadership of the NPA. Only after a first stage of national revolution was the party to instigate a socialist revolution and establish a communist state.

The NPA was started in 1969 in central Luzon with only 60 men— mainly young CPP-ML leaders from Manila, members of PKP partisan forces, and remnants of the Huk movement. It was formally established on March 24—the twenty-seventh anniversary of the original Huk movement—in order to stress the continuity of the Philippine revolutionary struggle. The adjective "new" was appended, however, to distinguish the NPA from the Huk movement's People's Liberation Army, which, according to the CPP-ML, had degenerated into revisionism and gangsterism.

The NPA first concentrated on pursuing agrarian reform in central Luzon and, to a lesser extent, enlisting support and establishing front organizations among leftist students, workers, and intellectuals, particularly in Manila. By 1972 it was estimated to have approximately 1,000 to 2,000 active fighters, 7,000 to 8,000 cadres, and 100,000 sympathizers. These were located mainly in central Luzon, Isabela Province in northern Luzon, and peninsular southeastern Luzon. After the declaration of martial law, which was justified in part by the need to suppress the "state of rebellion" led by the NPA, the government mounted strong counterinsurgency campaigns and over the 1973-74 period pushed the NPA out of most villages and into remote and often mountainous regions, substantially reducing the size of its support base. The government also eliminated most front organizations, arresting many of their leaders.

As a result, the NPA reorganized itself into more self-contained units and began to concentrate its efforts in remote rural areas where the government's presence was minimal. On Luzon, activity centered in the Sierra Madre in the northeast and in the adjacent Cagayan valley. Samar and Mindanao also became major targets. In each of these impoverished areas the NPA undertook to support local residents in disputes with the central government, local military and civilian officials, and landlords. For instance, beginning in 1976 the NPA became involved in the Chico River Dam dispute, siding with tribal minorities resisting development of their land. In most areas the communists were able to take advantage of peasant unrest over loss of land to corporate timber, fruit, sugar, and coconut enterprises and embraced issues relating to land reform.

Government initiatives did little to check the NPA. Over a dozen top CPP-ML and NPA leaders were captured or killed during 1976-77, including the party chairman, Jose Maria Sison, and the NPA chief, Bernabe Buscayno, alias Commander Dante. The government also mounted major anti-NPA campaigns in northern Luzon, on Samar, and elsewhere during the late 1970s. Ambushes and assassinations increased, however, and party cadres continued slowly to expand the geographical reach of the movement. Largely responsible for the lack of success in defeating the NPA was the group's decentralized organization that granted local commanders wide autonomy; Philippine geography; the armed forces' preoccupation with the Moro insurgency; and the discontent of many Filipinos with the adverse social, economic, and political conditions that they endured.

By early 1983 the NPA claimed to have units in well over one-half of the nation's provinces (see fig. 11). A paper prepared in 1982 by a private business club in Manila estimated that the NPA "has penetrated if not controlled 20 percent of the *barangays* [see Glossary] nationwide and can count on the sympathy if not the support of some 180,000 civilians." A government spokesman disputed those figures, however, stating that in only 3 percent of the *barangays* were 50 percent of the residents sympathetic to the NPA and capable of being mobilized, in only 5 percent of the *barangays* could 30 percent be considered to fall into that category, and in only 10 percent of *barangays* were 10 percent sympathetic. Notwithstanding the disagreement over the strength of the NPA and its support base, most sources, including the government, agreed that the communists were entrenched in the mountain provinces of northern Luzon, southern Quezon Province, peninsular southeastern Luzon, Samar, and eastern Mindanao.

Despite the NPA's apparently impressive showing, however, communist leaders admitted during the early 1980s that they were not in a position to bring down the government, nor would they be for many years. In recognition of this fact, the NPA has generally continued its "strategic defensive," working in small units and avoiding large-scale confrontations with the armed forces. In late 1982, however, larger units of NPA fighters, sometimes 200 or 300 strong, began to be re-

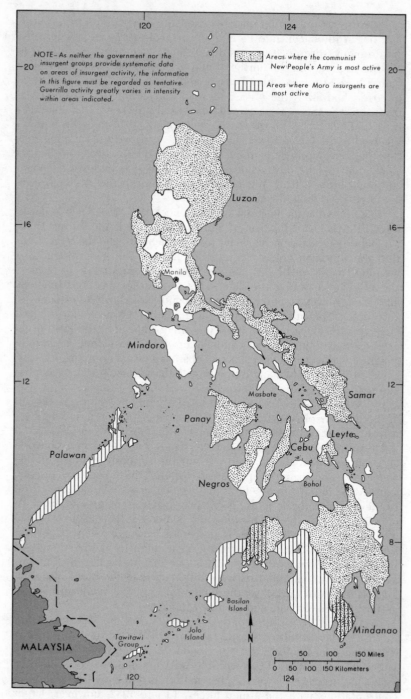

NOTE– As neither the government nor the
insurgent groups provide systematic data
on areas of insurgent activity, the information
in this figure must be regarded as tentative.
Guerrilla activity greatly varies in intensity
within areas indicated.

Areas where the communist
New People's Army is most active

Areas where Moro insurgents are
most active

Luzon

Manila

Mindoro

Masbate

Panay

Samar

Palawan

Cebu

Leyte

Negros

Bohol

Basilan
Island

Jolo
Island

Tawitawi
Group

Mindanao

MALAYSIA

N

| 0 | 50 | 100 | 150 Miles |

| 0 | 50 | 100 | 150 Kilometers |

Figure 11. A Geography of Guerrilla Activity, 1983

ported on Mindanao, where a major NPA campaign of expansion appeared under way. As of mid-1983 it was too early to judge whether these combat formations signaled a change in basic operational strategy or were simply isolated exceptions to the established pattern.

The CPP-ML organizational structure extended from the central committee on the national level through various subordinate units in regions, provinces, districts, and sections. Command was based in theory on the concept of democratic centralism, but communication between the movement's far-flung units was difficult, and local leaders often had considerable discretion. Information regarding the internal organization of the NPA could not be obtained. It was known, however, that the NPA distinguished areas in which it operated according to how securely the party could function within them. The safest, where the local population was controlled and organized politically by the NPA, were called guerrilla bases, around which were located zones known as fronts. Areas not secure enough to be called fronts were designated preparation zones.

NPA tactics generally followed a regular pattern. Cadres from a guerrilla base would move into a new territory, establishing a preparation zone. Mixing with the people, they lent assistance, such as planting or harvesting crops or providing medical care. When it was felt that propaganda teams would be well received, they were sent in to begin work on political consolidation and the establishment of secure bases and guerrilla fronts. The NPA claimed to have at least 36 fronts nationwide in 1983. After the cadre instituted a program of "social investigation and class analysis," those believed to be reluctant to support the communists were identified and usually eliminated—government officials, military and police contingents, unsympathetic community leaders, local criminals, and suspected informers being prime targets for assassination.

Although the NPA formed the dominant element in the communist strategy for promoting revolution, a second entity, the National Democratic Front (NDF), was also used as a united front vehicle to rally support for the cause. The NDF was essentially an umbrella structure having very little organizational substance. It included underground associations of peasants, youths, teachers, workers, and others. The CPP-ML and the NPA apparently controlled the NDF itself but not necessarily all constituent groups. Other groups not connected with the NDF, including some Roman Catholic social organizations, student groups, and associations representing the residents of the Tondo slum area of Metro Manila (see Glossary), were also believed to be infiltrated by communists. According to the NDF, it could call on a "secret army of activists" both in the countryside and in towns and urban areas. These activists were believed to be found among young professionals, university professors and students, mid-level government bureaucrats, and a few Catholic clergy and lay-workers.

As of mid-1983 it appeared that, although the CPP-ML and the NPA drew strongly on Maoist precepts and generally looked on China favorably, the Philippine communist insurgency was prosecuted essentially without foreign matériel or rhetorical support. In late 1982 a government spokesman acknowledged that the NPA was receiving no assistance from China. He also noted that the military had captured Soviet-made arms from the rebels but that there was no proof that the Soviet Union was aiding them. The party did maintain limited contact with certain foreign communist parties. A government release announcing rewards for the capture of 12 top communist leaders in 1982 identified two as being in China. Clandestine radiobroadcasts of the Communist Party of Malaya and publications of the Indonesian Communist Party occasionally commented on the activities of the CPP-ML. The NDF and some of its constituents also maintained contact with foreign organizations.

Most financial support was derived from extorting payoffs from firms and businesspeople operating in areas where the NPA was active. These included logging companies, mining corporations, plantations, traders doing business in the area, and small cottage industries. Representatives of such enterprises have commented that it was necessary to come to terms with the NPA if one wished to go about one's business in peace. The guerrillas also derived revenue from taxing residents in insurgent areas and growing marijuana in remote areas. Most weapons were captured or stolen from the Philippine armed forces, but some have been purchased from disloyal armed forces personnel. The NPA has been reported also to have purchased weapons from Moro insurgents and to have bought a small quantity of arms in the Middle East.

Moro Groups

Conflict between the central government and Moros in the south is often dated as beginning in October 1972, but violence had been on the upsurge in the area since the late 1960s, and tensions had been smoldering for decades. Some observers saw the modern conflict as part of a centuries-long struggle by Moros to assert their independence and preserve their cultural heritage. In this view, the Moro insurgency was part of a continuum of resistance that began in the sixteenth century when Spain attempted to colonize and convert Moros; the struggle persisted in fierce battles against the imposition of United States rule and continued to manifest itself in isolated uprisings even after independence.

The more immediate cause of insurgency, however, could be found in the worsening conditions of disorder and lawlessness in the region during the late 1960s, when violence associated with political disputes, personal feuds, and armed gangs began to proliferate. In this climate of civil turmoil, several violent incidents heightened tensions between the Moro and Christian communities, already in competition over land, economic resources, and political power. In addition, Moros had become increasingly alarmed by the level of immigration of Christians who had come from the northern portion of the archipelago and who were making Moros a minority in what they perceived as their own land. By mid-1972 partisan political violence, generally divided along religious lines, had gripped all of Mindanao and the Sulu Archipelago. After martial law was declared in September and all civilians were ordered to surrender their guns, spontaneous rebellions arose among Moros, who traditionally had "equated the right to carry arms with their religious heritage" and were suspicious of the government's intentions toward them.

In its initial phases the rebellion was a series of isolated uprisings that rapidly spread in scope and size, but one group, the Moro National Liberation Front (MNLF), maintained an organizing network in the Sulu Archipelago and on Mindanao that enabled it to develop a united front of partisan forces. Founded by Nur Misuari in 1969 to work for an independent Moro nation, the MNLF had contacts in both Libya and Sabah State, Malaysia, from which it derived funds and a supply route for weapons. By the end of 1973 most partisan Moro groups worked within the loosely unified MNLF framework.

The conflict reached its height in 1973-75 when the military arm of the MNLF, the Bangsa Moro Army, was able to field some 30,000 armed fighters. In order to keep the insurgency under control, the Philippine armed forces were expanded greatly, and some 70 to 80 percent of their total combat strength was committed to the south. Destruction and casualties, both military and civilian, were heavy.

In addition to military confrontation, the government used a variety of nonmilitary tactics to weaken the insurgency, including promoting factions and divisions among the insurgents, announcing new economic aid programs and political accommodations, and offering rebel commanders and troops incentives to surrender. These measures met with some success, particularly after the Sabah State government in Malaysia changed hands in mid-1975, resulting in a sharp decrease in the flow of arms to the insurgents. By 1976 the intensity of conflict had begun to wane.

Despite its setbacks, however, the MNLF had been successful in attracting the attention of several Islamic nations, timing its campaigns to coincide with international meetings of the leaders of those countries. In June 1974 the MNLF began sending delegates with observer status to these meetings. Sensitive to the dangers of increased foreign support, especially when the Philippines imported most of its oil from the Middle East, and burdened by the high costs of the continuing struggle with the Moro insurgency, the government entered into a series of negotiations with the MNLF, using the good offices of four Islamic nations selected by the Organization of the Islamic Conference (see Glossary).

Meeting in Libya in late 1976, the two sides signed the Tripoli Agreement, providing for the establishment of Moro autonomy in the southern Philippines "within the realm of the sovereignty and territorial integrity of the Republic of the Philippines." A cease-fire negotiated at the same time led to a sharp drop-off in fighting. By late 1977 the cease-fire had broken down, however, the MNLF accusing the government of changing the agreed areas of autonomy and allowing only token self-rule in the autonomous government structure due to be set up.

After the breakdown of the cease-fire, the government continued to make progress against the Moro insurgents, the forces of which had declined to an estimated 10,000 to 15,000 as of early 1983. A three-way split in the MNLF leadership in the late 1970s was responsible for some of the government's gains. Initially, the division produced two factions. The first and larger was led by the more militant Misuari; it was based in the Sulu Archipelago, drew support from the Maguindanao and Tausug ethnic groups, and favored a more confrontational stance. Misuari himself was most often based in Tripoli, Libya. The second faction was led by Hashim Salamat; it had the support of members of the Maranao ethnic group, which was most active in Mindanao, and favored a more moderate and conciliatory approach to the government. Salamat was also based in the Middle East, generally in Egypt or Saudi Arabia. Although Misuari continued to be recognized at international Islamic forums as the representative of the MNLF and the entire Moro insurgency, some elements of the partisan forces sided with Salamat, and battlefield cooperation and coordination suffered (see Relations with Other Selected Countries, ch. 4).

The MNLF was further divided by the defection of several prominent members, primarily pre-martial law politicians and community leaders. Two of these, former senator Salipada Pendatun and former congressman Raschid Lucman, went into voluntary exile—also in the Middle East—and formed their own antigovernment group, the Bangsa Moro Liberation Organization (BMLO). The Moro insurgency's negotiating posture with the government was weakened by these divisions. Insisting it could not be sure who really represented the bulk of the insurgents, the government took the opportunity to deal with representatives it believed would respond most favorably to officially sponsored initiatives.

Confused loyalties in the field, a drop-off of Middle Eastern as well as Malaysian support, war weariness, and offers of bounties to those who surrendered prompted many of the insurgents to turn themselves in. According to official figures, MNLF returnees numbered some 30,000 to 40,000 over the 1972-83 period; other sources placed that figure closer to 10,000, believing that many in the official estimates were imposters and repeaters who acted to take advantage of the government's generous incentives.

During the early 1980s the scale of fighting remained down in contrast to the mid-1970s, and the Philippine army commander, Major General Josephus Ramas, claimed in late 1982 that the MNLF had ceased to be a potent threat to the national security. The group's reliance on foreign-based leadership and a general lack of consensus over goals were said to be serious weaknesses. Its inability to secure substantial foreign material support, strains among ethnic Maranao, Maguindanao, Tausug, and Samal units, as well as weak grass-roots organization, have also been cited as impediments to increased effectiveness.

Despite its factionalism and organizational weaknesses, however, various elements of the Moro insurgency were still able to field an estimated 10,000 to 15,000 armed fighters in mid-1983, and skirmishes with government forces continued, occurring most frequently in Basilan, Sulu, and Tawitawi provinces where the groups still controlled large tracts of land. In a major confrontation on Pata Island in Sulu Province in early 1981, estimates of the civilian death toll alone ranged between 400 (the local Philippine Constabulary commander's minimum calculation) and 2,000 (based on refugee reports). The MNLF and other groups continued to finance weapons purchases by smuggling items such as locally produced rubber or Malaysian cigarettes over historic trade routes between Malaysia and the Philippines. Arms were most often bought, stolen, or captured from armed forces and militia units or obtained in Malaysia, where according to surrenderees, the MNLF maintained sanctuaries and training camps. The Malaysian government and the Sabah State government have strongly denied such reports, however.

The MNLF has generally repudiated independent Moro groups that claim identification with it and that have been held responsible for bombings in urban areas, ambushes, kidnappings for ransom, and extortion. The MNLF leadership in the city of Zamboanga has insisted that the group did not pursue a strategy of urban guerrilla warfare and struck only at military targets.

On the political front the Moro movement remained divided. The Misuari faction of the MNLF, if not the entire organization, had reverted to its demands for independence rather than autonomy. The MNLF became a full-fledged member of the Organization of the Islamic Conference in mid-1982. It was believed to have opened official missions in the name of the Bangsa Moro Republic in Libya and Syria at approximately the same time.

Several Moro activists favoring increased autonomy within the Philippine state attended a conference on Philippine Muslim solidarity held in Pakistan in early 1983. Their numbers included well-known figures living in exile who had previously been identified with Moro insurgent groups, as well as a Philippine government delegation led by former senators Demacao Alonto and Pendatun. Misuari and Salamat did not attend. Conference delegates signed a declaration calling for the complete implementation of the 1976 Tripoli Agreement. Specifically, they favored the establishment of a single autonomous regional government, which would presumably replace the two separate regional bodies set up by the Philippine government in 1979. Unlike the existing regional structures, however, the delegates wanted the new government entity to be 70-percent Moro, control the regional police and security forces, and have the powers to raise taxes and secure foreign loans.

The Outlawed Political Opposition

In addition to the Moro and communist insurgent groups, certain associations and persons that espoused political goals officially viewed as subversive have been outlawed or charged with criminal offenses. Most of the groups were initially organized with the objective of working to end martial law but have justified their existence after its termination by asserting that critical elements of the system remained in place. Some had apparently concluded that Marcos continued to dominate the political process and that neither electoral nor other legitimate means presented viable options for opposition activity. Although many nonetheless have remained committed to peaceful change, others have been willing to resort to violence if necessary.

Among the outlawed political opposition were a collection of groups charged by the government with being a "third force" of opposition aside from the Moro and communist insurgencies. In general, these groups were composed of fairly affluent, middle-class professionals, intellectuals, clergy, and seminarians. Most were members of the Catholic church and were located in or near Metro Manila. Not all members advocated the use of violence to achieve their goals, but by the late 1970s its use had become increasingly acceptable.

One of these was the United Democratic Socialist Party of the Philippines (Nagkakaisang Partido Demokratikong Sosyalista Pilipinas— NPDSP), which, according to the government, was originally established by anti-Marcos politicians who fled the country in the 1971-75 period. The group was sometimes referred to as the Socdems or the social democrats, in contrast with the national democrats, identified with the communist NDF. In late 1977 the NPDSP established on Mindanao an armed wing known as the Sandigan Army, and since late 1979 the small force—estimated to number fewer than 100 as of mid-1983—has been implicated in violence in eastern Mindanao. The Sandigan Army has also maintained a small following in the area around Metro Manila.

The NPDSP was believed to have three factions in the early 1980s. One was organized around Romeo Intengan, a Catholic priest who had been arrested in 1978 but was believed to be in Sabah State. This faction was reported to have maintained connections in Sabah State, Malaysia, and generally to be the most conservative of the three. Another faction apparently leaned toward establishing an alliance with the more leftist nationalist democrats, and still another faction seemed to be closely affiliated with anti-Marcos politicians in Manila.

Two groups that appeared to have connections with the NPDSP and the Sandigan Army claimed credit for violence in Metro Manila in 1979-80. The first was the "Light-a-Fire" movement believed to have set a series of fires in that area in October 1979. Its leader, Eduardo Olaguer, a prominent businessman, was arrested along with several others shortly thereafter, and the movement was quickly silenced. A second group, calling itself the April 6 Liberation Movement, claimed credit for bombings in Metro Manila during the August-October 1980 period. Named for the date of an anti-Marcos protest that occurred in Metro Manila on the eve of elections to the interim National Assembly in 1978, the April 6 Liberation Movement issued a statement that it was working for "the speedy overthrow of the Marcos dictatorship."

The ties between these "third force" groups and other opposition groups and figures were "influenced by ideological considerations and personal contacts." The government has also charged that with some groups the ties were much closer. After the April 6 Liberation Movement placed a bomb at a meeting in November 1980 of the American Association of Travel Agents, at which Marcos was present, the government issued arrest warrants for 30 leaders of the opposition, including former senators Benigno "Ninoy" Aquino, Jr., Jovito Salonga, and Raul Manglapus, all living in the United States. Others included members of the United States-based Movement for a Free Philippines (MFP), of which Manglapus was a leader in mid-1983. Aquino, Salonga, and Manglapus denied any connection with the perpetrators, although Aquino admitted that some "third force" groups had informed him of the plan to begin bombings and asked him to lead the movement. The MFP has also maintained close ties with the Philippines-based Christian Social Revolutionary Forces, or Christian Social Movement, which has also been identified with "third force" groups.

Other Dissident Actors

Opposition to the Marcos government has arisen among several groups in the nation, sometimes in the form of illegal or violent activity. Sources of such dissidence have included lay persons and members of the Catholic church hierarchy, students, labor organizations, urban slum dwellers, and tribal minorities.

Although opposition from religious groups has been generally peaceful and nonviolent, it was nonetheless viewed very seriously by the government. Almost all dissent arose from within the ranks of the Catholic church. Over 85 percent of the population was Catholic, and the church had the capacity to exert wide influence through its network of parishes, schools, and colleges, making it a very powerful institution. The church has been particularly important during the 1970s and early 1980s as a vehicle for popular expression when outlets such as political parties and the press were under varying degrees of government control.

The Catholic clergy itself was divided internally into activists and nonactivists; it was most often the first of these, according to the government, who have at times taken part in programs that intentionally or not, have given aid to communists or have been supported by them. Many activists have wholeheartedly accepted as part of the church's mission the need to strive for social justice as outlined in 1965 during the Second Vatican Council under Pope John XXIII. These members of the clergy have participated in social action projects among workers, urban squatters, rural agricultural workers, national minorities, and other groups—sometimes taking part in protests that have led to the arrests of priests and nuns, raids on church facilities, and deportations of foreign priests. Many of these clergy have publicly criticized the government and the military for human rights abuses and have advocated a major restructuring of society, the redistribution of wealth, and an end to policies intended to attract foreign private investment.

Activist priests, nuns, and lay-workers were well represented in the Association of Major Religious Superiors of the Philippines, an organization that presided over the various religious orders in the Philippines and operated Task Force Detainees, which maintained a watch over those it considered had been arrested for political offenses (see Public Order and Security Offenses, this ch.). Many were not native Filipinos, a fact that prompted some critics to charge that foreign clergy brought to the Philippines standards of activism and human rights more applicable to developed Western democracies than to the Philippines. Activist clergy were strongest in the southern areas of the nation.

Most activists took a reformist line, trying to work peacefully within the system; a small minority, however, have embraced more radical goals, at times reaching accommodation with the communists and working with alleged front organizations. A very few have come to advocate violence and the "Marxist option" for solving the nation's problems, and as many as 20 were believed to have joined the NPA by early 1983.

Positions taken by activists were often not shared by the mainstream of the Catholic clergy, however. Activists were far outnumbered by nonactivists who believed that the church should confine itself to administering to spiritual needs. The church's leading spokesman in the Philippines, Jaime Cardinal Sin, archbishop of Manila, has usually occupied a centrist stance, attempting to balance between the two extremes and keep some unity within the ranks of the clergy. Shortly after martial law was instituted, the church leadership, embodied in the Catholic Bishops Conference of the Philippines (CBCP), indicated that it would not openly oppose the martial law regime but would instead take up a position of what came to be known as "critical collaboration," speaking out when it believed necessary but trying to work with the government when possible.

By the late 1970s, however, several developments had caused the church leadership at times to undertake more active criticism of the government. These included arrests of priests, nuns, and lay-workers; raids on churches; increasing incidence of radicalization of the clergy; mounting government criticism of the Christian left; and alleged abuses by military and police officials against civilians, including Catholic clergy and lay-workers.

Increased criticism notwithstanding, the government has worked to keep church-state relations on an even keel, publicly stating that the church is an important factor in achieving national unity. Marcos has indicated his personal interest in working with the church to improve the economic and social welfare of the people. Cardinal Sin has also called for national reconciliation and for the government to work for the betterment of all Filipinos. Differences about how best to accomplish such tasks remained substantial, however, suggesting that elements within the church would persist in opposing and criticizing certain government policies and programs. In February 1983, for instance, the church released a pastoral letter that was highly critical of the government's economic development strategy, its human rights record, and the nation's political structure. In March 1983, in a speech in Metro Manila, Cardinal Sin called on the "First World countries" to stop supplying arms to the "authoritarian" Marcos government.

Student militancy has at times been given as one justification for the imposition of martial law, and student activism has since been watched closely to ensure that communists do not infiltrate or control campus organizations as happened in the pre-martial law period. Student activism resurfaced during the 1979-81 period. Although militancy was not on the scale experienced in the late 1960s and early 1970s, student unrest led to demonstrations over campus-related issues, such as the raising of tuition fees, the restoration of student councils and publications—banned in 1972—and the presence of outside security and law enforcement officials on campus. Student demonstrations over the pending visit of Chilean president Augusto Pinochet in 1980 reportedly influenced the decision of the government to cancel his visit. During some of these demonstrations, the government arrested student leaders alleged to represent communist front organizations. The government appeared to recognize, however, that the great majority of demonstrators were neither leftist nor communist inspired, and in late 1981 the minister of education and culture made efforts to placate their grievances, issuing guidelines for the reestablishment of student councils and publications. The Education Act of 1982 provided for campus security to be handled by contracted civilians unless disorder became uncontrollable. The act also held student leaders responsible for outbreaks of disorder or violence. Campuses generally were calm over the 1982 to mid-1983 period.

Labor organizations, union activity, and worker actions have officially been viewed as another potential source of disorder in the nation and as vehicles through which communists could gain influence. After declaring martial law, the government issued a ban on strikes in vital industries that effectively made virtually all labor actions illegal. A few strikes occurred nonetheless in various industries—mainly near Metro Manila—leading to arrests of strikers and union leaders. After lifting martial law, the government's handling of labor disputes was liberalized, but the minister of labor and employment retained the power to prohibit strikes in industries he deemed vital. Since that time, scattered illegal work stoppages and strikes have continued, some involving violence, but many without incident.

The government officially recognized only one national labor group, the Trade Union Congress of the Philippines, which attempted to work in cooperation with the government to achieve its goals (see Employment and Labor Relations, ch. 3). Other unions, some of which were affiliated with the Soviet-dominated World Federation of Trade Unions, were officially viewed with suspicion. Leaders of some of these groups have charged that the limitations on strikes and labor activity were really intended to attract foreign investment and to promote economic development at the cost of the workers. These persons have continued to press for increased worker militancy. In September 1980 the government arrested labor leaders threatening to stage a national strike and accused one organization, the May 1 Movement (Kilusang Mayo Uno—KMU), of being a communist front. In August 1982 constabulary and intelligence officials arrested several union officials associated with the KMU, accusing them of attempting to destabilize and overthrow the government during the 1981-82 period. The accused denied those charges, stating that what had been planned was to hold a national day of protest to publicize worker complaints.

Urban slum dwellers were another group that on occasion had resorted to violent opposition to government programs. The Tondo slum area of Metro Manila in particular has been cited as a potential source of discontent, and the area has been closely watched by police and security officials. Social activists, including clergy, have formed associations of Tondo residents to press their interests. These were especially active in the 1970s in resisting slum clearance projects. The government has accused some of these associations and their leaders of acting as communist fronts. Most residents of Tondo were considered squatters, being without legal title to their land.

Violent opposition to official development programs has also occurred among ethnic minorities—most without legal title to what they consider ancestral lands. These groups, sometimes aided by the NPA, have fiercely resisted the establishment of infrastructure projects, mining concerns, and corporate agribusiness in north central and northeastern Luzon, on Mindanao, and elsewhere, fighting to retain control of their lands.

The Armed Forces in the National Life

Philippine military tradition traces the formal beginnings of the national armed forces to the military arm of the revolutionary government, which was established in 1897 by Emilio Aguinaldo. The revolutionary army fought first for independence from Spain and then from the United States (see The Later Period of Spanish Rule, 1762-1898, ch. 1). Although it was dissolved in late 1899 after Aguinaldo recognized the futility of meeting the numerically superior and better armed United States forces in frontal engagements, Aguinaldo and other generals continued to wage guerrilla war against the United States until as late as 1903. According to their own ethos, the armed forces of the late twentieth century had inherited the people's mandate to the revolutionary army to defend the sovereignty of a Philippine nation in which Filipinos could achieve their aspirations for justice, order, and "the good life."

Philippine colors on view
Courtesy Tourist Research and Planning

There was no attempt made to reorganize a Philippine army when the United States took over the Philippines, but military and paramilitary forces played a role in the national life nonetheless. Units of the United States forces were maintained in the country to provide for external defense, and an element of those forces contained the Philippine Scouts, consisting of Filipino enlisted personnel and United States officers. The Philippine Constabulary (PC), established by the United States in 1901 to act as an insular police force patterned on military lines, played a more important role in the national life, however. It was at first manned by Filipinos and officered by United States personnel, but by 1917 a Filipino had been made PC chief, and 30 percent of the officers were Filipino; by 1933 Filipinos filled over 96 percent of officer ranks. The PC's scope of operation was virtually unlimited, personnel acting as jail guards, postmasters, and game wardens. They maintained telephone and telegraph lines, acted as inspectors of military science courses taught in schools and colleges, and escorted civilian officials to the backcountry. They played a central role in defending the interests of the propertied class. In the eyes of most Filipinos the PC was not a military institution per se, but its melding of police, paramilitary, and civilian functions provided a model for subsequently created armed forces.

The PC role in the national life waned during the late 1920s as civilian institutions began to develop, but military influence rose again after

251

the Commonwealth of the Philippines was established on November 15, 1935, and the Philippine army was organized the next year. The new army was closely patterned on the United States model. It was envisioned as a small, professional force of some 10,000 regulars, who were to be augmented by a reserve force to be built up to a strength of 400,000 by independence—promised for 10 years hence in 1946. Although the new army's structure seemed destined to guarantee it a rather low profile in the national life, its role in putting down a number of peasant revolts, as well as the growing Japanese threat, forced the army into a more prominent position in the late 1930s than was earlier anticipated necessary. The army was mustered into the service of United States forces during the 1941-44 period of the Japanese occupation, forming guerrilla forces that kept martial influence alive in the nation.

After World War II the armed forces' role in the national life waxed and waned, changes in large measure reflecting who was president and what security threat the nation faced. During the 1945-57 period armed forces personnel were actively involved in partisan politics, influencing election results in 1946 and 1949 in particular. Over the entire period they were generally able to retain control over internal decisionmaking, especially in the institutionally important areas of promotions and other personnel affairs. In the early 1950s career officers filled high government posts in the Ramon Magsaysay administration. Putting down the Huk rebellion involved the armed forces in the civilian government in central Luzon and led to a great expansion of the armed forces' civic action mission.

Despite their influence, however, the lack of a powerful national constituency for the armed forces was evidenced in a record of congressional penury in military appropriations and a tendency on the part of some to see militarization behind the armed forces' civil affairs programs. This attitude was particularly apparent during the 1958-65 period, which represented virtually a return to barracks for the armed forces. Under the administrations of presidents Carlos P. Garcia and Diosdado Macapagal, military and manpower budgets were reduced, and civic action was trimmed. The armed forces' leadership was kept relatively subordinate politically and was not included in the inner circles of power. Officers' careers were advanced, stalled, or ended by what many in the armed forces regarded as civilian interference in internal armed forces affairs.

In the 1966-72 period, the armed forces' influence rose again, in part because Marcos was a former officer in the army and comfortable with military men and in part because the level of civil unrest was rising. Military personnel again became involved in partisan politics, and a few were brought into the civilian administration. The armed forces' size and budgets grew, and Marcos greatly increased their civic action program, tapping the military's engineering, technical, and labor resources to aid in his program of national development.

National defense policy underwent a fundamental reassessment in the early 1970s, not only as a result of the armed forces' augmented civic role but also in response to a reevaluation of the nature of the threat facing the nation. Up to that time national defense had been tailored to a holding strategy, in which mobilized reserves would bolster a small standing force until the arrival of decisive outside assistance—from the United States under the conditions of the 1951 Mutual Defense Treaty Between the Republic of the Philippines and the United States of America (see Foreign Military Relations, this ch.). The contemporary threat was perceived to be one of internal insurgency and subversion, however, requiring a switch to a self-reliant defense posture. Developing self-reliance was also deemed important in light of United States retrenchment in Asia; it had additional appeal after the 1973 oil crisis because it focused on developing an economical defense capability that made use of local resources as much as possible and was affordable to a Third World, oil-importing nation.

The declaration of martial law set the stage for a much-enlarged role in the national life for the military, especially in areas troubled by insurgency. The military became involved in the administration of criminal justice nationwide, and particularly in the first years of martial law there was direct military involvement in the management of the economy. The military budget was increased substantially, and armed forces strength expanded threefold by 1981. Martial law was not rule by the military, however. Civilian supremacy was rooted in law and practice, and Marcos, as commander in chief, retained firm control over the armed forces.

After martial law was terminated in 1981, the military's role again waned somewhat, the armed forces withdrawing almost completely from involvement in the criminal justice system. Although some active-duty and retired officers had benefited personally during martial law, in general the military in the early 1980s played a very limited role in the national economy. As of mid-1983, however, in areas beset with insurgency, military and PC personnel continued to exercise authority over a wide range of affairs. Counterinsurgency strategy has also retained its stress on using tactics of both force and persuasion, maintaining the emphasis on the civic action mission.

The armed forces' evolving role in the national life has reflected the adaptation to twentieth-century Philippine experience of a model of military organization introduced by the United States before independence—the model being essentially that of a small, apolitical, civilian-controlled military that performed functions strictly limited to conventional defense against outside aggression. The armed forces' conception of its own institutional development, in which the historic role as defender against outside aggression became subordinate to the roles of defending domestic order and serving as the guiding force in national development, was summed up by Deputy Defense Minister Jose Crisol in 1980. He noted that the Philippines was a rural, underdeveloped nation, in which poverty, ignorance, injustice, and inequality were more dangerous to the state's authority than was armed dissent. Under these conditions the armed forces had to perform a dual role, performing both a conventional defense mission and a national development mission. In service of the latter, the armed forces should take part in government programs and reforms. When necessary, the military "should extend its operations into those areas of the national life where, for one reason or another, civilian authority has been inadequate." Crisol went on to say, as have numerous other military and government leaders, that the expansion of the armed forces' mission took place under complete civilian control and that the armed forces remained committed to the constitutionally mandated principal of civilian supremacy over the military.

External Defense

The nation faced no threat of external aggression in the early 1980s. Officials have voiced concern over the buildup of Soviet naval forces in the region and the presence of Vietnamese forces in Indochina, but these developments were seen more as potentially destabilizing to regional security in the long term than presenting a near-term threat. The Philippines has also viewed the expansion of Japanese military capability in the same light.

The Philippines had two territorial disputes in the early 1980s that had national security implications. The first of these concerned areas of shallow water in the South China Sea that have been identified as potential sources of petroleum deposits. There the nation maintained a presence on what it referred to as the Kalayaan Islands. These were part of the larger Spratly Islands, which were claimed in toto by the governments of China, Vietnam, and Taiwan. Malaysia has also laid claim to parts of the continental shelf underlying the southern Spratly group. Philippine armed forces first occupied three of the disputed islands in 1968 and have since fortified five others. As of the late 1970s some 1,000 marines were believed to be stationed on the islands, at least one of which had an airfield. As of mid-1983, however, Philippine military aircraft were not deployed to the Kalayaan Islands. By the early 1980s Vietnam also occupied several of the islands, and Taiwan one.

The government first put forth informal claims to the Spratly Islands in the mid-1950s. Formal claims were extended in 1978 in Presidential Decree 1596, which stated that islands and islets within a delimited area of the South China Sea were vital to the security and economic survival of the nation. These islands, 57 in all, were declared to be part of Palawan Province. The document asserted that the islands, which in fact were separated from the Philippines by a deep trench, constituted part of the national territory by virtue of their location on the continental margin of the Philippine archipelago. Claims of other nations were said to have lapsed by abandonment and to have been unable to prevail over Philippine claims on legal, historical, or equitable grounds.

Malaysia has interpreted a provision of the Philippine Constitution that defines Philippine national territory as encompassing lands to which the Philippines had historic rights as a potential basis for asserting a claim to Sabah State, Malaysia. At the time of the incorporation into Malaysia of the British-administered territories of Sarawak and Sabah on northern Borneo in 1962, the Philippines notified Britain that it had a claim to Sabah State because it formed part of the Sultanate of Sulu and had only been leased to British traders beginning in 1878. When Malaysia was formed in 1963, the Philippines broke relations, not reopening them until 1969. Marcos publicly renounced the claim in 1977, but Malaysia has insisted that total renunciation required a constitutional amendment. The Sabah issue was clouded by Philippine charges and Malaysian denials that Moro and other dissidents maintained sanctuaries in Sabah State.

Political Role

Evaluation of the armed forces' political role in the national life was open to very subjective assessment, depending on the observer. Most agreed, however, that the armed forces have provided Marcos' main power base and that he has accorded them a high priority in his administration. In the event of a threat to national stability, the armed forces, which appeared to be completely loyal to Marcos, were the single institution capable of restoring order. They would be sure to have a voice in resolving any succession crisis. According to Marcos, he had conferred with 12 top defense and military officials before proclaiming martial law, and all had agreed on a system of succession in the event he was disabled, pledging support for a civilian president at all times. One of those officials, Minister of National Defense Juan Ponce Enrile, represented the defense establishment on the Executive Committee formed in 1981 to provide for succession to the presidency should the necessity arise.

Many of the president's most trusted aides and advisers were connected with the defense establishment. In mid-1983 the most important of these were Enrile; General Fabian S. Ver, chief of staff of the armed forces and director general of the National Intelligence and Security Authority; and Lieutenant General Fidel Ramos, head of the PC, director general of the Integrated National Police, and vice chief of staff of the armed forces. Several active-duty and retired officers have also served in various government positions in the early 1980s, some in ambassadorships. In contrast to other Southeast Asian nations, however, the practice of assigning military officers to other ministries was not institutionalized; the few officers so assigned usually had been personally chosen by the minister of national defense or other high government officials.

During the martial law period armed forces units that were deployed nationwide took over many administrative functions formerly exercised by civilian officials. After martial law was lifted, however, the military presence was less visible in most parts of the country, and the civilian government had grown stronger. In addition, involvement in the criminal justice system has fallen sharply. Nonetheless, in areas where insurgency has been a problem, armed forces personnel have continued to take an active role in the administration of local affairs, both in conjunction with local officials and in their absence. In some areas, armed forces civic action programs were the only development projects under way.

The expansion of the role of some senior officers during the martial law period moved them into positions to cut red tape and to assume the role of patron in patron-client relationships as civilian politicians had traditionally done. Senior officers increasingly came to be called upon by lower ranking military personnel, civilian officials, relatives, and others for assistance in getting jobs, solving family problems, locating community development projects, or even having local officials replaced.

Civic Action and Military-Civilian Relations

A leading role in the armed forces' civic mission had been assigned to the Home Defense Program, a military-directed socioeconomic and civic action program that used the resources of a trained reserve citizen army for the purposes of national development. The Home Defense Program existed in its essential elements before martial law but took on a larger and more central role in the 1970s. The new role did not alter the underlying rationale of the program, which was to enhance military preparedness by building a trained military reserve force. Emphasis moved to improving public relations and contributing to development, however.

Three fields of civic action were defined in the Home Defense Program in the early 1980s: civic assistance, agromilitary activities, and community relations. A fourth field, reserve affairs and manpower development, remained both the core activity and the chosen instrument for promoting the others (see Organization and Training, this ch.). Direction and execution of the Home Defense Program lay with the assistant minister of national defense for home defense and the assistant chiefs of staff for home defense in each of the four service headquarters.

Civic action has become probably the most visible of the Home Defense Program activities. Under its aegis military units were involved in development work, such as the construction of roads and schools, disaster control and emergency relief, assistance in the maintenance and security of public utilities, and law enforcement and other support to local officials. The armed forces have also taken part in the National Livelihood Program (KKK—see Glossary), through which the Ministry of Human Settlements supplied financial and technical assistance for national development projects (see Income Distribution and Living Conditions, ch. 3).

Agricultural activities were among the earliest forms of civic action, a response to the agrarian nature of the Huk movement. The armed forces ran both "green revolution" projects and Socioeconomic Military Program farms to aid the national food production campaign by putting

*General Fabian S. Ver,
chief of staff of the
armed forces
Courtesy Embassy of the
Republic of the Philippines,
Washington*

idle military lands to work while providing training in agricultural skills. These programs have been a vehicle for assisting other government agencies in land resettlement projects and the distribution of public lands to landless farmers.

The community relations aspect of the Home Defense Program was concerned mainly with the information and public relations side of military-civil relations. A public information program was intended to foster popular confidence in the armed forces as a contributor to nationbuilding. It embraced activities "designed to win the hearts and minds of the people; to gain their cooperation, support and confidence; and to induce their participation in the attainment of military objectives and national goals." So-called mass base operations formed an important element in the program. They were intended to win the confidence of people believed vulnerable to subversion, to cushion the effects of military operations on the local population, and to mobilize local support in tactical military operations, including information gathering and involvement in security forces.

An intra-agency civil relations program has aimed at reeducating military personnel, enlisted as well as officer, to an awareness of the importance of military ties to the community and how this related to military conduct. Since the late 1970s this has been accomplished through a "motivational enlightenment program" intended to inform military personnel about Philippine history, culture, and society, as

257

well as official development goals. This was done to motivate greater loyalty and discipline. It was also aimed at imbuing armed forces personnel with attitudes and behavior patterns that would contribute to national development.

These programs notwithstanding, armed forces personnel have come under widespread criticism since the mid-1970s for abusive behavior toward civilians. There have been repeated allegations in both the Philippine and the international press of shoot-outs between different units, indiscriminate firing of weapons, arrogant misuse of authority, and physical violence being inflicted on civilians. On at least two occasions, local residents petitioned the national government to remove particular military units from their areas.

Government officials have acknowledged the validity of many of the charges against army and PC units and have run campaigns to tighten discipline and punish offenders. In the 1981 to mid-1982 period almost 800 military personnel were dismissed, almost 400 demoted, and another 324 punished or reprimanded. In late 1982 new and stricter measures were announced to deal with the problem. Uniformed soldiers and policemen were banned from entering public drinking places except when acting under orders. A rehabilitation brigade was set up to retrain military personnel charged with abusive behavior, and a general court-martial was established to handle cases of erring personnel. Observers generally agreed that the breakdown of discipline had neither affected armed forces internal cohesion nor signified dissatisfaction within armed forces ranks. They have also stressed, however, that abusive behavior has proved counterproductive to the armed forces' counterinsurgency and national development missions.

Relations between the armed forces and church officials and clergy, primarily those connected with the Roman Catholic Church, have been uneasy since martial law was imposed, disagreements arising mainly over what constituted subversion. The armed forces' leadership has stated that all citizens were subject to the law and has charged certain priests, nuns, and lay-workers with supporting subversion, asserting that many social action programs run by religious groups were subversive. The defense establishment has also expressed its resentment over allegations of military abuses by church groups. The Church-Military Liaison Committee was established in November 1973 to serve as a forum to resolve conflicts and misunderstandings between the two sides. Under its auspices, the military and religious organizations were able to reach agreement that "prior consultation" with religious superiors would occur before clergy or lay-workers were arrested. The church decided to withdraw from the committee in early 1983, however, stating that discussions had proved fruitless. The committee had met approximately 95 times to that date and was reported to have established regional chapters.

Manpower and Personnel

According to the Constitution, "The defense of the State is the prime duty of the Government and the people, and in fulfillment of this duty all citizens may be required by law to render personal military or civil service." The 1980 National Service Law provides the legal basis for conscription, requiring all citizens, male and female, to perform service in the military, civic welfare, or law enforcement starting from the fifth grade of elementary school. The new law was stated to have strengthened the spirit of the National Defense Act of 1935, which formerly provided the legal basis for conscription. As of mid-1983 the National Service Law had not been fully implemented.

Although during the mid-1970s the ranks of the armed forces were rapidly expanded through selective conscription, conscription has not been necessary during the early 1980s because volunteers have greatly outnumbered available slots. According to the commanding general of the army, there were 30,000 applicants for only 700 possible openings in 1982. This was not a surprising situation given the limited employment opportunities available to unskilled young adults, but the ratio was noteworthy considering that some 500 armed services personnel were killed in action in 1982.

The combined strength of the four armed services in mid-1983 was approximately 146,300. Maintaining that level proved no drain on potential manpower resources, because 57 percent of the population was estimated to be under the age of 20. Although armed forces strength had trebled since martial law was declared, the number of Philippine armed forces personnel per capita in 1982 was lower than that of the United States or any of the Philippines' Asian neighbors except Japan, Indonesia, and Papua New Guinea.

Personnel were drawn from all sections of the country and were fairly heterogeneous by class origin. Despite efforts to raise the level of recruitment in the southern parts of the nation, however, Moros continued to be underrepresented. Senior officers most often came from towns and cities, where standards of education are higher.

Once in the armed forces, persons from the same region of the country tended to associate with one another, although not usually in so exclusive a way as to form significant factions. Association was based primarily on common language or dialect, English being the standard medium of communication in the armed forces. Members of two groups— Ilocanos from President Marcos' home province and Visayans from the area of Imelda Marcos' origin—have maintained especially influential positions since the 1970s. Marcos has displayed a tendency to promote coregionalists to positions of power, as did many of his predecessors, and Ilocanos were prevalent at the highest levels of the defense establishment, in the upper ranks of police and armed services personnel stationed in Metro Manila, and in the Presidential Security Command.

Several observers of the Philippine armed forces have commented on the existence of factions within the officer corps, although all have cautioned that these did not appear to affect internal cohesion in the early 1980s. The first of these was based on commissioning source, officers being trained either in Reserve Officer Training Corps (ROTC) programs at national colleges and universities or at the Philippine Military Academy. Some friction has been reported between the two groups arising mainly from the fact that promotions were based on quotas assigned to reserve and regular officers, sometimes resulting in the promotion of persons perceived less qualified but eligible under the quota system. It was also the case that ROTC graduates were able to serve for 30 years from their time of commission, but academy graduates, having been commissioned upon entry to the academy, in effect served only 26 years.

Generational divisions and cleavages between combat and noncombat officers have also been noted. Rumors have circulated that certain younger officers have been displeased with corruption in the ranks of their superiors as well as in the government, but these could not be confirmed. Extra attention during the early 1980s to the welfare of younger officers who made up the majority of those serving in combat areas seemed to have been effective in diminishing complaints. There has also been an attempt to circulate field assignments throughout the officer corps.

Certain promotion and personnel practices have been credited with causing dissatisfaction within the officer corps. The first of these was the tendency of the government to assign to important posts "extendee" generals, who were given special dispensation to stay on past the legal retirement age. This occurred most often during the martial law period, when the government concluded that it would not be a good idea to change horses in midstream. The practice has continued to slow promotions, however, especially in the PC, where 10 of 13 regional commanders were extendee generals in late 1982. In mid-1983 serving officers had also complained of the practice of recalling retired generals to fill posts for which there were several qualified active-duty officers. In general, these practices were related to a tendency to bypass the traditional promotion system at the highest ranks. Boards were supposed to meet periodically to pass promotion recommendations to the chief of staff, who then channeled them to the minister of national defense and ultimately to the president. The president then acted on those recommendations, empowered to delete but not to add names. In practice, however, irregularities have been reported, certain officers receiving "hotline" promotions allegedly attributable to their personal connections.

Defense Spending and Industry

According to the latest available figures, the defense budget in 1980 was approximately ₱4,760 billion (for value of the peso—see Glossary). That figure represented 12.4 percent of total central government expenditures, down from a high of over 19 percent in 1976-77. The defense budget had grown over 800 percent since 1971 in current prices; when factoring in inflation, the rise was about 300 percent, total budget expenditures rising almost as fast in real terms. Military spending represented about 1.8 percent of the gross domestic product (GDP—see Glossary). The armed forces budget did not reflect United States Military Assistance Plan (MAP) grants or Foreign Military Sales (FMS) credits. The Philippines received approximately US$25 million in MAP grants in 1980-81, and the program was disbanded in 1981. A total of US$50 million in FMS credits was available to the Philippines in each of the five years covered by a base compensation package agreed on between the United States and the Philippines in 1979. Under improved credit terms another US$300 million was to be forthcoming during the 1984-88 period as was US$125 million in grant military assistance (see Foreign Military Relations, this ch.).

The national defense expenditures included allocations to the ministry, which funded its operations, as well as to programs designed to develop the local defense industry. These accounted for 35 percent of the total proposed budget for fiscal year (FY—see Glossary) 1983. The armed forces absorbed the remaining 65 percent of the total P8.8 million proposed for FY 1983, the army receiving the largest portion, followed by the PC, the navy, and the air force, in that order. Ninety-three percent of the armed forces' portion went to operational upkeep, providing for personnel costs, maintenance, spare parts, and ammunition. Expenditures per capita and per soldier were low compared with neighboring countries, and personnel have complained of insurgents being better armed than government forces. Over the 1975-79 period the nation imported arms valued at US$260 million, which came from the following sources: US$190 million from the United States, US$20 million from Britain, US$10 million from the Federal Republic of Germany (West Germany), US$5 million each from France and Italy, and the remainder from a variety of sources. The navy had fast attack craft on order from the Republic of Korea (South Korea) in mid-1983.

The development of a domestic defense industry was a basic priority under the armed forces' Self-Reliant Defense Posture (SRDP) program, which was initiated in 1974. Defense officials contracted SRDP projects with local manufacturers, encouraging the use of indigenous raw materials and local production capacity. One unique result of the program in 1980 was the development of a missile made from chemicals derived from coconut oil. Design criteria for SRDP projects stressed reliability and simplicity. Projects as of 1983 included the production of field combat rations; light seacraft; mortar tubes, sights, and ammunition; various sizes of other types of ammunition; grenades; communications equipment; and one-quarter-ton jeeps. One of the most important SRDP projects was the production of the M16-A1 rifle under agreement with the United States government and the Colt Armament Corporation. The SRDP program has also encompassed the assembly in the Philippines of helicopters and aircraft under license agreement. Export capability had been reached only in the early 1980s, and as of mid-1983 the total value of arms exports had been very small.

The Structure of the Armed Forces

Commonwealth Act 1, the National Defense Act of 1935, mandated the formation of the Army of the Philippines, comprising all eventual land, sea, air, and national police forces. The existing PC was abolished and used as the nucleus of the new army. The PC's air force became the air arm of the new army; a small maritime element, the Off-Shore Patrol, was added in 1939. Coincident with a reorganization of the government following independence, in 1947 the military forces were redesignated the Armed Forces of the Philippines. That organization was essentially an army command in which air force, maritime, and police internal security units were constituted as subordinate commands and had their own staffs. A more fundamental reorganization of the military establishment in 1950, brought about in part by the growing Huk insurgency, established four separate services—army, navy, air force, and national police (constabulary; not formally renamed Philippine Constabulary until 1959)—under a joint headquarters. The army continued to dominate the command structure, however, until about 1960 when the headquarters was changed into a truly joint command post. As of early 1983 the activities of the four armed services—army, navy, air force, and PC—continued to be governed by the National Defense Act of 1935 as well as by the New National Security Code, issued as a presidential decree in mid-1978. The latter was officially described as a compilation and translation into codal form of various presidential decrees, letters of instructions, general orders, and policies pertaining to national security and public order.

Philippine contingents gained combat experience while being dispatched abroad on three separate occasions. Philippine expeditionary forces served in South Korea under the United Nations (UN) Command between 1950 and 1955. Also under UN auspices air force officers and men were sent to the Republic of the Congo in 1963. From the mid-1960s until the early 1970s, the Philippine Civic Action Group, composed mainly of engineer, security, medical and rural community development teams, was active in the Republic of Vietnam (South Vietnam). The entire armed forces establishment has been mobilized for domestic counterinsurgency campaigns since the early 1970s.

After armed forces units suffered several setbacks and ambushes in late 1982, Marcos called on the defense establishment to reorganize combat forces in the field, eliminate unnecessary intervening headquarters, shift more personnel into combat assignments, and in general maximize combat efficiency. The National Security Council approved a plan that incorporated those changes in April 1983. Included in the plan was the creation of special elite forces in each of the four armed forces in order to strengthen counterinsurgency capability.

Organization and Training

Responsibility for national security was vested in the Ministry of National Defense. The main functions of the ministry were to provide the state all necessary protection against internal and external threats, direct and maintain law and order throughout the country, and perform whatever other functions were provided for by law. The task of preserving national sovereignty has been broadly interpreted since the 1970s as requiring the participation of the ministry in national development to cure underlying social and economic ills that were themselves perceived as threatening national security.

The minister of national defense is by law a civilian and a member of the cabinet. He has the duty of overseeing the Armed Forces of the Philippines and the national defense program. He also exercises executive supervision over bureaus, offices, and services under the jurisdiction of the ministry, including the Government Arsenal; the Office of Civil Defense; the Bureau of Coast and Geodetic Survey; the Philippine atmospheric, Geophysical, and Astronomical Services Administration; the Philippines Veterans' Affairs Commission; the Integrated National Police, and the National Police Commission.

The Constitution mandates civilian control of the military and establishes the president as commander in chief. The president also heads the National Security Council, which is a policymaking and advisory body for matters connected with national defense. Its members include the prime minister and the ministers of justice, national defense, media affairs, and foreign affairs. The director general of the National Economic and Development Authority and the armed forces chief of staff serve as technical advisers.

Operational control of the four branches is vested in the chief of staff of the armed forces. The chief of staff exercises command through the General Headquarters of the Armed Forces of the Philippines, which is located adjacent to the Ministry of National Defense in Manila. Immediately subordinate to him is a vice chief of staff, who is the commander of the PC and director general of the Integrated National Police, and a deputy chief of staff, who is his chief administrator. The chief of staff presides over the General Military Council, an advisory body to the commander in chief on defense matters. Other members of the council include the chiefs of each service and certain other designated general officers.

In mid-1983 the armed forces were in the process of reorganizing the operational command structure to streamline command procedures. Thirteen unified commands, directly subordinate to the armed forces headquarters, were to be established, each of which was to encompass (with minor exceptions) the territory included in one of the 13 regions of the civil administration. The new regional unified commands (RUCs) were to replace five combined commands formerly in existence. As of mid-1983, four of the 13 RUCs had been set up, one each in the Southern Mindanao, Eastern Visayas, Western Visayas, and Bicol regions. The RUCs were given the authority to coordinate all large-scale military actions. Their commanders reported directly to the chief of staff of the armed forces and exercised operational control over various units under them—army, navy, air force, or PC. Support functions, such as training and logistics, were left to the separate branches.

The armed forces maintained several military training institutions. Foremost of these was the Philippine Military Academy (PMA), founded in 1905 to train Filipino officers for the PC. Located at Fort del Pilar, Baguio, the academy trained future officers of all four services. It accepted cadets between the ages of 17 and 23 who were selected after taking a highly competitive examination to represent geographical constituencies around the nation. After a four-year course patterned on that of the United States Military Academy, graduates were assigned to different services according to quotas based on service requirements. Within the quota limits, cadets were given their preference, being asked in order of class standing; the PC was most often a cadet's first choice, reflecting the potential for developing supplementary income and local influence that came with the job. Those assigned to the navy and the air force usually attended orientation courses before being assigned to their units. Two bills in the interim National Assembly in 1983 proposed the creation of separate air force and naval academies to allow for more efficient training in those services; the PMA was felt to be oriented toward land-based officers.

Most reserve officers and some regular officers received their commissions through either the ROTC at selected universities or the course at the Armed Forces School of Reserve Commissions. The four-year ROTC program was a prerequisite for final probationary training, leading to commissioning as a reserve second lieutenant or, for a small number, regular commissions. Two-year course graduates qualified as candidates for reserve noncommissioned officer status. Commissions for women could be obtained through the Women's Auxiliary Training Corps at selected universities. Women were commissioned into the Women's Auxiliary Corps, of which each service had a counterpart. The Armed Forces School of Reserve Commissions was an officer candidate school open to enlisted men in the armed forces. Admission was highly selective and based mainly on examination.

The senior institution of tactical military education was the Command and General Staff School, which prepared officers of all services for command, staff, and managerial positions normally assigned to field-grade officers. The National Defense College conducted courses for senior officers and other government officials, as well as for civilian executives from industry, national organizations, and education. It was designed to provide the broad perspective necessary for national policymaking and to undertake research programs to contribute to the attainment of national goals. The armed forces also maintained the Research Center for National Defense and Development to provide continuous and intensive research on diverse subjects relating to national defense.

Army

The Philippine army was formally organized in 1936 after the United States accorded the Philippines commonwealth status, but it traced its origins to the army established in 1897 to fight for national independence. The army's structure included both operational and territorial commands under a conventional headquarters and staff organization located at Fort Bonifacio near Metro Manila. It was the largest of the four armed forces and in 1983 was commanded by a major general. The highest military rank, that of general, was held by an army officer who also held the post of chief of staff of the armed forces. Regular army strength in 1983 was an estimated 70,000 enlisted and officer personnel, representing approximately four times the army's strength in the early 1970s.

The major tactical units included four light infantry divisions, one unconventional warfare brigade, two engineer brigades, one light armored regiment, four artillery regiments, and a Hawk surface-to-air missile unit. In order to boost its counterinsurgency capability, in early 1983 the army reactivated the First Scout Ranger Regiment, which was composed of five ranger companies, two ranger battalions, and one mountaineering battalion. Despite the presence of divisional structures, operations were rarely if ever conducted in units larger than battalions. The army comprised infantry, armor, artillery, engineer, signals, and logistics branches.

Major ground forces arms included some 32 light tanks, approximately 165 armored personnel carriers and half-tracks, as well as light and medium artillery (see table 15, Appendix). The standard infantry weapon of the ground forces was the M16-A1 rifle, which was manufactured in the Philippines under license agreement. Most arms and equipment were of United States make or design, although since the 1970s sources of supplies have been diversified.

The army appeared to be moving toward the establishment of an elite ranger force to be deployed in varying sized units throughout regions where the NPA was active. Rangers were to be very lightly armed in order to be quick enough to pursue NPA guerrillas. Counterparts were found in the other three armed forces. Formerly, the army and other ground forces had been deployed in battalion combat teams that contained armor and artillery units. These had proved unsuited to jungle guerrilla warfare operations.

The army operated separate schools for its various arms and branches, all of which offered appropriate basic and advanced courses, as well as specialized technical courses. The Army School Center at Fort Bonifacio was open to both the army and the PC. The School for Combat Arms served artillery, armor, and infantry personnel; the School for Technical Services gave courses to signals, engineer, ordnance, quartermaster, and chemical service personnel; and the School for Administration and Finance offered courses in finance and administration.

Navy

Newest of the services, the navy traces its ancestry to the Off-Shore Patrol, which was formed as part of the army in February 1939. Redesignated the autonomous Philippine Naval Patrol in 1947, it became the Philippine Navy after the armed forces reorganization of 1950. Force levels of approximately 26,000 in 1983 included marine, coast guard, naval engineer, and naval air units. Headquarters of the navy was in proximity to its main base at Cavite on Manila Bay, where all major repairs and training activities were undertaken. The naval base complex at Subic Bay, facing the South China Sea west of Metro Manila, was probably without peer as a deep-water facility in the South Pacific. It continued to be used by United States naval forces in the early 1980s.

The navy's principal mission was related to protecting and policing the nation's more than 7,100 islands, which have a combined coastline double that of the United States and are distributed over the Philippines' claimed Exclusive Economic Zone (EEZ—see Glossary) of some 496,400 square nautical miles. The navy also had important support missions for the other armed forces and agencies of the government, especially in logistics roles around the islands. With its subordinate coast guard arm it was responsible for enforcement of maritime laws and regulations. The navy was also active in developing and maintaining maritime navigation and rescue facilities. Carrying out these missions, it has conducted antismuggling and antipoaching operations, naval reconnaissance, and interception of supply lines to Moro insurgents on Mindanao and nearby islands. It has joined other services in planning for joint operations and amphibious assaults.

Like the air force, the navy's combat forces—known collectively as the Naval Operating Force—were organized into three regional commands, one each for Luzon, the Visayan Islands, and the Mindanao-Sulu area. Consistent with the navy's mission, about three-fourths of fleet line vessels consisted of patrol boats and larger patrol craft (see table 16, Appendix). Larger vessels comprised seven frigates and 10 corvettes, all formerly United States craft. None of these was known to have a missile capability as of mid-1983, but six fast attack craft fitted with missiles were on order. Over 100 landing craft of various types and several support vessels ranging from oilers to a lighthouse tender formed the remainder of the navy's holdings. Mine countermeasures and antisubmarine warfare capability were virtually nonexistent, and the fleet contained no submarines. In mid-1983 the navy announced plans to acquire two additional frigates and as many as 50 locally produced patrol boats. Much of the navy's equipment was believed to be in need of upgrading and modernization.

Several other major subordinate commands, in addition to the Naval Operating Force, were under the navy headquarters. The Naval Shore Establishment was responsible for providing support for the fleet, ship maintenance and repair, as well as administrative, supply, and training support to all naval personnel. The coast guard, established in October 1967, was the navy's law enforcement arm and operated several coastal patrol craft. Its responsibilities included maritime affairs, such as testing and licensing seamen and vessels, providing navigational aids, and protecting life and property at sea. The coast guard maintained its own system of eight operational districts, and personnel numbered some 2,000 in mid-1983. The small naval air arm flew one search-and-rescue squadron with nine Islander aircraft and was assigned three helicopters and three patrol boats.

Two marine brigades, having a strength of approximately 6,800 in mid-1983, were trained to conduct amphibious operations. They were believed to be equipped with sufficient landing ships to mount and supply a full brigade-sized landing operation. In practice, however, the marines have generally been employed in assisting ground forces in counterinsurgency operations, for which duty they have been equipped with armored personnel carriers and howitzers. In 1982 a marine battalion was deployed to the city of Davao to strengthen forces fighting the NPA. The marines' performance there and elsewhere has earned them the reputation of being a well-disciplined and well-respected force.

Air Force

The Philippine Air Force was charged with providing aerial protection to the nation. It also performed air support roles for other forces, including counterinsurgency missions for the ground forces, search and rescue and reconnaissance for the navy, and transportation and communications for all services. The air force has also provided transportation and communications support to various government agencies, has regularly taken part in disaster relief and emergency operations in cooperation with civilian organizations, and has participated in national development programs.

The 21 operational squadrons of the force were organized into three air divisions that included a fighter wing, a strike wing, two transport wings, and one each composite, liaison, and special mission wings. Combat elements included three fighter squadrons, one each of F-8H Crusaders, F-5A Freedom Fighters and T-34A Mentors—the last jointly performing a training role. Additional combat elements comprised four counterinsurgency squadrons, of which three flew aircraft and one, helicopters. Other air elements included two search-and-rescue and reconnaissance squadrons, seven transport squadrons (one reserved for the president's use), and three training squadrons. Total aircraft numbered approximately 284, of which 134 were combat craft (see table 17, Appendix). Of the force's 72 helicopters, 18 were fitted for combat. The air force also operated three air defense sites and the air raid warning system. Air-to-air missiles included the United States-made Sidewinder, which was fitted to the F-8H Crusader.

All of the force's fighter aircraft were of United States origin, but the counterinsurgency elements also employed Italian aircraft. Transport and liaison craft have come from the United States, Australia, Britain, Japan, and the Netherlands. In line with the emphasis on self-reliance, in the late 1970s the Philippines began local production of several military aircraft under license agreements.

Air force strength was approximately 16,800 as of mid-1983. This included a commando-type security group numbering some 500, which was formed in 1982-83 as an emergency force that could be airlifted to strengthen security at air bases. The unit was assigned to duty in central Luzon in late 1982, replacing a PC battalion that had been pulled out for retraining. Major air bases in addition to Clark Air Base, which was used mainly by the United States air forces in the Philippines, included Basa Air Base in Pampanga Province, Fernando Air Base in Batangas Province, Sangley Point Air Base in Cavite Province, Mactan Air Base in Cebu Province, Edwin Andrew Air Base in Zamboanga del Sur Province, and Nichols Air Base in Metro Manila.

Flight training was conducted at the Air Force Flying School located at Fernando Air Base. Pilot output during the late 1970s was approximately 120 annually, a significant increase over previous years. The rise was intended to bring the complement of pilots up to authorized strength and to provide replacements for retiring personnel. Gunnery training was undertaken at the unit level.

Philippine Constabulary

The oldest of the nation's four armed forces, the PC was created in 1901 to preserve peace and order in the Philippines. It provided the nucleus of the first regular division of the Philippine army in 1936 and remained an element within the army (after 1946 as the Military Police Command) until 1950 when it was reestablished as a separate force; it was not formally renamed the Philippine Constabulary until 1959, however. PC strength in late 1980 was some 33,500, up over 45 percent since 1971.

Since 1959 the PC has formally constituted a national police force and essentially operated as a gendarmerie, holding primary authority for law enforcement and domestic security. In its law enforcement role it has maintained special units or task forces assigned to such crime prevention missions as land and close offshore aspects of smuggling and piracy, drug trafficking, "carnapping," and patrolling national and other highways. It had responsibility for large-scale crime, wide-area operations, and enforcing the peace and national laws in remote areas where other forces were nonexistent or ineffective. Since 1975 the PC has formed the nucleus of the Integrated National Police (see The Integrated National Police, this ch.).

The PC's task of maintaining domestic security has also encompassed combating insurgency and subversion—a role that after 1972 assumed major importance in areas where communist and Moro insurgents were active. In light of this, it was felt necessary in 1975 to merge certain small units of the PC into a bigger one for tactical deployment, the new formation being called the PC Brigade. As of mid-1983 the PC

Brigade, which at that time comprised 12 battalions, was being disbanded in response to Marcos' call for an increase in small-unit capability in all the armed forces. The brigade's personnel were being reassigned to fill out existing PC companies deployed throughout the nation.

Organized and equipped on military lines, the PC was headed in 1983 by a lieutenant general, who served concomitantly as the director general of the Integrated National Police. He was assisted by deputy chiefs for constabulary, police matters, and home defense. The constabulary staff comprised sections for personnel; intelligence; operations, organization, and training; logistics; plans; and the comptroller. The PC had a number of specialized elements. The Highway Patrol Group operated throughout the nation and had special responsibility for suppressing the traffic in stolen goods. The Civil Security Force Command enforced regulations governing firearms, explosives, and private security agencies. It also had the responsibility for the civilian security forces under the civilian home defense program. Other special units in the PC included the Crime Lab, the Criminal Investigation Service, and the Constabulary Support Command.

In mid-1983 the government announced plans to create the Special Action Force—a counterpart to ranger-style units formed by the other armed forces during the same period. The new unit was to possess airborne and mobile capability to combat terrorism, hijacking, and insurgency.

Most line forces were assigned to one of the 13 regional constabulary commands, under which were provincial commands as well as posts and stations staffed by PC companies and other detachments of varying sizes. One of the 13 regional commands was the PC Metropolitan Command (METROCOM), which has formed the nucleus of the integrated police forces for Metro Manila. As of mid-1983 it was uncertain what status, if any, the PC regional commands would retain when the armed forces' RUCs were completely established.

Reserves and Auxiliaries

National defense policy, particularly since 1972, has assigned a leading role to citizen forces of trained reservists and auxiliaries. Most elements of the reserve program had existed for a number of years, in some cases since before World War II, but new policies in the mid-1970s gave these programs a priority and commitment they lacked earlier. The expanded and improved program initiated under martial law preserved the citizen army concept embodied in the National Defense Act of 1935. This principle called for a defense based on a limited professional cadre backed up by a mass base of citizen reservists rather than a large conscript army. The expansion of reserve and auxiliary forces also reflected the government's commitment to increased self-reliance in national defense and to harnessing military training to promote national development. It formed an important element in the Home Defense Program.

According to the army reserve commander, Brigadier General Edon T. Yap, there were 1 million reservists nationwide in 1982. Yap stated that 15 to 17 battalions were capable of being mobilized within 72 hours and that an additional 15 home defense battalions organized provincially were battle worthy.

The core of the enlisted reserve program was the Trainee Program, under which a limited number of 20-year-old males were recruited to undergo military instruction for a six- to 18-month period. These were mostly out-of-school youths who were provided with housing and vocational training and were paid a small salary. A few reservists were veterans of the career military services, who were automatically placed on reserve until a certain age.

Other additions to the reserve force came from a variety of sources, including a compulsory military training and indoctrination course for all high school youth and the ROTC, which was open to physically fit college males. A counterpart organization for women, the Women's Auxiliary Training Corps, was voluntary. More specialized reserve programs included one under which certain key technicians and executives of utilities or companies deemed vital to the military received reserve commands and annual active-duty assignments in their specialties. All reservists periodically were required to undergo training and participate in mobilization exercises.

In addition to maintaining reserve forces, the Home Defense Program also called for the use of civilian auxiliary forces. These comprised the Integrated Civilian Home Defense Forces (ICHDF) and other groups that supported the ICHDF or contributed to defense and security in villages. The ICHDF was administered by the PC and had both armed and unarmed components. The largest of the armed elements were the Civilian Home Defense Forces (CHDF)—civilian volunteers organized on the local level to provide self-defense and assist the armed forces and the police. There were an estimated 71,000 persons serving in the CHDF in 1981. Most units were organized in areas troubled by insurgency.

Several special paramilitary forces composed of former rebels and others who had surrendered to the government were also incorporated into the ICHDF. These forces were located mainly in the south and were administered by local military authorities but were sometimes commanded by local political leaders. Other armed groups, including private and public security guards and watchmen as well as forces maintained by the Bureau of Forestry Development, the office of the Presidential Assistant for National Minorities (PANAMIN—see Glossary), logging firms, corporations, and others were also part of the ICHDF framework. All were legally answerable to the PC but in practice sometimes operated at the behest of military commanders, local officials, or others.

Unarmed components of the ICHDF included volunteer groups, such as the Red Cross and civic and religious associations that would be involved in disaster relief. Under the program, those employed in public works, transportation, and other government agencies have received training in civil defense and disaster relief. Groups of workers in cities have also received instruction on crowd control so they might function as auxiliaries to law enforcement during civil disturbances.

In general, the various armed components of the ICHDF were widely dispersed geographically and located in remote areas where few military and PC officers were stationed. Many had been given only rudimentary training, their internal organization and discipline not reaching military standards. Critics of the ICHDF have charged that several units contained local criminals and toughs who regularly abused the authority they enjoyed. The government has insisted, however, that the ICHDF performed an important counterinsurgency role and that any isolated abuses that have occurred have been dealt with severely.

Conditions of Service

The rank structure within the Philippine armed forces was very similar to that in counterpart units in United States forces (see fig. 12). There were, however, no warrant officer ranks in any of the four armed forces, and all four maintained seven enlisted ranks, rather than nine as in the United States system. Officer ranks corresponded to their United States counterparts, except that the top naval officer was called an admiral but was equivalent to a rear admiral in the United States Navy. The army, air force, and PC used the same rank terminology and insignia; the single full general in the nation was an army officer who had received his fourth star by virtue of his position as the chief of staff of the armed forces. Uniform khaki dress has been adopted for all services, the color of rank insignia rather than uniforms differentiating the separate services.

Pay, when combined with other emoluments in the armed forces, has traditionally been fairly competitive in relation to the civilian economy and the standard of living of the average Filipino, but it did not enable armed forces personnel, even the most senior officers, to live lavishly. Substantial increases in the kinds and levels of compensation were provided in the 1970s as a concomitant of the government policy of according priority to the development of the national defense establishment. This included not only increases in base pay scales and other fringe benefits but also improved allowances, housing, combat pay, and retirement and death benefits as well as enhanced promotional opportunities for senior officers. As of mid-1983 the Philippine armed forces had 90 officers of flag rank. Service emoluments included a commissary system established in 1973 and the Government Service Insurance system, which was extended in 1972 to include armed forces personnel.

Foreign Military Relations

The Philippines maintained its closest military relations with the United States. The relationship was based on three arrangements: the Military Bases Agreement of 1947; the Military Assistance Agreement

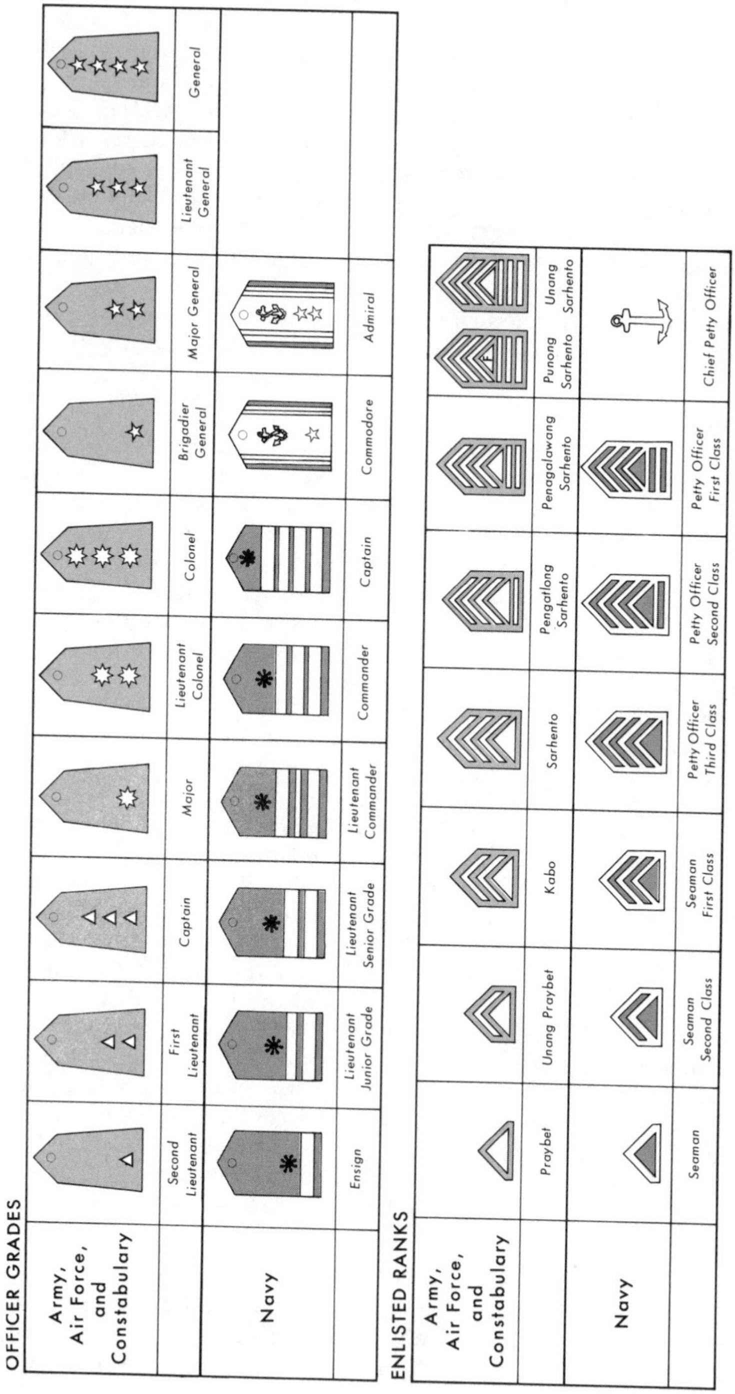

Figure 12. Ranks and Insignia of the Philippine Armed Forces, 1983

of the same year; and the Mutual Defense Treaty, signed in August 1951 and put into force in August 1952.

Under the 1947 Military Bases Agreement, the Philippines allowed the United States to maintain military installations in the nation. The original duration of the accord—99 years—was shortened in a 1959 amendment to 25 years with the proviso for a renewal if mutually agreed on at the termination of that period in 1991. Issues connected with the presence of the bases and United States forces were sometimes the objects of considerable controversy within the nation, two matters in particular—jurisdiction over criminal offenses and Philippine sovereignty—arousing widespread interest and sometimes opposition. Amendments in 1965 (put into effect in 1966) centered on revising arrangements over legal jurisdiction in criminal and civil matters to bring the agreement into closer accord with Philippine wishes. After long and difficult negotiation in the mid- and late 1970s, the bases agreement was again amended in 1979, reaffirming Philippine sovereignty over the bases. The 1979 amendments also provided for the installation of a Philippine commander at each United States base, reduced the areas for United States use on certain bases, provided for the Philippines to take over perimeter defense, assured the United States of unhampered military operations within the bases, and required a thorough review of all issues connected with the bases agreement to be undertaken every five years. In conjunction with the signing of the accord, President Jimmy Carter agreed to make his best effort to obtain a security assistance package of US$500 million for the five-year period of 1979-83. Security assistance was in the form of US$50 million in military assistance grants, US$250 million in Foreign Military Sales (FMS) credits, and US$200 million in Security Support Assistance. The last was to be used primarily to improve conditions around the bases, which were notorious for their red-light districts and consequent social problems.

In accordance with the amendment calling for a review of the bases agreement to be held every five years, United States and Philippine representatives began meeting in April 1983 and on June 1, 1983, signed the Memorandum of Agreement. Under provisions of the 1983 review, the United States agreed to seek prior consultation with the Philippines before establishing long-range missiles on United States bases in the nation or before using the bases for reasons outside the purposes of the Mutual Defense Treaty between the two nations or the Southeast Asia Collective Defense Treaty (sometimes called the Manila Pact—see Glossary) to which both nations and others, including Thailand, were signatories. Inclusion of the latter in effect provided for the use of the bases for operations in the defense of Thailand. The United States also agreed to give Philippine commanders increased access to facilities at the United States bases and pledged that United States personnel and dependents would respect Philippine law and abstain from political activity in the Philippines. In addition, the United States vowed to work further to improve social and economic conditions in areas surrounding the bases. Both parties agreed to amend portions of the military bases agreement concerning the jurisdiction of criminal cases in times of war. Coincident with the conclusion of the 1983 review, President Ronald Reagan promised to make his best effort to provide the Philippines with a security assistance package worth US$900 million to be disbursed over the 1984-88 period. The package comprised US$125 million in grant military assistance, US$475 million in economic assistance funds, and US$300 million in FMS credits. The terms of the FMS credits were considerably better than those for the 1979-83 period, having a 10-year grace period and a 20-year repayment period.

The United States maintained five military facilities in the Philippines. The two most important were the Subic Bay Naval Base (and associated units at Cubi Point, Zambales Province) and Clark Air Base, the largest United States military base outside the continental United States. Both were located northwest of Metro Manila. Other facilities comprised the John Hay Air Station in Benguet Province, the Naval Communications Station in Zambales Province, and Wallace Air Station in La Union Province. Philippine armed forces periodically engaged in joint training exercises with United States forces assigned to these bases, on both permanent and temporary status.

Under the terms of the 1947 Military Assistance Agreement with the United States, the Philippines has continued the military relationship between the two nations that has existed since the start of the American colonial period and has provided the Philippines with military equipment, training, and logistical support. The effect of such aid on the shaping of the Philippine armed forces would be hard to exaggerate. Although the country has diversified its military procurement somewhat since the mid-1970s and has adapted its force structures to meet domestic conditions, the impact of United States military influence on Philippine forces has remained strong. In the early 1980s the level of United States military aid combined with the need to maintain equipment compatibility made the United States the major supplier of Philippine military needs. During the 1950-82 period the United States funded military education for almost 17,000 Filipinos, 624 of these during the 1980-82 period. Most studied in United States military schools.

Under a separate program, Filipino students studied at the United States military academies. In general, there was at least one in each class at the United States Military Academy, as well as a smaller number in the United States Naval Academy at Annapolis, the Air Force Academy at Colorado Springs, and the Coast Guard Academy at New London.

The two nations' military relations were also based on the Mutual Defense Treaty. Under that treaty the Philippines and the United States each agreed that "an armed attack in the Pacific Area on either of the Parties would be dangerous to its own peace and safety . . ." Both nations pledged that in such an event each "would act to meet the common danger in accordance with its constitutional processes." There has been some complaint in official and other Philippine circles since the late 1970s that by specifying that either party must act according to its constitutional process, defense might not be automatic or prompt. The United States has given assurances, however, that it considers Philippine security vital to United States interests.

The Philippines and the United States were both signatories of the Southeast Asia Collective Defense Treaty of 1954. That treaty provided that each member would "act to meet the common danger in accordance with its own constitutional processes" in the event of armed attack against any member. If the threat to a member state's territorial integrity, sovereignty, or political independence came in a form other than direct attack, members pledged to consult on how to mount a common defense. The original signatories of the treaty were Australia, Britain, France, New Zealand, Pakistan, the Philippines, Thailand, and the United States. Pakistan withdrew in 1972, and in 1973 France ceased contributing to the structure formed by the treaty—the Southeast Asia Treaty Organization (SEATO). SEATO itself was phased out over the 1975-77 period. The treaty remained valid, however, and in mid-1983 continued to have ramifications for the use of United States facilities in the Philippines to repel aggression against Thailand should the government of Thailand request aid.

Relations with regional neighbors were conducted primarily within the framework of the Association of Southeast Asian Nations (ASEAN), members of which also include Indonesia, Malaysia, Singapore, and Thailand. ASEAN has no defense function, and its members have committed themselves to establishing a Zone of Peace, Freedom, and Neutrality in the region. The Philippine government has also supported this concept but, according to Marcos in 1983, until the ideal could be reached, the nation had to rely on the United States and work toward maintaining a balance of power in the region. Marcos noted that he had received encouragement from other ASEAN nations to maintain the United States facilities in the Philippines. Outside the ASEAN framework, the Philippines has conducted joint military training exercises on a bilateral basis with some regional neighbors.

Intelligence and Security Agencies

After the declaration of martial law, the number and scope of action of intelligence and security agencies expanded greatly. Many had overlapping functions and shared personnel.

The principal security agency was the National Intelligence and Security Authority (NISA), which was responsible to the National Security Council and the president for the preparation of foreign and domestic intelligence estimates to be used to formulate national policies. Its director general served as a technical adviser to the National Security Council and headed its secretariat. In mid-1983 the position was held by General Fabian S. Ver, who was also chief of staff of the armed forces. NISA was essentially a staff organization that supervised and coordinated the activities of various armed forces intelligence units and the National Bureau of Investigation. It also maintained contact with and drew on the resources of several other government bodies that performed intelligence functions. These included the Ministry of Finance, the Bureau of Internal Revenue, The Bureau of Land Transportation, the Customs Bureau, and agencies dealing with forestry and fishing.

Several armed forces organizations performed intelligence functions, but little has been made public of their organization or missions. In consequence, the division of responsibilities among the separate elements, as well as the institutional mechanisms, if any, that have been set up to coordinate their activities, was unclear. The Intelligence Service of the Philippine Armed Forces, whose operating units, known as Military Intelligence Units, were found throughout the country, presumably oversaw the activities of intelligence units maintained by the separate services. These included mainly the intelligence branches of the PC and the army, the former of which maintained regional intelligence groups throughout the nation and the METROCOM intelligence and security groups in Metro Manila, the latter of which had military security units stationed nationwide. Two other PC units, the Criminal Investigation Service and the Special Operations Group, as well as the Armed Forces Narcotics Command, also performed less clearly defined intelligence roles. The Presidential Security Command, located within the armed forces headquarters, also had some intelligence aspects.

The National Bureau of Investigation was a subordinate agency of the Ministry of Justice, patterned after the Federal Bureau of Investigation in the United States. The organization began as an investigative division in 1936 but was expanded and raised to full bureau status in 1947. It was originally intended to assist the local PC and police to cope with the tasks of crime detection and investigation, freeing them to concentrate on maintaining peace and order.

The bureau was organized into a headquarters under a director appointed by the president, an administrative element, and branches for investigation and technical services. The Investigative Branch comprised two divisions. The General Investigative Division performed investigative functions for the bureau's 13 regional offices. The Special Investigative Division dealt with investigative work in various specialized units of the bureau, including international crime, narcotics, fraud, graft and corruption, arson, and personnel background investigations. The Investigative Branch as a whole also was involved in naturalization procedures, name changes, determination of citizenship, service of warrants, and location of missing persons. The Technical Service Branch provided technical assistance in crime investigation techniques to local law enforcement personnel, courts, and other government officials. A records division served as the national repository for information concerning criminals and other matters of concern to law enforcement, the administration of justice, and national security.

Bureau personnel included agents, laboratory technicians, various technical specialists, and administrative staff. Recruitment was on the basis of rigid mental and physical examination. Bureau personnel generally had a reputation as being among the best and most efficient law enforcement agents in the nation.

Crime and the Criminal Justice System

Although national newspapers regularly carried sensational accounts of violent or exotic crimes, it appeared that crime was not an immediate problem for most Filipinos. Persons living in areas of insurgency and urban residents were more directly affected than others, however, and the government has tried to concentrate its resources in those areas. Nonetheless, crime has been on the rise nationwide since the mid-1970s, a development the government viewed quite seriously. In 1981, in order to combat crime more effectively and coordinate the activities of five elements of the criminal justice system—law enforcement, prosecution, courts, correctional institutions, and the community—the government established a national Peace and Order Council. Similar bodies were established at the regional, provincial, and city or municipal level to give due emphasis to the contributions of local officials and communities in counterinsurgency, antisubversion, and crime prevention and suppression.

The modern Philippine legal and judicial system contains elements of Roman law introduced during the long Spanish colonial experience and Anglo-Saxon law derived during the United States colonial administration. Procedural rules and general judicial techniques of the United States federal court system became the model for much of Philippine judicial practice, and contemporary United States legal experience has retained a formative influence over Philippine jurisprudence. The Spanish legal tradition has remained strongest in the field of civil law. A distinct Muslim legal tradition has long persisted among minority Moro communities of Mindanao and the Sulu Archipelago; courts were set up in the late 1970s in the two autonomous regions of Mindanao and the Sulu Archipelago to implement portions of the sharia (Islamic law), especially those dealing with family and inheritance matters.

Philippine jurisprudence also reflects an underlying cultural preference for arbitration by an individual leader rather than seeking remedy through litigation. In recognition of this, a mandatory *barangay* conciliation courts system has been initiated at the local level to facilitate the speedy implementation of justice. Ministry of Justice officials have provided *barangay* leaders with legal guidance to help them fulfill their role as arbitrators or conciliators. The system was intended to help ease the flow of minor complaints to the police.

Crime

One of the main reasons given for the declaration of martial law was the need to check escalating crime, violence, and lawlessness, which most observers agreed were serious problems in certain cities in the country, particularly in slum and nightclub areas of Manila. Widespread possession of illegal firearms, uncontrollable criminal syndicates, and undisciplined "private armies"—usually maintained as bodyguards by some politicians and wealthy families—were all identified as major contributors to the breakdown of peace and order in some areas. Moving after these targets in the first year of martial law, the government collected over 500,000 unlicensed weapons, disbanded 145 private armies, broke up numerous criminal gangs, and arrested approximately 30,000 persons, many of whom were criminals. These measures, combined with a midnight to 4:00 A.M. curfew, brought crime down rapidly and dramatically.

Available crime statistics were incomplete and sometimes inconsistent, but it appears that crime rates in general fell during the 1972-76 period but then began to rise again, crimes against both persons and property surpassing pre-1972 levels during the 1979-80 period. Various explanations have been suggested to explain the rise, including growing poverty, economic inequality, unemployment, and urbanization, as well as increased efficiency in police reporting. Some have laid the blame on "normalization" moves taken by the martial law government after the mid-1970s, especially the transfer of criminal cases from military to civilian courts and the lifting of the curfew in 1977.

Although cross-national comparison of crime rates was made difficult by differing reporting practices and varying degrees of completeness in coverage, a senior Philippines law enforcement official claimed in 1982 that crime rates in the Philippines in the late 1970s were far below those of Thailand, Singapore, and Malaysia, although somewhat higher than those of Indonesia. He also presented statistics suggesting that crime rates in Manila were dramatically lower than those of six large cities in the United States.

Crime rates appeared to be highest in urban areas as cities continued to attract the best and the worst from the rest of the country. Industrialization and economic development have not kept pace with the rapidly growing urban population, and resulting unemployment coupled with inadequate housing and services has forced a large part of the newcomers into slum and squatter settlements. In the early 1980s it was estimated that approximately one-fourth of the population of Metro Manila were squatters. Conditions in the rapidly growing cities on Mindanao, Davao in particular, have been complicated by the activity of insurgents in the area. Crime rates have also been high in the immediate vicinity of the two major United States military bases on Luzon, where social crimes, drug offenses, theft, and juvenile delinquency were problems. In the seas to the south of Luzon, long-standing piracy and smuggling continued to disrupt order.

As in many Third World nations, corruption has been a serious problem, and its elimination has been one of the government's goals since the declaration of martial law. Although recognizing that the phenomenon was to some extent rooted in the traditional cultural emphasis on interpersonal and kinship ties, the government has noted that corruption affected political and economic development adversely and would not be tolerated. The Constitution specifically mandates the creation of the Tanodbayan (Office of the Ombudsman) to receive and investigate complaints of official malfeasance. Set up in 1979, the Tanodbayan prosecuted its cases in a special court charged with handling graft and corruption cases, the Sandiganbayan (anticorruption court). The president has admitted, however, that although these institutions have processed several thousand complaints, much remained to be done.

Public Order and Security Offenses

The government maintains that it holds no political prisoners in the strictest sense of the term, because all its prisoners have been detained in connection with criminal offenses. These include public order offenses, such as subversion, rebellion, and possession of subversive materials or illegal firearms, as well as criminal violations, including arson and murder. In late 1982, according to Marcos, 551 persons—often referred to as public order violators—were being held for security offenses. Amnesty International and Philippine human rights groups, such as the Catholic-related Task Force Detainees, generally reported larger numbers of what they referred to as political prisoners, including in their totals some persons charged with common criminal offenses and not differentiating those advocating the violent overthrow of the government. These groups have charged that the government's figures did not reflect the number of individuals—for whom records rarely existed—who were detained for short periods of time by local armed forces units in the provinces. Task Force Detainees claimed that in 1982 alone there were at least 1,447 new arrests for "political offenses." All sources agreed that the number of detainees has steadily declined since the mid-1970s. Amnesty International estimated that the government had arrested over 50,000 people in the first three years of martial law, 6,000 of whom were still detained in 1975.

The legal basis for the handling of public order and security offenses is found in a variety of laws, including the Revised Penal Code, the 1957 Anti-Subversives Law, and the 1978 New Anti-Subversives Law. Other sources include Proclamation 1081, which declared martial law, as well as subsequent orders issued by the president. These empower the president and his designees—mainly the minister of national defense and the armed forces—to arrest, detain, and bring to trial persons committing security-related offenses, such as insurrection and subversion, as well as offenses arising from presidential orders that place limits on the rights of assembly, association, and expression. Under the 1973 Constitution, presidential orders immediately become part of the law of the land and retain their validity—even beyond the lifting of martial law—until they are modified, revoked, or superseded by subsequent presidential orders or by legislation of the interim or regular National Assembly. Under Amendment Six of the Constitution, the president is empowered to continue to issue "necessary decrees, orders, or letters of instruction" whenever in his judgment "there exists a grave emergency of a threat or imminence thereof, or whenever the interim Batasang Pambansa [National Assembly] or the regular National Assembly fails or is unable to act adequately on any matter for any reason . . ."

Those suspected of security-related offenses were generally arrested by intelligence or military officers in one of three ways: under warrant issued by a civil or military court, without warrant if a military commander believed the suspect would flee or endanger public order, or under a presidential commitment order that provided for arrest and detention without bail. Many defendants in security-related cases were held under the last category and could be released only under the orders of the president. Approximately 125 presidential commitment orders were issued in the first nine months of 1982. Arrest, search, and seizure orders issued by the president, the minister of national defense, or duly designated representatives were often used to justify legal action under martial law.

Regardless of how they were arrested, defendants charged with offenses such as subversion or rebellion were usually held without bail. Some prominent members of the opposition, however, have been released to house arrest when awaiting trial. Under the Constitution, habeas corpus protection is suspended for those charged with security offenses. Under Proclamation 2045, which terminated martial law, it remained suspended in the two autonomous Moro regions in the southern part of the nation. The Supreme Court has sometimes granted petitions for a habeas corpus hearing in security cases but has not released any defendants. In early 1983 the Supreme Court upheld the president's power to order the arrest and indefinite detention of persons charged with crimes against national security. The court also held that no court could inquire into the validity of a presidential commitment order issued by the president.

Detainees in national security cases came under the administration of the Command for the Administration of Detainees, located within the Ministry of National Defense. The majority were held in military stockades near Manila, but some were detained in local military camps or in civilian prisons. An extensive set of legal safeguards was in place to protect the rights of detainees. Despite these measures, the government has admitted that abuses against detainees have occasionally occurred and has expressed its determination to deal firmly with the perpetrators. Human rights groups and critics of the government, however, have alleged that the military intelligence units charged with investigation and suppression of subversion, insurrection, and rebellion often arrested suspects without regard for legal provisions, held persons incommunicado in private "safehouses" or military camps, and regularly used torture as a means of interrogation, particularly in the first stages of detention. These critics have also charged armed forces personnel with responsibility for "disappearances" of several persons.

The Integrated National Police

Up until the mid-1970s, when a major restructuring of the nation's police system was undertaken, the PC was responsible for law enforcement on a national level; independent city and municipal police forces took charge of maintaining peace and order on a local level, calling on the PC for aid when the need arose. The National Police Commission, established in 1966 to improve the administration and operation of local forces and to establish professional standards, had loose supervisory authority over the police. It was widely accepted, however, that this system had several defects, most noteworthy being jurisdictional limitations, disputes between police forces, lack of uniformity and coordination among forces, and partisan political involvement in appointments, assignments, promotions, and separations of police personnel.

In order to correct such deficiencies, the 1973 Constitution provides that "the State shall establish and maintain an integrated national police force, whose organization, administration and operation shall be provided by law." Several presidential decrees were soon issued, making operational the integration of police, fire and jail services in the more than 1,500 cities and municipalities in the country. The integration process began with the consolidation of the Metro Manila area forces in 1974 and was quickly followed by the integration of the remaining national forces.

On August 8, 1975, Presidential Decree 765 officially established the Philippine Constabulary-Integrated National Police (PC-INP) as an element of the Ministry of National Defense, mandating the PC to serve as the nucleus for the new organization and the Integrated National Police (INP) as its components. The PC, which by law remained one of the armed forces, was given the task of carrying out integration because ity had a well-developed nationwide command and staff structure. By law, the PC commander served jointly as the chief of the PC and the director general of the INP. As the PC commander, he reported through the armed forces chain of command, while as the head of the INP, he reported directly to the minister of national defense. The National Police Commission was transferred to the Ministry of National Defense, retaining its inspection, audit, and review authority but turning over responsibility for training and fixing salary schedules to the PC-INP.

The INP was organized into 13 units corresponding to the government's regional-level administration. Headquarters at the regional and the provincial levels were staffed by both PC and INP personnel. Provincial PC commanders held operational command over INP forces within the province, the only exception occurring in some areas of insurgent activity, where police at times were under the control of local mayors. Below the provincial level, INP forces were organized into districts, stations, and substations. The PC was responsible for patrolling rural areas.

The INP was assigned responsibility for public safety, protection of lives and property, enforcement of the laws, and maintenance of peace and order throughout the national territory. To carry out these responsibilities it was given powers "to prevent crimes, effect the arrest of criminal offenders and provide for their detention and rehabilitation, prevent and control fires, investigate the commission of all crimes and offenses, bring the offenders to justice, and take all necessary steps to ensure public safety." In practice, the PC retained responsibility for dealing with serious crime or cases involving jurisdictions far separated from one another, and the INP took charge of less serious crimes and local traffic, crime prevention, and public safety.

As of late 1980 the INP numbered some 51,000, about 5,000 of whom were fire and prison officials, and the remainder were police. This represented a ratio of approximately one police officer for every 1,100 inhabitants—a ratio that, according to the director general of the INP, provided only the barest minimum of coverage and was not sufficient to provide adequate police in urban areas. In practice, more police per capita were assigned to cities, where peace and order problems associated with rapid urbanization and modernization were most severe, leaving far fewer for less populated areas.

After integration, the government made a concerted effort to upgrade police standards, starting with establishing a uniform pay schedule to standarize salaries nationwide. Previously, remuneration in some locales had been insufficient for many police to live on, a factor sometimes cited as contributing to corruption among police. New equipment was also purchased, including service revolvers, fire trucks, police cars, and patrol boats. The INP Academy was set up in 1978 at Fort Bonifacio to provide officer cadets with a two-year study program. Entrance to the academy was very selective; in 1982 only 120 out of over 1,400 candidates were accepted. Regional training centers were also set up in the 13 regional PC-INP headquarters, and retraining courses were instituted for serving police. Notwithstanding these efforts, official campaigns during the early 1980s, which were aimed at combating police abuse and upgrading the image of the police, suggested that the INP still had room to raise its standards of conduct, performance, and appearance. The government insisted, however, that reports of police involved in violence or illegal acts were isolated incidents that blackened the good name of all officers.

Penal Law

Substantive criminal law is embodied in the Revised Penal Code as amended, which was enacted in late 1930 and has been in effect since January 1, 1932. The code is chiefly based on the Spanish Penal Code of 1870, which took effect in the Philippines in 1887. It also derives from acts of the Philippine legislature and its preindependence counterparts as well as from presidential decrees issued during the martial law period.

Criminal law from Spanish times to the present has rested on the classical or juristic school of criminal law, which considers human beings to be essentially moral creatures "with absolutely free will to choose between good and evil" and holds that as long as free will remains unimpaired, each person must answer for wrongful acts. This aspect of the criminal law, which stresses prevention and punishment of crime, has long been an object of reform efforts. An Official Code Commission created in 1947 to revise and codify existing civil and criminal law and to reflect "the progressive principles of law" recommended a new code of crimes based on the positivist philosophy that crime can be checked only by investigation and reform of the social, environmental, educational, economic, and psychological condition of the wrongdoer. In the late 1960s, a new Proposed Code of Crimes stressing the reformist elements in the positivist theory was drawn up to replace the penal code in use, but as of mid-1983 the new code had not been adopted, and the old remained in effect.

The penal code sets forth basic principles affecting criminal liability, establishes a system of penalties, and defines 14 classes of crimes. It lists aggravating and mitigating circumstances, providing, for instance, that age, physical defect, or acting under "powerful impulse causing passion or obfuscation" can affect criminal liability. Insanity or acting under irresistible force or uncontrollable fear are regarded by law as exempting circumstances.

Under the code, penalties are classified as capital (requiring a sentence of death), afflictive (six years to life imprisonment), correctional (one month to six years), and light (up to 30 days). This corresponds to the classification of crimes as grave felonies, punishable by capital or afflictive penalties; less grave felonies, punishable by correctional penalties; and light felonies, punishable by light penalties. Other penalties include disqualification, suspension, and fine. The Indeterminate Sentence Law of 1933 provides that sentences may be adjudged within a maximum and minimum range and establishes a pardons and parole board to administer early release on parole should a prisoner's behavior and likelihood of safe return to society warrant it. These provisions do not obtain for repeat offenders, persons sentenced to death or to life imprisonment, or those convicted of certain specified crimes, including treason, sedition, espionage, piracy, escape from confinement, or violation of previous parole.

Certain laws other than the Revised Penal Code establish criminal liability. These include an anti-hijacking law and an "anti-carnapping" law. Various presidential orders, decrees, and legislative acts also establish criminal violations.

Criminal Procedure

The sources of procedural criminal law are the Constitution, special laws, the Revised Penal Code of 1930, the New Rules of Court of 1964, and certain presidential orders and letters of instruction. These govern the pleading, practice, and procedure of all courts as well as admission to the practice of law. All have the force and effect of law. In October 1981 the minister of justice ordered the preparation of a new handbook for government prosecutors to ensure a clear, uniform, fair, and systematic administration of criminal justice; this document was expected to play an important role in determining the proper conduct of criminal procedure.

The Constitution guarantees every accused the rights of due process, presumption of innocence, prohibition against self-incrimination, and speedy trial. It protects the accused from ex post facto enactments, unreasonable search and seizure, double jeopardy, and cruel and unusual punishment. Habeas corpus protection is extended to all but those charged with invasion, rebellion, insurrection, or when the public safety requires it. Habeas corpus protection was suspended during martial law and as of mid-1983 remained suspended in the two autonomous Moro regions on Mindanao.

Criminal actions could be initiated by the offended party, by an official concerned, or by a prosecutor (termed a *fiscal* at the provincial levels of government and below). Pretrial proceedings consisted of a preliminary investigation in the case of more serious offenses to determine probable cause for arrest and preliminary investigation of the charge after arrest. Warrant for arrest was issued by a judge, and warrantless arrest by a peace officer could only be made under extraordinary circumstances. Investigation could be conducted by a trial judge, a *fiscal,* or other designated officials. In principle, persons were permitted bail except in certain very serious cases; in practice, pretrial detention was common.

Prosecution was carried out under the control and direction of the state prosecutor or a *fiscal;* both were able to exercise broad discretion in screening cases and affixing charges. At trial the accused had a constitutional right to counsel. If an individual could not afford counsel, the court was required to supply one. Trial procedure consisted of arraignment where the accused pleaded to the charge, the trial itself, and the judgment and sentencing by the court. The accused had the right to confront witnesses and compel the securing of witnesses on his own behalf. No jury was employed; the judge determined all question of law and fact and passed sentence. Judgment could be appealed by either party. The death penalty was automatically appealed to the Supreme Court. Probation instead of incarceration could be imposed when the court judged it proper.

As of mid-1983 the court system was in the process of reorganization. The 1981 Judicial Reorganization Law provided for the abolition of all courts below the Supreme Court, except for the Court of Tax Appeals and the Sandiganbayan. Three main levels of courts were to be substituted for the eight courts done away with. At the local level these comprised metropolitan trial courts, municipal trial courts, and municipal circuit courts. At the provincial level stood the regional trial courts and at the national level, the Intermediate Appellate Court. Courts at the local level had original jurisdiction over less serious criminal cases. More serious offenses were heard by the regional level courts, which also had appellate jurisdiction. Implementation of the new system has been effected only slowly, owing to administrative and financial constraints.

One administrative task slowing implementation was the necessity of appointing a new judiciary to staff the new system, for the dissolution of the old courts had legally abolished over 1,600 judgeships. This prompted a rash of criticism that the executive branch was using the act to overhaul the judiciary for political purposes. Provisions of the act empowering the president to appoint the new judges and to fix their salaries also came under attack. A petition to the Supreme Court to declare the act unconstitutional was dismissed in 1982. As of early 1983 it appeared that only a few judges had not been reappointed. After a scandal in 1982 in which it was revealed that the marks on the bar examination of the son of one Supreme Court justice had been tampered with, all 14 members of the court resigned, leaving Marcos with the task of appointing a new Supreme Court bench as well. In this instance, also, Marcos reappointed most of the sitting judges, accepting the resignations of only two.

The stated purpose of the 1981 Judicial Reorganization Law was to streamline court procedures, rationalize the court structure, and eliminate inept or corrupt judges from the judiciary. It was intended to cure a number of serious deficiencies in the court system, most importantly inefficiency, corruption, and a large backlog in cases. The reorganization, the first wholesale reform in 80 years, followed several partial reforms instituted in 1967 to cure the same problems. Restoring public confidence in the system of justice had also been a stated goal of martial law, during which period steps were taken to shorten pretrial procedures and make trials less vulnerable to delay tactics by the accused. Neither of these reforms nor the enactment of a strict statute of limitations setting time frames within which the court had to render a verdict or dismiss the case had proved effective, however, court backlogs continued to grow, and as late as 1982 cases frequently took two or three years to try.

Lawyers in the Philippines were organized under the Integrated Bar of the Philippines. Counsel for the indigent were usually secured through its legal aid offices, the government's Citizens' Legal Aid Office—organized in 1972 and active in several provinces—and various private organizations. Many of the private groups have been active in representing "social justice" causes and were staffed by volunteers. The oldest and largest of these was the Free Legal Assistance Group (FLAG), which was headed by former senators Jose Diokno and Lorenzo M. Tañada, both of whom were ranking members of the opposition. Another group, the Movement of Attorneys for Brotherhood, Integrity, and Nationalism (Mabini), has been active in undertaking special political causes, usually in opposition to the government.

The armed forces maintained an autonomous military justice system. Military courts were under the authority of the judge advocate general of the armed forces, who was also responsible for the prosecutorial function in the military courts. Military courts operated under their own procedures but were required to accord the accused the same constitutional safeguards as in criminal trials in the civil courts. In addition to regular courts-martial that had jurisdiction over armed forces and police personnel, the military also maintained special tribunals to try a broad range of security and public order offenses during the martial law period. After martial law was terminated, however, officials indicated that such cases would be returned to civilian jurisdiction as soon as possible, probably no later than December 1983. A special board of military prosecutors had been established to advise civilian prosecutors on how best to handle important security-related cases. In late 1982 as part of the official campaign to limit military abuses, Marcos signed an order to establish a general court-martial to try armed forces and police personnel in cases unrelated to military duty in order to speed up prosecution of those accused of abusive behavior should civilian courts not be able to try them quickly.

The Correctional System

Institutions for confinement of convicts and for the detention of persons awaiting trial included a variety of national prisons and penal farms as well as numerous local small jails and lockups. In general, the national prisons housed more serious offenders, and those serving short-term sentences were held in local facilities. The prison system at the national level was under the supervision of the Bureau of Prisons in the Ministry of Justice. The bureau was responsible for the safekeeping of prisoners and their rehabilitation through general and moral education and technical training in industry and agriculture. The bureau also oversaw the operation of prison agro-industries and the production of food commodities. Local jails were administered by the INP.

Prison conditions in the Philippines were generally poor, and life was harsh. Prisoners were sometimes held in isolation, but the government denied that any were held in solitary confinement. Inmates charged with security offenses were often given better accommodations: after the government transferred several public order violators from a military stockade to a civilian institution in early 1981, they went on a hunger strike to protest their new conditions. Several were later released, and most of the remainder returned to the military stockade.

As of 1981 the national prison population stood at 14,792. Figures for those held in local jails were not available but were believed to number far fewer. The nation's largest prison was the National Penitentiary at Muntinlupa, Rizal Province, which also operated the Manila City Jail. The penitentiary served as the central facility for those sentenced to death, life imprisonment, or long-term incarceration. It was divided into two camps to separate those serving maximum and minimum penalties. Combination prison and penal farms were located in Davao, Mindoro Occidental, and Palawan provinces and in Zamboanga on Mindanao. Specialized institutions were available for women and juveniles. A regional prison was opened in Leyte in the mid-1970s to help alleviate overcrowding at other institutions.

Prison inmates serving an indeterminate sentence were eligible for parole. After serving an established minimum sentence, they could apply to the Board of Pardons and Parole in the Ministry of Justice for release under terms and conditions of suspension the board deemed fit to impose. The board could also recommend to the president for pardon any prisoners it believed to have reformed and presented no menace to society.

*   *   *

A summary of Philippine political and security affairs as of 1981 can be found in *The Internal Situation in the Philippines: Current Trends and Future Prospects* by Larry A. Niksch and Marjorie Niehaus. Up-to-date information is available in weekly issues of the *Far Eastern Economic Review*. Data on the communist insurgency are located in the *Yearbook on International Communist Affairs*. *Philippine Society and Revolution* by Amado Guerrero—a pseudonym for Jose María Sison, former head of the Communist Party of the Philippines-Marxist Leninist, who has been in jail since 1977—provides insights on the ideology and goals of the communists. *Makibaka: Join Us in Struggle!* offers a radical leftist interpretation of Philippine society and documents antigovernment protests during the 1970s from that standpoint. The history of the Moro insurgency is treated in Thayil Jacob Sony George's *Revolt in Mindanao: The Rise of Islam in Philippine Politics*, as well as in Lela G. Noble's "Muslim Separatism in the Philippines, 1972-1981: The Making of a Stalemate."

Human rights and internal security issues are covered in yearly reports to the United States Congress by the Department of State, titled *Country Reports on Human Rights Practices*. Amnesty International's annual *Amnesty International Report* and *Report of an Amnesty International Mission to the Republic of the Philippines, 11-28 November 1981* are also valuable sources.

No single source providing a comprehensive treatment of the Philippine armed forces could be located. "Prelude to Martial Law: An Examination of Pre-1972 Philippine Civil-Military Relations," a doctoral dissertation by Donald Lane Berlin, chronicles the evolution of the armed forces' role in society, in particular highlighting their participation in nonmilitary affairs. Harold W. Maynard's "Views of the Indonesian and Philippine Military Elites" provides information, though somewhat dated, on personnel policies and attitudes. *The Armed Forces and Martial Law* by Jose Crisol offers a look at the armed forces' mission and place in the national life from the viewpoint of the defense establishment itself. "Church-Military Relations in the Philippines" by Robert L. Youngblood is a valuable source for data on both the Catholic church and the armed forces. The armed forces and the national security situation as of early 1983 are the subject of a series of articles in the March 10, 1983, issue of the *Far Eastern Economic Review;* these comprise "Eastern Davao Is the Hot Spot as NPA Ambushes Claim More Victims" by Sheilah Ocampo-Kalfors and "All the President's Men," "The Generals Watch the Favorites in the Succession Stakes," "How the AFP Got Out of MAP and into FMS—But Didn't Spend It All," and "Insurgency, Not Internal Threat, Is the Worry," all by David Jenkins.

Standard research tools for military affairs include annual editions of *The Military Balance,* prepared by the International Institute for Strategic Studies, and *World Armaments and Disarmament: SIPRI Yearbook,* assembled by the Stockholm International Peace Research Institute (SIPRI). Also valuable are the following annuals: *Jane's All the World's Aircraft, Jane's Armour and Artillery, Jane's Fighting Ships, Jane's Infantry Weapons, Jane's Weapon Systems,* and *Combat Fleets of the World.* Data on armamemt inventories and the defense industry are also available in *DMS Market Intelligence Report: South America/Australasia.* (For further information and complete citations, see Bibliography.)

Appendix A

Table 1. Metric Conversion Coefficients

When you know	Multiply by	To find
Millimeters	0.04	inches
Centimeters	0.39	inches
Meters....................	3.3	feet
Kilometers	0.62	miles
Hectares (10,000 m²) ...	2.47	acres
Square kilometers.......	0.39	square miles
Cubic meters............	35.3	cubic feet
Liters.....................	0.26	gallons
Kilograms	2.2	pounds
Metric tons	0.98	long tons
....	1.1	short tons
....	2,204	pounds
Degrees Celsius	9	degrees Fahrenheit
(Centigrade)	divide by 5 and add 32	

Table 2. Structure of Gross Domestic Product, 1960, 1971, and 1981 (value in billions of pesos; share in percentage)[1]

Sector	1960[2] Value	1960[2] Share	1971 Value	1971 Share	1981[3] Value	1981[3] Share
Agriculture, forestry, and fishing	3.6	31.9	14.8	29.5	69.2	22.5
Industry						
Mining...............................	0.1	0.9	1.2	2.4	9.7	3.2
Manufacturing......................	2.1	18.6	11.4	22.7	75.2	24.5
Construction........................	0.4	3.5	1.8	3.6	26.2	8.5
Utilities	n.a.	n.a.	0.4	0.8	3.3	1.2
Total industry[4]	2.6	23.0	14.8	29.5	114.4	37.3
Services						
Transportation, communications, and storage........................	0.6	5.3	2.2	4.4	19.6	6.4
Commerce	1.9	16.8	11.6	23.1	72.4	23.6
Other services.......................	2.6	23.0	6.8	13.5	31.5	10.3
Total services[4]....................	5.1	45.1	20.6	41.0	123.5	40.2
GROSS DOMESTIC PRODUCT[4]	11.3	100.0	50.2	100.0	307.1	100.0

n.a. —not available.
[1] For value of the peso—see Glossary
[2] Data for net domestic product, which excludes capital depreciation; utilities included with transportation, communications, and storage.
[3] Preliminary data.
[4] Figures may not add to total because of rounding.

Table 3. *Growth of Gross Domestic Product, 1960-82*
(in percentage change per year)

Sector	1960-71[1] Average	1972-76[2] Average	1977	1978	1979	1980	1981[3]	1982[4]
Agriculture, forestry, and fishing	3.9	4.7	4.6	4.9	4.6	4.9	3.8	2.5
Industry								
Mining	8.9	2.0	20.0	0.0	16.7	4.8	4.5	-13.0
Manufacturing	5.8	6.0	11.4	8.2	5.2	4.5	3.4	0.9
Construction	2.2	20.0	5.7	5.4	20.3	0.0	9.9	3.0
Utilities	n.a.	3.9	16.7	14.2	0.0	12.5	11.1	4.8
All industry	5.6	8.6	10.8	7.2	9.1	3.4	4.8	-6.1
Services								
Transportation, communications, and storage	4.9	12.1	7.7	7.1	2.2	4.3	4.2	3.3
Commerce	5.2	3.2	6.0	6.3	7.1	6.6	2.1	4.3
Other services	4.1	5.5	2.1	5.2	4.9	5.6	4.4	3.9
All services	4.6	5.1	4.9	6.0	5.7	5.7	3.7	4.0
GROSS DOMESTIC PRODUCT	4.6	6.3	7.0	6.8	6.7	4.4	3.8	2.4

n.a. —not available.
[1] Based on net domestic product, which excludes capital depreciation costs. Utilities included with transportation, communications, and storage. Growth rates calculated by comparing base year 1960 and ending year 1971.
[2] Geometric averages of annual growth rates for all years inclusive of 1972 and 1976.
[3] Preliminary government data.
[4] Estimates by private Philippine economic consultants.

Table 4. Financial Institutions, 1980

Institution	Assets[1] Value	Assets[1] Share	Number of Offices Head	Number of Offices Total
Central Bank................	65.4	21.1	1	1
Commercial banks				
Private....................	85.1	27.4	26	n.a.
Government.............	34.6	11.1	2	n.a.
Foreign...................	18.7	6.0	4	n.a.
Total commercial banks	138.4	44.5	32	1,503
Thrift banks				
Savings and mortgage	7.4	2.4	10	268
Private development...	1.6	0.5	43	154
Savings and loan	1.6	0.5	91	251
Total thrift banks.....	10.6	3.4	144	673
Rural banks.................	5.6	1.8	985	1,096
Specialized banks				
Development Bank of the Philippines	28.9	9.3	1	n.a.
Land Bank of the Philippines	5.2	1.7	1	n.a.
Philippine Amanah Bank	0.1	—	1	n.a.
Total specialized banks.................	34.2	11.0	3	92
Nonbank institutions				
Government insurance	18.5	6.0	2	n.a.
Private insurance	9.0	2.9	137	n.a.
Finance companies	11.9	3.8	342	531
Investment companies	5.0	1.6	62	62
Other investment institutions[2]...........	8.7	2.8	69	123
Trusts....................	1.7	0.5	n.a.	n.a.
Other[3]	2.1	0.6	782	838
Total nonbank institutions..........	56.9	18.2	1,394	1,554
TOTAL......................	311.1	100.0	2,559	4,919

— means negligible.
n.a. —not available.
[1] Value of assets in billions of pesos (for value of the peso—see Glossary); share in percentage.
[2] Chiefly investment houses.
[3] Including pawnshops, registered money brokers, securities brokers and managers, and loan associations.

Table 5. Consolidated Public Sector Budget, 1978-82[1]
(in percentage of gross national product)

	1978	1979	1980	1981	1982
Revenues					
National government					
Income tax	1.9	1.9	1.9	2.1	2.1
Profits tax.........................	1.2	1.2	1.4	1.1	1.1
Goods and services tax........	3.6	4.1	3.5	3.2	3.5
Import duties.....................	4.2	3.9	4.3	3.6	3.5
Export duties.....................	0.3	0.3	0.2	0.1	0.1
Other taxes.......................	1.2	1.3	1.2	1.2	1.1
Nontax revenues................	2.0	1.6	1.6	1.5	1.4
Total national					
government.................	14.4	14.3	14.1	12.8	12.8
Local government.................	1.2	1.2	1.2	1.1	1.2
Government corporations[2]	0.3	0.3	0.5	0.6	0.6
Total revenues	15.9	15.8	15.8	14.5	14.6
Expenditures					
Current expenditures					
National government	10.3	8.8	8.7	8.2	8.2
Local government..............	1.6	1.5	1.5	1.4	1.5
Total current					
expenditures................	11.9	10.3	10.2	9.6	9.7
Capital expenditures					
National government[3]	3.0	2.9	3.9	5.5	4.3
Local government..............	0.2	0.2	0.2	0.2	0.2
Government					
corporations....................	2.8	3.9	4.4	3.9	4.3
Total capital					
expenditures................	6.0	7.0	8.5	9.6	8.8
Total					
expenditures.............	17.9	17.3	18.7	19.2	18.5
Public sector deficit..................	–2.0	–1.5	–2.9	–4.7	–3.9
(Gross national product					
in billions of pesos)[4]	(178.1)	(220.9)	(265.0)	(305.5)	(326.9)

[1] Actual cash balances, except for 1981 and 1982, which are estimates based on the announced budget.
[2] Operating surplus only.
[3] Including financial investments.
[4] For value of the peso—see Glossary.

Table 6. Crop Production, Area Harvested, and Yield, 1964, 1971, and 1980[1]

Crop	Production (in thousands of tons)			Area Harvested (in thousands of hectares)			Yield (in tons per hectare)[2]		
	1964	1971	1980	1964	1971	1980	1964	1971	1980
Food crops									
Rice (rough)	3,843	5,343	7,504[3]	3,088	3,113	3,503	1.25	1.72	2.14
Corn (shelled)	1,293	2,008	3,176[4]	1,897	2,392	3,319	0.68	0.84	0.96
Bananas....................	755	1,034	3,977	216	227	317	3.49	4.56	12.52
Pineapples	156	234	1,287	27	28	64	5.83	8.34	20.43
Mangoes..................	95	138	374	49	41	39	1.96	3.40	9.50
Citrus fruit..............	61	63	131	28	18	25	2.16	3.32	5.24
Peanuts (unshelled)	14	19	50	25	33	55	0.57	0.58	0.91
Other fruits and nuts	213	257	522	73	59	74	2.92	3.94	7.08
Root crops[5]	1,553	1,221	3,470	288	246	487	5.39	4.96	7.13
Beans and peas	27	24	47	61	49	67	0.45	0.48	0.71
Vegetables	190	304	515	53	59	69	3.57	5.20	7.51
Other......................	45	79	387	12	13	85	3.80	6.13	4.60
Total food crops ...	8,245	10,724	21,440	5,817	6,278	8,104	32.07	43.47	78.73
Commercial crops									
Coconut/copra..........	1,550	1,679	4,570	1,483	2,049	3,126	1.05	0.82	1.46
Sugarcane	2,132	2,980	4,227	270	442	425	7.90	6.75	7.35
Abaca......................	134	105	172	211	155	236	0.64	0.67	0.73
Tobacco...................	63	56	39	96	76	56	0.65	0.74	0.69
Coffee.....................	39	50	145	42	54	109	0.94	0.91	1.32

Table 6.—Continued

Crop	Production (in thousands of tons)			Area Harvested (in thousands of hectares)			Yield (in tons per hectare)[2]		
	1964	1971	1980	1964	1971	1980	1964	1971	1980
Cacao..............	4	4	6	9	7	7	0.38	0.48	0.80
Rubber..............	6	21	68	20	23	54	0.30	0.91	1.25
Other..............	8	7	12	8	8	9	0.95	0.93	1.29
Total commercial crops	3,936	4,902	9,239	2,139	2,814	4,022	12.81	12.21	14.89
TOTAL..............	12,181	15,626	30,679	7,956	9,092	12,126	44.88	55.68	93.62

[1] Crop year beginning in July of the calendar year. Some 1980 data are preliminary.
[2] Calculated from unrounded data.
[3] 1981—7,723.
[4] 1981—3,247.
[5] Excluding potatoes, which are classified as vegetables.

Source: Based on information from Philippines, National Economic and Development Authority, National Census and Statistics Office, *Philippine Statistical Yearbook, 1981*, Manila, 1981, 264-68, 362-63; and Joint Publications Research Service, *South and East Asia Report*, JPRS 81311, No. 1168, July 19, 1982, 102-103.

Table 7. *Area Harvested and Yield of Major Crops by Region, 1979*[1]
(area in thousands of hectares; yield in tons per hectare
unless otherwise specified)

Region	Rice (rough)		Corn (shelled)		Coconuts[2]	
	Area	Yield	Area	Yield	Trees	Yield
Ilocas.................	321.5	1.99	47.9	0.69	2.3	33.8
Cagayan Valley......	416.1	2.04	330.4	0.99	1.0	37.3
Central Luzon.......	399.5	3.02	61.5	0.84	0.2	17.4
Southern Tagalog...	425.2	1.91	242.6	1.17	80.7	55.5
Bicol..................	286.0	2.09	160.0	0.70	29.5	40.8
Western Visayas....	468.4	2.00	208.5	0.74	14.7	25.1
Central Visayas	73.9	1.70	499.1	0.50	34.6	29.9
Eastern Visayas	171.4	1.49	154.7	0.88	54.2	23.6
Western Mindanao	147.1	2.79	222.3	0.77	36.4	38.5
Northern Mindanao	164.3	1.62	190.2	0.52	57.1	48.4
Southern Mindanao	176.9	2.46	747.6	1.39	48.6	27.5
Central Mindanao	418.5	1.58	462.2	1.07	27.6	32.5
TOTAL[3]	3,468.9	2.07	3,326.9	0.95	387.9	38.5

[1] Crop year beginning in July of calendar year; 1978 data for coconuts.
[2] Trees: millions of coconut trees, including nonbearing trees. Yield: number of coconuts harvested per tree, including nonbearing trees.
[3] Figures may not add to totals because of rounding; totals for yield are average yields calculated from unrounded data.

Source: Based on information from Philippines, National Economic and Development Authority, National Census and Statistics Office, *Philippine Yearbook, 1981*, Manila, 1982, 246-53.

Table 8. *Forestry Production, Exports and Conservation, 1966,*
1971, and 1980[1]
(in millions of cubic meters unless otherwise specified)

	1966	1971	1980
Production			
Logs	6.77	8.42	6.35
Lumber.......................	0.96	1.41	1.53
Plywood......................	0.19	0.64	0.52
Veneer	0.12	0.23	0.63
Total production	8.04	10.70	9.03
Exports			
Logs	3.75	7.02	0.72
Lumber.......................	0.01	0.15	0.74
Plywood......................	0.09	0.56	0.32
Veneer	0.07	0.13	0.19[2]
Total exports..............	3.92	7.86	1.97
Conservation (in thousands of hectares)			
Area destroyed..............	172.00	170.00	26.02
Area reforested.............	7.50	6.46	60.52
Net area reforested	−164.50	−163.54	34.50

[1] Crop year beginning in July of calendar year.
[2] 1979.

Source: Based on information from Philippines, National Economic and Development
Authority, *Pocketbook of Philippine Statistics, 1981*, Manila, 1981, 51; Philippines, National Economic and Development Authority, National Census and
Statistics Office, *Philippine Statistical Yearbook, 1981*, Manila, 1981, 293-96;
and *Fookien Times Philippines Yearbook, 1981-82*, Manila, 1982, 223.

Table 9. *Fishery Production and Net Exports, 1964, 1971, and 1980*

	1964	1971	1980
Production (in thousands of tons)			
Commercial	258	382	489
Municipal	283	543	1,048
Fish ponds[1]	63	98	136
Total production	604	1,023	1,673
Net exports[2] (in percentage of gross value of production)	−13	−8	5

[1] Including fish pens in lakes and rivers.
[2] Value of exports minus value of imports divided by the total production value.
Sources: Based on information from Philippines, National Economic and Development Authority, National Census and Statistics Office, *Philippine Statistical Year-book, 1981,* Manila, 1981, 230-33; and Philippines, National Economic and Development Authority, *Pocketbook of Philippine Statistics, 1981,* Manila, 1981, 102-05.

Table 10. *Structure and Growth of Manufacturing, 1972-80*
(in percentage)

Sector	1980 Share of Value Added[1]	1972-80 Annual Growth Rate[2]
Food............................	33.6	12.8
Petroleum and coal	14.2	5.8
Chemicals......................	9.7	3.6
Textiles.........................	8.7	5.8
Basic metals	4.0	11.0
Beverages	3.9	0.1
Wood and cork................	3.8	1.0
Metal products................	3.4	14.9
Nonmetallic minerals.........	2.7	3.5
Electrical machinery	2.6	14.8
Transport equipment.........	2.3	7.3
Other machinery	2.2	19.2
Footwear and garments......	2.0	−1.1
Tobacco products	1.9	−0.8
Paper products................	1.4	−6.5
Rubber products	1.3	5.5
Publishing and printing......	1.0	3.2
Furniture.......................	0.7	10.6
Leather products.............	0.1	4.8
Other...........................	0.5	−1.3
TOTAL....................	100.0	7.4[3]

[1] In current prices.
[2] In constant 1972 prices, comparing 1972 base year with 1980.
[3] Average.
Source: Based on information from Philippines, National Economic and Development Authority, National Census and Statistics Office, *Philippine Statistical Yearbook, 1981,* Manila, 1981, 186-89.

Table 11. *Production and Reserves of Major Minerals,*
Selected Years, 1971-81[1]
(in thousands of tons unless otherwise specified)

Mineral	Production			Reserves[2]
	1971	1980	1981	
Coal	40	324	370	103,000
Crude petroleum....	—	535	n.a.	n.a.
Copper concentrate	199	305	302	3,940,000
Chromite.............	150	354[3]	337[3]	73,000
Iron ores	1,381	—	—	4,070,000
Cement materials ...	3,948	10,100	n.a.	5,300,000
Silicon	34	104	n.a.	1,061,000
Gold (in tons)	20	20	18[3]	1,665,000
Silver (in tons)	60	61	47[3]	n.a.
Nickel.................	—	25	n.a.	1,479,000
Molybdenum.........	4	90	n.a.	71,000

— means none or negligible.
n.a. —not available.
[1] Production based on metal content of ore or concentrate; reserves are estimates of gross weight of mineral-bearing ores and are extremely tentative.
[2] December 1979.
[3] January through September only.

Table 12. *Primary Commercial Energy Consumption,*
1973, 1981, and 1987
(in millions of barrels of oil equivalent)

Kind of Energy	1973		1981		1987[1]	
	Volume	Percentage	Volume	Percentage	Volume	Percentage
Imported						
Oil.............	64.22	95.28	67.16	78.00	49.99	39.24
Coal...........	—	—	—	—	8.49	6.67
Nuclear	—	—	—	—	6.06	4.76
Total imported	64.22	95.28	67.16	78.00	64.54	50.67
Domestic						
Oil.............	—	—	1.37	1.59	6.35	4.99
Coal...........	0.14	0.21	0.90	1.05	15.08	11.84
Hydroelectric	3.04	4.51	6.42	7.46	15.76	12.37
Geothermal	—	—	4.75	5.52	17.80	13.97
Other[2]........	—	—	5.50	6.38	7.85	6.16
Total domestic	3.18	4.72	18.94	22.00	62.84	49.33
TOTAL...........	67.40	100.00	86.10	100.00	127.38	100.00

— means none or negligible.
[1] Target.
[2] Including bagasse, wood, and other sources.

Source: Based on information from Philippines, National Media Production Center, *Economic and Social Indicators: Philippine Profile, 1982,* Manila, 1982, 2.

Table 13. Balance of Payments, 1978-82
(in millions of United States dollars)

	1978	1979	1980	1981	1982[1]
Current account					
Receipts					
Exports[2]					
Copper	250	440	545	429	305
Other minerals	180	380	505	525	n.a.
Coconut products	872	965	781	718	638
Sugar products	213	239	590	454	n.a.
Forest products	323	484	420	344	n.a.
Other agricultural products	294	407	480	428	n.a.
Electrical equipment	253	412	671	838	1,010
Garments	326	404	500	618	564
Other nontraditional manufactures	497	704	937	1,153	2,019
Other exports	217	167	359	215	n.a.
Total exports	3,425	4,602	5,788	5,722	4,995
Tourism receipts	210	238	320	344	n.a.
Other service receipts	912	973	1,334	1,665	n.a.
Remittances	291	365	421	546	800
Other transfers	312	355	434	472	n.a.
Total receipts	5,150	6,533	8,297	8,749	n.a.
Payments					
Imports[2]					
Petroleum products	−1,015	−1,371	−2,226	−2,428	n.a.
Components for exports	−385	−525	−765	−813	n.a.
Fertilizer	−47	−91	−139	−105	n.a.
Other intermediate goods and raw materials	−1,467	−1,874	−1,974	−1,998	n.a.
Manufacturing equipment	−459	−590	−650	−623	n.a.
Transportation equipment	−389	−544	−533	−460	n.a.
Energy equipment	−262	−279	−290	−301	n.a.
Construction equipment	−58	−79	−100	−75	n.a.
Agriculture equipment	−19	−34	−28	−33	n.a.
Other capital goods	−214	−258	−385	−437	n.a.
Agriculture consumer goods	−339	−402	−541	−639	n.a.
Other consumer goods	−78	−94	−96	−40	n.a.
Total imports	−4,732	−6,141	−7,727	−7,952	−7,800
Interest payments	−304	−591	−846	−1,261	−1,811
Other service payments	−1,287	−1,375	−1,775	−1,839	n.a.
Total payments	−6,323	−8,107	−10,348	−11,052	n.a.
Current account balance	−1,173	−1,574	−2,051	−2,303	−3,347

Table 13.—Continued

	1978	1979	1980	1981	1982[1]
Capital account[3]					
Direct investment	171	99	45	407	259
Fixed-term loans					
Public............................	682	988	536	n.a.	n.a.
Private...........................	209	163	496	n.a.	n.a.
Total fixed-term loans........	891	1,151	1,032	1,332	n.a.
Short-term loans	168	−49	784	188	n.a.
Capital account balance	1,230	1,201	1,861	1,927	1,934
Other changes[4]	−112	−195	−191	−184	278
BALANCE OF PAYMENTS	−55	−568	−381	−560	−1,135

n.a. —not available.
[1] Preliminary estimates.
[2] Free on board (f.o.b.) value.
[3] Net flows, including repayments of principal.
[4] Changes in the value of foreign reserves because of price movements along with errors and omissions in the balance of payments.

Table 14. Direction of Trade and Capital Flows, Selected Years,
1972-82
(in percentage)

Country	Exports[1] 1972	Exports[1] 1982	Imports[2] 1972	Imports[2] 1982	Total Assistance (1978-81)[3]	Total Investment (1970-82)[4]
United States............	40.7	31.5	25.8	22.7	17.9	48.0
Japan.......................	33.5	22.9	31.1	20.0	30.6	18.0
West Germany..........	3.8	3.9	4.8	4.3	2.5	3.8
Hong Kong	1.3	3.9	1.0	2.7	n.a.	6.0
India.......................	—	3.9	0.2	0.1	n.a.	n.a.
Britain	2.4	3.8	3.8	2.1	-0.6	n.a.
Netherlands	7.1	3.5	1.5	1.1	0.8	4.2
Malaysia..................	0.1	3.5	1.4	1.5	n.a.	n.a.
South Korea.............	1.4	3.0	0.4	1.9	n.a.	n.a.
Singapore	0.8	2.2	0.9	2.8	n.a.	n.a.
Soviet Union	0.1	2.2	—	0.2	n.a.	n.a.
China......................	0.3	2.1	0.1	2.7	n.a.	n.a.
Australia..................	0.7	1.8	4.9	3.1	1.0	1.0
France	0.4	1.3	2.3	1.3	1.4	n.a.
Indonesia.................	0.3	1.1	0.7	1.9	n.a.	n.a.
Saudi Arabia.............	—	0.8	5.0	11.4	n.a.	n.a.
Thailand..................	0.2	0.3	1.1	0.4	n.a.	n.a.
Switzerland..............	—	0.2	0.6	0.7	0.6	2.9
Kuwait....................	—	0.2	1.8	3.6	n.a.	n.a.
Taiwan	1.7	1.9[5]	1.2	2.5[5]	n.a.	n.a.
Other......................	5.2	6.0	11.4	13.0	45.8[6]	16.1
TOTAL....................	100.0	100.0	100.0	100.0	100.0	100.0
(Total in billions of United States dollars...............	1.1	5.0	1.4	8.2	4.4	2.2

— means none or negligible.
n.a. —not available.
[1] Free on board (f.o.b.) value.
[2] Cost, insurance, and freight (c.i.f.) value.
[3] Actual receipts of official grants and officially guaranteed loans, having a grant element (see Glossary) of about 75 percent, less repayments on outstanding loans.
[4] Direct private investment in the Philippines, excluding flows out of the Philippines.
[5] 1981 share; 1982 unavailable.
[6] 32.8 percent from multilateral lenders, chiefly from the World Bank (see Glossary).

Table 15. Major Weapons of the Philippine Army, 1983

Type and Description	Country of Origin	In Inventory	On Order
Tanks			
Scorpion (light) with 76mm gun...............	Britain	28	—
M-41 Walker Bulldog (light) with 76mm gun	United States	4	—
Armored personnel carriers			
M-113A1 (amphibious)...........................	–do–	80	—
M-3 Half-track....................................	–do–	15	—
Chaimite..	Portugal	20	—
Armored infantry fighting vehicle (AIFV).....	United States	50	45
Howitzers and guns			
M-56 Pack 105mm...............................	Italy	120	—
M-101 105mm, towed	United States		95
M-114 115 mm	–do–	10	—
M-68 155mm......................................	Israel	16	—
Mortars			
M1 and M29 81mm	United States	n.a.	—
M2A1 107mm.....................................	–do–	n.a.	—
M75 60mm	Philippines	n.a.	—
M2 81mm (very similar to M29)	–do–	n.a.	—
Recoilless launchers			
M20 75mm	United States	n.a.	—
M60 90mm	–do–	n.a.	—
M40 106mm.......................................	–do–	n.a.	—
Helicopters			
Bell UH-1H Iroquois	–do–	60	—
Hughes 500D.....................................	–do–	8	10
PADC MBB BO-105*............................	Philippines	6	n.a.
Missiles			
Surface-to-air Hawk.............................	United States	n.a.	—

— means none.
n.a. —not available.
* Produced under license agreement with Messerschmitt-Bölkow-Blohm, Federal Republic of Germany (West Germany).

Table 16. Major Weapons Systems of the Philippine Navy, 1983

Type and Description	Country of Origin	In Inventory	On Order
Frigates			
Savage class; 1,590 tons displacement; armed with one 81mm mortar, Hedgehog antisubmarine launchers, six torpedo tubes; transferred first to Republic of Vietnam; acquired by Philippines in 1975	United States	1	—
Casco class; ex-Barnegat seaplane tenders; 1,766 tons displacement; armed with one 5-inch, three 40mm, two 20mm guns, six machine guns, two 81mm mortars; transferred first to Republic of Vietnam; acquired by Philippines in 1975..........	–do–	4	—
Cannon class; 1,220 tons displacement; armed with three 3-inch, six 40mm twin, two 20mm guns, 1 Hedgehog antisubmarine launcher, six torpedo tubes, depth charges; ex-Japanese navy..........	–do–	2	—
Corvettes			
Auk class; 1,090 tons displacement; armed with two 3-inch, four 40mm twin, four 20mm twin guns, three torpedo tubes, depth charges..........	–do–	2	—
PCE 827 class; 640 tons displacement; armed with one 3-inch, six 40mm guns, two torpedo tubes..........	–do–	7	—
Admirable class; 603 tons displacement; armed with one 3-inch, two 40mm, six 20mm guns..........	–do–	1	—

Table 16.—Continued

Type and Description	Country of Origin	In Inventory	On Order
Large patrol craft			
Katapangan class; 132 tons displacement; armed with two 20mm guns, two machine guns	West Germany	4	—
PC 461 class; 280 tons displacement; armed with one 3-inch, several 20mm guns, depth charges......	United States	2	—
Bessang Pass class; 75 tons displacement; for search and rescue	Japan	2	—
Bataan class; 150 tons displacement; one for search and rescue; one for command ship......	Singapore	2	—
PGM-39/71 class; 133 tons displacement; armed with two 20mm guns, two machine guns; one in coast guard......	United States	5	—
Fast attack craft			
PSMM 5 type; 250 tons displacement; armed with four missiles, one 3-inch, one 40mm gun, two machine guns	South Korea	—	6
Coastal patrol craft			
De Havilland series 9209; 15 tons displacement; fiberglass hull; armed with three machine guns	Australia	approx. 31	n.a.
Marcelo series; similar to De Havilland series; 22 tons displacement; fiberglass hull; armed with four machine guns	Philippines	n.a.	n.a.
Improved Swift type; 33 tons displacement; armed with four machine guns......	United States	approx. 13	n.a.

Table 16.—Continued

Type and Description	Country of Origin	In Inventory	On Order
Swift Mk I and Mk II; 22.5 tons displacement; armed with two machine guns..................	–do–	approx. 13	—
Abra type; 72 tons displacement; armed with two 20mm guns, one machine gun..............	Singapore	2	—
Amphibious forces			
Landing ship, medium (LSM)................	United States	4	—
Landing ship, tank (LST)...................	–do–	21	12
Landing ship, support (LSSL)...............	–do–	3	—
Landing craft, medium (LCM)...............	–do–	61	—
Landing craft, vehicle and personnel (LCVP)	–do–	7	—
Landing craft, utility (LCU).................	–do–	3	—
Landing vehicle, tank (LVTP4); with marines	–do–	n.a.	—
Landing vehicle, tank (LCTP5); with marines.....	–do–	n.a.	—
Landing vehicle, tank (LVTP-7); with marines.....	–do–	55	—
Aircraft			
Britten-Norman BN-2 Islander for search and rescue	Britain	9	—
PADC MBB BO-105 helicopter for search and rescue*	Philippines	3	—

— means none.
n.a. —not available.
* Produced under license agreement with Messerschmitt-Bolkow-Blohm, Federal Republic of Germany (West Germany).

Table 17. Major Weapons Systems of the Philippine Air Force, 1983

Type and Description	Country of Origin	In Inventory	On Order
Fighter aircraft			
Northrop F-5A, Freedom Fighter	United States	19	—
Northrop F-5E Tiger II	–do–	—	11
Vought F-8H Crusader	–do–	24	—
Light strike/trainer aircraft			
Beech T-34A Mentor	–do–	25	—
Counterinsurgency (COIN) aircraft			
SIAI-Marchetti SF-260W	Italy	16	—
North American T-28D	United States	32	—
Rockwell (North American) OV-10 Bronco	–do–	18	—
Search and rescue/reconnaissance aircraft			
Grumman HU-16B Albatross	–do–	4	—
Fokker F-27 Friendship/Maritime	Netherlands	3	—
Transport and utility aircraft			
Lockheed C-130H Hercules	United States	4	—
Douglas C-47	–do–	8	—
Lockheed L-100-20 Hercules	–do–	4	—
Fokker F-27 Friendship	Netherlands	8	—
Government Aircraft Factories (GAF) Nomad	Australia	12	—
Britten-Norman BN-2 Islander	Britain	6	—
PADC BN-2 Islander[1]	Philippines	16	n.a.
Boeing 707[2]	United States	1	—
British Aircraft Corporation BAC-111[2]	Britain	1	—
Fokker F-28 Fellowship[2]	Netherlands	1	—
NAMC YS-11[2]	Japan	4	—
Cessna O-1E Birddog	United States	n.a.	—
Cessna U-17A/B Skywagon	–do–	20	—
Cessna 210	–do–	3	—
Trainer aircraft			
Lockheed T/RT-33A Shooting Star	–do–	10	I
Cessna T-41D Mescalero	–do–	12	—
SIAI-Marchetti SF-260MP	Italy	30	I
Philippine Air Force T-160 Cali (Super Pinto)[3]	Philippines	n.a.	n.a.
Northrop F-5B Freedom Fighter	United States	3	—
Helicopters			
Bell UH-1H Iroquois (armed)	–do–	18	—
Bell UH-1H Iroquois[2]	–do–	4	—
Bell UH-1H Iroquois	–do–	43	—
Aérospatiale/Westland Puma[2]	Britain	1	—
Sikorsky S-62A[2]	United States	2	—
PADC MBB BO-105[4]	Philippines	4	5
Missiles			
Air-to-air Sidewinder (fitted to F-8s)	United States	n.a.	—
Air-to-ground (fitted to T-28s)	Philippines	n.a.	—

— means none.
n.a. not available.
[1] Produced under license agreement with Britten-Norman, Britain.
[2] In presidential squadron.
[3] Produced under license agreement with American Jet Industries, United States.
[4] Produced under license agreement with Messerschmitt-Bölkow-Blohm, Federal Republic of Germany (West Germany).

Appendix B

Mutual Defense Treaty Between the United States of America and the Republic of the Philippines

Signed at Washington August 30, 1951; Ratification advised by the Senate of the United States of America March 20, 1952; Ratified by the President of the United States of America April 15, 1952; Ratified by the Republic of the Philippines August 27, 1952; Ratifications exchanged at Manila August 27, 1952; Proclaimed by the President of the United States of America September 15, 1952; Entered into force August 27, 1952

The Parties to this Treaty,

Reaffirming their faith in the purposes and principles of the Charter of the United Nations and their desire to live in peace with all peoples and all Governments, and desiring to strengthen the fabric of peace in the Pacific Area,

Recalling with mutual pride the historic relationship which brought their two peoples together in a common bond of sympathy and mutual ideals to fight side-by-side against imperialist aggression during the last war,

Desiring to declare publicly and formally their sense of unity and their common determination to defend themselves against external armed attack, so that no potential aggressor could be under the illusion that either of them stands alone in the Pacific Area,

Desiring further to strengthen their present efforts for collective defense for the preservation of peace and security pending the development of a more comprehensive system of regional security in the Pacific Area,

Agreeing that nothing in this present instrument shall be considered or interpreted as in any way or sense altering or diminishing any existing agreements or understandings between the United States of America and the Republic of the Philippines,

Have agreed as follows:

Article I

The Parties undertake, as set forth in the Charter of the United Nations, to settle any international disputes in which they may be involved by peaceful means in such a manner that international peace and security and justice are not endangered and to refrain in their international relations from the threat or use of force in any manner inconsistent with the purposes of the United Nations.

Article II

In order more effectively to achieve the objective of this Treaty, the Parties separately and jointly by self-help and mutual aid will maintain and develop their individual and collective capacity to resist armed attack.

Article III

The Parties, through their Foreign Ministers or their deputies, will consult together from time to time regarding the implementation of this Treaty and whenever in the opinion of either of them the territorial integrity, political independence or security of either of the Parties is threatened by external armed attack in the Pacific.

Article IV

Each Party recognizes that an armed attack in the Pacific Area on either of the Parties would be dangerous to its own peace and safety and declares that it would act to meet the common dangers in accordance with its constitutional processes.

Any such armed attack and all measures taken as a result thereof shall be immediately reported to the Security Council of the United Nations. Such measures shall be terminated when the Security Council has taken the measures necessary to restore and maintain international peace and security.

Article V

For the purpose of Article IV, an armed attack on either of the Parties is deemed to include an armed attack on the metropolitan territory of either of the Parties, or on the island territories under its jurisdiction in the Pacific or on its armed forces, public vessels or aircraft in the Pacific.

Article VI

This Treaty does not affect and shall not be interpreted as affecting in any way the rights and obligations of the Parties under the Charter of the United Nations or the responsibility of the United Nations for the maintenance of international peace and security.

Article VII

This Treaty shall be ratified by the United States of America and the Republic of the Philippines in accordance with their respective constitutional processes and will come into force when instruments of ratification thereof have been exchanged by them at Manila.

Article VIII

This Treaty shall remain in force indefinitely. Either Party may terminate it one year after notice has been given to the other Party.

Bibliography

Chapter 1

Abaya, Hernando J. *Betrayal in the Philippines*. New York: Wyn, 1946.

Abubakar, Asiri J. "Muslim Philippines: With Reference to the Sulus, Muslim-Christian Contradictions, and the Mindanao Crisis," *Asian Studies* [Manila], 11, No. 1, April 1973, 112–28.

Abueva, Jose Veloso. "Ideology and Practice in the 'New Society'." Pages 32–84 in David A. Rosenberg (ed.), *Marcos and Martial Law in the Philippines*. Ithaca: Cornell University Press, 1979.

_____. "The Philippines: Tradition and Change," *Asian Survey*, 10, No. 1, January 1970, 56–84.

Adkins, John H. "Philippines 1971: Events of a Year, Trends of the Future," *Asian Survey*, 11, No. 1, January 1971, 78–85.

_____. "Philippines 1972: We'll Wait and See," *Asian Survey*, 13, No. 2, February 1973, 140–50.

Agoncillo, Teodoro A. *The Fateful Years: Japan's Adventure in the Philippines*. 2 vols. Quezon City: Garcia, 1965.

_____. *The Revolt of the Masses: The Story of Bonifacio and the Katipunan*. Quezon City: University of the Philippines, 1956.

Agoncillo, Teodoro A., and Oscar M. Alfonso. *A Short History of the Filipino People*. Manila: University of the Philippines, 1960.

Alfonso, Oscar M. "Taft's Views on 'The Philippines for the Filipinos'," *Asian Studies* [Manila], 6, No. 3, December 1968, 237–47.

Alip, Eufronio M. *Political and Cultural History of the Philippines*. Manila: Alip and Brion, 1950.

Averch, Harvey A., et al. *The Matrix of Policy in the Philippines*. Princeton: Princeton University Press, 1971.

Beckett, Jeremy. "The Defiant and the Compliant: The *Datus* of Magindanao under Colonial Rule." Pages 391–414 in Alfred W. McCoy and E.C. de Jesus (eds.), *Philippine Social History: Global Trade and Local Transformations*. Honolulu: University Press of Hawaii, 1982.

Blumberg, Arnold. "Belgium and a Philippine Protectorate: A Stillborn Plan," *Asian Studies* [Manila], 10, No. 3, December 1972, 336–43.

Carmen, Rolando V. del. "Constitutionality and Judicial Politics." Pages 85–112 in David A. Rosenberg (ed.), *Marcos and Martial Law in the Philippines*. Ithaca: Cornell University Press, 1979.

_____. "Philippines 1974: A Holding Pattern—Power Consolidation or Prelude to a Decline?" *Asian Survey*, 15, No. 2, February 1975, 136–47.

Casambre, Napoleon J. "The Response to Harrison's Administration in the Philippines, 1913–1921," *Asian Studies* [Manila], 7, No. 2, August 1969, 156–70.

Cheong, W.E. "The Decline of Manila as the Spanish Entrepôt in the Far East, 1785–1826: Its Impact on the Pattern of Southeast Asian Trade," *Journal of Southeast Asian Studies* [Singapore], 2, No. 2, September 1971, 142–58.

Coates, Austin. *Rizal: Philippine Nationalist and Martyr.* Hong Kong: Oxford University Press, 1968.

Coleman, Ambrose. *The Friars in the Philippines.* Boston: Marlier, Callanan, 1899.

Constantino, Renato. *Neocolonial Identity and Counter-Consciousness.* White Plains, New York: Sharpe, 1978.

Cruikshank, Bruce. "Continuity and Change in the Economic and Administrative History of 19th-Century Samar." Pages 219–50 in Alfred W. McCoy and E.C. de Jesus (eds.), *Philippine Social History: Global Trade and Local Transformations.* Honolulu: University Press of Hawaii, 1982.

Cushner, Nicholas P. *Landed Estates in the Colonial Philippines.* (Monograph series, No. 20.) New Haven: Southeast Asia Studies, Yale University, 1976.

Elliott, Charles Burke. *The Philippines to the End of the Commission Government: A Study in Tropical Democracy.* New York: Greenwood Press, 1968.

Evangelista, Oscar L. "Religious Problems in the Philippines and the American Catholic Church, 1898–1907," *Asian Studies* [Manila], 6, No. 3, December 1969, 248–62.

Foubert, Charles-Henri. *Les Philippines: Le réveil d'un archipel.* Paris: Editions L'Harmattan, 1980.

Friend, Theodore. *Between Two Empires: The Ordeal of the Philippines.* New Haven: Yale University Press, 1965.

Gagelonia, Pedro A. *Man of the Century: Biography of Jose Rizal.* Manila: Villanueva, 1964.

Gates, John Morgan. *Schoolbooks and Krags: The United States Army in the Philippines, 1898–1902.* (Contributions in Military History, No. 3) Westport, Connecticut: Greenwood Press, 1973.

Gowing, Peter G. *Muslim Filipinos: Heritage and Horizon.* Quezon City: New Day, 1979.

Hall, D.G.E. *A History of South-East Asia.* London: Macmillan, 1964.

Henze, Laura Jeanne. "U.S.-Philippine Economic Relations and Trade Negotiations," *Asian Survey,* 16, No. 4, April 1976, 319–37.

Hollnsteiner, Mary Racelis (ed.). *Society, Culture, and the Filipino.* 3 vols. Quezon City: Institute of Philippine Culture, Ateneo de Manila University Press, 1975.

Hunt, Chester L. "Philippine Values and Martial Law," *Journal of Southeast Asian Studies* [Singapore], 11, No. 1, March 1980, 110–21.

Ike, Nobutaka. "Urbanization and Political Opposition: The Philippines and Japan," *Asian Studies* [Manila], 7, No. 2, August 1969, 134–41.

Jesus, E.C. de. "Control and Compromise in the Cagayan Valley." Pages 21–38 in Alfred W. McCoy and E.C. de Jesus (eds.), *Phil-*

ippine Social History: Global Trade and Local Transformations. Honolulu: University Press of Hawaii, 1982.

Kerkvliet, Benedict J. *The Huk Rebellion: A Study of Peasant Revolt in the Philippines*. Berkeley and Los Angeles: University of California Press, 1977.

_____. "Land Reform: Emancipation or Counterinsurgency?" Pages 113–44 in David A. Rosenberg (ed.), *Marcos and Martial Law in the Philippines*. Ithaca: Cornell University Press, 1979.

_____. "Peasant Society and Unrest Prior to the Huk Rebellion in the Philippines," *Asian Studies* [Manila], 9, No. 2, August 1971, 164–213.

Krinks, Peter. "Old Wine in a New Bottle: Land Settlement and Agrarian Problems in the Philippines," *Journal of Southeast Asian Studies* [Singapore], 5, No. 1, March 1974, 1–17.

Lachica, Eduardo. *The Huks: Philippine Agrarian Society in Revolt*. New York: Praeger, 1971.

Landé, Carl H. *Leaders, Factions, and Parties: The Structure of Philippine Politics*. (Monograph series, No. 6.) New Haven: Southeast Asia Studies, Yale University, 1965.

Larkin, John A. *The Pampangans: Colonial Society in a Philippine Province*. Berkeley and Los Angeles: University of California Press, 1972.

Larkin, John A. (ed.). *Perspectives on Philippine Historiography: A Symposium.* (Monograph series, No. 21.) New Haven: Southeast Asia Studies, Yale University, 1979.

Le Roy, James A. *The Americans in the Philippines: A History of the Conquest and First Years of Occupation with an Introductory Account of Spanish Rule*. 2 vols. New York: AMS Press, 1970 (reprint).

Lightfoot, Keith. *The Philippines*. New York: Praeger, 1973.

Luna, Maria Pilar S. "General Artemio Ricarte y Garcia: A Filipino Nationalist," *Asian Studies* [Manila], 9, No. 2, August 1971, 229–41.

Macahiya, Ernesto R. "Footnote to Revolution and Social Change (The Philippine Case)," *Asian Studies* [Manila], 7, No. 2, August 1969, 142–55.

McCoy, Alfred W. "The Philippines: Independence Without Decolonization." Pages 22–65 in Robin Jeffrey (ed.), *Asia: The Winning of Independence*. New York: St. Martin's Press, 1981.

Machado, Kit G. "The Philippines 1978: Authoritarian Consolidation Continues," *Asian Survey*, 19, No. 2, February 1979, 131–40.

Mahajani, Usha. *Philippine Nationalism: External Challenge and Filipino Response, 1565–1946*. St. Lucia, Queensland: University of Queensland Press, 1971.

Majul, Cesar Adib. "Social Background of Revolution," *Asian Studies* [Manila], 9, No. 1, April 1971, 1–23.

May, Glenn Anthony. *Social Engineering in the Philippines: The Aims, Execution, and Impact of American Colonial Policy, 1900–1913*.

(Contributions in Comparative Colonial Studies, No. 2.) Westport, Connecticut: Greenwood Press, 1980.

Miller, Stuart Creighton. *"Benevolent Assimilation": The American Conquest of the Philippines, 1899–1903.* New Haven: Yale University Press, 1982.

Morga, Antonio de. *History of the Philippine Islands, from Their Discovery by Magellan in 1521 to the Beginning of the XVII Century; with Descriptions of Japan, China, and Adjacent Countries.* New York: Kraus, 1970 (reprint).

Nawawi, Mohd A. "Political Participation During the First Five Years of the New Society in the Philippines," *Journal of Southeast Asian Studies* [Singapore], 13, No. 2, September 1982, 270–78.

Neher, Clark D. "The Philippines in 1980: The Gathering Storm," *Asian Survey*, 21, No. 2, February 1981, 261–73.

––––––. "The Philippines in 1979: Cracks in the Fortress," *Asian Survey*, 20, No. 2, February 1980, 155–67.

Noble, Lela Garner. "Ethnicity and Philippine-Malaysian Relations," *Asian Survey*, 15, No. 5, May 1975, 453–72.

––––––. "Muslim Separatism in the Philippines, 1972–81: The Making of a Stalemate," *Asian Survey*, 21, No. 11, November 1981, 1097–1114.

––––––. "The National Interest and the National Image: Philippine Policy in Asia," *Asian Survey*, 13, No. 6, June 1973, 560–76.

––––––. "Philippines 1975: Consolidating the Regime," *Asian Survey*, 16, No. 2, February 1976, 178–85.

––––––. "Philippines 1976: The Contrast Between Shrine and Shanty," *Asian Survey*, 17, No. 2, February 1977, 133–42.

Overholt, William H. "Land Reform in the Philippines," *Asian Survey*, 16, No. 5, May 1976, 427–51.

Phelan, John Leddy, *The Hispanization of the Philippines: Spanish Aims and Filipino Responses, 1565–1700.* Madison: University of Wisconsin Press, 1967.

Reed, Robert R. *Colonial Manila: The Context of Hispanic Urbanism and Process of Morphogenesis.* (University of California Publications in Geography, 22.) Berkeley and Los Angeles: University of California Press, 1978.

Rosenberg, David A. "Introduction: Creating a 'New Society'." Pages 13–31 in David A. Rosenberg (ed.), *Marcos and Martial Law in the Philippines.* Ithaca: Cornell University Press, 1979.

Roth, Dennis M. "The *Casas de Reservas* in the Philippines," *Journal of Southeast Asian Studies* [Singapore], 5, No. 1, March 1974, 115–24.

––––––. "Church Lands in the Agrarian History of the Tagalog Region." Pages 131–54 in Alfred W. McCoy and E.C. de Jesus (eds.), *Philippine Social History: Global Trade and Local Transformations.* Honolulu: University Press of Hawaii, 1982.

Schurz, William Lytle. *The Manila Galleon.* New York: Dutton, 1959.

Shalom, Stephen Rosskamm. *The United States and the Philippines: A Study of Neocolonialism.* Philadelphia: Institute for the Study of Human Issues, 1981.

Soberano, Rawlein G. "The Philippine Independence Controversy from McKinley to Taft: The Politics of Accommodation," *Asian Studies* [Manila], 11, No. 2, August 1973, 114–27.

Stanley, Peter W. *A Nation in the Making: The Philippines and the United States, 1899–1921.* Cambridge: Harvard University Press, 1974.

Starner, Frances Lucille. *Magsaysay and the Philippine Peasantry: The Agrarian Impact on Philippine Politics, 1953–1956.* (Publications in Political Science, 10.) Berkeley and Los Angeles: University of California Press, 1961.

Stauffer, Robert B. "Philippine Corporatism: A Note on the 'New Society'," *Asian Survey*, 17, No. 4, April 1977, 393–407.

——. "The Political Economy of Refeudalization." Pages 180–218 in David A. Rosenberg (ed.), *Marcos and Martial Law in the Philippines.* Ithaca: Cornell University Press, 1979.

Steinberg, David Joel. *The Philippines: A Singular and a Plural Place.* Boulder: Westview Press, 1982.

Sturtevant, David R. *Popular Uprisings in the Philippines, 1840–1940.* Ithaca: Cornell University Press, 1976.

Suhrke, Astri. "Political Rituals in Developing Nations: The Case of the Philippines," *Journal of Southeast Asian Studies* [Singapore], 2, No. 2, September 1971, 126–41.

Sweet, David. "A Proto-Political Peasant Movement in the Spanish Philippines: The Cofrádia de San José and the Tayabas Rebellion of 1841," *Asian Studies* [Manila], 8, No. 1, April 1970, 94–119.

Tarling, Nicholas. *Sulu and Sabah: A Study of British Policy Toward the Philippines and North Borneo from the Late Eighteenth Century.* Kuala Lumpur: Oxford University Press, 1978.

Valdepeñas, Vicente B., Jr., and Gemelino M. Bautista. *The Emergence of the Philippine Economy.* Manila: Papyrus Press, 1977.

Villanueva, A.B., "Decentralization and Executive-Legislative Relations in the Philippines, 1961–1967," *Modern Asian Studies* [Cambridge], 12, No. 3, 1978, 377–92.

Villanueva, Honesto A. "The Independence Mission 1919: Independence Lies Ahead, *Asian Studies* [Manila], 9, No. 3, December 1971, 282–306.

Wickberg, Edgar. *The Chinese in Philippine Life, 1850–1898.* (Southeast Asia Studies, No. 1.) New Haven: Yale University Press, 1965.

Wolff, Leon. *Little Brown Brother: America's Forgotten Bid for Empire Which Cost 250,000 Lives.* New York: Kraus, 1970 (reprint).

Wurfel, David. "The Philippines." Pages 679–772 in George M. Kahin (ed.), *Government and Politics of Southeast Asia.* (2d ed.) Ithaca: Cornell University Press, 1965.

Youngblood, Robert L. "Government-Media Relations in the Philippines," *Asian Survey*, 21, No. 7, July 1981, 710–28.

―――. "The Philippines in 1981: From 'New Society' to 'New Republic'," *Asian Survey*, 22, No. 2, February 1982, 226–35.

―――. "The Philippines in 1982: Marcos Gets Tough with Domestic Critics," *Asian Survey*, 23, No. 2, February 1983, 208–16.

Zaide, Gregorio F. *The Pageant of Philippine History: Vol. I, from Prehistory to the Eve of the British Invasion.* Manila: Philippine Education, 1979.

―――. *The Pageant of Philippine History: Vol II, from the British Invasion to the Present Times.* Manila: Philippine Education, 1979.

―――. *Philippine Government: Development, Organization, and Functions.* Manila: Modern Book, 1965.

Chapter 2

Abad, Ricardo G. *Perspectives on Philippines Poverty: An Annotated Bibliography of Social Science Works, 1970–1980.* Quezon City: Ateneo de Manila University Press, 1982.

Achútequi, Pedro S. de, and Miguel A. Bernad. *The Religious Coup d'Etat, 1898–1901: A Documentary History.* Quezon City: Ateneo de Manila University Press, 1971.

―――. *Religious Revolution in the Philippines: The Life and Church of Gregorio Aglipay, 1860–1960.* 2 vols. Manila: Ateneo de Manila University Press, 1961.

Alfonso, Amelia B., Leda L. Layo, and Rodolfo A. Bulatao. *Culture and Fertility: The Case of the Philippines.* Singapore: Institute of Southeast Asian Studies, 1980.

Allen, J.P. "Recent Immigration from the Philippines and Filipino Communities in the United States," *Geographical Review*, 67, No. 2, April 1977, 195–208.

Ando, Hirofumi. "A Study of the Iglesia ni Cristo: A Politico-Religious Sect in the Philippines," *Pacific Affairs* [Vancouver], 42, No. 3, Fall 1969.

Angangco, Ofelia R., et al., *Status of Women in the Philippines: A Bibliography with Selected Annotations.* Quezon City: Alemar-Phoenix, 1980.

Aprieto, Pacifico N. "A Dictionary that Begins with the Letter F." Pages 226–27 in Betty Go-Belmonte (ed.), *Fookien Times Philippines Yearbook, 1981–82.* Manila; Fookien Times, 1982.

Aquino, Belinda A. (ed.). *Cronies and Enemies: The Current Philippine Scene.* (Philippine studies occasional paper, No. 5.) Honolulu: Center for Asian and Pacific Studies, Philippine Studies Program, University of Hawaii, 1982.

Barton, Roy F. *The Half-way Sun: Life among the Headhunters of the Philippines.* New York: AMS Press, 1978 (reprint.).

Baumgartner, Joseph (ed.). "The Cultural Minorities of the Philippines," *Philippine Quarterly of Culture and Society* [Cebu City], 2, Nos. 1–2, 1974, 1–101.

_____. "Philippine Cultural Minorities II," *Philippine Quarterly of Culture and Society* [Cebu City], 5, Nos. 1–2, 1977, 1–100.

Beltran, H.S., Jr. "Rural Education Revisited," *Diliman Review* [Quezon City], July-August 1982.

Bentley, G. Carter. "The Evolution of Muslim-Christian Relations in the Lanao Region, Philippines," *Dansalan Quarterly* [Marawi, Philippines], 3, No. 4, July 1982.

_____. "Islamic Law in Christian Southeast Asia: The Politics of Establishing Shari-a Courts in the Philippines," *Philippine Studies* [Quezon City], 29, 1981, 45–65.

Bulatao, Jamie. "Hiya," *Philippine Studies* [Quezon City], 12, No. 3, July 1964, 424–38.

Bulatao, Rodolfo A. "Attitudes Toward Divorce in a National Sample Survey," *Philippine Sociological Review* [Manila], 26, Nos. 3–4, July-October 1978, 239–43.

_____. "Ethnic Attitudes in Five Philippine Cities." Pages 196–205 in Mary Racelis Hollnsteiner (ed.), *Society, Culture, and the Filipino*, 2. Quezon City: Institute of Philippine Culture, Ateneo de Manila University Press, 1975.

Canoy, Reuben R. *The Counterfeit Revolution: Martial Law in the Philippines.* Manila: Philippine Editions, 1980.

Carner, George. "Survival, Interdependence, and Competition among the Philippine Rural Poor," *Asian Survey*, 22, No. 4, April 1982, 369–84.

Casal, Gabriel, et al. *The People and Art of the Philippines.* Los Angeles: Museum of Cultural History, University of California, 1981.

Casino, Eric S. *The Philippines: Land and Peoples, A Cultural Geography.* Manila: Grolier International, 1982.

_____. *The Jama Mapun, A Changing Samal Society in the Southern Philippines.* Quezon City: Ateneo de Manila University Press, 1976.

Castillo, Gelia. *Beyond Manila, Philippine Rural Problems in Perspective.* Laguna: University of the Philippines, 1977.

_____. *The Filipino Woman as Manpower: The Image and the Empirical Reality.* Laguna: University of the Philippines Press, 1976.

Cerdena, Criselda. "One-Quarter of Metro Manila's Residents are Squatters," *Philippines Daily Press* [Manila], June 25, 1982, 1, 6.

"Chinese Schools to Admit More Filipinos," *Manila Bulletin Today* [Manila], November 11, 1982, 28.

Concepcion, Mercedes (ed.). *Population of the Philippines.* Quezon City: Population Institute, University of the Philippines, 1977.

Constantino, Renato, *The Philippines: A Past Revisited.* Quezon City: Tala, 1975.

Cordero-Fernando, Gilda (ed.). *Being Filipino.* Quezon City: GCF Books, 1981.

Costa, Horacio de la, and John N. Schumacher. *Church and State: The Philippine Experience.* (Loyola papers, No. 3.) Quezon City: Ateneo de Manila University Press, 1978.

Dalton, Keith. "Health: The Undernourished Philippines," *Far Eastern Economic Review* [Hong Kong], 101, No. 35, September 1, 1978, 35.

Davis, William. *Social Relations in a Philippine Market.* Berkeley and Los Angeles: University of California Press, 1973.

Deats, Richard L. *Nationalism and Christianity in the Philippines.* Dallas: Southern Methodist University Press, 1967.

Demetrio, Francisco. *Christianity in Context.* Quezon City: New Day, 1981.

Development Academy of the Philippines. Task Force on Human Settlements. "Manila and Its Outlying Areas: Emerging Concepts and Issues," *Ekistics* [Athens], 39, No. 233, April 1975, 255–57.

Doeppers, Daniel F. "Changing Patterns of Aglipayan Adherence in the Philippines, 1918–1970," *Philippine Studies*, 25, 3d Quarter, 1977, 265–77.

_____. " 'Ethnic Urbanism' in Philippine Cities," *Annals of the Association of American Geographers*, 64, No. 4, December 1974, 549–59.

Doherty, John F. "Who Controls the Philippine Economy: Some Need Not Try as Hard as Others." Pages 7–35 in Belinda A. Aquino (ed.), *Cronies and Enemies: The Current Philippine Scene.* (Philippine studies occasional paper, No. 5.) Honolulu: Center for Asian and Pacific Studies, Philippine Studies Program, University of Hawaii, 1982.

Eder, James F. *Who Shall Succeed? Agricultural Development and Social Inequality on a Philippine Frontier.* Cambridge: Cambridge University Press, 1982.

Elwood, Douglas J., and Patricia L. Magdamo. *Christ in the Philippine Context.* Quezon City: New Day, 1971.

Encarnacion, Jose, Jr. *Income Distribution in Manila, Luzon, the Visayas, and Mindanao.* Quezon City: School of Economics, University of the Philippines, 1977.

Fabular, Leo D. "Chinese Community Rejects Charges," *Visayan Herald* [Cebu City], August 26, 1982, 1, 2.

Fauriol, Georges A. (ed.). *Population and Politics in the Philippines.* Washington: Center for Strategic and International Studies, Georgetown University, 1979.

Feria, Dolores. "A Look at the Educational GNP: Classified Brains for Hire," *Diliman Review* [Quezon City], May-June 1982.

Fernandez, Doreen G. *The Iloilo Zarzuela, 1903–1930.* Quezon City: Ateneo de Manila University Press, 1978.

Flavier, Juan M. *Back to the Barrios.* Quezon City: New Day, 1978.

Foronda, Marcelino A., Jr. *Kailukuan: Historical and Bibliographical Studies.* Manila: Philippine National Historical Society, 1976.

Frake, Charles O. *Language and Cultural Description: Essays.* Stanford: Stanford University Press, 1980.

George, Thayil Jacob Sony. *Revolt in Mindanao: The Rise of Islam in Philippine Politics.* Kuala Lumpur: Oxford University Press, 1980.

Gonzalez, Andrew B. *Language and Nationalism: The Philippine Experience Thus Far.* Quezon City: Ateneo de Manila University Press, 1980.

_____. "Language and Social Development in the Pacific Area," *Philippine Journal of Linguistics* [Manila], 10, June-December 1979.

Gowing, Peter G. "Christian-Muslim Dialogue in the Philippines, 1976–1981," *Islamocristiana* [Rome], 7, 1981, 211–25.

_____. *Muslim Filipinos: Heritage and Horizon.* Quezon City: New Day, 1979.

_____. "Towards Christian-Muslim Understanding in the Philippines," *Silliman Journal* [Dumaguete, Philippines], 25, No. 4, 1978, 339–58.

Gowing, Peter G., and Robert D. McAmis (eds.). *The Muslim Filipinos.* Manila: Solidaridad, 1974.

Green, Justin J. "Political Regime and Public Policy in the Philippines: Comparison of Bacolod and Iloilo Cities," *Journal of Asian Studies*, 36, No. 2, February 1977, 388–90.

Guthrie, George M. "A Social-Psychological Analysis of Modernization in the Philippines," *Journal of Cross-Cultural Psychology*, 8, No. 2, 1977, 177–206.

Guthrie, George M. (ed.). *Six Perspectives on the Philippines.* Manila: Bookmark, 1968. Hart, Donn V. *Compadrinazgo: Ritual Kinship in the Philippines.* DeKalb: Northern Illinois University Press, 1977.

_____. "Return to Caticugan, 1950–1979," *Philippine Studies Newsletter*, 7, No. 3, June 1979, 7–9.

Hart, Donn V. (ed.). *Philippine Studies: History, Sociology, Mass Media, and Bibliography.* (Occasional paper, No. 6) DeKalb: Center for Southeast Asian Studies, Northern Illinois University Press, 1978.

Hendershot, Gerry E. "The Plaza Complex and the Diffusion of Family Planning." Pages 27–38 in Mario D. Zamora, Donald J. Baxter, and Robert Lawless (eds.), *Social Change in Modern Philippines*, 19. Norman: Department of Anthropology, University of Oklahoma, 1978.

Herrin, Alejandro. *Population and Development Research in the Philippines: A Survey.* Quezon City: Philippine Institute for Development Studies, 1980.

Hiday, Virginia A. "Migration, Urbanization, and Fertility in the Philippines," *International Migration Review*, 12, No. 3, Fall 1978, 370–85.

Hoefer, Hans Johannes, et al. *Philippines.* Hong Kong: Apa, 1980.

Hollnsteiner, Mary Racelis. *The Dynamics of Power in a Philippine Municipality.* Quezon City: Community Development Research Council, University of the Philippines, 1963.

———. *The Filipino Woman: Her Role and Status in Philippine Society.* Quezon City: Institute of Philippine Culture, 1976.

Hollnsteiner, Mary Racelis (ed.). *Society, Culture, and the Filipino.* 3 vols. Quezon City: Institute of Philippine Culture, Ateneo de Manila University Press, 1975.

Ileto, Reynaldo C. *Pasyon and Revolution: Popular Movements in the Philippines, 1840–1910.* Quezon City: Ateneo de Manila University Press, 1979.

Ira, Luning B., and Isagani R. Medina. *Streets of Manila.* Manila: GCF Books, 1977.

Jacobson, Helga E. "Rural Traditions in an Urban Area: The Background to Change." Pages 99–110 in Mario D. Zamora, Donald J. Baxter, and Robert Lawless (eds.), *Social Change in Modern Philippines,* 19. Norman: Department of Anthropology, University of Oklahoma, 1978.

Jesena, Arsenio C. "The Sacadas of Sugarland." Pages 266–79 in Cynthia Nograles Lumbera and Teresita Gimenez-Maceda (eds.), *Rediscovery: Essays in Philippine Life and Culture.* Manila: National Bookstore, 1977.

Jocano, F. Landa. *Turburan: A Case Study of Adaptation and Peasant Life in a Visayan Barrio.* Quezon City: University of the Philippines, 1976.

Kaut, Charles. "Utang Na Loob: A System of Contractual Obligations among Tagalogs," *Southwestern Journal of Anthropology,* 17, No. 3, Autumn 1961, 256–72.

Keesing, Felix M. *The Ethnohistory of Northern Luzon.* Stanford: Stanford University Press, 1962.

Keyes, William J., and Clara Roldan Burcroff. *Housing the Urban Poor.* Quezon City: Institute of Philippine Culture, Ateneo de Manila University Press, 1976.

Lawless, Robert. "Population Growth in the Philippines." Pages 125–30 in Mario D. Zamora, Donald J. Baxter, and Robert Lawless (eds.), *Social Change in Modern Philippines,* 19. Norman: Department of Anthropology, University of Oklahoma, 1978.

LeBar, Frank N. *Ethnic Groups of Insular Southeast Asia, II: Philippines and Formosa.* New Haven: Human Relations Area Files Press, 1975.

Licuanan, Patricia B. "Beyond the Economics of Overseas Employment: The Human Costs," *Philippine Studies* [Quezon City], 30, No. 2, 1982, 262–71.

Lieban, Richard W. "Migration and Medicine: Population Movement and the Utilization of Urban Healers," *Philippine Quarterly of Culture and Society* [Cebu City], 4, December 1978, 228–38.

Llamzon, Teodoro A. *Handbook of Philippine Language Groups.* Quezon City: Ateneo de Manila University Press, 1978.

Lorenzo, Conrado Li, Jr. "The Population Program: Focus on Outreach." Pages 250–53 in Betty Go-Belmonte (ed.), *Fookien Times Philippines Yearbook, 1981–82.* Manila: 1982.

Lumbera, Cynthia Nograles, and Teresita Gimenez-Maceda (eds.), *Rediscovery: Essays in Philippine Life and Culture*. Manila: National Bookstore, 1977.

Lynch, Frank. "Big and Little People: Social Class in the Rural Philippines." Pages 181–89 in Mary Racelis Hollnsteiner (ed.), *Society, Culture, and the Filipino*, 2. Quezon City: Institute of Philippine Culture, Ateneo de Manila University Press, 1975.

————. "Folk Catholicism in the Philippines." Pages 227–38 in Mary Racelis Hollnsteiner (ed.), *Society, Culture, and the Filipino*, 2. Quezon City: Institute of Philippine Culture, Ateneo de Manila University Press, 1975.

————. "Social Acceptance Reconsidered." Pages 1–68 in Frank Lynch and Alfonso de Guzman II (eds.), *Four Readings on Philippine Values*. Quezon City: Institute of Philippine Culture, Ateneo de Manila University Press, 1974.

Lynch, Frank, and Alfonso de Guzman II (eds.). *Four Readings on Philippine Values*. Quezon City: Institute of Philippine Culture, Ateneo de Manila University Press, 1974.

McBeath, Gerald A. *Political Integration of the Philippine Chinese*. (Monograph, No. 8.) Berkeley: Center for South and Southeast Asia Studies, University of California, 1973.

McDonald, Crispina S. "Educational Change in Barrio San Julian, Pangasinan." Pages 55–65 in Mario D. Zamora, Donald J. Baxter, and Robert Lawless (eds.), *Social Change in Modern Philippines*, 19. Norman: Department of Anthropology, University of Oklahoma, 1978.

Maceda, Marcelino N. "Prospects for Development of the Non-Muslim Cultural Communities," *Silliman Journal* [Dumaguete, Philippines], 25, No. 4, 1978, 365–77.

Machado, Kit G., Richard Hooley, and Lawrence Reid. *Philippine Studies: Political Science, Economics, and Linguistics*. (Occasional paper, No. 8.) DeKalb: Center for Southeast Asian Studies, Northern Illinois University, 1981.

Madale, Nagasure T. (ed.). *The Muslim Filipinos: A Book of Readings*. Quezon City: Alemar-Phoenix, 1981.

Majul, Cesar Adib. *Muslims in the Philippines*. Quezon City: University of the Philippines Press, 1973.

Manalang, Priscilla. "Education and Poverty," *Diliman Review* [Quezon City], May-June 1982.

————. *A Philippine Rural School: Its Cultural Dimension*. Quezon City: University of the Philippines Press, 1977.

Maynard, Harold W. "Views of the Indonesian and Philippine Military Elites." Pages 123–53 in Sheldon W. Simon (ed.), *The Military and Security in the Third World: Domestic and International Impacts*. Boulder: Westview Press, 1978.

Mesa, José M. de. *And God Said, "Bahala Na!" The Theme of Providence in the Lowland Filipino Context*. Quezon City: Publishers Printing Press, 1979.

Miralao, Virginia. *Women and Men in Development: Findings from a Pilot Study.* Quezon City: Institute of Philippine Culture, Ateneo de Manila University Press, 1980.

Monteil, Cristina. *Rural Organizations and Rural Development in the Philippines.* Quezon City: Institute of Philippine Culture, Ateneo de Manila University Press, 1977.

Morais, Robert J. *Social Relations in a Philippine Town.* (Special report, No. 19.) DeKalb: Center for Southeast Asian Studies, Northern Illinois University, 1981.

Nance, John. *The Gentle Tasaday, A Stone Age People in the Philippine Rain Forest.* New York: Harcourt Brace Jovanovich, 1975.

Neher, Clark D. "The Role of Women in the Philippines," *Philippine Studies Newsletter*, 8, No. 1, March 1980, 5–7.

Ness, Gayl D. "Philippine Political Dynamics and Population Policy: Some Provocative Observations." Pages 28–53 in Georges A. Fauriol (ed.), *Population and Politics in the Philippines.* Washington: Center for Strategic and International Studies, Georgetown University, 1979.

Niksch, Larry A., and Marjorie Niehaus. *The Internal Situation in the Philippines: Current Trends and Future Prospects.* (Report No. 81-21F.) Washington: Congressional Research Service, Library of Congress, 1981.

Noble, Lela Garner. "The Moro National Liberation Front in the Philippines," *Pacific Affairs* [Vancouver], 49, No. 3, 1976, 405–24.

_____. "Muslim Separatism in the Philippines, 1972–1981: The Making of a Stalemate," *Asian Survey*, 21, No. 11, November 1981, 1097–1114.

Ocampo, Sheilah. "Guerrillas Gain in Paradise Lost," *Far Eastern Economic Review* [Hong Kong], 108, April 11, 1980, 19–21.

Omohundro, John T. *Chinese Merchant Families in Iloilo: Commerce and Kin in a Central Philippine City.* Quezon City: Ateneo de Manila University Press, 1981.

Ortigas, Irene, and Felix Regalado. *Society and Culture in the Rural Philippines.* Quezon City: Alemar-Phoenix, 1978.

Palanca, Ellen H. "The Economic Position of the Chinese in the Philippines," *Philippine Studies* [Quezon City], 25, 1st Quarter, 1977, 80–94.

Pernia, Ernesto M. "The Impact of Migration on Rural Areas in the Philippines," *Philippine Economic Journal* [Manila], 16, Nos. 1–2, 1977, 160–70.

_____. *Urbanization and Economic Development in the Philippines.* Quezon City: School of Economics, University of the Philippines, 1977.

_____. *Urbanization and Spatial Development in the Philippines: A Survey.* Quezon City: School of Economics, University of the Philippines, 1980.

_____. *Urbanization in the Philippines: Historical and Comparative Perspectives.* Honolulu: East-West Center, 1976.

_____. *Urbanization, Population Growth, and Economic Development in the Philippines*. Westport, Connecticut: Greenwood Press, 1977.

Philippines. Development Academy of the Philippines. *Measuring the Quality of Life: Philippine Social Indicators*. Manila: 1975.

Philippines. National Economic and Development Authority. National Census and Statistics Office. *1980 Census of Population, Preliminary Report*. Manila: 1980.

Porio, Emma, Mary Racelis Hollnsteiner, and Frank Lynch. *The Filipino Family, Community, and Nation: The Same Yesterday, Today, and Tomorrow?* Quezon City: Institute of Philippine Culture, Ateneo de Manila University Press, 1978.

Potter, David. "Participation as a Measure of Change: Urban *Compadrazgo*." Pages 111–31 in Mario D. Zamora, Donald J. Baxter, and Robert Lawless (eds.), *Social Change in Modern Philippines*, 19. Norman: Department of Anthropology, University of Oklahoma, 1978.

Pryor, R.J. *Migration and Development in South-East Asia*. Oxford: Oxford University Press, 1979.

Quisumbing, Lourdes R. "The Filipino Family and Philippine Society in the 1980s," *Asian Thought and Society: An International Review*, 7, March 1982, 32–39.

Recio, Dolores, et al. *The Social and Ethical Environment of Sterilization in the Philippines*. Quezon City: Institute of Philippine Culture, Ateneo de Manila University Press, 1978.

Romualdez, Philip. *The Mangyans of Mindoro*. Englewood Cliffs: Prentice-Hall International, 1978.

Rosaldo, Michelle Z. *Knowledge and Passion: Ilongot Notions of Self and Social Life*. (Cambridge Studies in Cultural System series, No. 4.) Cambridge: Cambridge University Press, 1980.

Rosaldo, Renato. *Ilongot Headhunting: A Study in Society and History*. Stanford: Stanford University Press, 1980.

Schlegel, Stuart A. "Muslim-Christian Conflict in the Philippine South." Pages 39–52 in Mario D. Zamora, Donald J. Baxter, and Robert Lawless (eds.), *Social Change in Modern Philippines*, 19. Norman: Department of Anthropology, University of Oklahoma, 1978.

_____. *Tiruray Justice: Traditional Tiruray Law and Morality*. Berkeley and Los Angeles: University of California Press, 1970.

Schumacher, John N. (ed.). *Readings in Philippine Church History*. Quezon City: Ateneo de Manila University Press, 1979.

Scott, James C. "Patron-Client Politics and Political Change in Southeast Asia." Pages 123–46 in Steffen W. Schmidt et al. (eds.), *Friends, Followers, and Factions: A Reader in Political Clientelism*. Berkeley and Los Angeles: University of California Press, 1977.

Scott, James C., and Benedict J. Kerkvliet. "How Traditional Rural Patrons Lose Legitimacy: A Theory with Special Relevance to Southeast Asia." Pages 439–58 in Steffen W. Schmidt et al. (eds.), *Friends,*

Followers, and Factions: A Reader in Political Clientelism. Berkeley and Los Angeles: University of California Press, 1977.

Scott, William Henry. *Cracks in the Parchment Curtain and Other Essays in Philippine History.* Quezon City: New Day, 1982.

_____. *On the Cordillera: A Look at the Peoples and Cultures of the Mountain Province.* Manila: MCS, 1969.

Shoesmith, Dennis. "The Glorious Religion of José Rizal: Radical Consciousness in a Contemporary Folk Religious Movement in the Philippines." Pages 149–79 in D.B. Miller (ed.), *Peasants and Politics: Grass Roots Reaction to Change in Asia.* New York: St. Martin's Press, 1978.

Smith, Peter C. "The Social Demography of Filipino Migrations Abroad," *International Migration Review,* 10, No. 3, Fall 1976, 307–53.

Statistical Yearbook, 1982. New York: United Nations Educational, Scientific, and Cultural Organization, 1982.

Steinberg, David Joel. *The Philippines: A Singular and a Plural Place.* Boulder: Westview Press, 1982.

Stinner, William F. "Modernization and Family Extension in the Philippines: A Social Demographic Analysis," *Journal of Marriage and the Family,* 41, No. 1, February 1979, 161–68.

_____. "Modernization and Household Size and Structure in the Urban and Rural Philippines," *Journal of Southeast Asian Studies* [Singapore], 13, No. 1, March 1982, 120–32.

_____. "Urbanization and Household Structure in the Philippines," *Journal of Marriage and the Family,* 39, No. 2, May 1977, 377–85.

Stone, Richard L. *Philippine Urbanization: The Politics of Public and Private Property in Greater Manila.* (Special report, No. 6.) DeKalb: Center for Southeast Asian Studies, Northern Illinois University, 1973.

Sturtevant, David R. *Popular Uprisings in the Philippines, 1840–1940.* Ithaca: Cornell University Press, 1976.

Sutlive, Vinson H., Jr. "A Comparison of Urban Migration in Sarawak and the Philippines," *Urban Anthropology,* 6, No. 4, Winter 1977, 355–69.

Szanton, Maria Christina Blanc. *A Right to Survive: Subsistence Marketing in a Lowland Philippine Town.* University Park: Pennsylvania State University Press, 1972.

Torres, Emmanuel. *Jeepney.* Quezon City: GCF Books, 1979.

Tubangui, Helen R., et al. *The Filipino Nation: A Concise History of the Philippines.* Manila: Grolier International, 1982.

Turner, Mark M. "Interpretations of Class and Status in the Philippines: A Critical Evaluation," *Cultures et développement* [Louvain], 10, No. 2, 1978, 265–96.

_____. "Urbanization and Class in the Ilocos Region," *Philippine Studies* [Quezon City], 30, No. 2, 1982, 204–30.

United Nations. Economic and Social Commission for Asia and the Pacific. Population and Social Affairs Division. *Population of the*

Philippines. (Country Monograph series, No. 5.) Bangkok: ESCAP, 1978.

Velez, Maria C. (ed.). *Images of the Filipina: A Bibliography.* Manila: Ala-Ala Foundation, 1975.

Vokey, Richard. "Criminals' New Society," *Far Eastern Economic Review* [Hong Kong], No. 105, September 21, 1979, 35–36.

Warren, James F. *The Sulu Zone, 1768–1898.* Singapore: Singapore University Press, 1981.

Watkins, D., and E. Astilla. "Self-Esteem and Social Class in the Philippines," *Journal of Psychology,* 102, July 1979, 211–14.

Wernstedt, Frederick L., and Paul D. Simkins. *Philippine Migration: The Settlement of the Digos-Padah Valley, Davao Province.* (Monograph series, No. 16.) New Haven: Southeast Asian Studies Program, Yale University Press, 1971.

Wernstedt, Frederick L., and J.E. Spencer. *The Philippine Island World: A Physical, Cultural, and Regional Geography.* Berkeley and Los Angeles: University of California Press, 1978 (reprint.).

Wernstedt, Frederick L., et al. *Philippine Studies: Geography, Archaeology, Psychology, and Literature: Present Knowledge and Research Trends.* DeKalb: Center for Southeast Asian Studies, Northern Illinois University, 1974.

Wery, Rene. *The Demand for Education in the Philippines.* Geneva: International Labour Office, 1977.

Wery, Rene, et al. *Population, Employment, and Poverty in the Philippines.* Geneva: International Labour Office, 1977.

Wickberg, Edgar. *The Chinese in Philippine Life, 1850–1898.* (Southeast Asia Studies, No. 1.) New Haven: Yale University Press, 1965.

Wurfel, David. "The Political Consequences of Population Growth in the Philippines." Pages 54–67 in Georges A. Fauriol (ed.), *Population and Politics in the Philippines.* Washington: Center for Strategic and International Studies, Georgetown University, 1979.

Yabes, Leopoldo Y. "The Language Policy Reconsidered." Pages 236–38 in Betty Go-Belmonte (ed.), *Fookien Times Philippines Yearbook, 1981–82.* Manila: Fookien Times, 1982.

Youngblood, Robert L. "Church Opposition to Martial Law in the Philippines," *Asian Survey,* 18, No. 5, May 1978, 505–20.

———. "Ideology and Christian Liberation in the New Society." (Paper prepared for the 2d International Philippine Studies Conference, Honolulu, June 1981.) Honolulu: 1981.

Zapanta-Manlapaz, Edna. *Kapampangan Literature: A Historical Survey and Anthology.* Quezon City: Ateneo de Manila University Press, 1981.

Chapter 3

Adkins, John H. "Philippines 1972: We'll Wait and See," *Asian Survey,* 13, No. 2, February 1973, 140–50.

Aprieto, Virginia L. *Fishery Management and Extended Maritime Jurisdiction: The Philippine Tuna Fishery Situation.* (Research paper, No. 4.) Honolulu: East-West Environment and Policy Institute, 1981.

Asia Pacific Centre. *Marketing Trends in the Asia Pacific Region: Economic Forecasts and Consumer Developments.* Aldershot, Hants, England: Gower, 1982.

Asia Yearbook, 1978. (Ed., Donald Wise.) Hong Kong: Far Eastern Economic Review, 1978.

Asia Yearbook, 1979. (Ed., Donald Wise.) Hong Kong: Far Eastern Economic Review, 1979.

Asia Yearbook, 1980. (Ed., Donald Wise.) Hong Kong: Far Eastern Economic Review, 1980.

Asia Yearbook, 1981. (Ed., Donald Wise.) Hong Kong: Far Eastern Economic Review, 1981.

Asia Yearbook, 1982. (Ed., Donald Wise.) Hong Kong: Far Eastern Economic Review, 1982.

Balance of Payments Statistics Yearbook, 1982. (Part 1.) Washington: International Monetary Fund, 1982.

Ballance, R.C. "The Philippines Barangay Water Program," *Ekistics* [Athens], 49, No. 296, September-October 1982, 407–09.

Baum, Dan. "Philippine Crops Withering in Worst Drought since '72," *Asian Wall Street Journal* [Hong Kong], April 14, 1983, 1.

Bautista, Romeo M., et al. *Industrial Promotion Policies in the Philippines.* Manila: Philippine Institute for Development Studies, 1979.

Bello, Walden, David Kinley, and Elaine Elinson. *Development Debacle: The World Bank in the Philippines.* San Francisco: Institute for Food and Development Policy, 1982.

Bowring, Philip. "The Poverty Puzzle," *Far Eastern Economic Review* [Hong Kong], March 27, 1981, 125–31.

Bowring, Philip, and Guy Sacerdoti. "Time for a Real Debate," *Far Eastern Economic Review* [Hong Kong], June 9, 1983, 54–66.

Browning, E.S. "Communist NPA Slowly Gains Influence in Philippines," *Asian Wall Street Journal* [Hong Kong], July 4, 1983, 1.

————. "Economic Woes: Military Abuses Fuel Support for NPA," *Asian Wall Street Journal* [Hong Kong], July 5, 1983, 1.

————. "Major Firms in Philippines Hit by Losses," *Asian Wall Street Journal* [Hong Kong], September 14, 1982, 1.

————. "Philippine Groups Attack IMF, World Bank," *Asian Wall Street Journal* [Hong Kong], April 23, 1983, 10.

————. "Philippines Seen Limping Behind World Recovery in '83," *Asian Wall Street Journal* [Hong Kong], May 12, 1983, 1.

"Business Lists Problems of National Development," Foreign Broadcast Information Service, *Daily Report: Asia and Pacific,* 4, No. 171 (FBIS-APA-82-171), September 2, 1982, P1-P6.

Carner, George. "Survival, Interdependence, and Competition among the Philippine Rural Poor," *Asian Survey*, 22, No. 4, April 1982, 369–84.

"Central Bank Criticizes IMF Lending Conditions," Foreign Broadcast Information Service, *Daily Report: Asia and Pacific*, 4, No. 189 (FBIS-APA-82), September 29, 1982, P3.

"Changing Attitudes to Housing Provision: BLISS in the Philippines?" (Part 1.) *Geography*, 68, No. 298, January 1983, 37–40.

Cheetham, Russell J., et al. *The Philippines: Priorities and Prospects for Development*. Baltimore: Johns Hopkins University Press, 1976.

Critchfield, Richard. *The Changing Peasant, Part VI: The Tenant*. (American Universities Field Staff. Fieldstaff Reports. Asia, No. 19.) Hanover, New Hampshire: AUFS, 1981.

Crone, Donald. "Emerging Trends in the Control of Foreign Investments in ASEAN," *Asian Survey*, 21, April 1981, 417–36.

Cueno, Armirda, et al. "Marketing System for Fruits in the Philippines: Some Practices and Problems," *Journal of Agricultural Economics and Development* [Laguna, Philippines], 11, No. 2, July 1981, 164–99.

Dagaas, Clarita T., and Edgardo M. Garcia. "Marketing System of Livestock, Poultry, and Eggs in the Philippines: Some Highlights on Practices and Problems," *Journal of Agricultural Economics and Development* [Laguna, Philippines], 11, No. 2, July 1981, 200–34.

Dumagat, F. L. "Some Reflections on the Factors of Effectiveness and Viability of Rural Organizations," *Journal of Agricultural Economics and Development* [Laguna, Philippines], 11, No. 1, January 1981, 23–45.

Eder, James F. *Who Shall Succeed? Agricultural Development and Social Inequality on a Philippine Frontier*. Cambridge: Cambridge University Press, 1982.

Erbe, Rainer. "Foreign Indebtedness and Economic Growth: The Philippines," *Intereconomics* [Hamburg], No. 3, May-June 1982, 125–32.

Faylon, L.P., et al. "Marketing System for Vegetables in the Philippines: Some Practices and Problems," *Journal of Agricultural Economics and Development* [Laguna, Philippines], 11, No. 2, July 1981, 129–43.

Federal Republic of Germany. Statistisches Bundesamt Wiesbaden. *Länderkurzbericht: Philippinen, 1982*. Stuttgart: Kohlhammer, 1982.

Food and Agriculture Organization. *Forest Resources of Tropical Asia*. (Tropical Forest Resources Assessment Project.) Rome: 1981.

Fookien Times Philippines Yearbook, 1981–82. (Ed., Betty Go-Belmonte.) Manila: Fookien Times, 1982.

Fookien Times Philippines Yearbook, 1982–83. (Ed., Betty Go-Belmonte.) Manila: Fookien Times, 1983.

Fredericks, L.J., and R.J.G. Wells. "Some Aspects of Tenancy Reform Measures in Southeast Asia," *Asian Survey*, 28, No. 6, June 1978, 644–58.

Gonzaga, Leo. "The Case for Inequality," *Far Eastern Economic Review* [Hong Kong], August 27, 1982, 44–45.

———. "The Dee Caper and Other Bouts of Stormy Weather," *Far Eastern Economic Review* [Hong Kong], March 27, 1981, 86–89.

———. "Fine Tuning for a Better Credit Picture," *Far Eastern Economic Review* [Hong Kong], March 26, 1982, 88–89.

———. "The Hesitation Waltz," *Far Eastern Economic Review* [Hong Kong], January 29, 1982, 50–51.

———. "Now the Rescuers Need Rescuing," *Far Eastern Economic Review* [Hong Kong], March 5, 1983, 96–97.

Gonzaga, Leo, and Guy Sacerdoti. "Operation Cold Comfort," *Far Eastern Economic Review* [Hong Kong], May 14, 1982, 86–88.

Government Finance Statistics Yearbook, 1982, 6. Washington: International Monetary Fund, 1982.

Grossholtz, Jean. "The Philippines: Midterm Doldrums for Marcos," *Asian Survey,* 8, No. 1, January 1968, 52–57.

———. "The Philippines: New Adventures with Old Problems," *Asian Survey,* 9, No. 1, January 1969, 50–57.

Hawkins, Edward K., et al. *The Philippines: Aspects of the Financial Sector.* Washington: World Bank, 1980.

International Financial Statistics Yearbook, 1982. Washington: International Monetary Fund, 1982.

International Labour Office. *Sharing in Development: A Programme of Employment, Equity, and Growth for the Philippines.* Geneva: 1974.

International Petroleum Encyclopedia, 1982. Tulsa: Pennwell, 1982.

Jayme, Vincente B. "Credit Management in Times of Uncertainty," *Philippine Business Review* [Manila], 15, No. 3, 3d Quarter 1982, 3–8.

Joint Publications Research Service—JPRS (Washington). The following items are from the JPRS series:

South and East Asia Report.

"Agricultural Production Down," *Philippines Daily Express,* Manila, June 27, 1982. (JPRS 81311, No. 1168, July 19, 1982,102–103.)

Banal, Conrado R., III. "World Bank on RP Development Plan," *Business Day,* Manila, August 23, 1982. (JPRS 81875, No. 1192, September 16, 1982, 76–85.)

"The Budget for 1982," *Business Day,* Manila, August 30, 1982. (JPRS 81785, No. 1192, September 16, 1982, 86–90.)

Dipasupil, Sonia G. "New Labor Law Anti-Labor Features Examined," *Philippine Collegian,* Manila, July 1, 1982. (JPRS 81503, No. 1177, August 10, 1982, 221–24.)

"Outlook for Employment Bleak," *Business Day,* Manila, August 31, 1982. (JPRS 81785, No. 1192, September 16, 1982, 91–95.)

"Philippines Plans 'Drastic Cut' in Expenditures," *Business Day,* Manila, November 8, 1982. (JPRS 82337, No. 1219, November 29, 1982, 73–75.)

Southeast Asia Report.

Aydinan, Abrino. "'82 GNP Growth: Below Expectations," *Business Day*, Manila, January 3, 1983. (JPRS 82681, No. 1241, January 19, 1983, 68–72.)

Genovea, Miguel. "Business Assured of Government Aid," *Business Day*, Manila, November 6, 1982. (JPRS 82371, No. 1222, December 2, 1982, 109–110.)

"Japanese Assisted Highway Project," *Philippines Daily Express*, Manila, May 7, 1983. (JPRS 83600, No. 1295, June 2, 1983, 27–31.)

Lacsamana, Joel D. "National Livelihood Program (KKK): Is It Really Working?" *Business Day*, Manila, December 29, 1982. (JPRS 82621, No. 1237, January 12, 1983, 55–59.)

Manlangit, Ros. "Farm Goods Trading to be Centralized," *Philippines Daily Express*, Manila, March 22, 1983. (JPRS 83348, No. 1280, April 27, 1983, 169–70.)

"New Law to Boost Exports," *Philippines Daily Express*, Manila, April 29, 1983. (JPRS 83587, No. 1294, June 1, 1983, 61.)

Pascual, Ruben J. "Review and Preview: Agriculture '82: A Bumper Crop of Problems," *Business Day*, Manila, January 14, 1983. (JPRS 82790, No. 1248, February 2, 1983, 11–15.)

Lachica, Eduardo. "Strict Loans Help Manila Avoid Default," *Asian Wall Street Journal* [Hong Kong], May 12, 1983, 1.

Lehner, Urban C. "Oil Glut Has Little Impact on Filipinos," *Asian Wall Street Journal* [Hong Kong], April 7, 1982, 1.

Lopez, Antonio. "Marcos' Land Reform: A Martial Law Bonus," *Asiaweek* [Hong Kong], January 9, 1981, 32–33.

McCue, Andy. "Labor Tensions Are Increasing in the Philippines," *Asian Wall Street Journal* [Hong Kong], June 9, 1982, 1.

———. "Marcos Again Ends Coconut Levy; Critics Hope Farmers Will Benefit," *Asian Wall Street Journal* [Hong Kong], August 30, 1982, 1.

———. "Philippine Assembly Passes a Bill Aimed at Preventing Violence Caused by Strikes," *Asian Wall Street Journal* [Hong Kong], June 2, 1982, 3.

———. "Philippine Government Devalues Peso by 7.3%" *Asian Wall Street Journal* [Hong Kong], June 24–25, 1983, 1.

———. "Philippines Cuts Back on 5 Major Projects," *Asian Wall Street Journal* [Hong Kong], June 22, 1983, 1.

———. "Silvero Falls on Hard Times in Philippines," *Asian Wall Street Journal* [Hong Kong], July 6, 1982, 1.

———. "Technocrats and Cronies Vie for Marcos's Favors," *Asian Wall Street Journal* [Hong Kong], August 27, 1982, 4.

———. "Turmoil over Dee Is Expected to Aid Philippines' Plan for Textile Firms," *Asian Wall Street Journal* [Hong Kong], February 3, 1981, 1.

Machado, Kit G. "The Philippines in 1977: Beginning a 'Return to Normalcy'?" *Asian Survey*, 18, No. 2, February 1978, 202–11.

_____. "The Philippines 1978: Authoritarian Consolidation Continues," *Asian Survey*, 19, No. 2, February 1979, 131–40.

"Marcos Is Short of Cash to Bail Out His Chums," *Economist* [London], April 23, 1983, 71–72.

"Marcos Speaks at Opening of National Assembly," Foreign Broadcast Information Service, *Daily Report: Asia and Pacific*, 4, No. 020 (FBIS-APA-83-020), January 28, 1983, P1-P9.

Nations, Richard. "A Chiller for Manila," *Far Eastern Economic Review* [Hong Kong], April 30, 1982, 40–41.

Neher, Clark D. "The Philippines in 1980: The Gathering Storm," *Asian Survey*, 21, No. 2, February 1981, 261–73.

_____. "The Philippines in 1979: Cracks in the Fortress," *Asian Survey*, 20, No. 2, February 1980, 155–67.

Niksch, Larry A., and Marjorie Niehaus. *The Internal Situation in the Philippines: Current Trends and Future Prospects*. (Report No. 81–21F.) Washington: Congressional Research Service, Library of Congress, 1981.

Noble, Lela Garner. "Philippines 1976: The Contrast Between Shrine and Shanty," *Asian Survey*, 17, No. 2, February 1977, 133–42.

Ocampo, Sheilah. "The Desperate Equation," *Far Eastern Economic Review* [Hong Kong], October 2, 1981, 32–35.

"Officials Denounce World Bank Agricultural Report," Foreign Broadcast Information Service, *Daily Report: Asia and Pacific*, 4, No. 241, (FBIS-APA-82-241), December 15, 1982, P2-P2.

Ofreneo, Rene E. *Capitalism in Philippine Agriculture*. Quezon City: Foundation for Nationalist Studies, 1980.

Ongpin, Jaime V. "The Future of the Philippine Mining Industry," *Asian Wall Street Journal* [Hong Kong], November 9, 1982, 8.

_____. "Letter to the Editor," *Asian Wall Street Journal* [Hong Kong], March 4-5, 1983, 4.

Organisation for Economic Co-operation and Development. *Geographical Distribution of Financial Flows to Developing Countries: 1978–1981*. Paris: 1982.

"Out of the Muddle, A Promise of BLISS," *Far Eastern Economic Review* [Hong Kong], February 16, 1979, 44–51.

Philippines. Central Bank of the Philippines. *Philippine Financial Statistics* [Manila], 12, No. 4, December 1981 (entire issue.).

Philippines. Ministry of Natural Resources. "Performance Report of the Ministry of Natural Resources on Its 7th Anniversary." (Report for the President, May 17, 1981.) Manila: 1981.

Philippines. Ministry of Natural Resources. Natural Resources Management Center. *Philippine Nature Resources Profile and Statistics*, 1. Manila: 1979.

Philippines. National Economic and Development Authority. *Philippine Development Report, 1980*. Manila: 1981.

_____. *Pocketbook of Philippine Statistics, 1981*. Manila: 1981.

Philippines. National Economic and Development Authority. National Census and Statistics Office. *NCSO Monthly Bulletin of Statistics* [Manila], March 1982 (entire issue.).

——. *Philippine Statistical Yearbook, 1981.* Manila: 1981.

——. *Philippine Yearbook, 1978.* Manila: 1979.

——. *Philippine Yearbook, 1981.* Manila: 1982.

Philippines. National Media Production Center. *Economic and Social Indicators: Philippine Profile, 1982.* Manila: 1982.

——. *The Philippines: Social Development, 1973–82.* Manila: 1982.

Philippines. Securities and Exchange Commission. *Business Day's 1,000 Top Corporations in the Philippines, 1981,* 13. Manila: Business Day, 1981.

"Philippines," *International Financial Statistics,* 36, No. 3, August 1983, 346–49.

"Philippines: Stand-By Arrangement and Compensatory Financing Facility, *IMF Survey,* 12, No. 5, March 7, 1983, 72.

Ravenholt, Albert. *Malnutrition in the Philippines.* (American Universities Field Staff. Fieldstaff Reports. Asia, No. 20.) Hanover, New Hampshire: AUFS, 1982.

"Realism Replaces Ambition," *Far Eastern Economic Review* [Hong Kong], November 20, 1981, 54–55.

Sacerdoti, Guy. "A Bailed-out Case," *Far Eastern Economic Review* [Hong Kong], March 24, 1983, 78–80.

——. "Beyond the Dotted Line," *Far Eastern Economic Review* [Hong Kong], March 24, 1983, 88–89.

——. "Cracks in the Coconut Shell," *Far Eastern Economic Review* [Hong Kong], January 8, 1982, 42–48.

——. "Deeper into Deficit," *Far Eastern Economic Review* [Hong Kong], December 17, 1982, 45–46.

——. "A Gulf Well Runs Dry," *Far Eastern Economic Review* [Hong Kong], March 3, 1983, 66–67.

——. "Manila Bails Itself Out," *Far Eastern Economic Review* [Hong Kong], April 21, 1983, 74–75.

——. "Manila Put on Standby," *Far Eastern Economic Review* [Hong Kong], April 7, 1983, 40–43.

——. "The No-Credit Risk," *Far Eastern Economic Review* [Hong Kong], July 16, 1982, 40–42.

——. "A Political Factor in the KKK Equation," *Far Eastern Economic Review* [Hong Kong], October 29, 1982, 34–36.

——. "Rescuer Needs Rescuing," *Far Eastern Economic Review* [Hong Kong], February 17, 1983, 38–40.

——. "Spending to Save," *Far Eastern Economic Review* [Hong Kong], July 21, 1983, 52–53.

——. "Virata Fights Back," *Far Eastern Economic Review* [Hong Kong], May 21, 1982, 64–66.

Sacerdoti, Guy, and Sheilah Ocampo. "Guthrie and the Angels," *Far Eastern Economic Review* [Hong Kong], November 19, 1982, 58–60.

Sacerdoti, Guy, and Malcolm Subhan. "Keeping Faith in Manila," *Far Eastern Economic Review* [Hong Kong], July 21, 1983, 50–52.

Saito, Katrine Anderson, and Delano P. Villanueva. "Transaction Costs of Credit to the Small-scale Sector in the Philippines," *Economic Development and Cultural Change*, 29, No. 3, April 1981, 631–40.

Shalom, Stephen Rosskamm. *The United States and the Philippines: A Study of Neocolonialism*. Philadelphia: Institute for the Study of Human Issues, 1981.

Silliman, G. Sidney. "The Philippine Court of Agrarian Relations in the Context of Martial Law," *Asian Survey*, 20, No. 6, June 1980, 634–47.

"Some Are Smarter than Others," (Part 1.) *Philippine Times*, December 10, 1979, 5.

"Some Are Smarter than Others," (Part 2.) *Philippine Times*, December 17, 1979, 10–11.

"Some Are Smarter than Others," (Part 3.) *Philippine Times*, December 24, 1979, 5.

"Some Are Smarter than Others," (Part 4.) *Philippine Times*, December 31, 1979, 5.

Soviet Union. Glavnoe upravlenie geodizii i kartograffi. *Filippiny, spravochnaia karta*. Moscow: 1982.

Standing, Guy, and Richard Szal. *Poverty and Basic Needs: Evidence from Guyana and the Philippines*. Geneva: International Labour Office, 1979.

Tagaza, Emilia. "Filipino Concern Over State Share Buying," *Financial Times* [London], March 11, 1983, 2.

_____. "Philippines: 'Pork Barrel' Projects vs. Budget Restraint," *Christian Science Monitor*, May 20, 1983, 6.

Valdepeñas, Vincente B., Jr., and Gemelino M. Bautista. *The Emergence of the Philippine Economy*. Manila: Papyrus Press, 1977.

Vries, Barend A. de. *Transition Toward More Rapid and Labor-Intensive Industrial Development: The Case of the Philippines*. (World Bank staff working paper, No. 424.) Washington: World Bank, 1980.

Vries, Barend A. de, et al. *Philippines: Industrial Development Strategy and Policies*. Washington: World Bank, 1980.

World Development Report, 1982. New York: Oxford University Press for the World Bank, 1982.

World Mines Register, 1981–82. San Francisco: Miller Freeman, 1981.

Wu, John C. "The Mineral Industry of the Philippines." Pages 779–96 in *Minerals Yearbook, 1980*. Washington: Bureau of Mines, U.S. Department of the Interior, 1982.

Wurfel, David. "The Philippines: Intensified Dialogue," *Asian Survey*, 7, No. 1, January 1967, 46–52.

Youngblood, Robert L. "The Philippines in 1981: From 'New Society' to 'New Republic'," *Asian Survey*, 22, No. 2, February 1982, 226–35.

Zamora, G.S., A.B. Agillon, and M.L. Sardido. "Fertilizer Marketing and Credit in the Philippines," *Journal of Agricultural Economics and Development* [Laguna, Philippines], 11, No. 2, July 1981, 268–91.

(Various issues of the following publications were also used in the preparation of this chapter: *Asian Wall Street Journal* [Hong Kong]; *Balance of Payments Statistics; Balance of Payments Yearbook; Business Asia* [Hong Kong]; *Economist* [London]; *Far Eastern Economic Review* [Hong Kong]; *Financial Times* [London]; Foreign Broadcast Information Service, *Daily Report: Asia and Pacific; Government Finance Statistics Yearbook; IMF Survey; International Financial Statistics;* Joint Publications Research Service, *South and East Asia Report* and *Southeast Asia Report; NCSO Monthly Bulletin of Statistics* [Manila]; and *Times Journal* [Manila].)

Chapter 4

Abueva, Jose Veloso. *Filipino Politics, Nationalism, and Emerging Ideologies.* Manila: Modern Book, 1972.

"And After Marcos? World Bank Report Raises Questions about the Political and Economic Future of the Philippines," *Asian Record,* 1, No. 9, December 1980, B1–B4 (supplement.).

"Aquino Assassination May Put Marcos on Spot," *Christian Science Monitor,* August 22, 1983, 1, 18.

Asia Yearbook, 1976. (Ed., Rodney Tasker.) Hong Kong: Far Eastern Economic Review, 1976.

Asia Yearbook, 1977. (Ed., Donald Wise.) Hong Kong: Far Eastern Economic Review, 1977.

Asia Yearbook, 1978. (Ed., Donald Wise.) Hong Kong: Far Eastern Economic Review, 1978.

Asia Yearbook, 1979. (Ed., Donald Wise.) Hong Kong: Far Eastern Economic Review, 1979.

Asia Yearbook, 1980. (Ed., Donald Wise.) Hong Kong: Far Eastern Economic Review, 1980.

Asia Yearbook, 1981. (Ed., Donald Wise.) Hong Kong: Far Eastern Economic Review, 1981.

Asia Yearbook, 1982. (Ed., Donald Wise.) Hong Kong: Far Eastern Economic Review, 1982.

Asia Yearbook, 1983. (Ed., Donald Wise.) Hong Kong: Far Eastern Economic Review, 1983.

Ayoob, Mohammed (ed.). *The Politics of Islamic Reassertion.* New York: St. Martin's Press, 1981.

Bowring, Philip. "Playing a New Tune: Marcos Keeps Up with Changing Political Times," *Far Eastern Economic Review* [Hong Kong], 115, No. 1, January 1, 1982, 8–10.

Branigin, William. "As Base Talks Near, Marcos' Opponents Call for U.S. to Get Out," *Washington Post,* May 4, 1983, A23.

_____. "Crackdown on 'Rebel Priests' Widens Church-State Rift in Manila" *Washington Post*, February 18, 1983, A28–A29.

_____. "Manila Broadens Legalistic Attack on Dissent," *Washington Post*, May 16, 1983, A14.

_____. "Opposition Sees Journalists' Trial as Sign of New Marcos Crackdown," *Washington Post*, February 20, 1983, A40.

Browning, E.S., and Andy McCue. "Manila's 'Mr. Clean' Wins Praise for Battling Cronyism," *Asian Wall Steet Journal* [Hong Kong], May 27–28, 1983, 1, 3.

Butterfield, Fox. "Aquino Was Warned 3 Times of Death Plots," *New York Times*, August 23, 1983, A9.

Campbell, Colin. "Manila Opposition Criticizes Inquiry," *New York Times*, August 24, 1983, A1, A3.

_____. "The Unarmed Opponents of Marcos Fear They May not Count," *New York Times*, August 27, 1983, A3.

Castro, Pacifico A. "The Philippines System of Government under the New Republic." Pages 31–32 in Betty Go-Belmonte (ed.), *Fookien Times Philippines Yearbook, 1981–82*. Manila: Fookien Times, 1982.

"Catholic Bishops Assail Marcos Regime," *New York Times*, February 17, 1983, A3.

Catholic Bishops Conference of the Philippines. "A Dialogue for Peace." (Joint pastoral letter.) Manila: February 20, 1983.

"Catholic Church Steps Up Criticism of Martial Law," Foreign Broadcast Information Service, *Daily Report: Asia and Pacific*, 4, No. 170 (FBIS-APA-79-170), August 30, 1979, P1–P2.

Chapman, William. "Opposition's Hope Shattered in Philippines," *Washington Post*, August 28, 1983, A23–A25.

Claver, Francisco F. "Prophecy or Accommodation: The Dilemma of a Discerning Church," *America*, April 26, 1980, 354–59.

"Columnist Deplores 'Sorry State' of Opposition," Foreign Broadcast Information Service, *Daily Report: Asia and Pacific*, 4, No. 147 (FBIS-APA-82-147), July 30, 1982, P3–P4.

"Crowds Mob Aquino Hearse; Cardinal Rejects Inquiry Role," *New York Times*, August 28, 1983, A1, A14.

Davies, Derek. "State of the Union," *Far Eastern Economic Review* [Hong Kong], 95, No. 6, February 11, 1977, 16–20.

Dodwell, David. "Marcos Seems Preoccupied with an Orderly Succession," *Asian Wall Street Journal* [Hong Kong], February 11, 1982, 7.

Edwards, John. "The First Amendment's Shield," *Far Eastern Economic Review* [Hong Kong], 110, No. 45, October 31, 1981, 14.

"Executive Committee's Role in Succession Noted," Foreign Broadcast Information Service, *Daily Report: Asia and Pacific*, 4, No. 153, (FBIS-APA-82-153), August 9, 1982, P1–P2.

"The Generals Watch the Favourites in the Succession Stakes," *Far Eastern Economic Review* [Hong Kong], 119, No. 10, March 10, 1983, 20–21.

Gigot, Paul A. "Flamboyant Imelda Marcos Accumulates Power, but Some Question Her Judgment," *Asian Wall Street Journal* [Hong Kong], January 7, 1983, 1.

Gonzago, Leo. "A Herald Tomorrow?" *Far Eastern Economic Review* [Hong Kong], 113, No. 28, July 3, 1981, 28–29.

Guthrie, George M. (ed.). *Six Perspectives on the Philippines.* Manila: Bookmark, 1968.

Gwertzman, Bernard. "Filipinos in U.S. Were Harassed, Ex-Aides Assert," *New York Times*, August 26, 1983, A1, A4.

———. "U.S. Would Cool Ties with Marcos if Guilt Is Found," *New York Times*, August 25, 1983, A1, A4.

Hoffman, David. "Marcos Blames Professional Killer in Aquino's Assassination," *Washington Post*, August 23, 1983, A1, A6.

Jeffrey, Robin (ed.). *Asia: The Winning of Independence.* New York: St. Martin's Press, 1981.

Jenkins, David. "All the President's Men," *Far Eastern Economic Review* [Hong Kong], March 10, 1983, 15–16.

Joint Publications Research Service—JPRS (Washington). The following items are from the JPRS series:

South and East Asia Report.

"Columnist Attacks 'Timid' Press," *Bulletin Today*, Manila, September 17, 1982. (JPRS 82031, No. 1203, October 20, 1982.)

"Columnist Examines Opposition," *Visayan Herald*, Cebu City, October 23–24, 1982. (JPRS 82337, No. 1219, November 29, 1982.)

"Government Battle Against Corruption," *Philippines Sunday Express*, Manila, June 13, 1982. (JPRS 81285, No. 1167, July 15, 1982.)

"Measures to Improve Political System," *Philippines Daily Express*, Manila, October 14, 1982. (JPRST 82177, No. 1210, November 5, 1982.)

"Nation's Conciliation Urged in View of Political Calm," *Times Journal*, Manila, October 15, 1982. (JPRS 82148, No. 1209, November 2, 1982.)

Southeast Asia Report.

"Columnist Calls for End to Graft," *Bulletin Today*, December 11, 1982. (JPRS 82710, No. 1243, January 21, 1983.)

"Freedom of Expression Urged," *Bulletin Today*, Manila, December 16, 1982. (JPRS 82710, No. 1243, January 21, 1983.)

"Marcos KBL Faction Attacks, Vivata Defends World Bank, IMF," *Bulletin Today*, Manila, April 22, 1983. (JPRS 83494, No. 1288, May 18, 1983.)

"PDP-LABAN Examined," *Bulletin Today*, Manila, March 6, 1983. (JPRS 83235, No. 1273, April 11, 1983.)

"Sin Outlines Church-State Council Idea," *Bulletin Today*, Manila, March 15, 1983. (JPRS 83348, No. 1280, April 27, 1983.)

"Tension Between Church, State on Human Rights," *Business Week*, Kuala Lumpur, July 6, 1979. (JPRS 74019, No. 836, August 16, 1979.)

"KBL Caucus Approves Government Reorganization," Foreign Broadcast Information Service, *Daily Report: Asia and Pacific*, 4, No. 142 (FBIS-APA-81-142), July 24, 1981, P1–P2.

Kerkvliet, Benedict J. (ed.). *Political Change in the Philippines*. Honolulu: University Press of Hawaii, 1974.

Lachica, Eduardo. "Few Snags Threaten Pact on U.S. Bases in Philippines," *Asian Wall Street Journal* [Hong Kong], March 24, 1983, 4.

———. "Reagan Begins to Look Beyond Marcos," *Asian Wall Street Journal* [Hong Kong], June 30, 1983, 4.

———. "Why Aquino Decided to Return to Manila," *Asian Wall Street Journal* [Hong Kong], August 25, 1983, 6.

Landé, Carl H. *Leaders, Factions, and Parties: The Structure of Philippine Politics*. (Monograph series, No. 6.) New Haven: Southeast Asia Studies, Yale University, 1965.

———. "Party Politics in the Philippines." Pages 85–131 in George M. Guthrie (ed.), *Six Perspectives on the Philippines*. Manila: Bookmark, 1968.

Lohr, Steve. "Filipinos Throng to Cortege for Aquino," *New York Times*, August 30, 1983, A3.

McCue, Andy. "Aquino Killed in Manila Airport," *Asian Wall Street Journal* [Hong Kong], August 22, 1983, 1, 5.

———. "Philippines and U.S. Agree on Sum of $900 Million for Military Bases," *Asian Wall Street Journal* [Hong Kong], June 1, 1983, 1–2.

———. "Philippines Welcomes Nakasone, Gets Few Benefits," *Asian Wall Street Journal* [Hong Kong], May 9, 1983, 1.

Machado, Kit G. "The Philippines in 1977: Beginning a 'Return to Normalcy'?" *Asian Survey*, 18, No. 2, February 1978, 202–11.

———. "The Philippines 1978: Authoritarian Consolidation Continues," *Asian Survey*, 19, No. 2, February 1979, 131–40.

Makalintal, Querube C. "The President and the Batasang Pambansa." Pages 74, 76–78 in Betty Go-Belmonte (ed.), *Fookien Times Philippines Yearbook, 1982–83*. Manila: Fookien Times, 1983.

Manglapus, Raul. *Philippines: The Silenced Democracy*. Maryknoll, New York: Orbis Books, 1976.

———. "Who Pulled the Trigger on Aquino?" *New York Times*, August 25, 1983, A19.

"Manila to Get $900 Million in Accord on Bases," *New York Times*, June 1, 1983, A6.

"Marcos Addresses Batasang on State of Nation," Foreign Broadcast Information Service, *Daily Report: Asia and Pacific*, 4, 145, (FBIS-APA-83-145), July 27, 1983, 1–6.

"Marcos Clarifies Government Position under Manila Pact," Foreign Broadcast Information Service, *Daily Report: Asia and Pacific*, 4, No. 034 (FBIS-APA-80-034), February 19, 1980, 1.

"Marcos Declares End to Martial Law Rule," Foreign Broadcast Information Service, *Daily Report: Asia and Pacific*, 4, No. 012 (FBIS-APA-81-012), January 19, 1981, 1–4.

"Marcos Discusses U.S. Trip, Internal Situation," Foreign Broadcast Information Service, *Daily Report: Asia and Pacific*, 4, No. 162 (FBIS-APA-82-162), August 20, 1982, P1–P9.

"Marcos Foe Slain as He Goes Home from Exile in U.S.," *New York Times*, August 22, 1983, A1, A8.

May, R.J. "The Philippines." Pages 211–32 in Mohammed Ayoob (ed.), *The Politics of Islamic Reassertion*. New York: St. Martin's Press, 1981.

Miller, Matt. "Aquino's Death Prompts Leftists' Overtures to Moderates," *Asian Wall Street Journal* [Hong Kong], August 24, 1983, 1.

"More on Marcos' Defense of Human Rights Record," Foreign Broadcast Information Service, *Daily Report: Asia and Pacific*, 4, No. 247 (FBIS-APA-82-247), December 23, 1982, P1–P2.

"More on Spokesman's Speech on Succession," Foreign Broadcast Information Service, *Asia and Pacific*, 4, No. 169 (FBIS-APA-82-169), August 31, 1982, P4–P6.

Morrison, Charles E., and Astri Suhrke. "The Philippines." Pages 232–64 in Charles E. Morrison and Astri Suhrke (eds.), *Strategies of Survival: The Foreign Policy Dilemmas of Smaller Asian States*. New York: St. Martin's Press, 1978.

Morrison, Charles E., and Astri Suhrke (eds.). *Strategies of Survival: The Foreign Policy Dilemmas of Smaller Asian States*. New York: St. Martin's Press, 1978.

Neher, Clark D. "The Philippines in 1979: Cracks in the Fortress," *Asian Survey*, 20, No. 2, February 1980, 155–67.

_____. "The Philippines in 1980: The Gathering Storm," *Asian Survey*, 21, No. 2, February 1981, 261–73.

Niksch, Larry A., and Marjorie Niehaus. *The Internal Situation in the Philippines: Current Trends and Future Prospects*. (Report No. 81–21F.) Washington: Congressional Research Service, Library of Congress, 1981.

Noble, Lela Garner. "Emergency Politics in the Philippines," *Asian Survey*, 18, No. 4, April 1978, 350–62.

_____. "Philippines 1975: Consolidating the Regime," *Asian Survey*, 16, No. 2, February 1976, 178–85.

_____. "Philippines 1976: The Contrast Between Shrine and Shanty," *Asian Survey*, 17, No. 2, February 1977, 133–42.

Ocampo, Sheilah. "Aquino Is Out, but Is He Free at Last?" *Far Eastern Economic Review* [Hong Kong], 108, No. 21, May 16, 1980, 10–11.

_____. "Back to the Streets," *Far Eastern Economic Review* [Hong Kong], 114, No. 43, October 16, 1981, 10.

_____. "The Dissenter's Voice," *Far Eastern Economic Review* [Hong Kong], 112, No. 17, April 17, 1981, 10–11.

──────. "Going It Together," *Far Eastern Economic Review* [Hong Kong], 115, No. 9, February 26, 1982, 30–31.

──────. "The Gun and the Crucifix," *Far Eastern Economic Review* [Hong Kong], 118, No. 50, December 10, 1982, 38–39.

──────. "The Heart of Imelda," *Far Eastern Economic Review* [Hong Kong], 115, No. 12, March 19, 1982, 22.

──────. "Judging the Judges," *Far Eastern Economic Review* [Hong Kong], 116, No. 20, May 14, 1982, 14–15.

──────. "Landslide Win for Marcos," *Far Eastern Economic Review* [Hong Kong], 112, No. 26, June 19, 1981, 13.

──────. "Marcos and the Church Militant," *Far Eastern Economic Review* [Hong Kong], 108, No. 20, May 9, 1980, 45.

──────. "Martial Law Marches On," *Far Eastern Economic Review* [Hong Kong], 106, No. 40, October 5, 1979, 24, 26.

──────. "The New Republic," *Far Eastern Economic Review* [Hong Kong], 112, No. 27, June 26, 1981, 16–17.

──────. "Of Priests and Politicians," *Far Eastern Economic Review* [Hong Kong], 106, No. 50, December 14, 1979, 38–39.

──────. "Philippines: The Seven-Year Itch," *Far Eastern Economic Review* [Hong Kong], 104, No. 26, June 29, 1979, 24–27.

──────. "A Pope among the Politicos," *Far Eastern Economic Review* [Hong Kong], 111, No. 8, February 13, 1981, 16–17.

──────. "The Prophet of Doom and Violence: Aquino's Claim that the Philippines Is Ripe for Revolution Prompts Skepticism," *Far Eastern Economic Review* [Hong Kong], 109, No. 34, August 15, 1980, 8–9.

──────. "Pushed into Purgatory," *Far Eastern Economic Review* [Hong Kong], 117, No. 37, September 10, 1982, 31–32.

──────. "Recipe for Succession," *Far Eastern Economic Review* [Hong Kong], 117, No. 33, August 13, 1982, 10–11.

──────. "Renewed Opposition," *Far Eastern Economic Review* [Hong Kong], 116, No. 19, May 7, 1982, 11–12.

──────. "Silence on the Succession," *Far Eastern Economic Review* [Hong Kong], 106, No. 45, November 9, 1979, 23.

──────. "A Stronger Strongman," *Far Eastern Economic Review* [Hong Kong], 111, No. 13, March 20, 1981, 24–25.

──────. "The Testing Time after Martial Law," *Far Eastern Economic Review* [Hong Kong], 111, No. 5, January 23, 1981, 8–9.

──────. "A United Opposition—But Only up to a Point," *Far Eastern Economic Review* [Hong Kong], 110, No. 43, October 17, 1980, 32.

──────. "The Wages of Discontent," *Far Eastern Economic Review* [Hong Kong], 104, No. 14, April 6, 1979, 18–21.

Ocampo-Kalfors, Sheilah. "More Sinned Against," *Far Eastern Economic Review* [Hong Kong], 119, No. 6, February 10, 1983, 10–11.

Ocampo-Kalfors, Sheilah, and Guy Sacerdoti. "Trouble for a Technocrat," *Far Eastern Economic Review* [Hong Kong], 120, No. 18, May 5, 1983, 44.

"Opposition Holds Talks on Possible Merger," Foreign Broadcast Information Service, *Daily Report: Asia and Pacific*, 4, No. 008 (FBIS-APA-83-008), January 12, 1983, P3.

"Opposition Party Leaders Issue Joint 'Manifesto'," Foreign Broadcast Information Service, *Daily Report: Asia and Pacific*, 4, No. 170 (FBIS-APA-80-170), August 29, 1980, P1–P3.

"Opposition Warns U.S. to Stop Backing Marcos," Foreign Broadcast Information Service, *Daily Report: Asia and Pacific*, 4, No. 010 (FBIS-APA-81-010), January 15, 1981, P1–P2.

"A Pact with the Devil Is No Pact at All," *Far Eastern Economic Review* [Hong Kong], 110, No. 43, October 17, 1980, 29.

Philippines. *The Philippine Constitution of 1973* (Amended). Manila: n.d.

"President's Spokesman Discusses Succession Issue," Foreign Broadcast Information Service, *Daily Report: Asia and Pacific*, 4, No. 168 (FBIS-APA-82-168), August 30, 1982, P1-P2.

Quinn-Judge, Paul. "Church Leader Warns Marcos on Aquino Inquiry," *Christian Science Monitor*, August 29, 1983, 4.

―――. "Philippines, U.S. Wait for Probe of Aquino Killing," *Christian Science Monitor*, August 24, 1983, 1, 18.

"The Review and Juan Ponce Enrile," *Far Eastern Economic Review* [Hong Kong], 102, No. 45, November 10, 1978, 28.

Romulo, Carlos P. "A Restatement of Philippine Foreign Policy." Pages 82–85 in Betty Go-Belmonte (ed.), *Fookien Times Philippines Yearbook*, 1981–82. Manila: Fookien Times, 1982.

Rosenberg, David A. "Liberty versus Loyalty: The Transformation of Philippine News Media under Martial Law." Pages 145–79 in David A. Rosenberg (ed.), *Marcos and Martial Law in the Philippines*. Ithaca: Cornell University Press, 1979.

Rosenberg, David A. (ed.). *Marcos and Martial Law in the Philippines*. Ithaca: Cornell University Press, 1979.

"Rule by Decree Lives On," *Far Eastern Economic Review* [Hong Kong], 113, No. 38, September 11, 1981, 18.

Sacerdoti, Guy and Rodney Tasker. "Death of a Senator," *Far Eastern Economic Review* [Hong Kong], 121, No. 35, September 1, 1983, 10–14.

Shalom, Stephen Rosskamm. *The United States and the Philippines: A Study of Neocolonialism*. Philadelphia: Institute for the Study of Human Issues, 1981.

Sin, Jaime L. "Cardinal Sin's Speech Before the CBCP." Baguio City: Catholic Bishops Conference of the Philippines, June 1981.

Solidum, Estrella D. "Philippine Perceptions of Crucial Issues Affecting Southeast Asia," *Asian Survey*, 22, No. 6, June 1982, 536–47.

"Some Are Smarter than Others," (Part 1.) *Philippine Times* [Manila], December 10, 1979, 5.

"Some Are Smarter than Others," (Part 2.) *Philippine Times* [Manila], December 17, 1979, 10–11.

"Some Are Smarter than Others," (Part 3.) *Philippine Times* [Manila], December 24, 1979, 5.

"Some Are Smarter than Others," (Part 4.) *Philippine Times* [Manila], December 31, 1980. 5.

Southerland, Daniel. "U.S. May Hold Marcos at Arm's Length, but Must Hold on to Bases," *Christian Science Monitor*, August 26, 1983, 1, 8.

"Speech Aquino Planned to Deliver," *New York Times*, August 22, 1983, A8.

Stauffer, Robert B. "Philippine Corporatism: A Note on the 'New Society'," *Asian Survey*, 17, No. 4, April 1977, 393–407.

Tagaza, Emilia. "How Tight Are Marcos' Reins on the Philippine Press?" *Christian Science Monitor*, June 23, 1983, 5.

Tan, Abby. "U.S., Manila Sign 5-Year, $900 Million Bases Pact," *Washington Post*, June 2, 1983, A23.

Tasker, Rodney. "Church Forms a United Front," *Far Eastern Economic Review* [Hong Kong], 95, No. 8. February 25, 1977, 20–21.

———. "Foreign Press under Scrutiny?" *Far Eastern Economic Review* [Hong Kong], 94, No. 46, November 12, 1976, 22–23.

———. "Islam Ready to Assert Pressure," *Far Eastern Economic Review* [Hong Kong], 103, No. 13, March 30, 1979, 14–15.

———. "Marcos Flays Pulpit Politics," *Far Eastern Economic Review* [Hong Kong], 94, No. 50, December 10, 1976, 10–12.

———. "The Moro Rebellion: Who Calls the Shots?" *Far Eastern Economic Review* [Hong Kong], 95, No. 2, January 14, 1977, 18–21.

———. "Muslim Peace Talks Run Aground," *Far Eastern Economic Review* [Hong Kong], 95, No. 9, March 4, 1977, 8–9.

———. "The President's New Clothes," *Far Eastern Economic Review* [Hong Kong], 110, No. 43, October 17, 1980 25–26.

———. "Support for a Strongman: Reagan Reinforces Marcos' Position, but Nagging Problems Remain," *Far Eastern Economic Review* [Hong Kong], 118, No. 44, October 29, 1982, 32–34.

———. "Time for Technocrats," *Far Eastern Economic Review* [Hong Kong], 113, No. 32, July 31, 1981, 8–9.

———. "Will He or Won't He: Whether or Not Aquino Returns to Manila, He Remains a Key Political Factor," *Far Eastern Economic Review* [Hong Kong], 121, No. 31, August 4, 1983, 28–31.

Tōnan Ajia Yōran, 1981. Tokyo: Tōnan Ajia Chōsakai, 1981.

"U.S. Buys Five More Years for Its Bases in the Philippines," *Christian Science Monitor*, June 2,1983, 3.

U.S. Catholic Conference. "Church-State Conflict in the Philippines," *JUSPAX*, 3, No. 1, March 1983, 2–3.

Vokey, Richard. "Anxiety over the Army's Role," *Far Eastern Economic Review* [Hong Kong], 111, No. 6, January 30, 1981, 28–31.

———. "Putting a New Face on Old Policies," *Far Eastern Economic Review* [Hong Kong], 105, No. 31, August 3, 1979, 14–15.

_____. "The Search for a Crown Prince," *Far Eastern Economic Review* [Hong Kong], 106, No. 48, November 30, 1979, 30–31.

Wideman, Bernard. "First Lady, Faults and All: Interview with Imelda Marcos," *Far Eastern Economic Review* [Hong Kong], 93, No. 32, August 6, 1976, 24-25.

Youngblood, Robert L. "Church Opposition to Martial Law in the Philippines," *Asian Survey*, 18, No. 5, May 1978, 505–20.

_____. "The Philippines in 1981: From 'New Society' to 'New Republic'," *Asian Survey*, 22, No. 2, February 1982, 226–35.

_____. "The Philippines in 1982: Marcos Gets Tough with Domestic Critics," *Asian Survey*, 23, No. 2, February 1983, 208-16.

(Various issues of the following publications were also used in the preparation of this chapter: *Asian Wall Street Journal* [Hong Kong], January 1980–June 1983; *Christian Science Monitor*, January 1982–June 1983; Foreign Broadcast Information Service, *Daily Report: Asia and Pacific*, January 1979–July 1983; *Keesing's Contemporary Archives* [London], January 1975–April 1983; *New York Times*, January 1980–June 1983; *Times Journal* [Manila], January 1980–October 1981; *Tōnan Ajia Yōran* [Tokyo], 1976–81; and *Washington Post*, January 1980–June 1983.)

Chapter 5

Amnesty International. *Report of an Amnesty International Mission to the Republic of the Philippines, 11–28 November 1981*. London: 1982.

Amnesty International Report, 1981. London: Amnesty International, 1981.

Aquino, Belinda A. "The Philippines under Marcos," *Current History*, 81, No. 474, April 1982, 160–82.

Armacost, Michael H. "Military Bases Agreement Review: Ambassador Armacost's Statement." Washington: United States Department of State, June 1, 1983.

Asia Yearbook, 1974. (Ed., Hiro Punwani.) Hong Kong: Far Eastern Economic Review, 1974.

Asia Yearbook, 1976. (Ed., Rodney Tasker.) Hong Kong: Far Eastern Economic Review, 1976.

Asia Yearbook, 1978. (Ed., Donald Wise.) Hong Kong: Far Eastern Economic Review, 1978.

Asia Yearbook, 1979. (Ed., Donald Wise.) Hong Kong: Far Eastern Economic Review, 1979.

Asia Yearbook, 1980. (Ed., Donald Wise.) Hong Kong: Far Eastern Economic Review, 1980.

Asia Yearbook, 1981. (Ed., Donald Wise.) Hong Kong: Far Eastern Economic Review, 1981.

Asia Yearbook, 1982. (Ed., Donald Wise.) Hong Kong: Far Eastern Economic Review, 1982.

Asia Yearbook, 1983. (Ed., Donald Wise.) Hong Kong: Far Eastern Economic Review, 1983.

Bacevich, Andrew J., Jr. "Disagreeable Work: Pacifying the Moros, 1903–1906," *Military Review*, 62, No. 6, June 1982, 48–61.

Berlin, Donald Lane. "Prelude to Martial Law: An Examination of Pre-1972 Philippine Civil-Military Relations." (Ph.D. dissertation.) Columbia: Department of Government and International Studies, University of South Carolina, 1982.

Berry, William Emerson, Jr. "American Military Bases in the Philippines, Base Negotiations, and Philippine-American Relations: Past, Present, and Future." (Ph.D. dissertation.) Ithaca: Graduate School, Cornell University, 1981.

Branigin, William. "As Base Talks Near, Marcos' Opponents Call for U.S. to Get Out," *Washington Post*, May 4, 1983, A23.

Cheetham, Russell J., et al. *The Philippines: Priorities and Prospects for Development*. Baltimore: Johns Hopkins University Press, 1976.

"Cleaning Up the Courts," *Asiaweek* [Hong Kong], January 28, 1983, 18.

Combat Fleets of the World 1982/83. (Ed., Jean Labayle Couhat.) Annapolis: Naval Institute Press, 1982.

Copley, Gregory R. (ed.) *Defense and Foreign Affairs Handbook*. Washington: Copley and Associates, 1981.

Cottrell, Alvin J. "Key U.S. Bases in the Philippines," *National Defense*, 67, No. 383, December 1982, 31.

Crisol, Jose M. *The Armed Forces and Martial Law*. Manila: Agro, 1980.

DMS Market Intelligence Report: South America/Australasia. Greenwich, Connecticut: DMS, 1982.

Durdin, Tillman. "Philippine Communism," *Problems of Communism*, 25, No. 3, May-June 1976, 40–48.

Fariñas, J. Rod (ed.). *Philippine Constabulary: 75 Years of Service to the Nation*. Manila: Constable and INP Journal, 1976.

Fookien Times Philippines Yearbook, 1981–82. (Ed., Betty Go-Belmonte.) Manila: Fookien Times, 1982.

Fookien Times Philippines Yearbook, 1982–83. (Ed., Betty Go-Belmonte.) Manila: Fookien Times, 1983.

Galicia-Hernandez, Carolina. "The Extent of Civilian Control of the Military in the Philippines: 1946–1976." (Ph.D. dissertation.) Buffalo: Graduate School, State University of New York at Buffalo, 1979.

George, Thayil Jacob Sony. *Revolt in Mindanao: The Rise of Islam in Philippine Politics*. Kuala Lumpur: Oxford University Press, 1980.

Goldrick, J.V.P., and P.D. Jones. "The Far Eastern Navies," *United States Naval Institute Proceedings*, 108, No. 3, March 1982, 60–65.

Government Finance Statistics Yearbook, 1982, 6. Washington: International Monetary Fund, 1982.

Guerrero, Amado. *Philippine Society and Revolution*. Oakland, California: International Association of Filipino Patriots, 1979.

Gunston, Bill (ed.). *Encyclopedia of World Air Power*. New York: Crescent Books, 1980.

Hewish, Mark, et al. *Air Forces of the World*. New York: Simon and Schuster, 1979.

International Bank for Reconstruction and Development. *The Philippines: Priorities and Prospects for Development*. Washington: World Bank, 1976.

International Financial Statistics Yearbook, 1981. Washington: International Monetary Fund, 1981.

Jane's All the World's Aircraft, 1980–81. (Ed., John W.R. Taylor.) London: Jane's, 1980.

Jane's Armour and Artillery, 1982–83. (Ed., Christopher F. Foss.) London: Jane's, 1982.

Jane's Fighting Ships, 1980–81. (Ed., John E. Moore.) London: Jane's, 1980.

Jane's Infantry Weapons, 1982–83. (Ed., John Weeks.) London: Jane's, 1982.

Jane's Weapon Systems, 1980–81. (Ed., John E. Moore.) London: Jane's, 1980.

Jenkins, David. "All the President's Men," *Far Eastern Economic Review* [Hong Kong], March 10, 1983, 15–16.

_____. "The Generals Watch the Favorites in the Succession Stakes," *Far Eastern Economic Review* [Hong Kong], March 10, 1983, 20–21.

_____. "How the AFP Got Out of MAP and into FMS—But Didn't Spend It All," *Far Eastern Economic Review* [Hong Kong], March 10, 1983, 19.

_____. "Insurgency, Not Internal Threat, Is The Worry," *Far Eastern Economic Review* [Hong Kong], March 10, 1983, 17–19.

Joint Publications Research Service—JPRS (Washington). The following items are from the JPRS Series:

   South and East Asia.

   "MNLF Commander Interviewed on Military Situation," *Arabia: The Islamic World Review*, London, July 1982. (JPRS 81503, No. 1177, August 10, 1982, 248–49.)

   "Nur Misuari Interviewed on Moroland," *Arabia: The Islamic World Review*, London, September 1982. (JPRS 82031, No. 1203, October 20, 1982, 68–69.).

   "View from Inside Guerrilla Heartland," *Arabia: The Islamic World Review*, London, July 1982. (JPRS 81503, No. 1177, August 10, 1982, 232–33.)

Jones, P.D., and J.V.P. Goldrick. "The Far Eastern Navies," *United States Naval Institute Proceedings*, 109, No. 3, March 1983, 57–63.

Keegan, John (ed.). *World Armies*. New York: Facts on File, 1979.

Kerkvliet, Benedict J. *The Huk Rebellion: A Study of Peasant Revolt in the Philippines.* Berkeley and Los Angeles: University of California Press, 1977.

Kroef, Justus M. van der. "The South China Sea: Competing Claims and Strategic Conflicts," *International Security Review,* 7, No. 3, Fall 1982, 305–29.

Lorimer, Norman. "Philippine Communism: An Historical Overview," *Journal of Contemporary Asia* [Stockholm], 7, No. 4, 1977, 462–85.

Mahajani, Usha. *Philippine Nationalism: External Challenge and Filipino Response, 1565–1946.* St. Lucia, Queensland: University of Queensland Press, 1971.

Makibaka: Join Us in Struggle! Netherlands: Friends of the Philippines, 1978.

"Manila to Get $900 Million in Accord on Bases," *New York Times,* June 1, 1983, A6.

"Marcos Comments on U.S. Bases Agreement," Foreign Broadcast Information Service, *Daily Report: Asia and Pacific,* 83, No. 107 (FBIS-APA-83-107), June 2, 1983, Pl.

Marcos, Ferdinand E. *The New Philippine Republic: A Third World Approach to Democracy.* Manila: National Media Production Center, 1982.

_____. "The Powers and Jurisdictions of Local Executives," *Constable and INP Journal* [Quezon City], 14, No. 2, February 1982, 2–9.

Maynard, Harold W. "Views of the Indonesian and Philippine Military Elites." Pages 123–53 in Sheldon Simon (ed.), *The Military and Security in the Third World: Domestic and International Impacts.* Boulder: Westview Press, 1978.

"Memorandum of Agreement." Washington: United States Department of State, June 1, 1983.

The Military Balance, 1982–83. London: International Institute for Strategic Studies, 1982.

"Military Bases Agreement Review: U.S.-Philippine Joint Statement." Washington: United States Department of State, June 1, 1983.

"New Courts, New Judges," *Asiaweek* [Hong Kong], April 9, 1982, 15.

Niehaus, Marjorie. "Philippine Internal Conditions: Issues for U.S. Policy." (Major Issues System, IB82102.) Washington: Congressional Research Service, Library of Congress, March 3, 1983.

Niksch, Larry A., and Marjorie Niehaus. *The Internal Situation in the Philippines: Current Trends and Future Prospects.* (Report No. 81–21F.) Washington: Congressional Research Service, Library of Congress, 1981.

Noble, Lela Garner. "Muslim Separatism in the Philippines, 1972–1981: The Making of a Stalemate," *Asian Survey,* 21, No. 11, November 1981, 1097–1114.

Ocampo, Sheilah. "The May Day Message from Labour," *Far Eastern Economic Review* [Hong Kong], May 11, 1979, 16–19.

Ocampo-Kalfors, Sheilah. "Easing Towards Conflict," *Far Eastern Economic Review*, [Hong Kong], April 28, 1983, 38–39.

————. "Eastern Davao Is the Hot Spot as NPA Ambushes Claim More Victims," *Far Eastern Economic Review* [Hong Kong], March 10, 1983, 20–21.

Philippines. National Economic and Development Authority. National Census and Statistics Office. *Philippine Yearbook, 1978*. Manila: 1979.

————. *Philippine Yearbook, 1981*. Manila: 1982.

Philippines. Office of the President. *Proclamation No. 2045: Proclaiming the Termination of the State of Martial Law Throughout the Philippines*. Manila: 1981.

Philippines. Public Information Office. *The Constabulary Story*. Manila: Bustamente Press, 1981.

Record, Jeffrey. "The Navy of the Philippines." Pages 334–53 in Barry M. Blechman and Robert P. Berman (eds.), *Guide to the Far Eastern Navies*. Annapolis: Naval Institute Press, 1978.

Robinson, Anthony (ed.). *Air Power*. New York: Ziff-Davis, 1980.

Romualdez, Eduardo Z. "The Military Bases in the Philippines: Background to the Recent Philippine-American Negotiations," *Kinaadman* [Cagayan de Oro, Philippines], 2, 1980, 1–41.

————. "Military Bases: The Issue of Criminal Jurisdiction," *Kinaadman* [Cagayan de Oro, Philippines], 3, 1981, 47–62.

Sivard, Ruth Leger. *World Military and Social Expenditures, 1982*. Leesburg, Virginia: World Priorities, 1982.

"A Storm over Sabah," *Asiaweek* [Hong Kong], December 3, 1982, 24–29.

Tan, Abby. "U.S., Manila Sign 5-Year, $900 Million Bases Pact," *Washington Post*, June 2, 1983, A23.

Tow, William T. "Asian-Pacific Alliance Systems and Transregional Linkages," *Naval War College Review*, 34, No. 5, September-October 1981, 32–54.

United States. Congress. 90th, 1st Session. House of Representatives. Committee on Foreign Affairs. *Collective Defense Treaties: With Maps, Texts of Treaties, a Chronology, Status of Forces Agreements, and Comparative Chart*. Washington: GPO, 1967.

United States. Congress. 97th, 1st Session. House of Representatives. Committee on Foreign Affairs. Subcommittee on Asian and Pacific Affairs and Subcommittee on Human Rights and International Organizations. *U.S. Policy Toward the Philippines*. Washington: GPO, 1982.

United States. Congress. 97th, 2d Session. House of Representatives. Committee on Foreign Affairs. Senate. Committee on Foreign Relations. *Country Reports on Human Rights Practices for 1981*. (Report submitted by the Department of State.) Washington: GPO, February 1982.

United States. Congress. 98th, 1st Session. Senate. Committee on Foreign Relations. House of Representatives. Committee on Foreign Affairs. *Country Reports on Human Rights Practices for 1982.* (Report submitted by the Department of State.) Washington: GPO, February, 1983.

United States. Department of Defense. Security Assistance Agency. *Congressional Presentation: Security Assistance Programs, FY 1983.* Washington: Department of Defense, 1982.

————. *Foreign Military Sales, Foreign Military Construction Sales, and Military Assistance Facts.* Washington: 1981.

"U.S. Buys Five More Years for Its Bases in the Philippines," *Christian Science Monitor,* June 2, 1983, 3.

Vokey, Richard. "Islands under the Gun," *Far Eastern Economic Review* [Hong Kong], May 8, 1981, 36–39.

Vreeland, Nena, et al. *Area Handbook for the Philippines.* (DA Pam 550–72.) Washington: GPO for Foreign Area Studies, The American University, 1976.

World Armaments and Disarmament: SIPRI Yearbook, 1975. Cambridge: MIT Press for Stockholm International Peace Research Institute, 1975.

World Armaments and Disarmament: SIPRI Yearbook, 1977. Cambridge: MIT Press for Stockholm International Peace Research Institute, 1977.

World Armaments and Disarmament: SIPRI Yearbook, 1978. New York: Crane, Russak for Stockholm International Peace Research Institute, 1978.

World Armaments and Disarmament: SIPRI Yearbook, 1979. London: Taylor and Francis for Stockholm International Peace Research Institute, 1979.

World Armaments and Disarmament: SIPRI Yearbook, 1980. London: Taylor and Francis for Stockholm International Peace Research Institute, 1980.

World Military Expenditures and Arms Transfers, 1970–1979. Washington: United States Arms Control and Disarmament Agency, 1982.

Yearbook on International Communist Affairs, 1969. (Ed., Richard F. Staar.) Stanford: Hoover Institution Press, 1970.

Yearbook on International Communist Affairs, 1972. (Ed., Richard F. Staar.) Stanford: Hoover Institution Press, 1972.

Yearbook on International Communist Affairs, 1980. (Ed., Richard F. Staar.) Stanford: Hoover Institution Press, 1980.

Youngblood, Robert L. "Church-Military Relations in the Philippines," *Australian Outlook* [Canberra], 35, No. 3, December 1981, 250–61.

(Various issues of the following publications were also used in the preparation of this chapter: *Asian Survey,* January 1972–May 1983; *Asian Wall Street Journal* [Hong Kong], January 1981–July 1983; *Asia Record,* January 1982–March 1983; *Asiaweek* [Hong Kong], January 1981–July 1983; *Christian Science Monitor,* January 1981–July 1983; *Far Eastern Economic Review* [Hong Kong], January 1972–July 1983;

Foreign Broadcast Information Service, *Daily Report: Asia and Pacific,* January 1978–July 1983; Joint Publications Research Service, *South and East Asia Report,* January 1970–December 1982, and *Southeast Asia Report,* January 1983–July 1983; *New York Times,* January 1981– July 1983; and *Washington Post,* January 1979–July 1983.)

Glossary

barangay—Malay term for boat; also came to be used for the communal settlements established by migrants who came from the Indonesian archipelago and elsewhere. The term replaces the word *barrio*, formerly used to identify the lowest political subdivision in the Philippines.

Colorum(s)—Folk Christian religious communities, derived from the 1839–41 Cofradía de San José movement, which spread through the islands thereafter and were the focus of resistance to American rule in the early twentieth century. Term derived from Latin phrase *per omnia saecula saeculorum* (world without end), which Catholic priests use to close their prayers.

debt-service ratio—In international finance, common measure of a nation's indebtedness, calculated as the ratio of long-term debt repayments (of interest and principal) to the total export earnings in a given year. A ratio of 20 percent is generally considered to be the upper limit of prudence, depending on the circumstances of the economy concerned. By Philippine law, the Central Bank must keep debt-service payments at less than 20 percent of the previous year's export earnings.

Exclusive Economic Zone (EEZ)—A wide belt of sea and seabed adjacent to the national boundaries where the state claims preferential fishing rights and control over the exploitation of mineral and other natural resources. Boundary situations with neighboring states sometimes prevent the extension of the EEZ to the full limits claimed. The Philippines claims a 200-nautical-mile EEZ.

fiscal year (FY)—Year ending June 30 through 1975; year ending December 31 thereafter. The transition period from July 1, 1975, through December 31, 1975, was a special fiscal period and has been added to FY 1975 in most cases.

grant element—The present value of a loan minus the discounted value of its contractual debt-service payments divided by the present value of the total loan. Generally, debt-service payments are discounted at a 10-percent rate of interest, and loans carrying a grant element of 25 percent and more are defined as concessional.

gross domestic product (GDP)—The total value of all final (consumption and investment) goods and services produced by an economy in a given period, usually a year.

gross national product (GNP)—GDP (*q.v.*) plus the income from overseas investments and wages, minus the earnings of foreign investors and workers in the home economy.

Huk—Short form of Hukbalahap, itself the abbreviated form of the Tagalog name for the guerrilla force established in 1942, known as the People's Anti-Japanese Army (Hukbong Bayan Laban sa Hapon). In 1946 renamed the People's Liberation Army (Hukbong Mapagpalaya ng Bayan).

International Monetary Fund (IMF)—Established along with the World Bank (*q.v.*) in 1945, the IMF is a specialized agency affiliated with the United Nations and is responsible for stabilizing international exchange rates and payments. The main business of the IMF is the provision of loans to its members (including industrialized and developing countries) when they experience balance of payments difficulties. These loans frequently carry conditions that require substantial internal economic adjustments by the recipients, most of which are developing countries. In late 1983 the IMF had 146 members.

kainginero(s)—Filipino term for one who practices shifting cultivation (*q.v.*). Originally referred to the upland tribal peoples but often used to refer to all peoples, including immigrants from the lowland areas, who practice this kind of farming.

KKK (Kilusang Kabuhayan at Kaunlaran—National Livelihood Program)—Government program under the guiding hand of Imelda Romualdez Marcos, through which concessional loans are made available to farmers and fishermen to help them improve their livelihoods.

Manila Pact—Synonymous with the Southeast Asia Collective Security Treaty establishing the Southeast Asia Treaty Organization (SEATO), signed in Manila in September 1954 by Australia, Britain, France, New Zealand, Pakistan, the Philippines, Thailand, and the United States.

mestizo—The offspring of Filipino and non-Filipino marriages; includes those of Spanish-Filipino parentage (Spanish mestizos) and Chinese-Filipino parentage (Chinese mestizos).

Metro Manila—Metropolitan Manila; also called the National Capital Region. Includes the cities of Manila, Pasay, Caloocan, and Quezon City and several other major population centers.

money supply—The value of cash, demand deposits, and some other forms of bank deposits (depending on the analytical definition). In the text of this study, the money supply includes quasi-money, i.e., savings deposits.

Moro—Spanish word for Moor; name given by Spanish to Muslim Filipinos and still used. Moros mostly inhabit southern and western Mindanao, the Sulu Archipelago, and Palawan and have not become assimilated into the mainstream of Philippine society.

Nonaligned Movement—Launched in 1961 as a loose grouping of nations seeking an independent foreign policy, supporting national liberation and independence movements, and not participating in any bilateral or multilateral military alliances involving the United States or the Soviet Union.

offshore bank—A foreign bank authorized to conduct only international transactions in foreign currencies.

Organization of the Islamic Conference—Established in 1971 to promote consultation, solidarity, and multifaceted cooperation among Islamic nations of the world.

PANAMIN (Presidential Assistant for National Minorities)—Government body assigned to protect the interests of all non-Muslim minority ethnic groups.

peso (₱)—Philippine currency, subdivided into 100 centavos. The value of the currency is quoted in terms of the United States dollar and since 1980 has been allowed to fluctuate basically according to transactions on the Manila foreign exchange market. One major exception occurred in June 1983, when the Central Bank announced that the peso had been devalued by 7.3 percent over one night. Average exchange rates per United States dollar were ₱ 7.51 in 1980, ₱ 7.90 in 1981, ₱ 8.54 in 1982, ₱ 11.00 in June 1983, and ₱ 11.02 in late August 1983.

Samahang Nayon(s)—Originally constituted as village-level pre-cooperatives in 1973; recognized in 1983 as full cooperatives. A Samahang Nayon is typically composed of smallholder farmers having fewer than seven hectares of property and residing within the same *barangay* (*q.v.*). Membership must be at least 25 persons. In early 1982 there were some 22,000 Samahang Nayons, some of which had been authorized to operate as commercial enterprises.

shifting cultivation—Farming characterized by the rotation of fields rather than crops, the use of short cropping periods and long fallow periods, and the maintenance of fertility by allowing natural vegetation to regenerate on fallow land. Clearing of newly or previously cropped land is often accomplished by burning. Also called slash-and-burn, swidden, or land rotation agriculture, which may refer to particular subtypes of shifting cultivation. Land ownership or rights of usufruct usually apply only while the cultivator is actually working the plot.

value added—The value of goods and services produced by an enterprise or economic sector minus the cost of raw materials, components, and services purchased from other firms or sectors.

World Bank—Informal name used to designate a group of three affiliated international institutions: the International Bank for Reconstruction and Development (IBRD), the International Development Association (IDA), and the International Finance Corporation (IFC). The IBRD, established in 1945, has the primary purpose of providing loans to developing countries for productive projects. The IDA, a legally separate loan fund but administered by the staff of the IBRD, was set up in 1960 to furnish credits to the poorest developing countries on much easier terms than those of conventional IBRD loans. The IFC, founded in 1956, supplements the activities of the IBRD through loans and assistance designed specifically to encourage the growth of productive private enterprises in the less developed countries. The president and certain senior officers of the IBRD hold the same positions in the IFC. The three institutions are owned by the governments of the countries that subscribe their capital. In 1983 the IBRD had over 140 members, the IDA had 130, and the IFC over 120. To participate in the World Bank group, member states must first belong to the International Monetary Fund (IMF—*q.v.*).

Index

Published Country Studies

(Area Handbook Series)

550-65	Afghanistan		550-151	Honduras
550-98	Albania		550-165	Hungary
550-44	Algeria		550-21	India
550-59	Angola		550-154	Indian Ocean
550-73	Argentina		550-39	Indonesia
550-169	Australia		550-68	Iran
550-176	Austria		550-31	Iraq
550-175	Bangladesh		550-25	Israel
550-170	Belgium		550-182	Italy
550-66	Bolivia		550-69	Ivory Coast
550-20	Brazil		550-177	Jamaica
550-168	Bulgaria		550-30	Japan
550-61	Burma		550-34	Jordan
550-83	Burundi		550-56	Kenya
550-50	Cambodia		550-81	Korea, North
550-166	Cameroon		550-41	Korea, South
550-159	Chad		550-58	Laos
550-77	Chile		550-24	Lebanon
550-60	China		550-38	Liberia
550-63	China, Republic of		550-85	Libya
550-26	Colombia		550-172	Malawi
550-91	Congo		550-45	Malaysia
550-90	Costa Rica		550-161	Mauritania
550-152	Cuba		550-79	Mexico
550-22	Cyprus		550-76	Mongolia
550-158	Czechoslovakia		550-49	Morocco
550-54	Dominican Republic		550-64	Mozambique
550-52	Ecuador		550-35	Nepal, Bhutan and Sikkim
550-43	Egypt		550-88	Nicaragua
550-150	El Salvador		550-157	Nigeria
550-28	Ethiopia		550-94	Oceania
550-167	Finland		550-48	Pakistan
550-155	Germany, East		550-46	Panama
550-173	Germany, Federal Republic of		550-156	Paraguay
550-153	Ghana		550-185	Persian Gulf States
550-87	Greece		550-42	Peru
550-78	Guatemala		550-72	Philippines
550-174	Guinea		550-162	Poland
550-82	Guyana		550-181	Portugal
550-164	Haiti		550-160	Romania

550-84	Rwanda	550-89	Tunisia
550-51	Saudi Arabia	550-80	Turkey
550-70	Senegal	550-74	Uganda
550-180	Sierra Leone	550-97	Uruguay
550-184	Singapore	550-71	Venezuela
550-86	Somalia	550-57	Vietnam, North
550-93	South Africa	550-55	Vietnam, South
550-95	Soviet Union	550-183	Yemens, The
550-179	Spain	550-99	Yugoslavia
550-96	Sri Lanka (Ceylon)	550-67	Zaire
550-27	Sudan	550-75	Zambia
550-47	Syria	550-171	Zimbabwe
550-62	Tanzania		
550-53	Thailand		
550-178	Trinidad and Tobago		

☆U.S. GOVERNMENT PRINTING OFFICE: 1984 -0- 421-658 (10002)

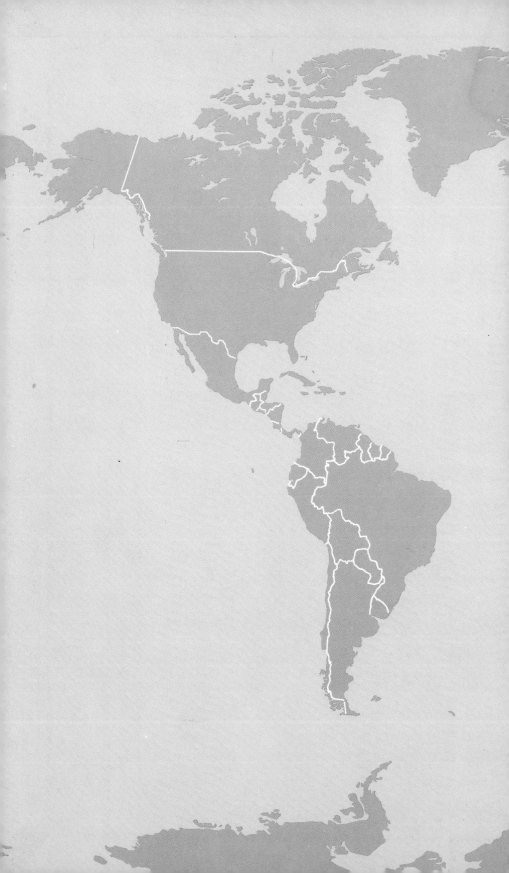